Software Processes and Life Cycle Models

Ralf Kneuper

Software Processes and Life Cycle Models

An Introduction to Modelling, Using and Managing Agile, Plan-Driven and Hybrid Processes

 Springer

Ralf Kneuper
Dr. Ralf Kneuper Consulting
Darmstadt, Germany

ISBN 978-3-030-07540-8   ISBN 978-3-319-98845-0   (eBook)
https://doi.org/10.1007/978-3-319-98845-0

This Springer imprint is published by the registered company Springer Nature Switzerland AG
The registered company address is: Gewerbestrasse 11, 6330 Cham, Switzerland

Foreword

A number of books have been written about software process improvement over the years, some of them quite good, some less so. Ralf has written a book that I will be happy to add to my library. Ralf has been involved with software process assessment and improvement for many years, so he has the experience necessary to speak knowledgeably about the topic. He is also addressing two topics that I think are important for systematic process improvement in today's world.

First, he is addressing agile methods. I became involved with agile nearly 20 years ago: I was asked to write a book chapter on Extreme Programming from the perspective of the Capability Maturity Model. I was impressed, surprised, and intrigued by the ideas captured in XP. While I would not agree with everything argued by the XP advocates, for the most part I found the XP practices appealing. I followed up with other agile methods, eventually becoming a Certified ScrumMaster. In my encounters with the agile community, I found a variety of perspectives, ranging from the "responsible center" to "fringe zealots".

I believe that agile methods have a great deal to offer the process community ... although there are those in both communities who downplay the contributions of the other. Process frameworks, such as CMMI, do not address every organizational need.

Software process as captured in the Software CMM, and now CMM Integration, focuses on building the capability of the organization to build systems. The emphasis is on operational excellence—meeting commitments, operating in an effective and efficient manner. There are other priorities that an organization could choose over operational excellence, such as innovation. In the custom software development world, operational excellence is crucial—but innovation cannot be ignored. In commercial software development, innovation may be the more important priority, yet meeting commitments is also useful.

Agile methods are focused on the needs of the software team to build a specific product in a specific context. As the agile experts all admit, you have to tailor the agile method to the unique needs of the project. If you tailor it too far, it may no longer be agile—but still be appropriate for the project's context. There are many good engineering and management practices embedded in the agile methods that can and should be adopted by the software community, even when "agility" is not a major driver for the project.

Nearly 20 years ago, I listened to Bob Martin tell a story at XP Universe about someone he ran into in the hall. That person thanked Bob, telling him that his company had adopted XP and were delighted with it. Bob asked what he thought about pair programming—we don't do pair programming ... well, what about the planning game—we don't do the planning game ... how's continuous integration working out for you—we don't do continuous integration. Bob then asked, well what do you do? And the answer: we don't document anything! Sitting in the audience I felt a strong sense of schadenfreude (joy in the misfortune of others). More than once I've had someone tell me, we're doing something stupid! Why? The CMM told us to! In following up, it was never something the CMM actually directed, it was what people felt they needed to do to check a box.

People in both the process and agile communities need to approach "the way we build software" with both humility and a sense of inquiry. How can we do a better job of building software? Frameworks such as the Software CMM and now CMMI have many good ideas for the organization that can help in deploying effective methods, such as Scrum, Extreme Programming, and Feature Driven Development. I hope that Ralf's insights into the good ideas ranging from plan-driven to agile will help software professionals come up with good answers to the questions that they ask.

Second, Ralf is addressing the software process from the perspective of the Software Engineering Body of Knowledge. SWEBOK is an attempt to capture the critical ideas fundamental to good software engineering. The IEEE Computer Society solicited inputs from the software engineering community in a transparent, open, consensus process on what we know about building software effectively and efficiently. Integrating these insights into your software process improvement initiatives should be useful and important.

There are many other good sources of insight into software engineering and management that could be cited, but these are two of the most influential and widely known. I will not claim to agree with everything said in the agile community or by the IEEE Computer Society—I'm well known not to agree with many in the process world! Even when we disagree, keeping an open mind to potential insights and integrating those into our thinking, even when it causes us to change our minds, is the highway to continual improvement. Basing our decisions on empirical evidence as to what really works is the core high maturity at levels 4 and 5, but that's a different book.

Dallas, Texas, August 2017   *Mark Paulk*

Preface

Since software is of growing importance in today's world, the importance of the processes used to create, maintain and run such software is growing in parallel. These processes may be defined in detail or not at all, but even a software development project or organization that does not explicitly define their software engineering processes will use processes implicitly to do their work.

However, an increasing proportion of software engineering organisations defines their "set of interrelated or interacting activities which transforms inputs into outputs" which is the ISO 9000 definition of processes. Such process definitions may take very different forms, from very traditional, plan-based approaches with lengthy and sequential phases for analysis, design, implementation and test to agile approaches where essentially the same activities are performed within very short and frequent cycles, today usually called sprints. Experience over the last decades has shown that the best way to reliably get excellent products is to ensure that excellent processes are used to create and maintain these products.

Software engineering as a discipline integrates a variety of tasks ranging from "classical" computer science to business-related topics, and can roughly be distinguished into *software technology* that addresses the methodical and technological aspects, and *organisation and management of software development*, which, among other tasks, includes different planning, measurement and controlling tasks. Good software processes help to bring these different tasks together, working towards the common goal of delivering high-quality products on time and in budget.

As software becomes a vital component of many systems and affects many aspects of our day-to-day life, the processes for creating, maintaining and running software become critical as well. To efficiently develop high quality software that addresses their needs, companies have to align software development and software management with their business goals and processes. To achieve this, certain guidelines are needed for development, defining the activities, results and roles needed in more or less detail. This is particularly obvious in the context of regulated and safety-critical environments, such as automotive, medical devices, or financial services, but in different, e.g. more agile environments, alignment of the development processes is similarly important, with the processes possibly taking a very different form, for example focussing on time to market rather than reliability.

Over time, plan-driven development and agile development have been developed as the two basic philosophies for software development. They both address the same objective of creating high-quality software in time and on budget, but with different emphasis. While agile development puts the emphasis on customer satisfaction and user benefit and tries to achieve these by making it easy to adapt work, plan-driven development puts more emphasis on requirements that have been identified in advance in order to achieve correctness and predictability. This results in different strengths and weaknesses of both philosophies, and in practice many development organisations use some combination of both.

Book Goals

Since process engineers and project managers face a diversity of approaches and standards that is hard to manage, defining and enacting appropriate processes constitute a challenging task that is often left to expertise and experience.

The book at hand therefore does not attempt to promote any specific approach, type of process, or model. Instead, it aims at delivering a big picture of the comprehensive field of software processes, covering in particular the essential topics:

- software process modelling
- software process models and life cycle models
- software process management, deployment and governance
- software process improvement (including assessment and measurement)

Furthermore, it can be used as a reference on software process models and notations, providing at least a brief overview of all the main approaches. The book also discusses the fundamental process principles, and presents an overview of current "hot topics" and emerging trends.

In particular, the book addresses the topics described in Chapter 8 "Software Engineering Processes" of the Software Engineering Body of Knowledge (SWEBOK® v3). To do so, it uses a uniform conceptual and terminological framework to present the software processes, explains the different topics by example, and shares experiences gathered over the years. The present book does not propose any new processes or methods. Its goal is to introduce software engineers into the topic of software processes to support the systematic development of high quality software in different and changing environments.

In discussing software processes and life cycle models, the focus lies on the benefits for development organisations and their customers that can be achieved, and what needs to be done in order to achieve them.

Conformance to relevant international standards is of course important as well, but should not be considered as the primary goal. Experience shows that most standards can be applied in very different ways, and a focus on compliance tends to lead to inefficient processes that are therefore difficult to deploy in the organisation. A focus on the benefits of the processes, on the other hand, using standards as a tool to where useful or required, will in general be far more helpful and, as a result, also easier to deploy.

Target Audience

This book is aimed at graduate students, researchers, and professionals. It can be used as a textbook for courses and lectures, for self-study, and as a reference. When used as a textbook, it may support courses and lectures devoted to software processes, but also as complementing literature for more basic courses, such as introductory courses on software engineering or project management.

Software engineering processes provide a structure and guidance to the software engineering activities, and it will be difficult to understand the structure without an understanding of the basic activities that are structured by processes. To make effective and efficient use of the different methods and techniques of software engineering, appropriate processes are needed. This book helps to understand and use these processes, to identify which processes are most appropriate in a certain environment, to document them and to introduce them into the organisation or project.

However, the book at hand does not try to be a general software engineering compendium or textbook. Readers should already have some fundamental knowledge about computer science, software engineering, and project management. Specific tasks, such as software development, architecture, and quality assurance, are not part of this book, and readers are expected to bring in basic knowledge of these topics. Furthermore, basic knowledge about software economics is beneficial.

Outline

The overall structure of the book can be found in Fig. 0.1. In Chap. 1, the foundations of the topic are introduced, covering the basic concepts, a historical overview, and an introduction to the terminology used.

Next, Chap. 2 covers the various approaches to modelling software processes and life cycle models, before Chap. 3 discusses the contents of these models, addressing plan-driven, agile and hybrid approaches.

The following chapters address different aspects of using software processes and life cycle models in an organisation, looking at the management of these processes (Chap. 4), their assessment and improvement (Chap. 5) and the measurement of both software and software processes (Chap. 6).

Working with software processes is usually supported by different kinds of tools, which is the topic covered in Chap. 7, before a look at current trends in software processes in Chap. 8 concludes the book.

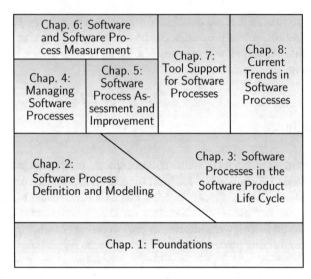

Fig. 0.1 Book outline

Relationship to SWEBOK®. The book is aligned with the *Software Engineering Body of Knowledge* (SWEBOK®) version 3, chapter 8 "Software Engineering Process" and, thus, provides a general introduction to the software process. SWEBOK® was created by the IEEE Computer Society, and its current version v.3 was published both as an IEEE guide and as ISO/IEC TR 19759:2015.

To some extent, the present book goes beyond the SWEBOK® contents by also providing insights into the topics of process selection and tailoring and by discussing emerging trends in the field of software processes. Furthermore, agile approaches are covered as well as plan-driven approaches, while SWEBOK has a strong emphasis on plan-driven development only.

Table 0.1 gives an overview of the top-level structure of the book and its relationship to SWEBOK®, Chap. 8.

Table 0.1 Relation of the present book to the topics covered by SWEBOK®, Chap. 8

SWEBOK® v3, Chap. 8	This book
Software Process Definition	Chapter 2, Chapter 4
Software Life Cycles	Chapter 3, Chapter 4
Software Process Assessment and Improvement	Chapter 5
Software Measurement	Chapter 6
Software Engineering Process Tools	Chapter 7

While Chap. 8 of SWEBOK® addresses software engineering processes as a topic of their own, several other chapters of the SWEBOK® also refer to software engineering processes. Table 0.2 lists the main relevant parts of SWEBOK® and where these topics are covered in the present book.

Table 0.2 Relation of the present book to the topics covered by SWEBOK®, Chap. 7 and 10

SWEBOK® v3	This book
Chap. 7, Sect. 2.1 *Process Planning*	Sect. 4.4
Chap. 7, Sect. 3.4 *Monitor Process*	Sect. 4.7, Sect. 6.5
Chap. 10, Sect. 1.3 *Models and Quality Characteristics*	Sect. 5.2
Chap. 10, Sect. 1.4 *Software Quality Improvement*	Sect. 5.4

Just like software engineers should think about what happens to their software after development is completed, so this book goes beyond development processes and looks at the entire software life cycle including operations, service management and maintenance, as well as the governance of software processes.

Terminology. Where possible, the terminology used is usually based on the current (in 2017) version of the *Software and Systems Engineering Vocabulary* (SEVOCAB) which collects definitions of terminology from various other norms and standards published by ISO, IEC, IEEE and PMI, and expands this collection by a number of additional definitions. SEVOCAB is publicly available from `https://pascal.computer.org`, and also published periodically as ISO/IEC/IEEE 24765.

In particular, the terminology from SEVOCAB is usually used in the definitions in this book. Where this standards includes several different definitions of the same term, this book usually selects that definition that is most appropriate in the context of software processes and life cycle models.

On the other hand, the same definition is sometimes used in several different standards. In this case, only the sources most relevant in this context are given, always including SEVOCAB if the definition is included in this standard.

Case studies and examples. To help to get a good understanding of the topics discussed, examples and case studies are provided. In particular, the following two companies will be used for the case studies:

Case Study 0.1. (CS AutoSystems) *CS AutoSystems* develops and produces various electronic control units (ECU) for cars, e.g. electric window lifters. These ECUs consist of hardware as well as software, and in some cases they are safety-relevant, leading to high demands on their reliability as well as on the validation of the systems.

The development department of CS AutoSystems is fairly small, with about ten developers (hard- and software).

Case Study 0.2. (CS Insurance InfoSys) *CS Insurance InfoSys* is a large IT service provider, with about 1000 developers. The organisation develops and runs the information systems for its parent, a large insurance company. To a minor extent, it also acquires software from external suppliers which is then run in the data centre of CS Insurance InfoSys.

Both case studies are based on a combination of real, existing companies even though the companies as described do not exist in this form. Nevertheless, everything described in the case studies has actually happened in existing companies.

Example 0.1. Apart from these two case studies companies that will be used in case studies repeatedly across the entire book, various other examples will be used to illustrate the concepts introduced.

At the end of each chapter, references to further reading are included for those who want to go into more detail of one of the topics covered.

Also at the end of most chapters, some exercises are included to help get a better understanding of the concepts covered. These exercises do not just ask to repeat any contents described in the book but refer to applying and interpreting this contents in a certain context, sometimes the reader's own work environment. As a result, these exercises have rarely, if ever, a unique correct answer.

There are many norms and standards relevant in the field of software processes and this book addresses many of them. A list of the most important such norms and standards can be found in the appendix.

Acknowledgements. Many thanks go to Marian Benner-Wickner, Ernest Wallmüller, Eckhard Wirth and the anonymous reviewers for their feedback on various drafts of this book.

Many thanks also go to the copyright owners of the figures included. Unfortunately, not all copyright owners managed to answer this request, and I therefore had to remove a few figures I would have liked to include.

The author thanks the International Electrotechnical Commission (IEC) for permission to reproduce Information from its International Standard IEC 61508-3:2010. All such extracts are copyright of IEC, Geneva, Switzerland. All rights reserved. Further information on the IEC is available from http://www.iec.ch. IEC has no responsibility for the placement and context in which the extracts and contents are reproduced by the author, nor is IEC in any way responsible for the other content or accuracy therein.

Trademarks.

- ITIL® is a (registered) Trade Mark of AXELOS Limited. All rights reserved.
- PRINCE® is a (registered) Trade Mark of AXELOS Limited. All rights reserved.
- PRINCE2 Agile® is a (registered) Trade Mark of AXELOS Limited. All rights reserved.
- Capability Maturity Model®, Carnegie Mellon® and CMM® are registered in the U.S. Patent and Trademark Office by Carnegie Mellon University.
- CMMI and SCAMPI are registered marks of CMMI Institute LLC.
- Team Software Process, TSP, Personal Software Process, PSP and IDEAL are service marks of Carnegie Mellon University.
- PMI® and PMP® are registered marks of Project Management Institute, Inc.
- V-Modell® ist eine geschützte Marke der Bundesrepublik Deutschland. (V-Modell® is a registered mark of the Federal Republic of Germany.)
- SAFe® and Scaled Agile Framework® are registered trademarks of Scaled Agile, Inc.
- The Open Group® and TOGAF® are registered trademarks of The Open Group.
- IBM® is a registered trademark of International Business Machines Corporation.
- CORBA®, Object Management®, OMG®, and UML® are registered trademarks and BPMN™, Business Process Modeling Notation™, and Unified Modeling Language™ are trademarks of the Object Management Group.
- COBIT® is a registered trademark of the Information Systems Audit and Control Association and the IT Governance Institute.
- IEEE® iis a registered trademark of the Institute of Electrical and Electronics Engineers, Inc.
- Microsoft® is a registered trademark of Microsoft Corporation.

About the author. Ralf Kneuper got a diploma in mathematics from the Univ. of Bonn, Germany, in 1985, and a Ph.D. in Computer Science from the Univ. of Manchester, UK, in 1989. Since then, he has worked with various companies on software quality assurance, quality management and software processes. Currently, he works both as an independent consultant on software quality management, process improvement and data protection, and as a professor of Business Informatics and Computer Science at the IUBH Internationale Hochschule in Germany. He has published extensively on CMMI, process improvement and process quality.

Contents

Chapter 1
Foundations

Abstract *Software engineering* aims at developing software systems in an efficient and systematic manner. As part of software engineering, *software processes* and *life cycle models* provide a framework for the various activities, defining how and when to perform these activities, specifying the roles involved and the results to be created. Since there are many different approaches to developing software, with many different software engineering methodologies and techniques, there exists a similar multitude of software processes and life cycle models that has grown over decades, and today we face a large number of approaches addressing the whole software product life cycle or selected parts thereof. In this chapter, we lay the foundation for the present book, providing an overview of the topic, context information and motivation, and outline the problems and challenges coming along with software processes. Furthermore, we provide a short history of software processes, and define the main concepts and terminology used.

1.1 Background

Before covering any aspects of software processes and life cycle models in detail, this section gives a first overview of some basic concepts and the main challenges to be addressed. This will help to provide the general background for the later discussions going into more detail for the individual topics.

1.1.1 Basic Concepts

Software processes and software development. Software development is a complex task, consisting of many individual activities that need to be coordinated. This is where software processes and life cycle models come into play, providing an infrastructure to coordinate and manage these various activities.

© Springer Nature Switzerland AG 2018
R. Kneuper, *Software Processes and Life Cycle Models*,
https://doi.org/10.1007/978-3-319-98845-0_1

SWEBOK 3.0 [9] provides an overview of these topics involved that range from the more technical ones to methodical and organisational topics, such as:

- Software requirements
- Software design
- Software construction
- Software testing
- Software configuration management
- Software quality

These and further tasks are carried out in (almost) all software development efforts, even though the way, order, and frequency of performing these tasks differs. (Defined) software processes aim at bringing order into chaos by structuring these tasks.

In the previous paragraph, the term "effort" was used deliberately instead of the more common "project", since not all development is done in projects, for example, maintenance work is often not done as part of a project. Therefore, the term "development effort" will be used in the remainder of this book to cover both project and non-project work.

It is also important to note that even if a development organisation does not explicitly define or manage its processes, it still *uses* them, and therefore defines them at least implicitly. The organisation may not have any software process *model*, but it certainly does have processes, be it grown, implicit processes or explicitly defined ones.

Software processes, software process models and life cycle models. In this context it is important to emphasize the difference between (software) processes and (software) process models. A process model is a representation of a process, describing how the process is performed (descriptive model) or how it is expected to be performed (prescriptive model) at a selected level of granularity. A process is a much wider concept, and above all consist of the actual performance of the relevant activities, which may or may not be described by a model.

In this sense, all software organisations use processes to develop their software, be it an explicitly modelled and standardized process or an implicit process that changes every time.

Software process models and life cycle models, on the other hand, are two similar concepts, but with different focus: life cycle models define the main steps (often called phases or stages) in the software life cycle and their sequence, in particular in the software development life cycle. Software process models provide more detail, breaking the main steps down into sub-steps, and adding information about the results generated and the roles involved. Therefore, software process models often describe only an individual process rather than the entire life cycle.

The challenge of objectively evaluating software processes. One of the basic properties of the software life cycle, in particular of software development, is that it is always performed in a different context, with unique properties such as task at hand, team available and its qualification and background, requirements on speed of delivery and reliability of results, and so on. As a result, it is usually not possible to evaluate and compare different processes and life cycle models for the same task in a genuinely objective way. In that sense, software development is more similar to social science than to natural science where experiments can be performed and repeated, and are expected to lead to very similar results.

While the quest for "the best" way to develop software is generally accepted as an important task, different researchers and practitioners coming from different backgrounds and evaluating software processes in different contexts come to very different results, as shows the multitude of very different processes and methodologies that is in practical use. To some extent, it is possible to correlate certain processes with certain contexts, e.g. noting that agile processes are more suitable for an environment which is constantly changing, while plan-driven processes are more suitable for a stable environment with high requirements on the reliability of the result.

This leads to a situation where software development processes and methods are not just a topic of scientific investigation but just as much a matter of belief, with sometimes almost religious discussions about the pros and cons of certain approaches, as for example the discussion about the relative merits of agile and plan-driven development.

Of course, this book cannot take a fully neutral stance in these discussions either, but tries to present the main concepts behind the different processes, and pointing to the different contexts where these processes might be more or less suitable.

1.1.2 The Purpose of Explicitly Using Software Processes

Initially, the main purpose of making software processes explicit as software process models was to provide a structure for software development, defining a framework for software development tasks and methods, breaking down this increasingly complex task into smaller sub-tasks to help planning and monitoring work, to support cooperation and communication between the different people and groups involved, and to ensure quality of the result. Starting in the 1980s, the models were additionally created to improve and automate (parts of) the development process which led to more detailed descriptions or models of the software processes involved.

Basic uses of software process models (according to Curtis, Kellner and Over). In 1992, Curtis et al. summarised the then current state of the art in software process modelling and described five basic uses of software process models:

- "*Facilitate human understanding and communication* requires that a group be able to share a common representational format
- *Support process improvement* requires a basis for defining and analyzing processes
- *Support process management* requires a defined process against which actual project behaviors can be compared

- *Automate process guidance* requires automated tools for manipulating process descriptions
- *Automate execution support* requires a computational basis for controlling behavior within an automated environment." [14, p. 76]

Software processes as a means to convince third parties of the quality of the software. Software process models are also needed to convince others, such as customers or regulatory bodies, of the quality of the software. Even if the software itself was perfect, this would not be sufficient if there was not some form of proof or at least strong argument to show this. Using appropriate software development processes is often considered as such a strong argument. This applies first of all if properties such as reliability, safety and security are important, while properties such as usability and functional suitability are comparably easy to evaluate by just examining or testing the software.

Standards discussing the reliability, safety or security of (software) systems therefore usually include a number of requirements on the processes used to develop these systems, as discussed in more detail in Sect. 3.11.

Software processes and IT governance. The main purpose of software processes and life cycle models is to support the goals and strategy of the organisation that develops and/or uses software—which of course need to be defined first. Whether an organisation wants to provide very reliable and fast (development or software-based) service to its customers, whether it wants to provide a standardised service at low price, or whether it aims for some other goals, the organisation's strategy needs to be supported by the software processes used.

This leads to the need for corporate and IT governance, both for internal reasons to ensure that the company as a whole and IT in particular are moving in the right direction, implementing the company objectives, and for external reasons to comply to relevant laws and regulations such as the Sarbanes-Oxley Act (SOX) in the USA, or ISO 26262 for functional safety in the automotive industry. Similarly, an increasing amount of software has an impact on the safety of its environment, and therefore relevant regulations must be satisfied in development in order to be allowed to deploy the software later on.

The main reason for using software processes and software process models as part of IT governance is that they can help to increase the predictability of processes and their results, and in particular the transparency of the work done. These obviously are important benefits from the viewpoint of (senior) management that wants to know and to control what is happening in an organisation, as well as from the viewpoint of external regulatory bodies who want to ensure that distributed products are safe, or want to prevent fraud.

In this context, however, it is important to remember what was said in the preface of this book about the distinction between focussing on compliance to relevant standards vs. focussing on company and customer benefits, using standards as a tool: experience shows that it is far more efficient and often even more effective for compliance to focus on defining and implementing processes that first of all help the company, and by the way also satisfy relevant standards, rather than starting with an emphasis on the standards.

Processes for risk management. Closely related to IT governance is risk management, another common reason for defining and managing software processes, and emphasised in common standards such as ISO 9001:2015, COBIT, SOX, and ISO 31000:2009. On the one hand, the systematic definition and management of software processes can help to reduce the risks involved in these processes. Looking at this relationship the other way round, high risks involved in a software process are one indicator that this process should be defined and managed very systematically, while other, low-risk processes may be performed in a more ad-hoc way.

Software processes in small development efforts. It is often assumed that defined software processes are mainly or only adequate for large, long-lasting development efforts. This, however, is not true. Of course, small and agile development efforts will need different kinds of software processes to be successful, but if adequate processes are used, these development efforts will also benefit considerably, specifically if a fast start of development is important. At the same time, development teams in small development efforts are more likely to object to a set of processes that they did not select themselves and that they might not see as genuinely helping them. Therefore it is particularly important in small settings to ensure that the processes really make the team's life easier and does not just add bureaucracy.

Case Study 1.1. (CS Insurance InfoSys) Apart from a number of large projects, *CS Insurance InfoSys* also has a large number of small projects, mostly working according to an agile methodology, some of which are expected to start very quickly. In order to be able to do so, a set of processes was defined that do not define the steps in detail but that provide a framework for agile development, defining the main steps to perform, the tools needed and templates to use them etc.. Based on these definitions, it was possible to set up a standard development environment, called the *project-out-of-the-box*, allowing to set up new projects more or less immediately, and to focus on the content of the project from the beginning, rather than spending a lot of effort and time to define and set up such an environment.

1.1.3 Software Processes and their Evolution

Software processes as an explicit topic of study have been around since the late 1970s and different movements appeared and disappeared over time.

Plan-driven development. In "the old days", simple sequencing of the individual activities shaped the initial software process models, using well-defined artefacts resulting from one phase and handed over to the next phase. Since this was the type of software development process that was introduced first, it is better known as the "classical" software process, but since this name does not really describe the ideas behind it, the name "plan-driven" will be used in this book.

As the software business evolved over time so did the software processes. It soon became clear that strictly sequential life cycles were not sufficient, and iterations and increments were introduced, still trying to plan work in advance as far as possible. While this type of development is often called the "classical" way of working, this does not really provide any information about how work performed, which is why we here talk about "plan-driven" development instead, to emphasise the core property that in this type of development, one tries to plan work as far as possible in advance. This implies that the requirements need to be identified in advance, which is why this way of working is also called "requirements-driven". Note that a plan-driven or requirements-driven way of working does allow iteration, but with the limitation that these iterations and their contents are largely planned in advance.

However, these traditional software processes showed limitations, such as lacking flexibility toward changes, over-documentation, and poor performance, and they also introduced some bureaucracy. In response, some initiatives aimed at replacing the "old-fashioned heavy-weight processes" by more agile approaches of software development.

Agile and plan-driven development. This led to a situation in which agile approaches were discussed and researched intensively [16, 17] and their benefits were preached in a close-to-dogmatic manner. There was an avalanche of success stories trying to make everybody ashamed who did not adapt agile methods. On the other hand, proponents of plan-driven development fought against this newfangled, unstructured way of working, often supported by the fact that many projects used this new label "agile" as an excuse for truly unstructured development, using a code-and-fix approach leaving out the documentation. A cultural conflict resulted which still is not fully resolved, due to dogmatics on either side. Nevertheless, while agile development still is growing in importance, there is also growing understanding that both approaches have the common goal of building quality software efficiently, with a different focus applicable in different environments, and a need for some combination of both approaches in many cases, the so-called hybrid development models.

In this context, Murphy et al. [41, VI.D] found development teams welcome agile software development approaches while project managers tend to be reluctant toward buying-in agile methods, as they prefer to have more control over the work performed, like it is provided by traditional plan-driven approaches. (It certainly does not help to convince project managers that they risk losing their job if development is done by self-organised teams.)

Related to the contrast between agile and plan-driven development is the discussion about the importance and interpretation of risk management and IT governance in software processes. Particularly in financial and safety-related environments, these topics have grown in importance and now often take high priority, be it for internal or legal reasons.

While it is certainly true that there is some conflict between agile development on the one hand, and classical risk management and IT governance on the other, this does not imply that agile development is impossible in such a context. In many cases, it is still possible and helpful to use a hybrid approach in such a context, based on a defined framework for self-organisation rather than strict guidelines that might lead to considerable bureaucracy.

Standardisation of processes. Related to but not identical with the relationship between agile and plan-driven development, one can observe two major streams regarding standardisation: while large companies and companies working in regulated environments typically adopt standardised processes, often based on relevant general standard and norms, small companies working outside regulated environments tend to reject these standardised approaches. Instead, they often go for individual, ad hoc approaches, claiming to follow agile development but not always applying the internal discipline involved in genuine agile development.

Industry and technology trends. Another important factor influencing the evolution of software processes is of course the evolution of the software industry and the related technology. New trends provide new opportunities but also new challenges for the software processes used to implement these trends. Some of the main current trends affecting software processes, both for development and operations, are:

- digitalisation and cyber-physical systems
- cloud computing
- increasing service orientation, both on the level of technology and of customer expectations, resulting e.g. in service-oriented architecture (SOA) and micro-services
- closer cooperation between development and operations, e.g. continuous deployment and DevOps
- increasing relevance of safety and security
- globalisation with different cultures working together, sometimes within the same project
- increasing relevance of off-the-shelve products where the configuration of standard components and services becomes more important than genuine development
- increasing importance of the development of small mobile apps.

Software process variety. As a result of this evolution, there is a large variety of different software processes and life cycle models around, both in practical usage and as published, sometimes standardised, models. Still, practitioners and researchers search for approaches and new models appear on a regular basis.

This is confirmed by various studies. For instance, a study conducted in 2015 [53] and identified more than 60 different process models being used. Apparently, there is a specific process for each situation. Different sources, including scientific studies [53, 55] as well as more practitioner-oriented studies [33, 54] show a trend toward the development and use of *hybrid approaches*, e.g. a waterfall model combined with different agile methods and practices, and even agile methods are adopted to a particular context. The dissemination of process models will be discussed in more detail in Sect. 3.13.

1.1.4 Managing Software Processes

In order to use software processes, they need to be managed adequately. Since such management processes operate on other processes, they are sometimes called *meta-processes* similar to the meta-models introduced later. This section gives a first introduction to the issues to address in software process management which will be covered in more detail in Chap. 4.

In order to achieve their objectives, software organisations need to manage their software processes in a systematic way. This section gives a first introduction to the main topics in software process management. Most of these topics will be discussed in more detail later in this book, mainly in Chapters 4 and 5.

Defined vs. performed process. For a variety of reasons, there is a difference between the *defined* process and the *performed* process performed by development teams. Already in 1986, Parnas and Clements [44] analysed problems with the "ideal [design] process" and explained why it is impossible to fully follow such an ideal process in software development. However, they stated that one could still "fake" it by providing the appropriate documentation after the fact. According to [44], this is partly done to sedate project managers and clients giving them the illusion of a project ran to the letter, but mainly because such an ideal process provides helpful guidance even if not all of it can be implemented.

The main target, of course, is to ensure that there is no major difference between the performed and the defined process, i.e. that the performed process conforms to the defined process.[1] This is true for agile as well as plan-driven approaches, as can e.g. be seen from the argument that a project "is not really using Scrum" (or any other agile methodology) because it does not conform to some agile practice or other.

Process selection and tailoring. Project managers often select a development approach on a per-project basis, usually grounded in their personal experience and preferences [35, 55], which limits project comparability and knowledge transfer.

Organisations therefore tend to define the approach and the processes to be used. While in the past, this tended to be a very detailed definition, today many organisations prefer to set a framework within which the projects define their own processes. The challenge for the organisation in this context is to find a balance, setting the limits sufficiently tight to ensure that different projects can learn from each

---

[1] Obviously, the two variants cannot be identical because the performed process contains a lot of detail that—for good reason—is not contained in the defined process, such as the individuals filling the various roles.

other, developers moving from one project to another can get productive fast, and the projects can be adequately monitored from the management point of view. At the same time, different projects have different side conditions, teams, and tasks, and therefore need to organise themselves and adapt to their specific conditions, implying that the organisational limits should be fairly wide.

Example 1.1. In a software development company, different project types are defined based on their size. A general development process is defined on a high level that applies to all project types. Depending on the project type, certain activities and checkpoints of the general process may be optional so that individual projects may decide themselves whether or not to use them.

Since the architecture of any system developed needs to integrate into the overall architecture, the definition of the high-level architecture to be used leads to a strictly controlled checkpoint. After that, projects are fairly free to define their own detailed approach, using an agile or plan-driven methodology.

Process and product quality. One of the central concepts of most current approaches to quality management is the hypothesis that good processes will lead to good resulting products. This is a hypothesis and not a general statement or theorem since it is not possible to prove that it is correct, due to many outside influences to be taken into account and the fact that there is no general agreement about what makes a "good" process. For example, proponents of agile and plan-driven development will generally agree on the hypothesis, but will have very different opinions about which processes are "good".

This hypothesis can be formalised by the formula $Goal \approx f(Process, Context)$, where "the goal can be any relevant product, service, or project property" [40, p. 22] such as the time taken for certain development steps or the number of bugs in the final product, and f is some function. However, with the current state of software engineering f is a non-deterministic function, i.e. given the same process and the same context (assuming this is possible) it still is not guaranteed that the goal is satisfied to the same extent.

Apart from the process as discussed above, the function f also depends on the development context including topics such as the application domain, the experience of the testers and other participants, or the programming language and tools used. Although not stated explicitly in [40] in this discussion, the process should therefore depend on the context, and the same process may lead to very good results in one context and very bad ones in a different context. Put differently, "the best process" does not exist in general but always depends on the context, including for example the people that perform the process, and any improvement activities should be adapted to the context rather than complaining about a difficult environment, as often happens.

Software Process Improvement (SPI). In order to address the resulting issues and to provide companies with better development models, software processes should be subject to (continuous) software process improvement (see [30]) programs. SPI has been around for decades and is a frequently discussed topic. For instance, Horvat et al. [28] consider SPI as crucial for all companies—regardless of their size—to succeed in the market. At the same time, Henderson-Sellers [26] considers comprehensive improvement initiatives as a "waste of time", and Staples et al. [51] provided a rationale why companies do not adopt normative approaches like CMM(I). Comparable to the software process, SPI is also shaped by diversity and a recently conducted study [36] shows new (non-standardised) approaches proposed on an annual basis.

Software processes and knowledge management. A common feature of most software processes is that they require a fairly large amount of knowledge to perform. The tasks of managing these processes or supporting them via tools therefore has a considerable overlap with knowledge management, and many concepts from knowledge management can be applied to support software processes [31]. For example, it certainly is no coincidence that the Scrum methodology was first introduced in a publication on knowledge management ([52], cf. Sect. 3.5.2).

One can distinguish two basic approaches to knowledge management, codification and personalisation of knowledge [25]. With codification, knowledge is documented in the form of guidelines, procedures or, in our case, software process models and repositories. For knowledge that is fairly structured and mature, this can work very well and form the basis of supporting the work via tools. However, this does not always apply and some knowledge is too complex too manage by documenting it. In this case, the challenge is to manage such knowledge as implicit or tacit knowledge using personalisation of the knowledge, ensuring that employees build up the experience needed, that they exchange experiences even if the knowledge involved cannot be made explicit.

One can recognise these different strategies also in software development processes. Plan-driven development builds mainly on the codification strategy, defining the relevant steps in advance, while agile development puts more emphasis on personalised knowledge.

The relationship between software processes and knowledge management will be discussed in more detail in Sect. 4.9.

Software processes and people. Software processes are largely performed by people, with only small parts automated or at least strongly prescribed. Therefore, the role of these people, their motivation and qualification, have a strong influence on success and need to be taken into account in the design of software processes. One of the first to discuss this aspect of programming was Gerald M. Weinberg in his classic [56].

The people aspect of software processes includes two different viewpoints:

- On the one hand, a very restrictive definition of the processes to be performed will reduce the motivation and the creativity of the developers involved, who typically feel a strong need for freedom in their work. An early criticism of this viewpoint can be found in [15] which introduced the term "peopleware" to emphasize the importance of people in the development of software.

Part of the reason why agile methodologies have become widely accepted is that they tend to put more emphasis on the people performing software development and allowing them a lot of freedom about how to perform their work.

- On the other hand, cooperation within teams is very difficult without agreed and defined rules about who is to do or deliver what, and when to do so. This definition may take different forms, with a thoroughly defined standard process of the organisation at one end of the spectrum, and a set of internal rules agreed within a Scrum team at the other end, including e.g. a "definition of done" that defines what it means for a task to be "done", specifying for example the minimum amount of coding and documentation needed.

1.1.5 Software Process Models and Meta-models

As long as processes and their descriptions are essentially used by humans, in particular by project managers and developers, a fairly low level of formality is sufficient and the processes may be described in an ad-hoc way in natural language, with only limited structure. As far as communication between humans is concerned, a structured but informal process description may actually be more helpful than a more formalised description.

Once we want to support these processes using tools, or to analyse them in any systematic way, we need some form of formal description of the processes. This is where meta-models come into play, i.e. models that define the notation to be used for (software process) models.

As a result, different levels of process description are needed:

- the process execution level refers to the execution of the process, the individual documents created, the activities performed etc.
- the process description level goes up one level of abstraction, defining the process models and the document types, the activity types and so on, thus fixing the objects to be used on the process execution level.
- the process meta-model level goes up another level, containing the description of the concepts used to define the document types, activity types etc., i.e. the objects on the process description level.

These different description level are defined in a more formal way in the Meta Object Facility (MOF), as will be described in Sect. 2.1.3.

1.2 The Software Process Ecosystem

In order to work with software processes and life cycle models, it is not sufficient to have the processes and models themselves but an entire ecosystem around them is needed. Apart from the management of such processes and models, and the meta-models needed (which were all described above), there is a number of additional components that together form such a software process ecosystem. Some of its main building blocks are:

- *tools* to define, manage and perform software processes and life cycle models. Such tools may be used for general standard process models such as ITIL, V-Model XT, CMMI or PRINCE2, or on the level of the organisational or project process model, possibly derived from a general standard model. Therefore, the tools used to define and manage the general standard process models are sometimes made available to the organisations and teams that use these models, as e.g. done for the V-Model XT (see Sect. 2.4.4).
- *training* is an important task in order to get a process model deployed and used. Again, this may happen on different levels, either on the level of general standard process models which often include defined training courses in addition to the models themselves, or on the lower level of individual organisations that want to deploy a certain process and therefore need to train their members in the use of this process.
- *certification infrastructure* when certification regarding a model is to be possible, which is mainly relevant for public process standards, again including ITIL, V-Model XT, CMMI and PRINCE2. Such a certification may refer to individuals and their competencies regarding the process model, or to an organisation and its correct implementation of the process model, see Sect. 5.4.5 for more detail.

Case Study 1.2. (CS Insurance InfoSys) As part of their effort to define and use software processes, CS Insurance InfoSys initially selected Lotus Notes as a tool in which software process definitions were created and made available to all roles involved in development. Later, the same tool was also used to define the processes in the IT services and operations group.

In order to enable the development teams to use the defined processes, a training programme was set up. The main component of this training programme were two one-day trainings, one giving an overview of the life cycle model and how to find detailed information about various processes within the tool. The second training class focussed on CMMI as the reference model used, covering the main requirements of the model and how these are to be satisfied by the software process model used. The main purpose of this second training was to give an understanding of the main ideas behind the software process model and ensure that tailoring of the model was done adequately. Gradually, more than half of all project team members attended at least one of these training classes, which helped to spread the ideas widely even to those that had not attended the training.

Example 1.2. As part of the development of the V-Model XT, tools were built that help edit and adapt the model itself, and to tailor it based on a set of predefined criteria, see Sect. 2.4.4. The editor was mainly used by the team developing the V-Model XT, but made publicly available to support user organisations that want to perform advanced tailoring of the model. The tailoring assistant, on the other hand, is meant for basic tailoring of the model and therefore mainly used by organisation using the V-Model XT.

In addition to the model itself, a set of training classes was set up to support V-Model XT, leading to a certification of the participants. This involves a basic training and certification aimed at project managers and quality managers (V-Modell XT Pro), and an advanced training aimed at process engineers which puts the focus on the meta-model and the tailoring of the model (V-Model XT PIng). A third level of certification for process assessors is currently only available to members of the organisations developing V-Model XT.

Apart from these certifications of individuals, there are two levels of certification for organisation: on the first level, certification confirms that the organisational process model is compliant to the standard model V-Model XT. The second level goes beyond that and also certifies that the organisation correctly applies the compliant organisational process model.

1.3 Historical Overview

Software processes and software process models have been topics of investigation for more than 60 years now. This section provides a brief overview of this history and the different evolution stages of software processes.

Apart from their changing purpose, one of the main influences on software life cycle models was the hardware and software technology available at different times, such as the software engineering tools (compilers, development environments etc.). For example, publications in the 1950s talk about "computer system development" rather than "software development". During that time, software was not usually developed separately from the hardware it was to run on, but in a joint effort. Standard, off-the-shelf hardware became gradually available in the 1960s after IBM had standardized the computer interfaces with the computer family System /360 from

IBM. Closely related is the fact that computing time (and memory) initially was very expensive compared to manpower. This lead to completely different trade-offs between analysing code and testing it compared to today since recompiling and retesting code after each minor change was simply too expensive. [32]

1.3.1 The Early Days

Initial thoughts about how to develop software started more or less from the beginning, keeping in mind that software development initially consisted solely of programming. First ideas about how to go about programming can already be found in the series of reports on coding [22] by Herman H. Goldstine and John von Neumann. These reports arose from their work on the then new EDVAC computer which (like the ENIAC from 1948 onwards [24]) stored its programs in memory and did not need the manipulation of switches and cables for programming. Reference [22] introduced a flow diagram language and then, for a number of mathematical problems, presented flow diagram solutions and derived the appropriate code.

Only a few years later, in 1956, Herbert D. Benington [3], at the time an engineer in the SAGE project, one of the largest and most complex software projects at the time, provided the first explicit representation of a software development life cycle. This model described a linear life cycle with phases such as *Program Specifications* and *System Evaluation*, as shown in Fig. 1.1.

Waterfall models. In spite of Benington's work and a few other similar publications, there was not much interest in software processes at the time. This changed to some extent with Winston W. Royce's paper [48] published in 1970 which describes a software development life cycle. That paper is often referred to as *the* main reference on the waterfall model with a strict sequence of phases. Yet, Royce in [48] actually addressed feedback loops explicitly stating that a linear waterfall (which he described in the early part of his paper, see Fig. 1.2) was not sufficient.

The term "waterfall model" was introduced later in [2] referring to Royce's paper, and became well-known following Barry W. Boehm's book [5] which used the waterfall model as a foundation for estimation, project monitoring and similar tasks.

The V-Model. The V-Model is an enhancement of the linear life cycle, using a V-shaped graphical representation to add emphasis to the systematic verification and validation of results. It was first described in 1979 by Boehm to show "the context of verification and validation activities throughout the software life cycle" [4].

In the V-Model, the life cycle is split into two branches: the left-hand branch contains the requirements, analysis, and design tasks, leading to coding at the bottom of the "V". In the right-hand branch, the system is integrated, tested and verified. These phases each refer to one of the requirements, analysis and design phases, and their task is to verify that the developed products correctly implement the result of the relevant left-hand phase.

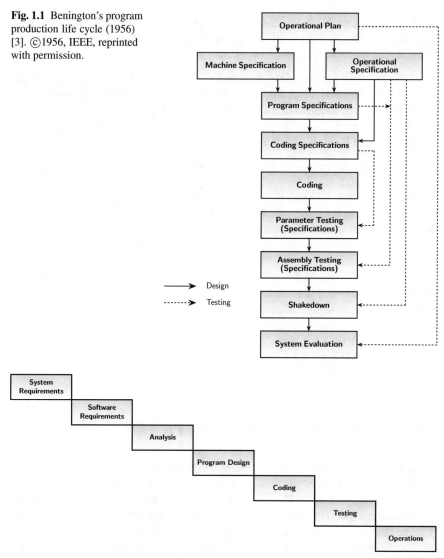

Fig. 1.1 Benington's program production life cycle (1956) [3]. ©1956, IEEE, reprinted with permission.

Fig. 1.2 Royce's waterfall model

Iterative and incremental development. Simple forms of iterative and incremental development involving the use of a prototype were used more or less from the start, see e.g. the descriptions above of the work by Benington and by Royce. Gerald M. Weinberg is cited describing a project in 1957 that did already use iteration where "the technique used was, as far as I can tell, indistinguishable from XP" [37, p. 48]. As described by [37], there was also various other work using iterative or incremental development soon after that.

One should note, however, that the terms "iterative" and "incremental" development are not clearly defined, allowing a number of very different interpretations. Early interpretations included

- creating a prototype or preliminary version, as described by Benington and Royce
- stepwise refinement of an initial abstract model of the system, as described by [58], the first publication describing iterative development
- stepping back one (or more) phases in order to correct any earlier results as necessary, e.g. in Royce's waterfall model

Different types of iterative and incremental development will be discussed in more detail in Sect. 3.2.5.

Even though iterative and incremental development was used even at that early time, it was not in common use. This is at least partly due to the fact that computing time was far more expensive than it is today, and therefore balancing the cost of computing time versus developer time led to very different results compared to today.

Independent of that, software processes and life cycle models did not come into focus until the 1980s. First, the basic building blocks of software processes had to be created, such as structured and other development methods. These involved the description of the required functionality, e.g. using function trees or hierarchical process descriptions using input, processing and output, and further components to support data modelling, e.g. using entity relationship diagrams, and modelling of data and control flows of software programs.

1.3.2 The 1980s: The Rise of Software Processes

In the 1980s, process management became more prominent, not just in software development but in industry in general. For example, the first version of the ISO 9000 series was published in 1987, and a few years later initial versions of IT-specific models such as CMM [45, 46], ITIL [10] and the German software process V-Model [29], predecessor of the V-Model XT (see Sect. 3.4.2), were published. The first *International Software Process Workshop* (ISPW, now called *International Conference on Software and Systems Process* (ICSSP)) took place in 1984 [47], the series of *European Workshops on Software Process Technology* (EWSPT) started in 1991 (initially under a different name, cf. [19]). Apart from the general industry trend, two specific trends led to this increased focus on software processes. At first the discussion on the "software crisis" arose once more due to the increasing size and complexity of software systems and the resulting problems to deliver on time, in quality and in budget—or quite often to deliver at all. Furthermore, object-oriented development (beyond object-oriented programming) started to gain momentum in industry, which led to a need for new development methods, software processes, and life cycle models.

The main focus of research and development on software processes during this time was on process modelling, tailoring, and tool support, such as Process-Centered Software Engineering Environments (PCSEE, see e.g. [23]), Computer-Aided Software Engineering (CASE) or Integrated Project Support Environments (IPSE). The main goal of this work was usually to automate the overall development process or at least parts thereof.

The published software process models during this time mostly concentrated on large and complex systems, often consisting of hard- and software and/or in a military environment. Therefore, large "heavy-weight" processes were taken for granted, describing the development steps in detail and sometimes even trying to enforce the defined process using tools. Leon Osterweil's seminal paper [43] describes this approach quite well as "programming the process".

This also applied to object-oriented development: development methods changed, structured analysis and design turned into object-oriented analysis and design and eventually UML, but even here development processes were typically defined in a lot of detail, as for instance in the (Rational) Unified Process discussed in Sect. 3.4.1.

1.3.3 The 1990s and Early 2000s: Lightweight and Agile Processes

As a reaction to the growing importance of software processes, there was also a backlash stating that such processes are too restrictive on the developers. Another major concern was the linear structure of the common process models, which did not allow for iterations, even though the concept of iterative development was not new and had been in use for some time. As part of this backlash, some of the newer life cycle models did explicitly support (frequent) iterations, for example prototyping [18], Boehm's spiral model ([6]; cf. Sect. 3.2.5.2) and, a few years later, Rapid Application Development (RAD) [38]. This movement toward iterative development and less restrictive processes grew stronger during the 1990s, leading to *light-weight processes*. Several new development approaches were introduced, such as Scrum (see Sect. 3.5.2), Extreme Programming (XP, see Sect. 3.5.5), Dynamic Systems Development Method (DSDM), the Crystal family of methods [13], Feature Driven Development (FDD, see [12, 42]), and many more. In various shapes and with different focal points, these methods extended the original concept of iterative and incremental development and introduced the concepts now known as Agile Methods, such as intensive communication within the project, fast feedback, few external rules for the way of working etc. A similar movement against a plan- and process-driven way of working also occurred in industrial production, where *Lean Production* had become quite important, mainly initiated by [57]. Many ideas introduced by lean production were later adapted by the agile software development methods.

Initially, these processes were usually called "light-weight'' as opposed to the fairly detailed "heavy-weight" processes. With the publication of the Agile Manifesto (see Sect. 3.5.1 or [1]) in 2001 the new term *agile methods* was introduced and immediately accepted widely. The common values and principles of agile methods as summarised in the agile manifesto helped them to gain considerable importance, even though there were many fundamental and sometimes very emotional discussions about the adequacy of classic, plan-driven versus agile development approaches. Fortunately, both sides gradually came to understand that both approaches have their strengths and weaknesses, and therefore are appropriate for different types of projects. In particular, as for example Boehm and Turner elaborated in [8], both approaches do not necessarily contradict each other but in many cases a combination of both is the best solution.

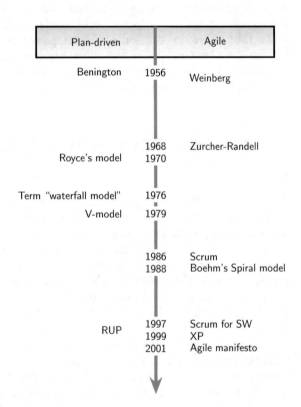

Fig. 1.3 Major milestones in the history of software life cycle models

1.3.4 Recent Trends

There is a wide spectrum of recent trends in software processes, and Chap. 8 will discuss some of these in more detail:

- Software process lines

- Process intelligence and process mining
- Statistical process control
- Process simulation
- Continuous delivery and DevOps

This section will give a short overview of other current software process trends:

Agile, plan-driven and hybrid life cycles. Although the discussions have become slightly less dogmatic, the questions about which approach is "better" and which criteria to choose to select one of the many available models of course stays relevant.

In order to be able to make reliable statements about the adequacy of different types of process or life cycle models, systematic investigation, without trying to promote one approach or another, is starting (see e.g. [8, 39]), but there certainly still is a long way to go.

Agile in-the-large. To address the difficulty that agile approaches are often well-suited to small development teams but difficult to handle in larger teams, a number of new methodologies are being investigated and introduced to scale agile development to larger teams and entire companies. This topic will be covered in more detail in Sect. 3.5.9.

IT Governance. Since governance in general and IT governance in particular are growing in importance in many companies, this of course also affects software processes. So far, this mainly affects operations and service management processes, but gradually software development processes start to be addressed as well. See Sect. 4.8 for more information about this topic.

Global and distributed software processes. A trend that runs counter to the trend of agile development is the globalisation of software processes, both development and service and operations processes. The main reasons for this trend are cost pressure, trying to make use of lower salary levels in other, mainly Asian, countries, as well as the availability of qualified resources in those countries.

In software services and operations, there is an additional reason for this trend, namely the possibility to provide around-the-clock services more easily, and to speed up resolution of incidents and problems by "following the sun", passing any incidents and problems which are still open at the end of the working day on to colleagues in some other time zone which only just start work.

Of course, distributing work around the world like this will have a major influence on the software processes used, for example making face-to-face communication more difficult and requiring more documentation. Section 4.10 will cover this topic in more detail.

Open source development. A closely related challenge to software engineering and the processes used is the increasing relevance of open source development. Open source development teams are often distributed around the world, which means the difficulties in communication are similar to those described above for global and distributed software processes.

Additionally, open source development typically has a higher risk of developers not being available or delivering late due to other commitments and priorities. The processes used therefore need to support sufficient flexibility to cope with this challenge.

Raymond discussed some of the major challenges involved in open source software development, introducing the distinction between the "cathedral" and the "bazaar" approach (cf. Sect. 3.5.8).

Configuration of software rather than development. A sign of the increasing maturity of software development is the trend to configure software from existing components, rather than develop everything from scratch. Although the basic development life cycle stays the same, the priorities and the distribution of effort changes considerably, leading to more emphasis on integration and testing and less on coding.

Processes for new technologies and application areas. With the change in technology and software application areas, the processes needed to develop the software also need to change. Digitalisation and other technology trends such as app development, cloud computing, cyber-physical systems, product lines and big data also influence the software processes needed for development and operations, typically with a combination of the need for fast reaction to changing requirements, high reliability and ease of use of the resulting software products.

1.4 Terminology and Basic Concepts

In this section, we introduce the main terminology and basic concepts needed to talk about software processes, software process models and life cycle models. Wherever possible and adequate, definitions will be taken from relevant norms and standards, in particular from SEVOCAB *Systems and software engineering—Vocabulary*.

SEVOCAB collects vocabulary from a large number of different standards into a single document, adding further terminology as considered relevant. Most definitions in the remainder of this book can therefore be found in this standard. Unfortunately, due to its role as a collection of vocabulary, the definitions included are not always consistent. Where relevant, such inconsistencies will be pointed out below, and usually only that definition that the author considers most widely used or most relevant in the context of software processes will be included.

However, since this section concentrates on defining the various terminology used later, it is not easy reading. Readers may therefore consider to just skim over this section, and come back later to read specific parts of it in detail when the relevant terms are used.

1.4.1 General Terminology

We start with some general terminology regarding the environment of software processes:

Definition 1.1 (System). *Combination of interacting elements organised to achieve one or more stated purposes. (ISO/IEC 15288:2015, SEVOCAB)*

In the context of software processes, we are mainly interested in systems that consist of or at least include software:

Definition 1.2 (Software). *All or part of the programs, procedures, rules, and associated documentation of an information processing system. (SEVOCAB)*

Although software can also be developed in an ad-hoc, unsystematic manner, in this book we are mainly interested in software development performed using a systematic engineering approach:

Definition 1.3 (Software engineering). *Application of a systematic, disciplined, quantifiable approach to the development, operation, and maintenance of software; that is, the application of engineering to software. (SEVOCAB)*

Software processes form only a small part of software engineering, but this is a very central part, providing a framework of when and how to apply the various methods defined by software engineering.

1.4.2 Process Terminology

We now come to one of the main terms in this context, the "process":

Definition 1.4 (Process). *Set of interrelated or interacting activities which use inputs to deliver an intended result. (ISO 9000:2015, SEVOCAB)*

Processes are therefore often described as consisting of input, processing and output (IPO), leading to the high-level notations used for processes described in Sect. 2.3.3. While this description is useful for many purposes, it leaves out the important fact that a process should have a goal as well—that is why a process delivers an *intended* result according to the definition above.

A process may be *performed*, *enacted* or *executed*. There is no standard distinction between these terms, except that *process execution* often (but not always) refers to automated processes, executed by a machine. Following [40, Glossary], the term *process enactment* will be used in this book to describe that a process is enacted by humans, machines, or a combination of both. The term *process execution* will be used if the process is executed by machines (only). The term *process performance* will be used as synonymous with process enactment, but in general, the term process enactment will be preferred because process performance also describes the extent to which enactment of a process achieves its purpose (ISO/IEC 33001:2015, SEVOCAB).

Processes can be broken down into sub-processes, activities and tasks as follows:

Definition 1.5 (Task). *Required, recommended, or permissible action, intended to contribute to the achievement of one or more outcomes of a process. (ISO/IEC 12207:2008, SEVOCAB)*

Definition 1.6 (Activity). *Set of cohesive tasks of a process. (ISO/IEC 12207:2008, SEVOCAB)*

Definition 1.7 (Sub-process). *A process that is part of a larger process. (CMMI® v1.3 [11])*

Even though it is not stated explicitly in this definition, a task is usually considered as the smallest unit of work that is not split any further in (project) management. These smallest units of work are sometimes also called process steps or atomic processes (e.g. [40, p. 11]) or process elements (e.g. CMMI v1.3).

A closely related term is the "procedure":

Definition 1.8 (Procedure). *Specified way to carry out an activity or a process. (ISO 9000:2015, SEVOCAB)*

Documented versions of such procedures are commonly called "standard operating procedures" (SOP) , in particular in regulated environments such as the production of pharmaceutical products.

The entity relationship diagram in Fig. 1.4 provides an overview of these terms and their relationships.

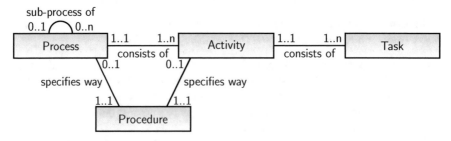

Fig. 1.4 Relationship between processes and related terms

While a process is defined as a set of activities and describes the details of the individual process steps, their input and output and how to combine them, the life cycle addresses a slightly different aspect, focussing on the combination and in particular the temporal relationship of the various processes and activities:

Definition 1.9 (Life cycle). *Evolution of a system, product, service, project or other human-made entity from conception through retirement. (ISO/IEC 12207:2008, SE-VOCAB)*

The PMBOK® Guide contains the very similar definitions of the *product life cycle*, defining it as a *series of phases* that represent the evolution of a product, as defined here for the life cycle, and of the *project life cycle*, a series of phases that a project passes through.

To manage a life cycle, it is often described in the form of a model, leading to the life cycle models as one of the core concepts of this book:

Definition 1.10 (Life cycle model). *Framework of processes and activities concerned with the life cycle, which can be organised into stages, and which acts as a common reference for communication and understanding. (ISO/IEC 12207:2008, SEVOCAB)*

Since most processes are performed repeatedly, we need to be able to distinguish between the process itself and the individual instance of the process:

Definition 1.11 (Process instance). *Single specific and identifiable execution of a process. (ISO/IEC 33001:2015, SEVOCAB)*

As discussed in more detail in Sect. 2.1.4, the main components of a process definition are usually the roles involved and the products created, in addition to the activities performed. The concept of roles is introduced in order to define responsibility for groups of activities and tasks without referring to individuals. A role is then assigned to individuals as part of project planning. Depending on factors such as the specific role under consideration, the size of the project etc., a role may be assigned to one or more individuals, and an individual may be assigned one or more roles within a project.

Definition 1.12 (Role). *A defined function to be performed by a project team member, such as testing, filing, inspecting, coding. (PMBOK® Guide; SEVOCAB)*

Rather than assigning responsibility for certain activities and tasks directly to a role, this may be done indirectly by assigning the responsibility for a product (which is created or modified by a certain activity or task) to a role.

Typical roles in software processes are developer, tester or project leader. Roles are assigned to individuals, but this is rarely a 1:1-relationship. The same role may be assigned to multiple individuals, e.g. there usually are several developers in a project, or the same individual may fill multiple roles, e.g. in a small project the project leader may also be a developer and perhaps a tester.

According to this definition, qualification requirements are not explicitly part of the concept of a role, but in the context of process definition or improvement it is often useful to explicitly identify the qualifications needed.

Definition 1.13 (Product). *An artefact that is produced, is quantifiable, and can be either an end item in itself or a component item. (PMBOK® Guide; SEVOCAB)*

Instead of "product", the term "work product" is often used, as for example in CMMI®.

1.4.3 Software Process Terminology

To stick closely to the definition of processes introduced above, we define software processes as follows:

Definition 1.14 (Software process). *A process that forms part of the life cycle of software.*

Typical software processes include core processes such as requirements analysis, design, and implementation, but also processes later in the life cycle such as maintenance and operations, and supporting processes such as quality assurance and project planning.

SWEBOK® uses "software process" as an abbreviation for "software engineering process", but uses a very similar interpretation to our "software process" above.[2]

There are many different (and sometimes contradictory) definitions of the term "software process". SEVOCAB does not define it at all but defines the similar "software development process". An alternative definition is added here that relates the software development process to the software development life cycle:

Definition 1.15 (Software development process).

1. *Process by which user needs are translated into a software product. (SEVOCAB)*
2. *A software process that is performed (fully or at least partly) during the development part of the software life cycle.*

Reference [40] defines (software) processes only in the context of an "engineering-style" development.[3] Compared to that definition, our definition is more general and allows for undefined and unsystematic software processes as well.

Like processes in general, software processes can be combined in a life cycle. Following SWEBOK®, we distinguish between the software development life cycle and the software product life cycles:[4]

Definition 1.16 (Software development life cycle (SDLC)). *Life cycle that includes the software development processes used to specify software requirements and transform them into a deliverable software product. (Based on SWEBOK)*

Definition 1.17 (Software (product) life cycle (SPLC)). *Life cycle that includes the software development life cycle plus additional software processes that provide for deployment, maintenance, support, evolution, retirement, and all other inception-to-retirement processes for a software product, including the software*

---

[2] "...software engineering processes are concerned with work activities accomplished by software engineers to develop, maintain, and operate software ..." [9, p. 8-1].

[3] "A software process is a goal-oriented activity in the context of engineering-style software development." [40, p. 8]

[4] SEVOCAB defines neither of these terms but introduces the term *software development cycle* instead, which is defined as the "period of time that begins with the decision to develop a software product and ends when the software is delivered".

configuration management and software quality assurance processes that are applied throughout a software product life cycle.

A software product life cycle may include multiple software development life cycles for evolving and enhancing the software.
(Based on SWEBOK)

In the following, we will also use the abbreviation *software life cycle* instead of software product life cycle.

When talking about *applications* rather than software in general, the term "application life cycle" is also commonly used, in particular in the context of *Application Life Cycle Management (ALM)*.

(Software) life cycles are often broken down into smaller components called phases or stages:

Definition 1.18 ((Life cycle) phase). *Collection of logically related life cycle activities. During development, a phase usually culminates in the completion of a major deliverable. (Adapted from the definition of project phases in PMBOK® Guide; SEVOCAB)*

We follow here the tradition to define a phase as a collection of *logically* related activities, as opposed to a collection of activities that are *temporally* related, i.e. performed within the same *stage*:

Definition 1.19 (Stage). *Period within the life cycle of an entity that relates to the state of its description or realization. (SEVOCAB)*

As the examples below show, the definitions of phase and stage often overlap, i.e. activities belonging to the same phase tend to be performed within the same stage, and vice versa. However, the term "phase" can also be used to group activities that are performed across the entire project, such as project or configuration management, or activities such as requirements analysis that are mainly done in the requirements phase but continue to be performed almost until the end of the development project.

Typical project phases mentioned in SEVOCAB are for example concept phase, requirements phase, design phase, implementation phase, test phase, and installation and checkout phase. After development, phases such as the operation and maintenance phase and finally the retirement phase follow. Different life cycle models can mainly be distinguished by the different sequences of phases that they describe. In Chap. 3, this topic will be covered in more detail.

The end of a phase is often defined as a stage gate:

Definition 1.20 (Stage gate). *A review at the end of a stage in which a decision is made to continue to the next stage, to continue with modification, or to end a project. (based on the definition of phase gate in PMBOK® Guide and SEVOCAB)*

In order to keep the terminology consistent, the term "stage gate" is used here instead of the term "phase gate" as defined in the PMBOK® Guide.

A concept very similar to a stage gate that has become fairly popular in the development of technical systems and software is the quality gate:

Definition 1.21 (Quality gate). *A defined set of results and activities to be completed at a certain point within development such as the end of a stage, in combination with a formal review to verify that all expected results have been prepared in adequate quality, and all expected activities have been performed.*

Such a formal review usually results in a decision about whether and how to continue work, similar to the stage gate. In comparison, quality gates are slightly more general since they may be be performed somewhere in the middle of a stage as well as at its end. On the other hand, a quality gate explicitly includes the expected results and activities, but of course these are implicitly part of the concept of a stage gate as well.

Both stage gates and quality gates are interpreted as "gates" to be passed before work can continue. They are fairly common in development of technical systems, but rarely with the strict interpretation that work is not allowed to continue until the gate has been passed. Since gates are used to explicitly close a development step, the term is mainly used in plan-driven development, while they do not fit well with the concept of agile development.

On a smaller scale, quality gates are also commonly used in agile development, for example in the "definition of done" of a backlog item as described in Sect. 3.5.2.

Definition 1.22 (Milestone). *A significant point or event in the project. (PMBOK® Guide; SEVOCAB)*

Milestones are often used to measure progress and therefore usually defined by the significant point or event in combination with the planned point in time when the milestone is to be reached. A milestone review is then performed to verify that the significant point or event has indeed been reached, e.g. a defined set of results been created in adequate quality. Payment of the project is sometimes based on achieving certain milestones, i.e. for each milestones, a defined percentage of the overall project price is due to be paid by the customer.

Both stage gates and quality gates can be considered as special kinds of milestones.

Although the term "milestone" is mainly used in plan-driven development, the completion of an iteration in agile development might be considered as a milestone as well.

Another term related to the life cycle is the "methodology". SEVOCAB contains two similar definitions of this term as follows, where in particular the second one points to the close relationship to (software) processes:

Definition 1.23 (Methodology).

1. *A system of practices, techniques, procedures and rules used by those who work in a discipline. (PMBOK® Guide; SEVOCAB)*
2. *Specification of the process to follow together with the work products to be used and generated, plus the consideration of the people and tools involved, during an information-based domain (IBD) development effort. (ISO/IEC 24744:2014; SEVOCAB)*

In the agile community, the term "methodology" is wide-spread while terms such as "software process" or "life cycle model" are mainly used for plan-driven approaches.

Where possible, the terms "software process", "software life cycle" and "methodology" will be distinguished in this book, but in many cases the distinction is not really clear. In such cases, the term "software process" will be used.

1.4.4 Model and Meta-model Terminology

The term "model" has many different meanings. In the context of software processes and software process models, this term is used in its meaning as an abstract or conceptual model, and in this book we will only use it with that meaning.

Definition 1.24 (Model).

1. *Representation of a real world process, device, or concept. (SEVOCAB)*
2. *An abstract representation of an existing entity or an entity to be created, where entity denotes any part of reality or any other conceivable set of elements or phenomena, including other models.*
   With respect to a model, the entity is called the original. (IREB® Glossary [21])

Definition 1.25 (Descriptive and prescriptive models). *If a model represents an existing entity, it is called a* descriptive *model. If it represents an entity that is to be created, it is called a* prescriptive *model.*

The two definitions of models from SEVOCAB and from the IREB® Glossary essentially describe the same concept, but the second one emphasizes the fact that a model may not only describe the existing real world but also the real world as it is to be created. In the context of process modelling as discussed here, this is an important distinction and we will need to deal with both variants.

Nevertheless, the difference between descriptive and prescriptive models is solely a difference in the purpose but not necessarily in the contents of the model. In process modelling, the two models actually often form a cycle, as described e.g. in [40, p. 21]: a descriptive model is analysed and improved, leading to a prescriptive model. This prescriptive model is deployed, and therefore eventually describes the process as it is actually performed.

A software process model typically describes the way software is to be developed, and in this case it is a prescriptive model. However, software process models can also describe how software is actually developed, in order to analyse and improve this process, in which case it is a descriptive model.

One of the main challenges in defining a prescriptive model is not the definition itself but to make sure that the model is actually used (deployment). This topic will be covered in Sect. 4.6.

Note that from a constructivist view, the definition above is quite inadequate since it assumes that the modelled "real world" exists independent of the person creating or using the model rather than being constructed by the modeller (see e.g. [49]). However, in this context we will ignore this issue.

Following Stachowiak's *General Model Theory* a model is characterised by three properties [34, 50]:[5]

- Mapping property: a model is a mapping or representation of some entity.

  - In the case of software process models, the modelled entity is the software process, either as it is supposed to be performed (prescriptive model) or as it is actually performed (descriptive model).

- Reduction property: a model is a reduction of the represented entity and does not contain all attributes of the original. If this was not the case, the model would be identical to or a copy of the original.

  - In the case of software process models, we for example do not want to include the specifics of one particular development effort into the model, such as the names of the developers (rather than their respective roles) or the specific requirements to be implemented in this case.

- Pragmatic property: a model is created for a certain purpose, which implies that *the* correct model of some original does not exist. There are many possible models and their adequacy depends on the purpose of the model. The pragmatic property therefore addresses the usefulness of a model and guides which aspects of the original are left out in the model.

  - Again looking at the case of software process models, we first have to identify what we want to do with a certain model. If we plan a prescriptive model we need to define which rules to be included in the model we really want to apply to all projects, and which rules should be defined as optional. If the process model is to be passed to the customer, we may want to leave out certain content that would be included in a process model for internal use only.

In order to describe a model, we need to define how this is to be done, and what terminology may be used. In other words, we need a model of the model, a meta-model (also called a process scheme, see e.g. [40, p. 12]:

Definition 1.26 (Meta-model).

1. *Specification of the concepts, relationships and rules that are used to define a methodology. (ISO/IEC 24744:2014; SEVOCAB)*
2. *Model defining the concepts and their relations for some modelling notation (ISO/IEC 15909-2:2011, SEVOCAB)*

While the first definition concentrates on the use for definition of a methodology and therefore is more directly related to software processes, the second is more general and refers to the definition of general models.

---

[5] These properties are also used in the IREB requirements engineering glossary [21] to describe the concept of a model.

As an example, a meta-model may define that a software process model is to be defined using a strictly defined structure of activities, products and roles etc., or it may allow fairly unstructured text in natural language. Different approaches to define software process models and meta-models will be discussed in Chap. 2.

An alternative term that is sometimes used instead of "meta-model" is the "notation" used to describe a model.

1.4.5 Process Model Terminology

1.4.5.1 The process cube

The concept of a process involves some very different views, which can be represented as different dimensions shown by the process cube in Fig. 1.5.

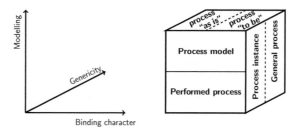

Fig. 1.5 The process cube

"Performed process" vs. "Process model". A very common mistake is to refer to the "process" when actually talking about the process model which is only part of the overall process. Apart from the model, the process also includes the process as it is actually performed, which may or may not be the same as described in the model. Put differently, the process model describes the *explicit* understanding of the process, while the performed process describes the *implicit* understanding. As a result, both components of the process are actually optional, since a process may be modelled but not (yet) performed, or—more common—it may be performed but not modelled.

"Process 'as is' " vs. "Process 'to be' ". At first sight, this distinction might seem to be the same as the previous one. However, a process model may be descriptive, describing the process "as is", or it may be prescriptive, describing the process "to be". Similarly, even if a process has not been modelled, there exists an implicit expectation of how the process should be performed, the process "to be".

"General process" vs. "Process instance". Most processes exist on two different levels: there is the level of the individual instance, where the process is performed once, and the level of the general process as it is performed repeatedly, across dif-

ferent instances. Although this distinction is mainly relevant on the level of the performed process, it also applies to the process model which may refer to the details
of an individual instance, or be specified in a more abstract format for all instances.

Apart from helping to understand the concept of a process and its different aspects or dimensions, the process cube also helps to visualise many tasks within
process management which are concerned with the relationship between different
components within the process cube, such as comparing them or transitioning between these components. It will therefore be used later in this book to visualise
various process management tasks.

1.4.5.2 Standard processes and tailoring

A commonly used concept regarding processes is the standard process:

Definition 1.27 (Standard process). *Set of definitions of the processes used to
guide processes in an organisation. (SEVOCAB; ISO/IEC 33001: 2015)*

The standard process is often defined on the level of an organisation, or sometimes
more general as a public standard or norm, and applies to all instances of the process,
in all or at least many projects and teams of the organisation. Locating it in the
process cube, a standard process is a general process / process model / process "to
be".

Adapting a standard process to a specific environment is called "tailoring":

Definition 1.28 (Process tailoring). *Making, altering, or adapting a process description for a particular end. (SEVOCAB)*

The "particular end" of tailoring is usually the definition of a process to be used in a
specific project or, more general, in a smaller environment than the original standard
process.

The definition of tailoring leads to the following obvious definition of the tailored
process:

Definition 1.29 (Tailored process). *Process developed by tailoring a standard process. (ISO/IEC/IEEE 33001:2015,SEVOCAB)*

Other definitions of tailoring are more restrictive and only include "cutting off"
everything that is not needed. However, sometimes moving from a standard process
to the process used in a specific project also includes adding tasks, work products
and other contents to the process that is specific to this individual case, e.g. because
a different technology is used.

Tailoring may occur on different levels as shown in Fig. 1.6, here in two steps
from a general standard process to an organisational standard process, and from the
organisational standard process to the project's tailored process. In principle, more
tailoring levels are possible but are rarely needed. In the process cube, a tailored
process is a process model / process "to be" like the standard process, but depending
on the level of tailoring it may still be a general process or a process instance.

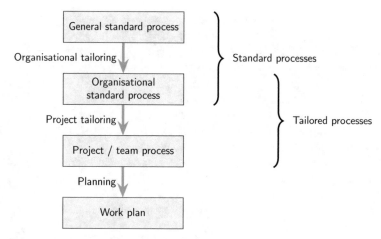

Fig. 1.6 Standard processes and tailored processes

Figure 1.6 also includes the step of project planning which adds further information to the project process such as the resources used, dates, or the information that certain steps need to be repeated multiple times (e.g. if the software product contains multiple modules, then module test must be performed for each of them). Except for large projects, the steps of project tailoring and planning are however usually integrated, with little or no separate documentation of the project process.

In the context of maturity models (described in Sect. 5.5), the related term "defined process" is also commonly used to describe a process that is tailored from the set of standard processes according to the organisation's tailoring guidelines, has a documented and maintained process description, and contributes process improvement information to the organisation's process assets. Such a defined process is considered to achieve capability level 3 according to these models.

Case Study 1.3. (CS Insurance InfoSys) CS Insurance InfoSys has defined two different project types which have different life cycle models, a V-shaped model (see Sect. 3.2.2) and a Scrum-based model (see Sect. 3.5.2), with defined criteria on when to use which of these models. For each of these life cycle models, there is a set of documented standard processes, with some overlap between them. In the process cube, these standard processes are process models, describing the general process "to be". However, not all aspects of the process that are expected to be implemented are also documented in the standard processes (general performed process "to be"), for example the cooperation with all other stakeholders such as the central IT security group, central architecture group etc..

When a project starts, it selects and adapts (tailors) the life cycle model and the processes to be used, and documents these in the project plan. The project plan again describes the model of the processes "to be", but this time for an individual instance (if the process is performed only once per project) or a reduced general process (if the process is performed multiple times within the project). Again, certain aspects of the process instance are "to be" performed without being modelled/planned.

Looking at a process that is performed only once, say database design in a project using the V-shaped model, we see the performed process "as is" for an individual instance. At the end of the month, the project leader creates a project report stating how this process was performed, i.e. the status report describes a process model of the process instance "as is". The same aspect of the process, but possibly with a different result, is described by the project quality manager when he performs an audit on this process and reports the result.

Going one step up, looking at the different projects within CS Insurance InfoSys and how they perform the various processes, leads to the general performed processes "as is". At the end of the year, there is a quality management review of these various processes reporting how the processes were actually performed, in particular which deviations from the standard processes were identified, leading to the general process model "as is".

1.4.6 Major Phases Within Software Life Cycles

To some extent, all software life cycles contain the same major software engineering phases even though the details and the ordering of these phases may be quite different. This section gives a short overview of these phases which will later form the main building blocks of the various life cycle models. Remember that, according to Def. 1.18, a phase contains a collection of *logically* related activities which may or may not be temporally related.

One of the first steps in most software life cycles is (requirements) analysis:

Definition 1.30 (Requirements analysis). *Process of studying user needs to arrive at a definition of system, hardware, or software requirements. (SEVOCAB)*

While waterfall-type life cycle models attempt to perform the entire requirements analysis at the beginning of a development effort, iterative and incremental life cycle models, to a varying degree, start with parts of requirements analysis but then perform some or all of the other development activities before continuing with requirements analysis.

Building on the results of requirements analysis, the solution must be designed:

Definition 1.31 (Design). *Process of defining the software architecture, components, modules, interfaces, and data for a software system to satisfy specified requirements. (SEVOCAB)*

As needed, different levels and types of design may be distinguished such as preliminary design, detailed design, functional design, architectural design, interface design etc..

After design, the design results are implemented:

Definition 1.32 (Implementation). *Process of translating a design into hardware components, software components, or both. (SEVOCAB)*

To ensure that the implemented system works as expected, it is usually tested:

Definition 1.33 (Test). *Activity in which a system or component is executed under specified conditions, the results are observed or recorded, and an evaluation is made of some aspect of the system or component. (SEVOCAB)*

Note that according to this definition, the term "test" requires the system to be executed. Occasionally, a wider definition of testing is used which also includes other forms of analysing the system, in particular reviews and static analysis.

Once a software system has been implemented and tested, it is deployed:

Definition 1.34 (Deployment). *Phase of a project in which a system is put into operation and cutover issues are resolved (SEVOCAB)*

There are many variations of naming and exact content of this development step, such as roll-out or transition.

Finally, the system is put into operations in order to be actually used:

Definition 1.35 (Operations). *Ongoing execution of activities that produce the same product or provide a repetitive service. (SEVOCAB)*

This definition is somewhat wider than needed in this context, since operations of software systems will provide a (repetitive) service but not any physical products.

Two closely related tasks that, to varying degrees, need to be performed across the entire development effort are verification and validation (sometimes abbreviated as "V& V"):

Definition 1.36 (Verification). *Confirmation, through the provision of objective evidence, that specified requirements have been fulfilled (ISO/IEC 12207:2008, SEVOCAB)*

Definition 1.37 (Validation). *In a life cycle context, the set of activities ensuring and gaining confidence that a system is able to accomplish its intended use, goals and objectives. (ISO/IEC 12207:2008, SEVOCAB)*

The main difference between both tasks is that verification builds on an existing specification of a result and checks ("verifies") that a result has been created according to this specification. As an example, the results of the test phase may be verified by checking that all stated software requirements are being tested. This same test may then verify that the software requirements have been implemented correctly.

Validation, on the other hand, starts from the informal stakeholder needs as a reference and checks that the result supports those needs. As a result, validation of the initial requirements, e.g. using reviews, is an important step, since these initial requirements by definition cannot be verified but will form a basis for all later verification steps. In regulated environments where the final system will need some form of legal confirmation in order to be allowed to be used, the term "validation" is often used specifically for all tasks needed to prepare for getting such a legal confirmation.

To better distinguish between verification and validation, it is often said the validation is concerned with "doing the right thing", while verification is concerned with "doing things right". ITIL uses different wording and looks at it from a different angle but discusses the same concepts in its distinction between "fitness for purpose" (utility), which is checked by validation, and "fitness for use" (warranty), which is checked by verification.

Closely connected with verification is the concept of traceability. In order to verify that a certain result conforms to a certain part of a specification, it must be clearly defined which result is expected to implement this part of the specification, and which part of the specification contains the requirements on this result.

Definition 1.38 (Traceability). *Degree to which a relationship can be established between two or more products of the development process, especially products having a predecessor-successor or master-subordinate relationship to one another. (SE-VOCAB)*

Traceability is usually mainly used in the context of requirements traceability where results are related to the appropriate requirements.

1.4.7 Other Relevant Terminology

Another term that is very relevant in the discussion of (software) processes is "quality", since one of the main goals of explicitly working with processes is to improve the quality of the resulting products.

Definition 1.39 (Quality). *Quality is the degree to which a set of inherent characteristics fulfils requirements. (ISO 9000:2015)*

Of course, there are many different approaches to defining the term "quality", see e.g. Garvin's description of five different approaches to defining quality in [20]: (1) the transcendent approach of philosophy; (2) the product-based approach of economics; (3) the user-based approach of economics, marketing, and operations management; and (4) the manufacturing-based and (5) value-based approaches of operations management.

Apart from applying the concept of quality to products such as software, it can be applied to many other entities such as processes themselves, to process models, meta-models and to services. In this context, we are mainly interested in the quality of processes:

Definition 1.40 (Process quality). *Ability of a process to satisfy stated and implied stakeholder needs when used in a specified context. (ISO/IEC 33001:2015, SEVO-CAB)*

In order to evaluate and perhaps measure the quality of any such entity, the concept of quality must in general be defined in more detail. For example, the quality of software processes and software process models will be discussed in more detail in Sect. 5.2, the quality of software in Sect. 6.3.2.

Most (but not all) software development is performed within projects:

Definition 1.41 (Project). *A project is a temporary endeavour undertaken to create a unique product, service, or result. (PMBOK® Guide, Fifth Edition; SEVOCAB)*

Software processes form a large part of the work performed in software projects, and (defined) software processes will provide a basis for planning and managing a software project.

The distinction between work performed as a project and other work is not always clear-cut. In general, development of a new software system will lead to a "unique" product and therefore be performed as a project, while maintenance of an existing software system typically will be a routine activity rather than a project. Enhancement of an existing system, adding further functionality, may be performed either way, depending on the kind and size of the enhancement. However, since the work needs to be planned and managed in both cases using similar methods, the distinction is of limited importance.

Finally, a concept that will occur in different contexts within the discussion of software processes is the "risk":

Definition 1.42 (Risk). *Uncertain event or condition that, if it occurs, has a positive or negative effect on one or more project objectives*
(PMBOK® Guide, Fifth Edition; SEVOCAB)

Although according to this definition, a risk may describe an uncertain event with a positive effect, the term is usually used to refer to uncertain events with negative effects.

A risk has two important parameters that are used to evaluate or quantify it: the size of the potential (positive or negative) effect, and the probability that this effect actually occurs. These two parameters can then be combined in various ways to quantify the risk, e.g. by taking their product to receive the expected value (in the statistical sense) of the size of the effect.

Further Reading

Reference [7] provides a good overview of the development of the main ideas of software engineering since the 1950s, which of course have a strong influence on and interaction with the software engineering processes.

More specific, [32] describes the historical development of software processes and their fundamental ideas from Benington in 1956 onwards.

Specific aspects of the history of software processes are described in more detail in [23] and [37]. While [37] investigates the development of iterative and incremental development and demonstrates how this was used from the 1950s onwards, much earlier than most people would expect today, [23] describes the history of tool support using Process-Centered Software Engineering Environments.

A good summary of how the Agile Manifesto came into being can be found in [27].

Not exactly a document to read but nevertheless very useful as a reference is the standard SEVOCAB *Systems and software engineering—Vocabulary* (SEVOCAB) which collects definitions of terminology from various other norms and standards.

Exercises

1.1. For each of the eight components of the process cube, explain its meaning and provide a practical example.

1.2. To what extent would it have been possible to use Scrum and similar methodologies using the technology available in the 1960s?

1.3. Identify three items of software development knowledge where the codification strategy of knowledge management works best, and three items where the personalisation strategy works best.

1.4. What are the main risks of working with defined software processes and life cycle models? What are the main risks of not doing so?

1.5. What are the main elements that together form a process?

References

1. K. Beck, M. Beedle, A. v. Bennekum, A. Cockburn, W. Cunningham, M. Fowler, J. Grenning, J. Highsmith, A. Hunt, R. Jeffries, J. Kern, B. Marick, R. C. Martin, S. Mellor, K. Schwaber, J. Sutherland, and D. Thomas. Manifesto for agile software development. Available online at http://agilemanifesto.org (last access 2017-07-19), October 2001.
2. T. E. Bell and T. A. Thayer. Software requirements: Are they really a problem? In *Proceedings of the 2nd International Conference on Software Engineering, San Francisco, California, USA, October 13-15, 1976.*, pages 61–68, 1976.
3. H. D. Benington. Production of large computer programs. *IEEE Annals of the History of Computing*, 5(4):350–361, 1983.
4. B. W. Boehm. Guidelines for verifying and validating software requirements and design specifications. In *Euro IFIP 79*, 1979.
5. B. W. Boehm. *Software Engineering Economics*. Prentice-Hall, Englewood Cliffs, 1981.
6. B. W. Boehm. A spiral model of software development and enhancement. *IEEE Computer*, 21(5):61–72, 1988.
7. B. W. Boehm. A view of 20th and 21st century software engineering. In *International Conference on Software Engineering*, pages 12–29, 2006.
8. B. W. Boehm and R. Turner. *Balancing Agility and Discipline: A Guide for the Perplexed*. Addison-Wesley Professional, Aug. 2003.

9. P. Bourque and R. Fairley, editors. *Guide to the Software Engineering Body of Knowledge (SWEBOK®), Version 3.0.* IEEE Computer Society, 2014. Available online at http://www.swebok.org (last access 2018-01-07).

10. Central Computer and Telecommunications Agency (CCTA). *Service level management.* H.M.S.O., 1989.

11. M. B. Chrissis, M. Konrad, and S. Shrum. *CMMI for Development: Guidelines for Process Integration and Product Improvement.* Addison Wesley, 3rd revised edition, 2011.

12. P. Coad, E. Lefebvre, and J. De Luca. *Java Modeling In Color With UML: Enterprise Components and Process.* Prentice Hall International, 1999.

13. A. Cockburn. *Crystal Clear. A Human-Powered Methodology for Small Teams.* Addison-Wesley Longman, 2004.

14. B. Curtis, M. I. Kellner, and J. Over. Process Modeling. *Commun. ACM*, 35(9):75–90, Sept. 1992.

15. T. DeMarco and T. Lister. *Peopleware. Productive Projects and Teams.* Dorset House, 1987.

16. T. Dingsøyr, S. Nerur, V. Balijepally, and N. B. Moe. A decade of agile methodologies: Towards explaining agile software development. *Journal of Systems and Software*, 85(6):1213–1221, 2012. Special Issue: Agile Development.

17. T. Dybå and T. Dingsøyr. Empirical studies of agile software development: A systematic review. *Information and Software Technology*, 50(9–10):833–859, 2008.

18. C. Floyd. A systematic look at prototyping. In R. Budde, K. Kuhlenkamp, L. Mathiassen, and H. Züllighoven, editors, *Approaches to Prototyping; Proc. Namur*, pages 1–18. Springer, 1984.

19. A. Fuggetta, R. Conradi, and V. Ambriola, editors. *First European Workshop on Software Process Modeling : CEFRIEL, Milan (Italy), 30-31 May 1991.* Associazione Italiana per l'Informatica ed il Calcolo Automatico, Working Group on Software Engineering, 1991. cf. http://trove.nla.gov.au/work/22457426.

20. D. A. Garvin. What does "product quality" really mean? *MIT Sloan Management Review*, 26(1), 1984.

21. M. Glinz. *A Glossary of Requirements Engineering Terminology, Version 1.6.* International Requirements Engineering Board (IREB), May 2014. Available online at https://www.ireb.org/en/cpre/cpre-glossary/ (last access 2018-02-28).

22. H. H. Goldstine and J. von Neumann. Planning and coding of problems for an electronic computing instrument. Technical Report Part II, Vol. 1–3, Institute of Advanced Study, Princeton, New Jersey, 1947.

23. V. Gruhn. Process-centered software engineering environments. A brief history and future challenges. *Annals of Software Engineering*, pages 363–382, 2002.

24. T. Haigh, M. Priestley, and C. Rope. Engineering "the miracle of the ENIAC": Implementing the modern code paradigm. *IEEE Annals of the History of Computing*, pages 41–59, 2014.

25. M. T. Hansen, N. Nohria, and T. Tierney. What's your strategy for managing knowledge? *Harvard Business Review*, pages 106–116, March–April 1999.

26. B. Henderson-Sellers. Method engineering: Theory and practice. In *Information Systems Technology and its Applications. 5th International Conference ISTA'2006*, volume 84 of *Lecture Notes in Informatics*, pages 13–23. Gesellschaft für Informatik, 2006.

27. J. Highsmith. History: The agile manifesto, 2001. http://agilemanifesto.org/history.html (last access 2018-01-07).

28. R. V. Horvat, I. Rozman, and J. Györkös. Managing the complexity of SPI in small companies. *Software Process: Improvement and Practice*, 5(1):45–54, March 2000.

29. H. Hummel. The life cycle methodology for software production and the related experience. In W. Ehrenberger, editor, *Approving Software Products. Proc. of the IFIP WG 5.4 Working Conference*. North-Holland, 1990.

30. W. S. Humphrey. *Managing the Software Process.* SEI Series in Software Engineering. Addison-Wesley Professional, 1989.

31. R. Kneuper. Supporting software processes using knowledge management. In S. Chang, editor, *Handbook of Software Engineering and Knowledge Engineering*, volume 2, pages 579–608. World Scientific Publishing Co., 2002.

32. R. Kneuper. Sixty years of software development life cycle models. *IEEE Annals of the History of Computing*, 39(3):41–54, 2017.

33. A. Komus, M. Kuberg, C. Atinc, L. Franner, F. Friedrich, T. Lang, A. Makarova, D. Reimer, and J. Pabst. Status quo agile 2014. http://www.status-quo-agile.net/ (last access 2018-01-07), 2014.

34. T. Kühne. What is a model? In J. Bezivin and R. Heckel, editors, *Language Engineering for Model-Driven Software Development*, number 04101 in Dagstuhl Seminar Proceedings, Dagstuhl, Germany, 2005. Internationales Begegnungs- und Forschungszentrum für Informatik (IBFI), Schloss Dagstuhl, Germany.

35. M. Kuhrmann and D. M. Fernández. Systematic software development: A state of the practice report from Germany. In *International Conference on Global Software Engineering*. IEEE, 2015.

36. M. Kuhrmann, C. Konopka, P. Nellemann, P. Diebold, and J. Münch. Software process improvement: Where is the evidence? In *International Conference on Software and Systems Process*. ACM, 2015.

37. C. Larman and V. R. Basili. Iterative and incremental development: A brief history. *IEEE Computer*, June 2003.

38. J. Martin. *Rapid Application Development*. Macmillan, 1991.

39. B. Meyer. *Agile! The Good, the Hype and the Ugly*. Springer, 2014.

40. J. Münch, O. Armbrust, M. Kowalczyk, and M. Sotó. *Software Process Definition and Management*. Springer, 2012.

41. B. Murphy, C. Bird, T. Zimmermann, L. Williams, N. Nagappan, and A. Begel. Have agile techniques been the silver bullet for software development at Microsoft? In *International Symposium on Empirical Software Engineering and Measurement*. ACM/IEEE, 2013.

42. Nebulon USA LLC. Agile software development using Feature Driven Development (FDD). http://www.nebulon.com/fdd/index.html.

43. L. Osterweil. Software processes are software too. In *Proceedings of the Ninth International Conference on Software Engineering*, 1987.

44. D. L. Parnas and P. C. Clements. A rational design process: How and why to fake it. *Transactions on Software Engineering*, 12(2):251–257, Feb. 1986.

45. M. C. Paulk, B. Curtis, M. B. Chrissis, and C. V. Weber. Capability maturity model[SM] for software, version 1.1. Technical Report CMU/SEI-93-TR-024, Software Engineering Institute, Carnegie Mellon University, 1993.

46. M. C. Paulk, C. V. Weber, S. M. Garcia, M. B. Chrissis, and M. Bush. Key practices of the capability maturity model[SM] for software, version 1.1. Technical Report CMU/SEI-93-TR-025, Software Engineering Institute, Carnegie Mellon University, 1993.

47. C. Potts, editor. *Proceedings of a Software Process Workshop, February 1984, Egham, UK*. IEEE Computer Society, 1984.

48. W. W. Royce. Managing the Development of Large Software Systems. In *Proceedings, IEEE Wescon August 1970*, pages 1–9, 1970.

49. R. Schuette and T. Rotthowe. The guidelines of modeling—an approach to enhance the quality in information models. In T.-W. Ling, S. Ram, and M. L. Lee, editors, *Conceptual Modeling— ER '98. 17th International Conference on Conceptual Modeling, Singapore, November '16-19, 1998. Proceedings*, number 1507 in Lecture Notes in Computer Science (LNCS), 1998.

50. H. Stachowiak. *Allgemeine Modelltheorie*. Springer, 1973.

51. M. Staples, M. Niazi, R. Jeffery, A. Abrahams, P. Byatt, and R. Murphy. An exploratory study of why organizations do not adopt CMMI. *Journal of Systems and Software*, 80(6):883–895, 2007.

52. H. Takeuchi and I. Nonaka. The New New Product Development Game. *Harvard Business Review*, Jan. 1986.

53. G. Theocharis, M. Kuhrmann, J. Münch, and P. Diebold. Is water-scrum-fall reality? On the use of agile and traditional development practices. In P. Abrahamsson, L. Corral, M. Oivo, and B. Russo, editors, *Product-Focused Software Process Improvement, 16th International Conference, PROFES 2015*, pages 149–166. Springer, 2015.

54. VersionOne. State of agile survey. Available online at `http://stateofagile.versionone.com/` (last access 2018-03-19), 2006–2016.
55. L. R. Vijayasarathy and C. W. Butler. Choice of software development methodologies—do project, team and organizational characteristics matter? *IEEE Software*, 33(5):86–94, 2015.
56. G. M. Weinberg. *The Psychology of Computer Programming*. Van Nostrand Reinhold, 1971.
57. J. P. Womack, D. T. Jones, and D. Roos. *The Machine That Changed the World : The Story of Lean Production*. Harper Perennial, Nov. 1991.
58. F. W. Zurcher and B. Randell. Iterative multi-level modeling—a methodology for computer system design. In *Proc. IFIP Congress 68*, pages 138–142. IEEE CS Press, 1968.

Chapter 2
Software Process Definition and Modelling

Abstract In order to define or model software life cycles and processes, a suitable notation is needed, also called meta-model, language or vocabulary. Depending on the type and purpose of the model, different notations are available and needed. All of them contain a number of basic components such as activities, work products and roles, but different notations expand these basic components in many different forms. This chapter provides an overview of the main concepts of such notations and their main properties, and gives an overview of the main notations and languages available for describing software process models and life cycle models. These notations range from high-level templates to describe processes in a semi-structured format using natural language such as a wiki, mainly useful for models to be used by humans, to formal notations that can be supported by tools. Furthermore, we provide an overview of different methods to develop software processes.

2.1 Introduction

This chapter covers the various approaches to defining and modelling (software) life cycles and processes. The main topic therefore is not the contents of the processes but the notations used to describe them. These notations are often described as meta-models, i.e. as models describing the format of a (process) model, as introduced in Def. 1.26.

One might think that only one meta-model should be needed to describe any process model, but in practice, almost every common model comes with its own notation or meta-model. Apart from the "not-invented-here" effect, this is also due to the fact that different process models may have very different purposes, leading to different information about the model that needs to be captured. For example, a meta-model may just support one type of activity, or it may distinguish several types such as high-level activities (e.g. phases) and low-level activities (tasks) which are considered atomic and cannot be broken down further.

© Springer Nature Switzerland AG 2018

R. Kneuper, *Software Processes and Life Cycle Models*,

https://doi.org/10.1007/978-3-319-98845-0_2

Furthermore, process models may address different target groups such as developers or a quality management/assurance group, but also support tools and software engineering environments, which leads to very different requirements on the model notation.

Therefore, there is no "best" notation but how good a notation is depends largely on the purpose of the models to be described.

2.1.1 Basic Concepts

Usages of defined process modelling notations. So why do we need defined notations for describing processes rather than just plain text? Plain text may suffice in some simple cases but for more complex use cases, this obviously is not enough: using a defined format will in many cases make work easier both for the reader and the author of a process description because this usually leads to a clearer structure, and a better understanding of what certain symbols mean. Relevant use cases where a defined notation is at least very helpful include:[1]

- explicit, structured description of different levels of process, for example starting with high-level phases and stages, and breaking these down into (sub-)processes, activities and tasks
- automated selection of the parts of the process model to be displayed, such as those relevant for a certain role or a certain phase of the project
- representing or displaying the same process descriptions in different formats for different purposes, for example alternatively as HTML hypertext and in a linear format for printing
- exchanging process descriptions between different tools
- automated support for various other tasks, such as for the analysis of the process description, for tailoring or even for process execution.
- defining clear criteria as a basis for checking processes and their implementation, e.g. as part of an assessment or audit.

Syntax and semantics of a language. Since notations and meta-models form specific types of languages, it is helpful to keep in mind the standard language definition concepts of abstract syntax, concrete syntax, and semantics. The abstract syntax defines the basic building blocks used in a language, in this case for example stages and activities. The concrete syntax defines the symbols used to represent these building blocks, such as rectangles or a certain text format to represent a stage. Finally, the semantics describe the meaning of these building blocks of a language, defining for example what is meant by a "stage". Considering the semantics of a notation becomes particularly important when exchanging information between different tools.

---

[1] Remember that we are talking about the different use cases for defined process *notations*, not for process descriptions. Even though both groups of use cases of course do overlap, and some usages of process descriptions are only possible with a defined notation, they are not identical.

Different notations might interpret the same term, for example "work product", differently, so that a work product in one notations does not necessarily translate into a work product in the second notation.

An additional concept for the definition of a language that is just as important but not always made explicit regards its *pragmatics*, i.e. the guidance on when and how to use the language and its constructs. For example, a description of a process step in a very formal language may be syntactically and semantically correct, but not useful in from a pragmatic point of view if it is to be read and used by humans rather than tools. For programming languages, these pragmatic issues are often addressed by programming guidelines.

In the following, we will sometimes refer to these concepts in order to describe software process or life cycle notations and meta-models.

Using notations for business and application processes. In the context of software engineering, process notations are used in at least two different roles: apart from the definition of software processes, the topic of the current book, such notations are also used for the analysis phase within software development, to describe the business or other application processes which are to be supported by software. Since in many cases, the software processes are not that different from application processes, such process notations from business or application modelling can also be used to describe software processes, as e.g. discussed in Sect. 2.3.2 and 2.3.4.

2.1.2 Properties of Process Meta-Models

There are a number of properties which can be used to distinguish different meta-models and which help to decide which meta-model to use in a certain context:

- *level of abstraction/of detail*: life cycle models such as the waterfall model are on a fairly high level abstraction, including major steps such as the development phases, but without addressing the details such as the individual activities or artefacts to be created. Such an abstract or coarse-grained model is mainly helpful to get an overview of a process or life cycle, while a more fine-grained model provides the detail needed for its actual implementation. This level of detail of the models is guided by the notation used, for example whether it supports the single attribute "name" for a phase, or whether it supports or even requires detailed attributes and templates for the definition of the work products to be created.
- *degree of structuredness*: closely related to the level of abstraction is the degree of structuredness. The same process defined on the same level of detail and with the same process steps, results etc. may be described as an unstructured, plain text, or in a more or less structured format, explicitly distinguishing between different process steps, listing the results to be created, and so on. For complex processes, structuredness also includes the distinction between different description levels, e.g. between high-level phases or stages down to activities and tasks.
- *ease of use* which applies both to

- process authors, making it easy for them to describe and tailor the process and to ensure consistency between different parts of the description, and to
- process users who at least want to easily find and interpret the process model description and its notation

- *degree of formality*: a software process notation or meta-model and its syntax and semantics may be described in a very formal way, fixing it in an exact, mathematical format, or it may not be explicitly described at all, as done in the "modelling" of the waterfall model by Fig. 1.2.

  Since a high degree of formality tends to lead to a reduced ease of use, it is usually only used if the process model is to be supported by tools which require this formality, e.g. to support process tailoring, to represent the model in different formats, and to transfer the model between different tools.

- *Process enactment, execution or simulation support*: apart from supporting the description of processes for human readers, models can help to enact a process, e.g. based on a work-flow engine, or even to execute parts of the process automatically. An important difference is that support for process enactment includes the modelling of actual process results, while support for process definition only needs to define the types of such process results.

  Similarly, a process model may allow to simulate the process, in order to analyse it for understanding and improvement. All these forms of support will be based on a high degree of formality, but a high degree of formality alone does not guarantee that these forms of support are possible.

- *graphical vs. text-based notation*: in contrast to the previous properties, this property only considers the concrete syntax of the modelling language. Two different notations might both use the abstract syntax concept of an activity, but one might represent such an activity graphically as a rectangle with the name of the activity written inside, while the other notation uses a text-only format for the same purpose. In actual fact, most notations use a mixture of graphical and text elements, typically providing an overview of the processes and internal or external relationships using graphical elements, and adding detail using text. Where automated tools are used to represent a process, the same description may alternatively be represented as a diagram (for human readers) or in a text format (e.g. to exchange the relevant information between tools).

Requirements for process modelling notations. Based on previous work by Rombach and Verlage, [23, §4.3.2] describes the following requirements for process modelling notations:

- *R1 Natural representation:* If relevant properties and aspects can be represented in a natural way, this helps to identify and to verify them.
- *R2 Support of measurement:* In order to evaluate the processes, suitable measurements are needed which should be supported by the process model.
- *R3 Tailorability of model:* An important aspect of process models is that they can be adapted ("tailored") to the specific requirements of the individual environment and process instance.

- *R4 Formality* is needed in order to support and analyse the process models with tools, and to achieve a clear semantics and therefore a common understanding by the people involved.
- *R5 Understandability*, as described above, is to some extent in conflict with formality, but of course it is important that models are reasonably easy to understand. Even if they are mainly used by tools, it is important to be able to understand them in order to validate the models.
- *R6 Executability* refers to the possibility to interpret and execute the process model by a machine. Of course, since not all process models are meant for execution this requirement is not always relevant. Since—similar to R4—it tends to stand in conflict with R1 and R5, this requirement often has low priority.
- *R7 Flexibility* is needed to allow the representation of unexpected and creative work as part of a process.
- *R8 Traceability*, finally, ensures that the relationships between different process components can be represented and this traced back, for example, is a design document is to be based on a certain requirements document, the notation should support the representation of this information.

Different Types of Meta-models and Notations. To group the many different types of meta-models and notations, we will distinguish three groups as shown in Fig. 2.1 and described in more detail in the remainder of this chapter.

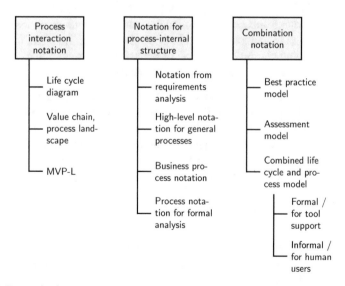

Fig. 2.1 Types of software process meta-models and notations

- *Process interaction notations* (or meta-models) help to model multiple processes and their interactions and relationships. They are mainly useful to define the life cycle, on a high level of abstraction, and the resulting models are therefore called "life cycle process models" in [23, §2.3]. The main objects of these meta-models are the phases or stages that make up the life cycle. These high-level notations typically use some graphical notation, with little or no definition of the syntax and semantics used.

- Notations for the process-internal structure, on the other hand, help to model one of the processes under consideration in more or less detail. The main objects of these notations therefore are the standard components of activities, results, and roles. In [23, §2.3], the resulting models are called "engineering process models".
- Combination notations, as the name suggests, combine the high-level overview of the life cycle and the details of the individual processes within one notation.

2.1.3 Meta-meta-modelling

Just like a meta-model is needed to describe the notation used for models, a meta-meta-model is needed to describe the notation used for meta-models, and such meta-meta-models will be discussed in the current subsection. Today, the main notation used for this task is the *Meta Object Facility (MOF)*, while the first widely used notation was the *CASE Data Interchange Format (CDIF)*. Both will be introduced below.

One of the challenges in this context is the need to bootstrap the hierarchy of meta-models: of course, the meta-meta-model needs some notation as well, leading to a meta-meta-meta-model and so on. The two formats described here resolve this challenge by using a notation on the level of the meta-meta-model that can also be used to describe itself, so that no higher level is needed.

The CASE Data Interchange Format (CDIF). CDIF was published in 1994 by the Electronic Industries Alliance (EIA), a former US-based standards and trade organisation. As the name indicates, CDIF was developed to help exchange data between different CASE tools which typically use different notations or meta-models as a basis. It therefore does not directly address software process models but it is closely related. An overview of its architecture and the relevant documents is given in [15].

Today, CDIF is rarely if ever used but has been replaced by the Meta Object Facility.

The Meta Object Facility (MOF). MOF is an Object Management Group (OMG) standard that describes the multiple levels needed in meta-modelling, also published as ISO/IEC 19508:2014.

MOF supports the description of various widely-used languages, mainly UML and BPMN, both also defined by OMG standards. Particularly important in this context is the support for the *Software Process Engineering Metamodel (SPEM)* which will be described in Sect. 2.4.2. Similar to CDIF, the main purpose of MOF is to provide a basis for tool support for such modelling languages, including the exchange of models between different tools.

Although MOF does not fix a certain number of levels in meta-modelling,[2] it is usually used with four levels, as shown in Fig. 2.2.

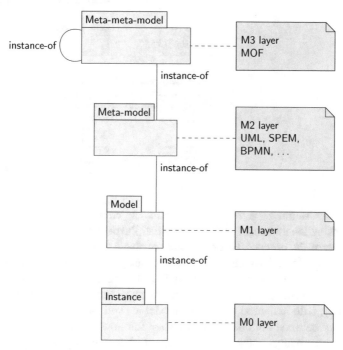

Fig. 2.2 The Meta Object Facility (MOF), 4-level representation

To resolve the challenge mentioned above that each level of modelling ought to be defined using a meta-model, leading to an infinite recursion of meta-models, the MOF language only consists of a small number of basic constructs such as classes and their relationships which can then be used to describe itself.

2.1.4 Core Contents of Software Process Models

The core elements of probably all software process (meta-)models are the products to be created, the activities to create these products, and the roles responsible. These core elements can be found in more or less any software process model, and they are often extended by templates for the various products created, and methods describing how to perform the activities, see Fig. 2.3.

---

[2] Actually, a minimum number of two levels is needed in order to distinguish between models and meta-models.

Fig. 2.3 Core elements of
software process models

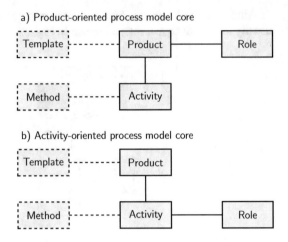

When describing an activity and the products created by that activity, there is
some information that clearly belongs to either the description of the activity or the
description of the product. However, there is also a considerable amount of information that could go into either of the two descriptions, such as the methods to be
used or the roles responsible. Putting such information in both description would
be possible in principle, but is clearly not recommended because of the resulting
redundancy, with increased size of the model as well as a considerable risk of in-
consistency between both descriptions. Therefore, one needs to decide whether to
represent the products or the activities as the leading components, and based on this
decision one can distinguish between product-oriented and activity-oriented process
models, see Fig. 2.3.

While this distinction between product-oriented and activity-oriented process
models in this context is only described as a question of modelling, the same question is relevant with respect to process control. Process control may also be product-
oriented, monitoring that the expected work products are produced at the right time
and with the right quality, or process control may be activity-oriented, monitoring
that the right activities are performed at the right time and with the right quality, in
the expectation that this will eventually be more effective to create good products.

ISO/IEC TR 24778:2010. This standard describes a simple structure for describing software processes, consisting of the following elements:

- title
- purpose
- outcome
- activities
- tasks
- information items (containing any other information needed in a description but
  not included in the previous elements)

Since the goal is to provide a description structure to be used in other standards, the standard includes guidelines on how to phrase these description of the various elements, in some cases prescribing the exact wording. On the other hand, products are only briefly addressed as specific types of outcomes, while roles are not addressed at all.

2.1.5 Further Contents of Software Process Models

Apart from the core elements of software process models as shown in Fig. 2.3 above, there are many more elements that are often included in process models. Which elements need to be included of course depends on the purpose of the model. As long as the model is only to be used as guidance for human process performers, less detail will be needed than if the model is also to be used for analysis or automated support.

As an example aiming for more detailed guidance for humans, as well as some basic analysis and possibly some automated support, [23, p. 11] lists the following main elements of process models:

- description of an identifiable activity or a group of activities
- description of the product flow (i.e., input and output products for activities)
- description of the control flow between processes (i.e., the enactment or execution sequence)
- description of a refinement (i.e., the definition of a hierarchy of processes)
- description of the relationships to techniques, methods, tools
- description of the relationship to roles.

Another information that should usually be included are the restrictions on tailoring a certain component of the model, starting with the statement whether a certain part of the process description is mandatory or optional / tailorable.

A general meta-model. A general or "neutral" meta-model used for comparing different life cycle models was introduced in [25], see Fig. 2.4. This general meta-model is an extension of the one shown in Fig. 2.3, dstinguishing between phases and activities, and adding information regarding the methods supporting an activity, as well as standards and guidelines, and notations, to be used for results.

2.2 Notations for Modelling the Interactions Between Processes

High-level modelling notations covering multiple processes are commonly used to describe life cycle models, usually in a graphical format as for example shown in Fig. 1.1 and Fig. 1.2. However, these life cycle models usually use an ad hoc rather than some defined notation, as the two examples mentioned show. One of the few

Fig. 2.4 A general software
life cycle meta-model [25].
©1999, Springer-Verlag,
reprinted with permission.

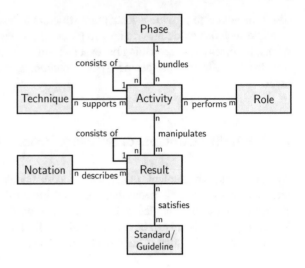

exceptions is the value chain notation which is quite common in business process
modelling but only occasionally used for software processes.

2.2.1 Value Chain Diagrams and Process Landscape Diagrams

These related notations come from business process modelling and are used to provide an overview of different (or all) processes within an organisation and the interfaces between them. They are useful to show the role certain process such as the
software processes play in the overall organisation, while the processes themselves
will have to be described in some other format, e.g. one of the notations described
below. An example of such a process landscape can be found in Fig. 2.5, showing
the process used by an IT service provider, including several value chains.

2.2.2 The Multi-View Process Modeling Language (MVP-L)

The *Multi-View Process Modeling Language (MVP-L)*[3] is a language for describing (software development) processes in a formal way, describing their external
behaviour without looking at their internal structure, quite similar to abstract data
types. MVP-L was mainly developed by H. Dieter Rombach and his colleagues, first
at the Univ. of Maryland, USA, as part of the TAME project (which will be described
in somewhat more detail in Sect. 5.7), and later at the Univ. of Kaiserslautern, Germany. The name of this notation was selected to point out that the notation supports

---

[3] This short summary of MVP-L is based on [23, §4.4] and the language report [8].

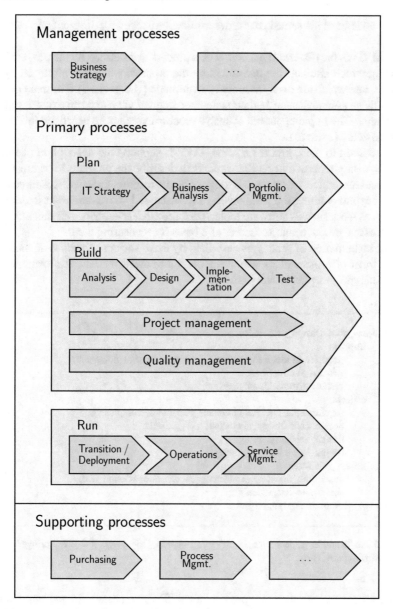

Fig. 2.5 A sample process landscape for an IT service provider

multiple views of the same process description, as needed for different purposes and roles.

In MVP-L, the (external) behaviour of a process is described by the product flow, showing which artefacts are consumed by the process, which are produced by the process, and which are both consumed and produced (i.e. revised). The main properties of these artefacts, such as their status, are defined via entry and exit criteria and invariants.[4] The implementation of such a process may then be described informally in more detail if wanted.

In addition to these *process models*, MVP-L supports the description of related aspects, using in particular *product models* to describe the products to be created by the processes, and *resource models* to describe the resources needed. Resource models go beyond defining the roles involved as discussed above, and refer to other resources as well, such as software tools. *Attribute models* describe relevant attributes of processes, products and resources as a basis for measuring them.

The instantiation of processes described by these various models is documented in the form of project plans which import the relevant models. An example of a small such project plan is shown in Fig. 2.6.

```
project_plan  Design_project_2 is
    imports
        product_model Requirements_document, Design_document;
        process_model Design;
        resource_model Design_group;
    objects;
        requirements_doc: Requirements_document("complete");
        design_doc: Design_document("non_existent");
        design: Design(0, 2000);
        design_team: Design_group(0);
    object_relations;
        design(req_doc=>requirements_doc, des_doc=>design_doc,
            designer=>design_team);
    end project_plan  Design_project_2
```

Fig. 2.6 An example project plan in MVP-L notation [23, §4.4]. ©2012, Springer-Verlag, reprinted with permission.

This project plan refers to a project called "Design_project_2" and imports two different product models which describe the structure of the two product objects that are included in the plan, one of which exists and is complete at the beginning of the project. Furthermore, the project plan includes the process object "design" which is an instance of the process model "Design" also imported by the plan. The definition of this process model contains two parameters, which is why two values

---

[4] An invariant of a process is a property or predicate that is expected to be satisfied when the process is started, and—assuming it was satisfied at the beginning—is guaranteed to be satisfied at the end of the process.

for these parameters are passed to the object "design". Similarly, the resource "design_team", an instance of the resource model "Design_group", is part of the project plan. Finally, the object relationships are defined, such as the relationship between the object "req_doc" defined as input in the process model "Design", and the object "requirements_doc" in the project plan.

2.3 Detailed-Level Modelling Notations for Individual Processes

In this section, we discuss the different notations used to describe individual processes in detail, several of which are not specific to the description of software processes but originate from business processes and other application areas. Since even with these notations, it is important to be able to model multiple processes, some of them support process hierarchies with one top-level process which may then be broken down into sub-processes, which themselves may be broken down into sub-sub-processes, and so on.

2.3.1 Process Patterns

Process patterns are a bottom-up description of processes, starting from a specific context and task or problem and suggesting a solution to this task. In that sense, process patterns are quite different from most other process descriptions since they do not focus on the processes as such but on solutions to selected problems.

The concept is based on design patterns (which in turn were originally introduced in architecture) and was first transferred to process patterns by James Coplien in [9]. Although Coplien described process patterns for software development processes, these patterns are not specific for software processes and can be used to describe processes in other application areas as well.

Coplien used the pattern

- problem
- context
- forces
- solution
- resulting context
- design rationale

to describe 38 process patterns, for example the pattern "Size the organisation" to address the question how big the development organisation should be.

Based on [2], we define patterns as follows:

Definition 2.1 (Pattern, Anti-pattern). *A* pattern *is a description of a general solution to a common problem or issue from which a detailed solution to a specific problem may be determined.*

A process pattern *is a pattern which describes a proven, successful approach and/or series of actions for performing a certain process.*

An anti-pattern *is a description of an approach to solving a common problem that in time proves to be wrong or highly ineffective.*

A process anti-pattern *is an anti-pattern for performing a certain process.*

This definition introduced the new concept of (process) anti-patterns which describe solutions that have turned out to be *unsuitable* to solve the relevant common problem. In contrast to patterns, a defined structure such as the one described above is rarely used for anti-patterns. Instead, the description is usually reduced to the problem to be solved (possibly including some context), the (unsuitable) solution, and possibly the "design rationale", i.e. the reasoning why the solution is unsuitable.

Process patterns and the OOSP. In [2], Scott Ambler used the notation of process patterns to describe software processes for object-oriented development. Despite its title, [2, 3] covers the concept of process patterns rather briefly and concentrates on describing the *Object-Oriented Software Process* (OOSP) instead, using three different levels of process patterns: on the bottom level, there are *task process patterns* which describe individual tasks such as detailed modelling or technical review. *Stage process patterns* describe individual development stages. Finally, *phase process patterns* describe one of the four project phases of OOSP.

Despite being named "patterns", the descriptions of task and phase process patterns in [2] do not actually follow a standard pattern, in contrast to the stage process patterns which use the pattern

- Initial context
- Solution
- Solution: project tasks
- Resulting context
- Secrets of success
- Process check-list

to describe the stages within a phase.

2.3.2 Modelling Notations from Requirements Analysis

An obvious choice for modelling software processes is to use the same notation as for business and application processes, as used e.g. as part of requirements analysis.

2.3.2.1 Modelling notations from structured analysis and design

In the 1970s and 1980s, requirements were usually documented using a notation from the various structured analysis and design techniques around, such as control-flow and data-flow diagrams and state charts (if not documented in natural language), and these notations therefore were also used to describe software processes.

Of course, such general notations do not provide any specific support for software processes but on the other hand they allowed to use the same notation for all company processes.

Today, control-flow diagrams are still occasionally used to model processes, typically as an addition to a definition in natural language, but in most cases the extended forms of EPK or BPMN diagrams are used. As discussed in Sect. 2.3.4, these notations are quite common for modelling business processes but rarely used for software processes.

The (Hierarchical) Input-Processing-Output notation (H)IPO. As described in Def. 1.4, the core components of a process are its input, the activities or processing performed on this input, and the resulting output. Different variants of this structure are used to model processes, including the HIPO notation that was fairly common in structured analysis, and some more modern variants that will be discussed in Sect. 2.3.3 below.

In HIPO, a process was modelled as a table with one column describing the input data to the process, the second column describing the processing steps performed on these input data, and the third column describing the resulting output data. To start with, the processing steps were often themselves quite complex, and may therefore be broken down hierarchically into sub-processes which were then modelled in the same way (similar to the sub-processes as supported by business process notations such as BPMN).

IDEF3. An older notation for processes that also can still occasionally be found is *IDEF3*, a member of the IDEF family of design notations and methods which was based on SADT (see [22]). In IDEF3, processes are described by process flow diagrams, using a different syntax but the same concepts as other process flow descriptions. Additionally, IDEF3 supports *Object State Transition* diagrams, a variant of state transition diagrams with process activities as transitions between object states.

2.3.2.2 Modelling notations from UML

Today, structured notations for the description of software requirements have largely been replaced by UML, and similarly, UML notations are occasionally used to describe software processes, where structured techniques would have been used in the past.

The main UML diagram type used for modelling software processes is the activity diagram, a variant of the classical flow-charts. To add more detail, other UML diagram types such as sequence diagrams can be used. If the process is to be supported by tools, the underlying data structures also need to be modelled, which is often done using class diagrams.

A comparison of several UML-based languages for describing software processes can be found in [6].

2.3.3 High-Level Notations for General Processes

There are a number of general, i.e. not software-specific notations to describe processes which help to give a high-level overview of the relevant process rather than provide details. Most of these notations are extensions or variations of the Input–Processing–Output (IPO) pattern as introduced above. These properties are usually described using some more or less structured form of natural language, without any formalization of the content.

Three of these notations that are widely used (even though mostly outside the world of software processes) will be described in the following: SIPOC, ETVX and turtle diagrams, plus the process representation that was introduced with the 2015 release of ISO 9001.

Another high-level notation is for example described in SWEBOK [7, Fig. 8.2]. In addition to the usual IPO pattern, this notation explicitly includes entry criteria checking that the input is adequate, and exit criteria for the process output.

2.3.3.1 The Entry-Task-Verification-Exit (ETVX) notation

Entry-Task-Verification-Exit (ETVX) is a notation that was introduced at IBM in the 1980s and can be used to provide a quick overview of a process, for example in a card-like format such as that shown in Fig. 2.7. It describes a process in terms of

- its entry condition, i.e. a conditions that is expected to be true before the process has started
- the task that it performs
- the verification steps performed on the task and its results
- its exit condition which is guaranteed to be true after the process has finished.

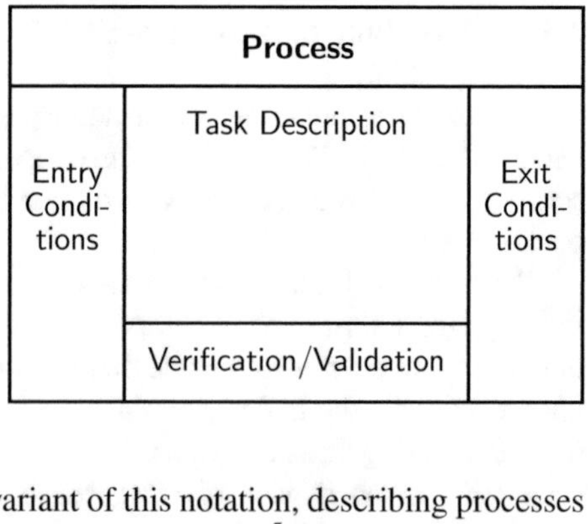

Fig. 2.7 The Entry, Task, Verification, and Exit (ETVX) process notation

W. Humphrey in [19, Chap. 13] used a variant of this notation, describing processes in terms of Entry, Exit, Feedback, Task and Measurement.[5] Later, the ETVX no-

---

[5] This variant additionally used a rather different concrete syntax, describing the processes in a purely text-based format without the graphical representation shown in Fig. 2.7.

tation was commonly used at the Software Engineering Institute (SEI), for example in their description of the Cleanroom processes, see Sect. 3.3. Another variant of ETVX is discussed in [17, p. 117] which describes ETVX as a process control model where the results of any task are validated before they are passed on.

Another variant of ETVX which is fairly well-known is the EITVOX notation which adds input and output descriptions.

2.3.3.2 Turtle diagrams

Another high-level process representation is the *turtle diagram*, first published in [5]. It is also a variation of the input-process-output pattern and fairly well known in the automotive industry. Fig. 2.8 shows the structure of these diagrams.

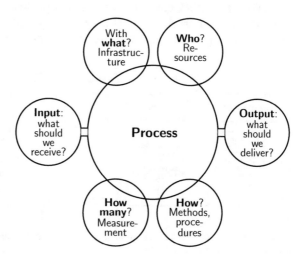

Fig. 2.8 The turtle process notation

2.3.3.3 The SIPOC notation

SIPOC is a process notation that is commonly used in Six Sigma (cf. Sect. 8.2) and describes a process in terms of Suppliers, Inputs, Process, Outputs and Customers ([16], [24, Sect. 7.1.4]). It can be represented either in a graphical format or as a table, with one column for each of the five components. As an example, Table 2.1 describes the Scrum sprint process in the latter format. (See Sect. 3.5.2 for more information about Scrum.)

Table 2.1 Scrum sprints in SIPOC notation

Supplier	Input	Process	Output	Customer
Project stake-holders (end users etc.), product owner	Product backlog	Sprint planning, daily scrum, sprint review, sprint retro-spective, development	Increment	Project customer, product owner

2.3.3.4 Schematic representation of processes according to ISO 9001

A variant of the SIPOC notation is suggested by ISO 9001:2015 as shown in Fig. 2.9. In addition to SIPOC, this representation puts particular emphasis on defining process controls and check points at appropriate points in the processes, helping to ensure that the process is indeed performed as intended.

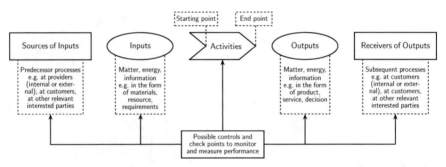

Fig. 2.9 Process representation according to ISO 9001:2015. Reprinted with permission of DIN Deutsches Institut für Normung e.V.[6]

2.3.4 Notations for Modelling Business Processes

Looking at (business) processes in general, there are a few widely accepted standard notations that may also be used to describe software engineering processes. One of these notations, the value chain diagram, provides a high level view of the processes and was therefore already introduced in Sect. 2.2. In the following, a number of BPM notations for describing individual processes are introduced. All these nota-

---

[6] Relevant for the application of DIN standards is the edition with the most recent release date, which is available from Beuth Verlag GmbH, Am DIN Platz, Burggrafenstraße 6, 10787 Berlin, Germany.

tions are based on very similar concepts, even though they vary considerably in the details of notation and expressibility:

- *(extended) Event-driven Process Chains* (EPC and eEPC), part of the ARIS toolset, used to be the standard notation for business processes but have been overtaken during the last couple of years by BPMN. The core of an (e)EPC describes the flow of activities within a process.
- *Business Process Model and Notation* (BPMN) is the most widely used notation today. It also describes the flow of activities within a process, with a similar syntax as (e)EPCs, but is more expressive than the other notations listed here since it allows a number of additional constructs such as a large number of events types (timer events, messages sent or received, error events etc.).
- *BPMN Collaboration and Choreography Diagrams* go one level of abstraction above BPMN process diagrams, defining the cooperation of different organisations and the dependencies between messages exchanged between them. Figure 2.10 shows a simple example of such a collaboration diagram, modelling the collaboration between a customer and a contractor in the early phase before a project is started. Optionally, the internal processes within the customer organisation and the contractor organisation may be included in the diagram, but the main benefit of this diagram type is the modelling of the collaboration between the two organisations as represented by the messages exchanged by the two "pools" representing the organisations.[7]

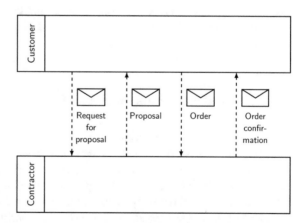

Fig. 2.10 Sample BPMN collaboration diagram

- *Petri nets* are less expressive than BPMN process models and eEPCs, but they are easier to analyse. They are rarely used directly for process modelling but if any automated analysis of the process is required, BPMN diagrams or eEPCs are usually translated into Petri nets first. This loses some information (e.g. in the

---

[7] If you know UML, you may have noted that collaboration diagrams are quite similar to UML sequence diagrams, using a different concrete syntax but built upon very similar concepts.

case of BPMN most event information is lost) but the core activity flow can be translated without problems.

- *UML Activity diagrams* use a different notation but essentially describe the same kind of activity flow as BPMN diagrams and (e)EPCs. They are mainly used in combination with other UML diagrams to model requirements and design of a system to be built.
- *Business Process Execution Language* (BPEL) differs from the other notations described above in that it aims to describe processes in sufficient detail to automate them. This is done by specifying actions as references to web services, including the necessary information to call these services via their interfaces.

All these business process notations (apart from value chain / process landscape diagrams) are very adequate for strongly structured processes, consisting of a defined flow of atomic activities, as holds true for many business processes. Therefore, these or similar notation are sometimes used to describe processes for software operations and IT service management. Software development processes, on the other hand, typically contain far less structure and are therefore difficult to model in any such notation. [14] contains a somewhat more detailed analysis of the possibilities and limitations of BPMN for modelling software processes.

As a result, business process notations are rarely used to model the overall software processes, but occasionally used for modelling individual sub-processes, e.g. within a textual description of a process to provide more detail. Obviously, this is mainly done for processes that allow or require a lot of structure, often because they involve several interacting stakeholders. Examples are the handling of incidents and service requests by a service desk, or the handling of bug reports and change requests within a development project.

2.3.5 Process Notations for Formal Analysis

This section describes a few formal notations for processes which can then be used to model and analyse the complex interactions between different process components. In contrast to most other models described in the current chapter, these notations are not intended for prescriptive process modelling but for purely descriptive modelling, to be used for analysis and simulation of the processes.

However, since these notations themselves are fairly complex as well, they are not widely used but they can help to explain and understand the behaviour of organisations and their processes.

2.3.5.1 Process Algebras

Process algebras are used to model systems consisting of multiple processes that run in parallel and may communicate via channels. This is a very formal, mathematical approach that was mainly developed to model the behaviour of operating systems or within networks. Process algebras are rarely used in the context of software process modelling but as shown in [28], they can be used to describe and analyse these processes. Due to its formality, this notation certainly is not adequate to be used by humans, but it can form a basis for analysis and comparison of software process models, as well as tool support.

2.3.5.2 System Dynamics

System dynamics is an approach to the analysis and design of complex systems, taking into account the interaction and feedback loops that exist in most such systems. The use of system dynamics for software engineering was first introduced by Tarek Abdel-Hamid and Stuart E. Madnick in [1], and later taken up by the popular books [30, Chap. 4] and [10].

At the core of system dynamics, systems are represented by different reservoirs which are connected by pipelines. For example, in a simple representation a project may consist of one reservoir containing the work to be done, and one reservoir containing completed work. Since the speed of the flow from one reservoir to the next is limited, this is described by the rate of flow. Unfortunately, this rate of flow is not a constant but depends on a number of factors such as the size and experience of the team. The experience of the team, in turn, depends on the work that has already been completed, and therefore changes over time, depending among others on the rate of flow. This is a simple case of a feedback loop. By identifying and quantifying the interactions involved, based on experience data where possible, one tries to get a better understanding of these interactions and of the results of any decisions taken.

2.4 Combined Modelling Notations Combining High-Level and Detailed-Level Modelling

A type of model that is fairly common in software engineering is a life cycle model providing a high-level view of when to perform which process, combined with a set of descriptions defining these processes in detail. This can be done in a fairly simple form, consisting of a diagram showing the life cycle model, plus a textual description of the processes involved. An alternative that is mainly used if some form of tool support is wanted is the use of a detailed meta-model, often XML-based. Three such meta-models will be discussed below, all of which define open, standardised formats, in order to allow the exchange of process data between different tools.

2.4.1 Life Cycle Diagram Plus Textual Process Documentation

A fairly simple form of defining processes is the documentation of the life cycle as a graphic, without defined syntax or semantics, plus the documentation of the processes themselves as plain text (including hyper-links as appropriate), typically using some basic structure but again no defined syntax or semantics. This format is easy to prepare and to read, and therefore quite common, probably the most common format used for process definitions. As long as it is only used as guidance for human process performers, and the process itself is not too complex, this format can be quite sufficient. The meta-model used in such a process definition is rarely explicitly defined but usually very similar to that of Fig. 2.3, with just some minor variations or additions.

In most cases, a hyper-text format is used, making it easy to document and follow cross-references within the text. A useful starting point for such a process documentation is a process landscape diagram as described in Sect. 2.3.4 below, with the various processes connected from the diagram via hyper-links.

An advantage of such a textual description format is that no tools are needed for editing or reading such a process model beyond standard office software. This also makes the distribution of the model quite easy, in particular to outside users such as customers or suppliers. When a more complex format is used, such a simple textual representation sometimes needs to be created via export functions which can then be distributed outside the organisation as needed.

Wikis. A common format for textual process representations is the definition of processes in a wiki, sometimes including semantic web technologies (see e.g. [4, 11]). Like process definitions in general, wikis can be used on two different levels, either on the level of the organisation to document organisational processes or, more common when using a wiki, on the level of the individual development effort. One of the main advantages of wikis is that they are very easy to use, both for authors and for readers of the documents.

Wikis are therefore particularly common in agile development, with a focus not on prescribing how to perform the process but to collect the guidelines *agreed within the development effort*, as well as further supporting descriptions of how to perform certain steps. In such an environment, there is usually no defined author of these descriptions but all team members are allowed to edit the descriptions as they see fit, using the wiki as a knowledge management tool. Furthermore, such wikis commonly go well beyond documenting the process to be used and also act as a repository for other project documentation, thus supporting collaboration within the development effort.

If the wiki is used to document the organisational software processes, a more restricted wiki software is usually used that supports a role concept, with at least two different roles for readers and authors of the process documentation.

One of the advantages of using a wiki (or similar tools) for process documentation is that it is easy to access, which among other advantages helps to ensure that process performers always work with the current version of the documentation.

Additionally, a wiki makes it easy to integrate the handling of process improvement ideas and the discussion of the processes themselves, using the standard wiki discussion functionality.

Electronic Process Guide. A concept very similar to a wiki, but on a slightly different technical basis, is the web-based Electronic Process Guide (EPG) as described in [20], [23, Sect. 2.5.2]. The goal of an EPG is to provide a well-structured representation of processes, making extensive use of hyper-links and allowing users to find information easily, e.g. by providing suitable search functions. The representation should be based on standard web technology.

2.4.2 The Software & Systems Process Engineering Meta-Model (SPEM)

The *Software & Systems Process Engineering Meta-Model (SPEM)* is an OMG standard [26] that is explicitly based on the Meta Object Facility (MOF) (cf. [26, p. 1]) and implemented as an UML profile[8] and, as the name suggests, describes a meta-model for defining software and systems processes, and for exchanging such process models between different tools.

History of SPEM. SPEM grew out of work by IBM, Rational Software (later taken over by IBM), and several other companies, on the basic concepts used for defining and maintaining the *(Rational) Unified Process* (RUP). SPEM 1.0 was published in 2002, then under the name "Software Process Engineering Metamodel", and based on UML 1.4. A minor update version 1.1 was published in 2005. This meta-model was revised by IBM in the context of ongoing development of the RUP after IBM had taken over Rational Software, leading to the *Unified Method Architecture* (UMA) meta-model used for the IBM Rational Unified Process [27]. UMA, in turn, was then integrated into SPEM leading to SPEM 2.0 which also was based on the new UML version 2.

In parallel to and interacting with this work on the SPEM meta-model, the *Eclipse Process Framework* (EPF) project developed open source tool support for SPEM, including the EPF Composer for authoring software processes based on SPEM as well as a number of process models based in SPEM such as OpenUP, an open source variant of RUP (cf. 3.4.1). Table 2.2 shows an overview of the relationship between these different topics.

In order to allow tool support for SPEM, its concepts are defined by an XML Schema (in SPEM 1.x, an XML DTD was used).

A fundamental concept of SPEM is the distinction between *method* and *processes*, as e.g. shown in Fig. 2.11. For example, work products are defined as part of the method content, while their use is defined as part of the process.

---

[8] UML profiles define extensions of standard UML to adapt it to particular domains.

Table 2.2 SPEM and related topics

	OMG	Eclipse / EPF	IBM Rational
Tool		EPF Composer (cf. Sect. 7.2.1)	Rational Composer
Process model		UP, OpenUP (cf. Sect.3.4.1)	RUP (cf. Sect.3.4.1)
Meta-model	SPEM		UMA

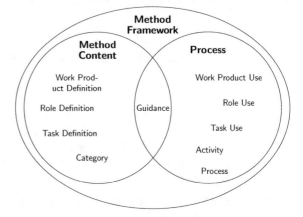

Fig. 2.11 Key SPEM terminology mapped to method content vs. processes ([26, Fig. 6.5]) ©2008, Object Management Group OMG, reprinted with permission.

Due to its tool support, SPEM initially became fairly popular. However, there is criticism that the meta-model too is complex but does not sufficiently support performance of processes defined using SPEM, see e.g. [6, Sect. 4.1].

2.4.3 Software Engineering Metamodel for Development Methodologies (SEMDM) ISO/IEC 24744

In order to provide better (compared to SPEM) support for modelling processes as well as performing the modelled processes, the *Software Engineering Meta-model for Development Methodologies (SEMDM)* was developed and published as ISO/IEC 24744. It is one of the few models that supports the actual enactment of the process as well as modelling the process as such, and therefore can for example be used for process performance or compliance checking.

SEMDM is not based on UML but uses the concept of powertypes, i.e. classes whose instances are subclasses of a given class, and therefore does not need a multi-layer model architecture such as MOF.[9]

---

[9] See [18] for more information about the use of powertypes for meta-modelling.

2.4.4 V-Model XT Meta-Model

V-Model XT is a software development life cycle and process model that was created on behalf of the German government. As a basis for this models and the tool support, an XML-based meta-model was defined which will be covered in more detail below. The V-Model XT itself will be described in Sect. 3.4.2.

To understand the meta-model as described below, it is important to realise that V-Model XT puts particular emphasis on *tailoring*. To help support tailoring, the contents of the model is split into 22 process modules ("Vorgehensbausteine") such as requirements definition, software development, or contracting (either from the customer or from the supplier viewpoint). A simple initial tailoring step consists of selecting those process modules that are relevant for a certain project.

Since the meta-model is very complex, it is structured into several packages as shown in Fig. 2.12.

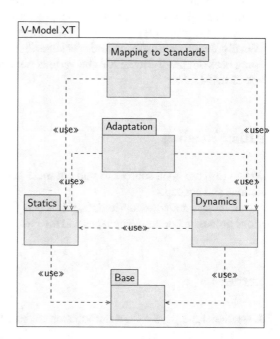

Fig. 2.12 V-Model XT package structure (translated version of [21, Abb. A.1]). ©2011, Springer-Verlag, reprinted with permission.

- The *Base* package defines the structure of the model *documentation*, such as the chapters, and the method and tool references that are part of the model.
- The *Statics* package defines the *process modules* and their basic components, such as the activities, products and roles, including their relationships and dependencies.
- The *Dynamics* package builds on the statics package and mainly defines the order in which to perform the different activities contained in that package. There are two core concepts used to do so: *decision points* ("Entscheidungspunkt") define

that a decision is to be taken about whether to proceed, based on the products completed at this point in time, and therefore similar to a milestone. The order in which these decision points are performed is defined by a *project execution strategy* ("Projektdurchführungsstrategie") which allows quite different types of life cycle, including a V-shaped approach as the name suggests but also a more iterative approach.

- The *Adaption* package defines in more detail when and how to tailor the model based on standardised criteria. To do so, it defines different project types, depending on whether the model is to describe the contractor side of a project, the customer side of a project, or a combination if both roles are based within the same organisation. These project types can be refined into project type variants. The third main concept in this package are the project characteristics which for example define whether the project is to develop an off-the-shelf product, whether a prototype is to be created, etc.

  The information contained in this package is later used for tailoring tool support, which allows an automated initial project-specific tailoring by selecting the project type, project type variant and the project characteristics (cf. Sect. 7.2.1).

- Finally, the *Mapping to Standards* package allows to add, as a reference, the mapping between the V-Model XT and various standards such as DIN EN ISO 9001 or CMMI-DEV.[10]

Further Reading

[13] and [29] are good sources to find out more about the various business process notations and concepts.

Even though no longer up-to-date, [12, Chap. 2] gives an extensive overview of various process modelling languages and the concepts behind them.

Exercises

2.1. Section 1.3.1 gave a short introduction to the waterfall model. On which layer of the MOF model (as described in Sect. 2.1.3) does this description belong? Sketch out the contents of the three other layers as applicable here.

2.2. Take a fairly simple process that you know well and perform regularly. Model this process using several different notations introduced in this chapter, e.g. ETVX, turtle diagram, SIPOC, (high-level) BPMN (if you know that notation), and process patterns.

---

[10] Since keeping such a mapping up-to-date whenever one of the two models involved is changed, most of these mappings are rather outdated but still included because at least they give a first impression of the relationship between the different models.

Once you have created these models, compare their usefulness and the effort needed to produce them.

2.3. Identify and compare the abstract syntax, the concrete syntax, and the semantics of a) the notation used to describes Royce's waterfall model in Fig. reffig:royce-waterfall b) the ETVX notation as introduced in Sect. 2.3.3.1 c) the SPEM notation as introduced in Sect. 2.4.2. Which parts of these notations are similar, where are the main differences?

2.4. What are the advantages and disadvantages of using a single notation for describing different processes within an organisation vs. combining different notations?

References

1. T. K. Abdel-Hamid and S. E. Madnick. *Software Project Dynamics. An Integrated Approach.* Prentice Hall, Englewood Cliffs, 1991.
2. S. W. Ambler. *Process Patterns. Building Large-Scale Systems Using Object Technology.* Cambridge University Press, 1998.
3. S. W. Ambler. *More Process Patterns. Building Large-Scale Systems Using Object Technology.* Cambridge University Press, 1999.
4. O. Armbrust and S. Weber. Wiki-basierte Dokumentation von Software-Entwicklungsprozessen—Erfahrungen aus der industriellen Praxis. In H.-G. Hegering, A. Lehmann, H.-J. Ohlbach, and C. Scheideler, editors, *Informatik 2008. Beherrschbare Systeme—dank Informatik Band 1*, volume 133 of *GI Edition. Lecture Notes in Informatics*, pages 320–326, 2008.
5. Automotive Industry Action Group (AIAG). *ISO/TS 16949:2002 Implementation Guide*, 2003.
6. R. Bendraou, J.-M. Jééquel, M.-P. Gervais, and X. Blanc. A comparison of six UML-based languages for software process modeling. *IEEE Transactions on Software Engineering*, 36(5):662–675, 2010.
7. P. Bourque and R. Fairley, editors. *Guide to the Software Engineering Body of Knowledge (SWEBOK®), Version 3.0.* IEEE Computer Society, 2014. Available online at http://www.swebok.org (last access 2018-01-07).
8. A. Bröckers, C. M. Lott, H. D. Rombach, and M. Verlage. MVP-L language report version 2. Interner Bericht 265 / 95, AG Software Engineering, Fachbereich Informatik, Universität Kaiserslautern, Feb. 1995.
9. J. O. Coplien. A generative development-process pattern language. In J. O. Coplien and D. C. Schmidt, editors, *Pattern Languages of Program Design*, pages 183–238. Addison-Wesley, 1995.
10. T. DeMarco. *The Deadline: A Novel about Project Management.* Dorset House Publishing Company, 1997.
11. F. Dengler, S. Lamparter, M. Hefke, and A. Abecker. Collaborative process development using semantic mediawiki. In K. Hinkelmann and H. Wache, editors, *WM2009: 5th Conference on Professional Knowledge Management*, GI Edition. Lecture Notes in Informatics, pages 97–106. Gesellschaft für Informatik e.V. (GI), 2009.
12. J.-C. Derniame, B. Ali Kaba, and D. Wastell. *Software Process: Principles, Methodology and Technology.* Number 1500 in Lecture Notes in Computer Science. Springer, 1999.
13. M. Dumas, J. Mendling, M. La Rosa, and H. A. Reijers. *Fundamentals of Business Process Management.* Springer, 2013.

14. M. Dumas and D. Pfahl. Modeling software processes using BPMN: When and when not? In M. Kuhrmann, J. Münch, I. Richardson, A. Rausch, and H. Zhang, editors, *Managing Software Process Evolution*, chapter 9, pages 165–183. Springer, 2016.
15. R. G. Flatscher. An overview of the architecture of EIA's CASE Data Interchange Format (CDIF). *Informationssystem-Architekturen. Rundbrief des GI-Fachausschusses 5.2*, 3(1):26–30, 1996. http://wi.wu-wien.ac.at/rgf/9606mobi.html (last access 2017-06-28).
16. J. Fogal. Process improvement using intelligent Six Sigma. In C. Kahraman and S. Yanik, editors, *Intelligent Decision Making in Quality Management*, pages 363–387. Springer, 2016.
17. T. Gilb and D. Graham. *Software Inspection*. Addison-Wesley, 1993.
18. C. Gonzalez-Perez and B. Henderson-Sellers. A powertype-based metamodeling framework. *Software & Systems Modeling*, 5(04):72–90, 2006.
19. W. S. Humphrey. *Managing the Software Process*. SEI Series in Software Engineering. Addison-Wesley Professional, 1989.
20. M. I. Kellner, U. Becker-Kornstaedt, W. E. Riddle, J. Tomal, and M. Verlage. Process guides: Effective guidance for process participants. In *Proc. 5th Int'l. Conf. on the Software Process: Computer Supported Organizational Work*, pages 11–25. Software Process Association Press, 1998.
21. M. Kuhrmann, T. Ternité, and J. Friedrich. *Das V-Modell® XT anpassen*. Informatik im Fokus. Springer, 2011.
22. R. J. Mayer, M. K. Painter, and P. S. deWitte. *IDEF Family of Methods for Concurrent Engineering and Business Re-engineering Applications*. Knowledge Based Systems, Inc., 1992. Available online at http://www.idef.com/?ddownload=296 (registration required, last access 2017-01-08).
23. J. Münch, O. Armbrust, M. Kowalczyk, and M. Sotó. *Software Process Definition and Management*. Springer, 2012.
24. K. Muralidharan. *Six Sigma for Organizational Excellence*. Springer India, 2015.
25. J. Noack and B. Schienmann. Objektorientierte Vorgehensmodelle im Vergleich. *Informatik-Spektrum*, pages 166–180, 1999.
26. Object Management Group (OMG). Software & Systems Process Engineering Meta-Model Specification (SPEM), Version 2.0. Available online at http://www.omg.org/spec/SPEM/2.0/ (last access 2017-12-20), April 2008.
27. A. K. Shuja and J. Krebs. *IBM Rational Unified Process Reference and Certification Guide*. IBM Press, 2008.
28. Y. Wang and G. King. *Software Engineering Processes. Principles and Applications*. CRC Press, 2000.
29. M. Weske. *Business Process Management. Concepts, Languages, Architecture*. Springer, 2nd edition, 2012.
30. E. Yourdon. *Rise & Resurrection of the American Programmer*. Yourdon Press, PTR Prentice Hall, 1996.

Chapter 3
Software Processes in the Software Product Life Cycle

Abstract Apart from the different formats of software process descriptions and life cycle models as discussed in the previous chapter, there are many different types of such models. The basis for these models is formed by several fundamental life cycles, in particular sequential models such as the waterfall model or the V-shaped model, and iterative-incremental models such as the spiral model or Scrum. These fundamental life cycles can be varied in many forms, or extended by adding information leading to detailed process models such as the (Rational) Unified Process. The models can also include different sets of processes, where at one end of the spectrum, software processes support software development by structuring the different development-related activities. At the other end of the spectrum, software processes also provide a more comprehensive perspective, e.g. including operation and IT service management, or interfacing with organisational and administrative tasks. Depending on the purpose of the model, there are some very different types of process reference models available, including for example method-driven life cycle models, agile methodologies, process assessment models. In this chapter, we survey these different types of software processes and their role in the software life cycle. We provide a categorization of software processes, introduce the basic life cycle models, and present some selected reference models.

3.1 Introduction

Having introduced different formats for describing software processes and life cycle models in the previous chapter, the current chapter describes the contents of these models. There is a huge variety of different such models with very different approaches, leading to the "frameworks quagmire" as it was called in [77, 91].

Similar to the previous chapter but in contrast to most other chapters of this book, this chapter focusses on software process *models*, while the processes as actually performed will be discussed again in the following chapters.

© Springer Nature Switzerland AG 2018
R. Kneuper, *Software Processes and Life Cycle Models*,
https://doi.org/10.1007/978-3-319-98845-0_3

3.1.1 Distinctive Properties of Software Process and Life Cycle Models

There are many very different types of software process and life cycle models. The following properties help to distinguish between these different models types:

- *purpose:* the purpose of the model of course strongly influences its contents and structure. It may be created to get a general understanding of how software is developed in a certain context, for training purposes, to standardise development across one or several organisations, to improve development work, to ensure certain properties such as safety and security from the customer or the government point of view, etc.

  The purpose also implies whether to describe the process as-is, or whether to describe the process to-be, incorporating improvement of the process, for example as part of some organisational (process) improvement project, or even to completely re-engineer the process.

- *process scope:* this ranges from models such as COBIT, which attempt to cover the entire work to be performed by the IT of an organisation, via product and service life cycle models such as ITIL and ISO/IEC/IEEE 12207, to models that cover the *development* work such as the V-Model or Scrum, and finally to models addressing only one (or at least a small number) of processes such as Test Maturity Model integration (TMMi) for testing.

- *organisational scope*: a different way to look at the scope of a framework is to look at the organisational roles included: the framework may cover the work to be done by a development organisation, or it may look at the same work from the customer point of view, with typical tasks such as selecting the supplier (i.e. the development organisation) and defining the work to be done. Alternatively, it may combine both views, which is particularly relevant if customer and supplier belong to the same organisation.

  Yet another alternative is for the framework to describe work from the point of view of the IT service provider, including operations and service management.

  Closely related is the question whether the model applies to an individual project or team, or whether it applies to an entire organisation,or even goes beyond that level, for example describing an industry or national standard. A different way to look at this is to ask how similar different projects are expected to work (within an organisation or beyond): is the purpose to try and ensure that all projects work in a very similar way, making the exchange of results or people between projects easier, or does it try to allow development teams a lot of freedom, fixing just a few core concepts.

- *level of detail*: as already discussed in the context of modelling notations and meta-models, there is a large range starting with simple life cycle models that essentially name the different phases and define their sequence, but provide little or no detail. Somewhat more detail is provided by methodologies such as Scrum that define a framework for the relevant processes, but also without going into a lot of detail.

At the other end of the scale are detailed life cycle and process reference models such as RUP or V-Model XT that add descriptions of the individual tasks, sub-tasks and roles, and provide templates for the results to be created.

- *degree of flexibility*: software process models vary regarding the degree of flexibility they allow, as shown in Fig. 3.1.

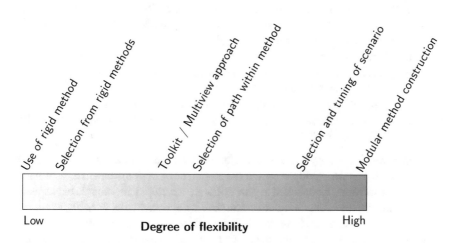

Fig. 3.1 The degree of flexibility of software process models (adapted from [44, Fig. 3.1]). ©1994, North-Holland / Elsevier, reprinted with permission.

A model may quite rigidly describe a fixed sequence of steps to perform and results to produce, making it easy to define but difficult to use if the task at hand and its environment do not fully satisfy the underlying assumptions of the model. At the other end of the scale, the model may describe the processes in terms of basic building blocks which are then used to build a specific software process as needed in any particular instance.

- *degree of obligation*: closely related but not identical to the degree of flexibility is the degree of obligation which defines the extent to which a process model and its components are obligatory. A process definition, or, more fine-.grained, a given part of a process definition, may be *suggested*, leaving it to the process performers to decide whether they are going to work according to it.

  A higher degree of obligation is a process definition that is *recommended* or *expected*. In this case, the process performers are expected to work according to the process definition unless there is a convincing reason not to do so.

  Finally, a process definition may be *required*. Of course, one should usually still allow to deviate from a required process definition but in this case there needs to be a very convincing reason to do so, which should have to be confirmed by some higher management or decision level.

- *underlying philosophy*: the main distinction here is between the plan-driven approaches on the one hand, and the agile and lean approaches on the other hand, with many organisations using some mixture between these two.

[88] describes these two approaches to software development from the viewpoint of how the processes are controlled, and distinguishes the following different forms of process control:

– *defined process control*, based on planning the work to be done and then implementing this plan. This works well if the environment and the requirements are well-defined, and the process to be controlled is reasonably predictable.
– *empirical process control*, on the other hand, applies to processes that "are imperfectly defined, generate unpredictable and unrepeatable outputs" [88]. In this case, process control needs to be based on transparency of the process, frequent inspections to check where the process is going, and adaptation if it is not giving the expected results.

    Of course, as proponents of agile development the authors of [88] clearly prefer empirical process control, and this approach is described as one of the foundations of Scrum.

• *application area:* some models are specifically adapted to a certain application area, focussing for example on the development of systems consisting of hardware and software, as opposed to pure software development; models may specifically address the development of software or systems with very high requirements on safety, security or reliability, or they may address software projects which contain little development but a lot of configuration and integration, such as the adaptation of a standard Enterprise Resource Planning (ERP) system to a specific organisation. An important property of the application area is its stability—how quickly does the technical and organisational environment change? Put differently: how much innovation is the model expected to support?
• *organisational environment:* closely related to the application area is the organisational environment, distinguishing different models e.g. by the size of the development teams supported. For example, most agile methodologies are not appropriate for development teams that go beyond 10 to 15 team members, and additional techniques and processes are needed ("scaling agile", see Sect. 3.5.9). Another organisational influence on the software process and life cycle models is the (geographical) distribution of the development teams involved. A set of software processes used by globally distributed teams will need to define cooperation in more detail, while the members of a development team where all members work in the same place may informally agree on many of these issues over coffee.

    Finally, there may be a number of contractual and legal requirements which need to be taken into account in the definition of software processes. The customer may have a number of requirements on the way work is performed, and put these into the contract, e.g. fixing certain intermediate deliverables in a development project.
• *method neutrality* (method (in)dependence): while many software process and life cycle models try to be neutral regarding the development methods used, other models focus on supporting a specific method and integrate these methods into the life cycle or process.

An example of the first group is the the German V-Model XT (see Sect. 3.4.2) whose predecessors even included a separate document describing different methods that could be used for various process activities.

To achieve method-independence, the process models usually have to focus on the results to be delivered, with little consideration about how they were created. However, full method-independence is not really achievable, since in many cases there is a close relationship between process and method, and the method to a considerable extent defines the tasks to be done and their order.

Some models therefore are tied to a certain development method or, put differently, some methods come with their own software process (model). For example, this is the case for the *Cleanroom* method as introduced in Sect. 3.3.

All of the models mentioned in this description will be described later in this book, mostly in the current chapter. It is important to keep in mind that a larger or smaller scope, a higher or lower level of detail etc. does not by itself make a framework generally better (or worse) but this depends on what one wants to use them for. Depending on the context, one or the other variant may be better suited.

The definition or selection of software process and life cycle models in a certain context will be covered in Sections 4.3 to 4.4.

3.1.2 Software Product Life Cycle

In Sect. 1.4.3 we introduced the distinction between a software development life cycle (SDLC) and a software (product) life cycle SPLC. A SDLC includes the software development activities from requirements specification to delivery, while the SPLC starts with inception of the software and ends with its retirement. In addition to this larger scope, a SPLC typically also puts more emphasis on the relevant interfaces and necessary cooperation beyond development, e.g. between development and operation.

The main difference between a SPLC and a SDLC is the inclusion of maintenance and enhancement in the SPLC:

Definition 3.1 (Maintenance). *Process of modifying a software system or component after delivery to correct faults, improve performance or other attributes, or adapt to a changed environment. (SEVOCAB)*

Definition 3.2 (Enhancement). *Modification to an existing software product to satisfy a new requirement. (Named "maintenance enhancement" in SEVOCAB)*

In many cases, it is difficult to decide when exactly "maintenance" and "enhancement" start. According to these definitions, maintenance starts with delivery and enhancement similarly when the product "exists, but what about agile development? Here, one could argue that this is the case starting with the end of the first sprint or iteration since this provides the first delivery of the product.

Case Study 3.1. (CS Insurance InfoSys) In the past, CS Insurance InfoSys took about 48 hours to deploy a new version of their core sales system, which happened four times per year. Since they usually performed the deployment at the weekend when insurance agents were not in their offices, this was quite adequate. However, as customers started to ask for insurance agents to visit them at the weekend, and in particular the insurance company wanted to allow customer self-service via internet, shutting the core system down for four weekends per year was no longer acceptable and the insurance company started a major project to streamline and automate all delivery processes and bring the time needed for deployment down to a few hours.

The main focus of the project was to automate the deployment processes, taking many ideas from continuous deployment and DevOps (cf. Sect. 8.3). Nevertheless, since only a small part of the overall delivery chain was made "continuous", and in particular the development projects continued to deliver a new release four times per year, this was not a full implementation of the concepts of continuous deployment and DevOps yet.

Laws of software evolution. One of the first systematic investigations of the software processes *after* initial development has been completed was performed by Meir M. (Manny) Lehman and led to his *laws of software evolution* [58, 59]. These laws describe observations about the evolution of most software that is in practical use.[1] The laws have gone through some evolution themselves and their final version was described in [59] as follows:

1. *Continuing change*: an E-type program that is used must be continually adapted else it becomes progressively less satisfactory.
2. *Increasing complexity*: as a program is evolved its complexity increases unless work is done to maintain or reduce it.
3. *Self regulation*: the program evolution process is self regulating with close to normal distribution of measures of product and process attributes.
4. *Conservation of organisational stability (invariant work rate)*: the average effective global activity rate on an evolving system is invariant over the product life time.
5. *Conservation of familiarity*: during the active life of an evolving program, the content of successive releases is statistically invariant.

---

[1] For this purpose, Lehman distinguished three different types of software. S-programs are programs whose function can be exactly specified in advance, such as a mathematical calculation. S-programs are therefore unlikely to change over time, but in practice are rather rare. P-programs can also be specified in advance, but in practice are not feasible to be fully implemented, for example because the underlying problem is NP-hard. (NP-hardness is a concept from complexity theory that formally defines a certain degree of difficulty to compute tasks efficiently.) The most common group of programs, however, are the E-programs that "mechanize a human or societal activity" [58, p. 1062], and these are the programs that are addressed by the laws of software evolution.

6. *Continuing growth*: functional content of a program must be continually increased to maintain user satisfaction over its lifetime.
7. *Declining quality*: E-type programs will be perceived as of declining quality unless rigorously maintained and adapted to a changing operational environment.
8. *Feedback system*: E-type programming processes constitute multi-loop, multi-level feedback systems and must be treated as such to be successfully modified or improved.

While the laws themselves are mainly descriptive, they do of course have implications on the processes used to develop and maintain software, which is particularly obvious in the case of the eighth law. Since the laws do not address individual releases but the evolution of software across different releases, these implications mainly refer to the overall product life cycle processes rather than the development life cycle within a project. Nevertheless, agile development to some extent makes use of the observations included in these laws by putting particular emphasis on managing this evolution across different sprints, in particular managing continuing change and increasing complexity.

3.1.3 Organisational Software Processes

In addition to the life cycles discussed above which focus on an individual project or product, there are a number of process and life cycle models that refer to an entire IT organisation. This section will provide a short introduction to these models.

The COBIT life cycle model. A very general model covering the entire IT processes and their governance is COBIT which will be described in more detail in Sect. 4.8.2. COBIT includes the well-known basic life cycle Plan-Build-Run as for example used in the process landscape in Fig. 2.5, extending it by an additional phase "Monitor":

- *Plan*: plan what software, or IT in general, is needed in the organisation.
- *Build*: build the needed software by developing it oneself, or acquiring it from a supplier. Acquisition may refer to software individually developed for the organisation, or standard software products.
- *Run*: once the software is available, it is put into operation, including IT service management, maintenance etc.
- *Monitor*: as mentioned above, this phase is not usually part of this high-level SPLC but specific to COBIT. It includes the various activities needed to monitor progress, measure and assess the processes used etc.

In COBIT, this SPLC is used to structure the process reference model which supports COBIT's main objective, the governance and management of enterprise IT.

The IT Infrastructure Library (ITIL) service life cycle. The *IT Infrastructure Library*[2] looks at the software product life cycle from a different viewpoint, concentrating on the services provided by or using the software. This results in the service life cycle shown in Fig. 3.2, consisting of five service phases:

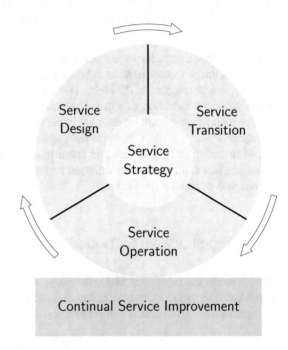

Fig. 3.2 ITIL service life cycle

- *Service Strategy* is concerned with the questions of which services are needed, and how to finance these services, e.g. whether to charge for an IT service per user or per business transaction.
- *Service Design* includes the processes needed to design the needed services.
- *Service Transition* addresses the transition of designed services into operation.
- *Service Operation* refers to the various processes that are needed to support a service in operation. This includes the ITIL processes that are probably the best-known and most widely used processes such as Incident Management and Problem Management. Once a service is in operation, one often identifies improvements of this service, or even new services to be provided, which leads back to Service Design.
- *Continual Service Improvement*, finally, contains a number of processes that help to continually improve the services delivered, including standard quality management methods such as the Plan-Do-Check-Act-Cycle (cf. Sect. 5.4.2) and the use of measurements.

---

[2] The model ITIL itself will be covered in more detail in Sect. 3.8.1. Here, we only look at the ITIL service life cycle.

IT security. IT security does not consist of an individual model, but there are a number of different models that address this topic. Some of them do so on the level of the individual product or project, but many on the level of the overall organisation and its IT infrastructure. Section 3.11 will provide an introduction to this topic and the different types of processes and process models used in this context.

IT architecture. Similar to IT security processes, the IT architecture processes are largely performed on the organisational level, ensuring that different development efforts fit together. Probably the best-known approach to managing and governance and management of IT architecture is *The Open Group Architecture Framework* (TOGAF), which will be discussed in more detail in Sect. 4.8.5.

3.1.4 Software Development Life Cycle

A SDLC is a part of a SPLC as described in the previous section. At the same time, it is often embedded in a system development life cycle, since software is often developed as part of an overall system to be built. In a simple form, this could already be seen in some very early life cycle models such as Benington's program production life cycle (Fig. 1.1) and Royce's waterfall model (Fig. 1.2). Although a different wording is used in these examples, the embedding of a SDLC in a system development life cycle usually starts with identifying the system requirements, from which (possibly with some intermediate steps such as system design) the software requirements are derived, starting the SDLC. The results of the SLDC are then fed back into the system development life cycle and integrated into the overall system.

In the remainder of this chapter, the most important SLDCs will be introduced without a strict distinction between a software development life cycle and a system development life cycle.

3.1.5 Software Life Cycle Processes According to ISO/IEC/IEEE 12207

ISO/IEC/IEEE 12207 is an international standard that contains a process reference model structuring the software life cycle into different processes. The purpose of this model is to provide a common reference for activities such as defining and modelling or assessing the processes described. It also forms the starting point for a number of some other, more detailed process standards such as for ISO/IEC/IEEE 15939 which defines the measurement process. By introducing a common terminology, ISO/IEC/IEEE 12207 helps to ensure that standards as well as other, e.g. internal, documents use the same names for the same software processes, with the same meaning. In ISO/IEC/IEEE 12207, the meaning of the processes is defined by providing, for each process, a purpose statement, a list of outcomes, and set of activities and tasks. It deliberately does not go down to the level of methodologies but leaves it open to the users of the standard to select suitable methodologies to implement the processes.

Process categories. The previous version ISO/IEC 12207:2008 explicitly included two different groups of processes, namely system life cycle processes and software specific processes, where the system life cycle processes were largely identical to those in ISO/IEC/IEEE 15288. The current version ISO/IEC/IEEE 12207:2017 concentrates on the *software* processes, therefore merged some of the processes from the previous version, and distinguishes the following categories of software processes. An overview of the processes within these categories can be found in Figure 3.3.

- *Agreement processes* address the cooperation and agreement with other organisations.
- *Organisational project-enabling processes* are performed on the level of the development organisation and provide the environment needed to perform projects.
- *Technical management processes* ("Project processes" in the previous version) refer to different aspects of (project) management and are therefore performed on the level of a project.
- *Technical processes* describe the various processes or phases within a software product life cycle, from stakeholder requirements definition to software disposal.

Process assessments. Apart from the usages mentioned above, ISO/IEC/IEEE 12207 is used as a basis for the process assessment model contained in ISO/IEC 15504-5 (SPICE) which can be used to assess the maturity of software processes within an organisation. This will be described in more detail in Sect. 5.5.4.

ISO/IEC/IEEE 15288. The closely related standard ISO/IEC/IEEE 15288 provides a very similar process reference model but refers to *system* life cycle processes rather than software life cycle processes. Since software is often part of a larger system, both standards are closely aligned.

3.1.6 Categories of Software Process and Life Cycle Models

The categories of models used in this chapter are not based on any specific criteria such as level of detail or application area but on a mixture of such criteria, trying to define categories that are relevant for the practical use of the models:

Basic life cycle models. These models describe the basic sequence of phases and activities and contain little detail about the processes involved, e.g. few or no roles and (work) products. Main examples are the waterfall, V-shaped or iterative approach. To be used in practice, more detail needs to be added, possibly leading to one of the following categories of models. See Sect. 3.2 for more details.

Software life cycle processes

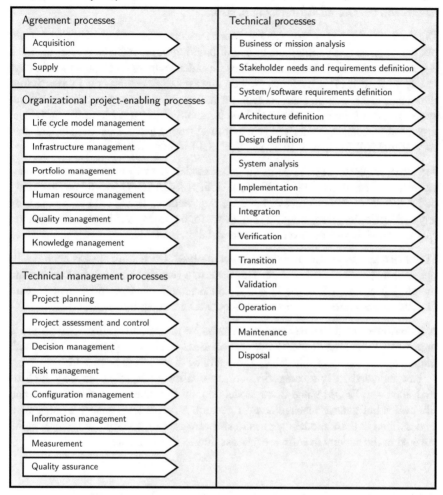

Fig. 3.3 Software life cycle processes as defined in ISO/IEC/IEEE 12207:2017

Methodology-driven life cycle and process models. As the name suggests, these models are based on some specific development methodology and provide some more detail, typically defining the main activities, roles and/or work. Examples are structured development methodologies (SSADM, SSADT etc.), formal development methodologies and Cleanroom, see Sect. 3.4.

Agile methodologies. Although one could see agile process and life cycle models as a specific case of methodology-driven models, they typically differ by their emphasis on self-organising teams, with little prescriptive modelling of the processes.

Therefore, these models, with Scrum as the best-known and most widely used example, will be covered separately in Sect. 3.5.

Detailed, product-type process reference models. The models described so far put the emphasis on defining the temporal ordering of the main activities, with just a general outline of these main activities. In order to apply these processes in day-to-day work, it is often useful to provide more detail, breaking down the activities into small tasks, defining the contents of the resulting work products and the responsibilities of the roles involved. This is usually fairly specific to the individual organisation, sometimes derived (via tailoring) from a general standard model such as V-Model XT, Hermes or RUP. See Sect. 3.4 for more information.

Maturity models. In contrast to the other models described here, maturity models such as CMMI and SPICE (ISO/IEC 15504, ISO/IEC 330xx) do not explicitly define any life cycle or process, but state requirements that should be satisfied by any such definition, and provide a framework for deploying and implementing them. Maturity models will be covered in more detail in Sect. 3.7.

IT service management and operations models. Once software has been developed, it must be deployed and run. This leads to a very different set of processes and therefore process models, the IT service management and operations models, with ITIL as the best-known example. See Sect. 3.8.1 for more information.

Application-specific collections of process requirements. Finally, there are a number of models for specific application-areas, typically application areas with high financial, safety or other risk. These will be discussed in Sect. 3.12.

Not included in this categorization are quality management models such as ISO 900x and EFQM since these models do not describe software processes and life cycles but quality management in general. Nevertheless, quality management as described in these models applies to software as well, and they will therefore be covered in the context in software process improvement in Chap. 5.

3.1.7 Categorizing Process Models by Level of Detail

A different categorization of process models was defined by Humphrey in [45], based on the different levels of detail of the models:

- *Universal models* (U models) provide a high-level overview of the process. Examples are the waterfall model (see Sect. 3.2.1) or the spiral model (see Sect. 3.2.5.2). In this book, such models will be called *basic* life cycle models.
- *Worldly models* (W models) provide more detail and define for example the main tasks to be performed, the roles responsible for these tasks, the sequence of the tasks and the main results to be created.
- *Atomic models* (A models) provide even more detail, describing the process on a procedural level to ensure strong consistency and perhaps to be able to automate

the process. Examples of such atomic models are the (Rational) Unified Process (see Sect. 3.4.1) and the German V-Model XT (see Sect. 3.4.2).

These terms should not be confused with the U-shaped model (V-shaped model) and the W-shaped model described in Sect. 3.2.2 below.

3.2 Basic Software Development Life Cycle Models

We start the discussion of individual models with the basic software development life cycle models which form the foundation for later, more detailed process models. The most important basic models are

- waterfall model: one of the best known models, often used in its very strict form as an argument for agile and against plan-driven approaches
- V-Model: also describes a sequential, plan-driven approach but represents it in a V-shape in order to put more emphasis on validation and verification
- component-based model: puts particular emphasis on separating the temporal and the logical relationship between different processes, often represented as some form of matrix
- prototyping: not a complete model but may be used to extend another model by adding a reduced version of the life cycle early in the overall life cycle
- iterative, incremental and evolutionary models: extend the concept of prototyping by not just building a single prototype but repeatedly cycling through (parts of) the overall life cycle to gradually build up the product needed

3.2.1 Waterfall Models

The waterfall model is the easiest and oldest explicit life cycle model, as described in Sect. 1.3.1. It consists of a sequence of phases such as analysis, design, implementation and test, with little or no overlap between consecutive phases. Like a waterfall, once a certain phase has been reached there is no going back to a previous phase, as shown e.g. in Fig. 1.1. Therefore, waterfall models are often used in combination with stage or quality gates.

Definition 3.3 (Waterfall model). *Model of the software development process in which the constituent activities, typically a concept phase, requirements phase, design phase, implementation phase, test phase, and installation and checkout phase, are performed in that order, possibly with overlap but with little or no iteration. (SEVOCAB)*

Although the waterfall model is, or at least was, quite common in theory, usage of a strict waterfall sequence is very rare in practice, and this was already true well before agile development became wide-spread. In most practical cases, stepping back at least some of the time is necessary in order to correct errors or to deal with changed requirements. Therefore, even Royce's model which is often considered as the first waterfall model, did actually include stepping back at least one phase, see Fig. 1.2. Furthermore, in the same publication, Royce stated that this model will only work for very simple cases, and discussed various forms to include iteration in the waterfall model.

Nevertheless, projects based on the waterfall model at least try to follow a sequence of life cycle phased, and stepping back is usually considered a necessary evil that cannot always be prevented but that is kept to a minimum.

Waterfall model with overlapping phases. A variant of the strictly sequential waterfall model is the waterfall model with overlapping phases, as shown in Fig. 3.4.[3] This variant of the waterfall model has the advantage of including a certain amount

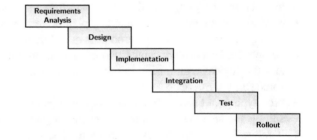

Fig. 3.4 Overlapping waterfall model

of stepping back a phase in the planning, which will be needed in many cases anyway, and to support the fact shown from practical experience that often some parts of one phase are completed and it would be useful to move on, while other parts of the work to be performed in the same phase are still in work.

Sequence of waterfalls. Occasionally, large projects lasting several years are based on a single run through the waterfall, but this has become very rare, hardly ever used except for system development projects with a large proportion of hardware development or system roll-out, where any form of iteration becomes far more difficult than for pure software development.

Wherever feasible, at least a simple form of incremental development is usually used today, with several consecutive waterfalls each lasting several months as shown in Fig. 3.5.

---

[3] Occasionally, the waterfall model with overlapping phases is also called *Sashimi*, using a Japanese term for thinly sliced raw fish arranged on a plate, with slices overlapping each other. Like "Scrum", this metaphor was introduced by [97]. However, the term is not used with a consistent meaning, since other authors use the same term for iterative development with short cycles but no overlap, such as a sequence of sprints.

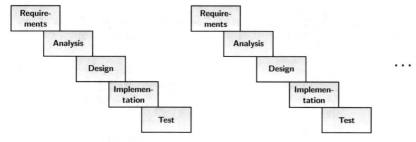

Fig. 3.5 Sequence of waterfalls

3.2.2 The V-Model

In order to put more emphasis on the verification and validation tasks compared to the waterfall model, Boehm in [15] described a V-shaped (sometimes also called U-shaped) model now often called the V-Model[4], (see Sect. 1.3.1).

To achieve this emphasis on the verification and validation tasks, the V-Model breaks down the linear life cycle into two branches, see e.g. Fig. 3.6: the left branch contains the various requirement, analysis, and design tasks, leading to the coding phase a the bottom of the V. In the right branch, the system is integrated, tested and verified. These phases each refer to one of the requirements, analysis and design phases, and their task is to verify that the developed products correctly implement the result of the relevant phase.

V-shaped models are particularly common in development of technical and safety-related systems. For example, IEC 61508-3 defines the V-shaped model shown in Fig. 3.6 for developing software as part of electrical/electronic/programmable electronic (E/E/PE) safety-related systems. (See Sect. 3.11.2 for more information on IEC 61508.)

The W-Model One criticism of the V-Model is that, in spite of its emphasis on verification and validation, testing and other quality assurance tasks start too late, and the V-Model does not sufficiently support the early preparation of testing, nor the early review and analysis of design documentation.

This criticism led to the W-Model that put more emphasis on early verification activities by overlapping a second "V", leading to a "W"-like shape of the model. Actually, there are at least two variants of the W-Model as shown in Fig. 3.7: Herzlich in 1993 introduced the W-Model, putting the focus on explicitly adding the analysis and test activities to be performed for each phase. A similar W-Model was described e.g. in [93] but here the left-hand branch of the second "V" contains the

---

[4] In German-speaking countries, the term "V-Model" is actually used for three related but different concepts: apart from referring to the V-shaped models described here, it is occasionally also used as an abbreviation for "Vorgehensmodell" (software process model). Additionally, there is a national standard called V-Modell XT (see Sect. 3.4.2) which describes one specific such software process model.

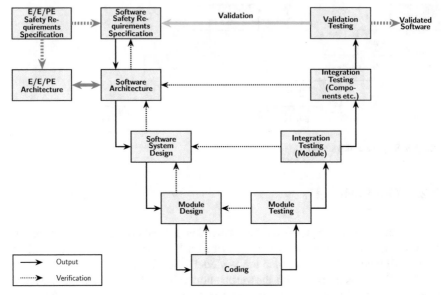

Fig. 3.6 Development life cycle (V-Model) as defined in IEC 61508-3:2010 ed.2.0. ©2010 IEC Geneva, Switzerland. http://www.iec.ch

test preparation and planning activities, while the right-hand branch contains debugging and changing following the various test activities.

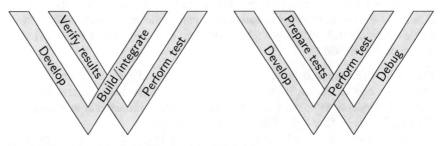

Fig. 3.7 Herzlich's (left) and Spillner's (right) W-Model

Case Study 3.2. (CS AutoSystems) As is quite common in the development of technical software and systems, CS AutoSystems has decided to use a V-shaped life cycle model. Since the systems developed by CS AutoSystems typically consist of the three components housing, printed circuit board (PCB) and software, the following model was defined:

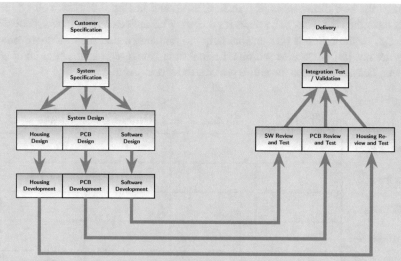

As the name suggests, the customer specification is usually provided by the customer, but often needs to be refined in order to add missing information or clarify stated requirements.

Based on the customer specification, a system specification is created that adds technical details.

The design is created on two levels: first, the overall system is designed. Then, the individual components housing, PCB and software are designed, either as separate documents or as chapters within the system design document, depending on the size of the design.

Each of these components is developed, reviewed and tested separately, before they are integrated, tested and validated as an overall system.

Not included in this model is the iteration that is used in the projects where several prototypes need to be delivered to the customer (A sample, B sample etc.). Since the exact iteration differs from project to project, this was left out of the model and is included by repeating the relevant phases as needed.

3.2.3 Component- or Matrix-Based Models

Component-based models[5] were first introduced in the 1990s to describe object-oriented development. The basic idea is to represent the temporal and the logical relationship between between different tasks or activities separately, often repre-

---

[5] There is no standard name used for this type of process model. The name "component-based model" is used occasionally and will therefore be used here, but from this author's point of view, "matrix-based" may be a better name.

sented as the two dimensions of a matrix, as shown in Fig. 3.8. Each cell of the matrix describes the work to be done for the process, such as requirements analysis or design, in the relevant phase. This helps to emphasise that most of these processes are not just performed within a limited time-frame such as the beginning of a project, but rather across the entire project, though in varying intensity.

	Phase 1	Phase 2	Phase 3	Phase ...
Process 1				
Process 2				
Process 3				
Process 4				
Process 5				
Process ...				

Fig. 3.8 Component-based models

The best-known example of component-based development models is the RUP which will be described in Sect. 3.4.1. Another, less well-known example is the Object-Oriented Software Process (OOSP) as introduced in Sect. 2.3.1.

3.2.4 Prototyping

Prototyping builds on a plan-driven development approach but adds some iterative aspects, with a prototype as a "learning vehicle providing more precise ideas about what the target system should be like" [40, p. 3]. In prototyping, only selected properties of the intended system are taken into consideration, e.g. a prototype may be built in order to evaluate the user interface of the system, and therefore ignore other important properties such as performance or security. Alternatively, the purpose of a prototype may be to evaluate a technical solution to a specific problem, ignoring the user interface of the system.

Definition 3.4 (Prototype). [6] *An experimental model, either functional or non-functional, of the system or part of the system (SEVOCAB)*

---

[6] The term "(function) prototype" is also used in programming with the very different meaning of declaring the input and output types of a function, also known as the signature. A third meaning of the term "prototype" is the prototype design pattern. In this book, however, the term "prototype" will only be used in the meaning of the experimental model as defined here.

Since for a reasonably complex system, it is difficult to understand in advance what is needed and what is technically feasible, Brooks recommended (well before agile development) to "Plan to throw one away: you will, anyhow" [21, Chap. 11].

To support the target of learning from a prototype, the following steps are recommended [40]:

- *Functional selection* defines the part of the overall system that is to be included in the prototype. This selection mainly depends on what one wants to learn from the prototype.
- *Construction* refers to the building of the prototype.
- *Evaluation* is in some way the most important step since this is where the actual learning from the prototype occurs.
- *Further use* refers to what happens with the prototype after it has been evaluated. The prototype may now be no longer needed since it has completed its purpose of enabling learning about the system to be built.

Exploratory vs. experimental prototypes. Depending on how and when the prototype is to be used, different kinds of prototype are distinguished [40][7]:

- An *exploratory prototype* is used in the initial phase of development, with the main purpose of helping to identify the requirements on the system to be developed. It is above all a communication medium that helps to get a common understanding about expected system properties between developers or analysts on the one side, and stakeholders or users on the other.
- An *experimental prototype* is used somewhat later, once at least an initial set of requirements has been identified. Its main purpose is to experiment with the current solution (initial requirements, design, technical solution, etc.) in order to validate it, e.g. checking the technical feasibility. The distinction between exploratory and experimental prototypes is not very always clear-cut but it helps to understand the different emphasis of the two kinds of prototype.

Since the main goal pf prototypes is to get a better understanding of a particular aspect of the system under development, it may be quite adequate to build several prototypes in parallel, addressing different open questions.

Prototypes in systems engineering. A slightly different kind of prototypes is used in systems engineering. In this case too, prototypes may be exploratory or experimental, but in many cases one of the main characteristics of a prototype is that it is produced using one-off components and production methods rather than the mass production machinery to be used later on, once the product design has been validated. The use of a small number of such prototypes is quite common in systems engineering, such as an alpha and a beta prototype. Due to the effort and cost involved, however, one rarely goes beyond a small number of prototypes, and iterative

---

[7] Floyd in [40] actually distinguishes *three* kinds of prototypes, namely exploratory and experimental prototypes as described here, and evolutionary prototypes as described below. Since the definition of a evolutionary prototype refers to a different aspect of a prototype and starts off as an exploratory or experimental prototype, the classification of prototypes has been adapted as described in the following.

development such as described below and quite common for software development is rather uncommon in hardware or systems development.

Evolutionary vs. throw-away prototypes. Depending on what happens with the prototype after the initial evaluation, one can also distinguish between *evolutionary* and *throw-away* prototypes. An evolutionary prototype starts from an exploratory or experimental prototype but after evaluation, it is revised repeatedly to finally evolve into the target system. Evolutionary prototyping is therefore a step towards iterative or incremental development. A throw-away prototype, on the other hand, is no longer used but thrown away after evaluation.

A major risk with throw-away prototypes is that customers may see the user interface which satisfies their requirements, and assume that the system is almost complete, with little understanding that this actually is a throw-away prototype, with no adequate design, and development of the system itself has only just started. When using throw-away prototypes, it is therefore important to make this very clear to the customers.

Rapid prototyping. A commonly used term in this context is "rapid prototyping", where the focus lies on creating feedback early and rapidly. As a result, the main difference between rapid prototyping and exploratory prototyping is that rapid prototyping is limited to throw-away prototypes.

Definition 3.5 (Rapid prototyping). *Type of prototyping in which emphasis is placed on developing prototypes early in the development process to permit early feedback and analysis in support of the development process.*
(SEVOCAB)

Case Study 3.3. (CS Insurance InfoSys) A medium-sized project had the task to develop an XML interface which would allow customers to order a (large and complex) service, plus a web application that would support the administration of these service orders.

While little benefit was seen in building a prototype of the XML interface, a prototype of the user interface of the web application was considered helpful. This prototype included the series of web pages included in an interaction with the application, without any functionality built in. A few sets of input data were hard-coded into the prototype so that users could get an understanding of the application and how it would be used.

The used feedback on the prototype helped to identify some less obvious functions that had not been identified in the initial requirements analysis. Furthermore, it showed that the user interface had been built on standard style guidelines, with a limited number of data and functions on any individual web page. However, since the users were to be power users of the system, they complained that the dialogues too long, consisting of too many pages in sequence. Instead, they preferred to completely fill the web pages with data, far beyond what would usually be adequate, so that they could enter or edit all relevant data using a very small number of web pages.

3.2.5 Iterative, Incremental and Evolutionary Development

Expanding on the concept of prototyping as described above, most development life cycle models include some form of loop in which certain steps are performed repeatedly. Such loops are usually called "iterations", and the life cycle models are called iterative, incremental or evolutionary development.

The main advantage of using such iterations is that they help to reduce risk by getting fast feedback on the work performed. Different types of iteration provide different types of feedback, ranging from "the new code did not break any existing functionality" to "the new functionality genuinely satisfies the user's needs".

Iterations that include the delivery / deployment of new functionality have the additional advantage that the new functionality is made available to the users soon after it has been developed, and therefore starts to provide the expected benefit early on.

3.2.5.1 Basic concepts

Unfortunately, the terms iterative, incremental and evolutionary development are not clearly distinguished, and often used as synonyms. SEVOCAB provides the following relevant definitions which are "standard" in the sense that they are contained in a relevant standard document, but unfortunately not in the sense of being generally accepted and used, and there is a large variety of interpretations of these terms in different publications.

Definition 3.6 (Increment). *A tested, deliverable version of a software product that provides new or modified capabilities. (SEVOCAB)*

Definition 3.7 (Iteration).

1. process of performing a sequence of steps repeatedly
2. a single execution of the sequence of steps in (1)

(SEVOCAB)

Definition 3.8 (Incremental development). *Software development technique in which requirements definition, design, implementation, and testing occur in an over-*

*lapping, iterative (rather than sequential) manner, resulting in incremental comple-
tion of the overall software product. (SEVOCAB[8])*

Definition 3.9 (Incremental life cycle, iterative life cycle). *A project life cycle
where the project scope is generally determined early in the project life cycle, but
time and cost estimates are routinely modified as the project team understanding
of the product increases. Iterations develop the product through a series of repeated cycles, while increments successively add to the functionality of the product.
(PMBOK® Guide; SEVOCAB[9])*

Together, these definitions indicate the essential differences between iterations
and increments: an iteration refers to the sequence of steps which is repeatedly performed and may or may not include the delivery of a new version of the software
product. In other words, the result of an iteration may be a new increment if the
iteration includes all the necessary steps for such a delivery. Alternatively, it may
consist of a more limited set of development steps, such as iterating the requirements analysis steps, or the sequence *correction of bugs–test–delivery*, which leads
to repeated new deliveries but no new increments.

As shown in Fig. 3.9, there are many different types of iterative development,
mainly distinguished by the development steps which are included in the iteration.
The most simple (and possibly the most common) form, which is not usually considered as iterative development at all, only includes coding and testing in the loop,
with the first iteration including the full functionality and all later iterations correcting any bugs found in testing.

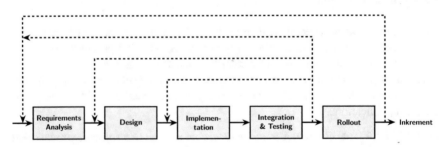

Fig. 3.9 Different types of iteration

An extended form which can genuinely be called incremental development also
includes coding and testing in the iteration, perhaps some design, but where new
functionality (that has been analysed and designed) is added with each iteration.
An example is the "daily build" or "nightly build" where the software is re-built

---

[8] Note that SEVOCAB does not define the terms "iterative development" or "evolutionary development".

[9] The terms "incremental life cycle" and "iterative life cycle" are both included in SEVOCAB, as
separate entries but with identical definitions. However, the term "evolutionary" life cycle is not
included in SEVOCAB.

each day (or night), usually followed by a large set of automated tests to ensure that the changes did not break any of the existing functionality. This started to be used in the early 1990s, e.g. at Microsoft (see [31, Chap. 5]), but now has largely been replaced by continuous integration where a full build plus test is performed with each modification. Only for large systems, where a full build plus test of the main functionality would take too long for the developer to wait for the results, daily builds are still used.

Sequence of waterfalls revisited. A simple form of iteration consists of performing several waterfalls in sequence, each resulting in a new increment, as shown in Fig. 3.5. While each waterfall or iteration may be completed before the next waterfall starts, an alternative approach is to allow the different waterfalls to overlap, with little or possibly no distance between the completion of a certain stage within one iteration and the begin of the same stage in the next iteration, see Fig. 3.10. This variant is commonly used if different teams are responsible for the different stages, ensuring that no team is idle between iterations.

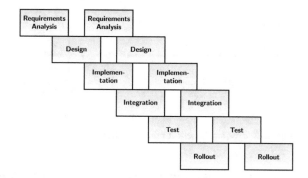

Fig. 3.10 Overlapping sequence of waterfalls

Another variant of performing several waterfalls in sequence is the "staged delivery" where requirements analysis, often also high-level design, is separated out of the iterating cycle, as shown in Fig. 3.11. This is particularly usedful if a requirements documentation is needed beforehand as part of a request for proposals or to reply to such a request.

Fig. 3.11 Overlapping sequence of waterfalls with initial requirements analysis

Benefits of incremental development. As mentioned before, the main benefit of iterative development is the reduction of risk by collecting early feedback. Incremental development has the additional advantage that any new functionality can be put into production very soon after having been implemented, thus providing the relevant benefit early on. The example shown in Fig. 3.12 shows this quite well: while the cost rise more or less linearly over time, the benefits of a system under development only materialise when the developed functionality is rolled out to users. As the resulting curve shows, the sum of the benefits over time (mathematically speaking: the integral of the benefits curve) becomes much larger with short release cycles.

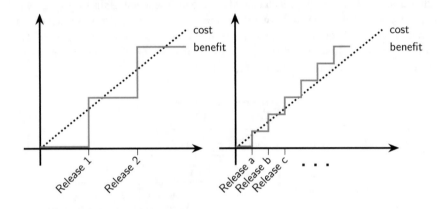

Fig. 3.12 Cost and benefit for long vs. short release cycles

Of course, this discussion leaves out the fact that releases themselves incur costs, and more releases therefore incur more costs. In incremental development it therefore becomes important to reduce the costs incurred per release, allowing more frequent releases and thus higher benefits over time.

Stepwise refinement A specific variant of an iterative (but not incremental) life cycle is stepwise refinement, where development starts with an abstract model of the system and gradually adds detail [107]:

Definition 3.10 (Stepwise refinement). *Software development technique in which data and processing steps are defined broadly at first and then further defined with increasing detail. (SEVOCAB)*

Stepwise refinement therefore is an iterative life cycle where the full intended functionality is described at an abstract level (specification) from the start, rather than being added step by step, as is common e.g. in agile development. Each iteration then adds the detail needed. This implies that a stepwise refinement approach shares with sequential development the difficulty that requirements have to be identified in advance, and this approach therefore is not in common use. A special case where stepwise refinement can be quite useful is in the application of formal methods for software development, where small refinement steps from (formal) specification to code allow to prove the correctness of these transformation steps, which would not be feasible if the entire transformation was done in one large step [49].

3.2.5.2 Boehm's spiral model

Boehm's spiral model was the first model to explicitly describe an iterative life cycle [16, 17, 18]. As can be seen in Fig. 3.13, the main emphasis of this approach is the reduction of risks by analysing risks in every iteration, and mitigating these risks e.g. by using prototypes.

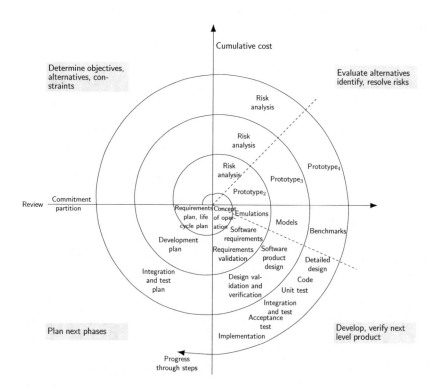

Fig. 3.13 The Spiral model. [16]. ©1986, IEEE, reprinted with permission.

Later, Boehm revised this model repeatedly, leading e.g. to [18] and to the *Incremental Commitment Spiral Model* (ICSM) [19].

In SEVOCAB, the concept of a spiral model has been generalised to describe any iterative model, but without Boehm's emphasis on identifying and managing risk:

Definition 3.11 (Spiral model). *Model of the software development process in which the constituent activities, typically requirements analysis, preliminary and* *detailed design, coding, integration, and testing, are performed iteratively until the software is complete. (SEVOCAB)*

3.2.5.3 Release trains

A variant of an incremental model that can be seen as a first step towards agile development [84] is the *release train* in which releases are delivered using a regular pattern, e.g. one release per quarter. Like "real" trains (at least in theory), release trains run on schedule and deliver the release on time. If there are any problems that prevent the delivery of the agreed functionality on the agreed date, release trains use the concept of a time-box and stick to the date, delivering whatever has been completed and is ready for delivery at that time.

Another advantage of this concept is that it helps to coordinate different teams working on different parts of the same system.

Example 3.1. A medium-sized bank uses a large core system developed and maintained by the internal IT organisation. This core system consists of about ten subsystems supporting the different types of accounts and loans offered by the bank, as well as common functionality such as the management of customer information. For each subsystem, there is a separate development team.

Since there are major dependencies between the different subsystems, a common release schedule was defined, with releases every four months. Each release started with a planning and analysis phase defining the functionality to be delivered and identifying the dependencies between the subsystems, and completed with an integration testing phase testing the integration between the subsystems. In between, each team was responsible for the development of their respective subsystem.

The basic agreement was to use time-boxes and deliver on time, even if that implied that certain functionality had to be moved to a later release. However, this could not always be implemented since occasionally, major functionality that had been developed could not be integrated in time. In these cases, the release had to be delayed after all.

Even for smaller changes that could have been moved to a later release from the viewpoint of the bank, this was not always technically possible since the configuration management initially did not allow to remove such a change once it had been committed and integrated. By strengthening the use of the configuration management system, this difficulty could eventually be overcome.

The concept of release trains has recently gained importance as a tool to coordinate multiple agile teams, mainly as part of the *Scaled Agile Framework (SAFe)* (see Sect. 3.5.10).

3.2.6 An Anti-Pattern: Code-and-Fix

Code-and-fix is a development model that is fairly commonly used, described e.g. in [16] and [65, Sect. 7.2]. The basic characteristics of code-and-fix development are little or no specification and design, and little systematic testing. Development starts—perhaps after a little specification—with coding, based on a general idea of what is needed. This code is then fixed or modified repeatedly until the customer is satisfied (or perhaps has just given up hope).

The advantage of this approach is obvious: there is very little overhead for planning, documentation, design etc., all effort goes into coding the product and you can "show something" almost immediately. Furthermore, it is very easy to learn. The disadvantages, at least for non-trivial projects, are just as obvious: the risk that you will not be able to deliver anything useful is high, and it is difficult to track progress or assessing quality. If there are any major flaws in the design approach, they tend to show up late but are difficult to fix and you will probably have to redo everything. Due to constant fixing, the design tends to degenerate and maintenance is very expensive.

Even though code-and-fix is fairly common, people using it would rarely admit to it. At first sight, there is little difference between code-and-fix development and agile development, and many people who actually use code-and-fix will claim to do agile development—after all, they leave out the documentation. However, a closer look shows that genuine agile development is quite disciplined and therefore very different from code-and-fix, including a strongly test-driven approach and close cooperation with the stakeholders, resulting on a focus on getting feedback on work results very early (see e.g. [7]).

3.2.7 Digression: the Six Phases of a (Big) Project

Not quite serious but still amazingly well-known is this project life cycle model which exists in many variants, here in a variant taken from Wikipedia[10]. It seems to look familiar to many people working in projects:

1. Enthusiasm,
2. Disillusionment,
3. Panic and hysteria,

---

[10] https://en.wikipedia.org/wiki/Six_phases_of_a_big_project, last access 2017-07-07.

4. Hunt for the guilty,
5. Punishment of the innocent, and
6. Reward for the uninvolved.

3.3 Methodology-Driven Life Cycle and Process Models

While many life-cycle and process models try to be method-neutral, some other models are closely related to the development method used. This section provides a short overview of such methods and models.

Structured development. In the 1970s and 1980, a number of structured development techniques was introduced by various authors, including SSADM, SADT, Yourdon structured method, and many others. These structured techniques used some variant of the waterfall life cycle, adding a number of concepts for analysis (e.g. functional decomposition), design (e.g. strong cohesion within modules— loose coupling between modules) and programming (e.g. restricted use of GOTO, systematic use of block structures and loops).

Additionally, the various structured development techniques included different collections of diagrams and tools assigned to the different life cycle phases, such as flow-charts, data-flow diagrams, data dictionaries, and the Hierarchical Input-Processing-Output (HIPO) notation.

Formal development methods Formal development methods were widely discussed in research in the 1980s and 1990s, see e.g. [35, 50]. The idea behind these formal methods is to specify the requirements on a system in a formal language with clearly defined semantics, and then prove, in the mathematical sense, that the implementation satisfies the specification.

Although (as the name indicates) formal methods are first of all *methods* for software development, to use them the software processes must be defined in a way to support this formal approach. In particular, formal methods require a very linear life cycle, with strong emphasis on identifying requirements up-front since later changes can break the proofs of implementation correctness.

As a result, formal methods are occasionally used in the development of systems with very high requirements on reliability but rarely elsewhere. (See [51] for a more extensive discussion of the difficulties involved in the use of formal methods.) In some standards, the use of formal methods is required for systems with very high requirements regarding safety or security, for example the Common Criteria (*Common Criteria for Information Technology Security Evaluation*, published as ISO/IEC 15408, cf. Sect. 3.11.3) or the standards DO-178B/ED-12B and DO-178C/ED-12C (*Software Considerations in Airborne Systems and Equipment Certification*, cf. Sect. 3.11.2).

Cleanroom. Closely related is the Cleanroom software engineering which combines formal development methods with an emphasis on iterative development and with statistics-based testing, with the goal to reduce the number of bugs built into a system, and increase the percentage of bugs found in testing [72, 62].

A full description of Cleanroom can be found in [62] where the processes involved are defined using the ETVX notation introduced in Sect. 2.3.3.1.

Again, this approach became quite well-known but was little used outside the development of systems with very high reliability requirements.

Design thinking. Design thinking is not specific for software but applies to design of products and systems in general, of course including software products and systems. The main purpose of design thinking is to get an understanding of what users really need, and to provide innovative solutions to that need. It is not one specific method but there are a number of different but similar methods that address design thinking, for example the *Stanford Design Innovation Process* which breaks down design thinking into the following steps: [46]

- *Empathise* with users to understand them, their needs, and the problems to be solved
- *Define* the needs of the users and the resulting problem to be solved
- *Ideate* is about generating ideas to solve the problems, deliberately taking a very wide view of possible solutions and typically using some form of brainstorming techniques
- *Prototype* the best problem solutions found
- *Test* the prototype solution to refine the prototype solution iteratively.

A variant of this process is the *GV Design Sprint* which also describes a five-step design process, where one (design) sprint lasts five days and consists of the steps Map–Sketch–Decide–Prototype–Test.

3.4 Detailed, Combined Software Life Cycle and Process Models

This section provides an overview of some common process reference models, consisting of a combination of software process and life cycle models. In most cases, these models go beyond the development processes in the narrow sense, and include related processes and topics such as project management, quality management, and safety and/or security.

3.4.1 The (Rational) Unified Process

With the growing importance of object-oriented development, a number of different methods for object-oriented analysis, design and programming were published in the early 1990s by different authors. Eventually, these different methods were unified into a common language, the *Unified Modelling Language (UML)*. However, such a modelling language does not define when and how to use the various types of models and diagrams that can be expressed, which led to the definition of the *Unified Process (UP)* [48, 54].

Since most of the work on the Unified Process was performed at the company Rational Software, a provider of software development tools, this original version was named the *Rational Unified Process (RUP)*. RUP was formally defined using the UMA meta-model, which is closely related to SPEM (cf. Sect. 2.4.2).

RUP is a component-based model and therefore distinguishes between the work to be done (described as work-flows in RUP, equivalent to the processes as shown in Fig. 3.8) and the time when to do this work (described as phases).

The Rational Unified Process contains the four phases *Inception*, *Elaboration*, *Construction* and *Transition*, where each phase will usually be broken down into multiple iterations. Therefore, RUP is sometimes described as "serial in the large", and "iterative in the small" because of the iterations within the phases.

Even though RUP describes an iterative, incremental approach to software development, is is not an agile approach but contains strong guidance on when and how to perform what work. The authors of RUP explicitly state that the belief that software development "should be organized around the skills of highly trained individuals" with little "guidance in policy and procedure" is "badly mistaken" [48, preface].

Over time, more and more detail was added to RUP, including descriptions on how to support the process using (Rational) development tools. The final version 7.0 was published in 2005. Today, RUP is still fairly well-known but no longer supported by Rational or its parent company IBM. In addition to RUP, a number of variants of the Unified Process were published, the best-known being *OpenUP* and the *Agile Unified Process* as described below.

OpenUP. One of the main variants of the Unified Process is the *OpenUP* which was published by the Eclipse Foundation [37] (originally under the name *Basic Unified Process*). OpenUP is based on a reduced version of RUP, more adapted to agile development, which was made freely available by IBM in 2006, a few years after it had taken over Rational Software. OpenUP uses the same basic concepts as RUP, including the four phases *Inception*, *Elaboration*, *Construction* and *Transition*, and the same component or matrix structure.

Enterprise Unified Process (EUP) and Agile Unified Process (AUP). Following his work on process patterns and the *Object-Oriented Software Process (OOSP)*, Scott Ambler adapted the UP to turn into the *Enterprise Unified Process*, which added two phases at the end of RUP, *Production* and *Retirement*, leaving out *Elaboration* [5]. A second adaptation of UP, also by Scott Ambler, was the *Agile Unified Process*, a light-weight variant of UP based on agile practices. Even though this was first published in 2005 and Ambler stopped work on it already in 2006 [6], AUP became fairly well-known and widely-used.

3.4.2 The German V-Model XT

The V-Model XT[11] is a software process and life cycle model that was developed on behalf of the German government and is expected to be used for major projects commissioned by German government agencies. It derives its name from the V-Model as described in Sect. 3.2.2 and includes an entire product suite consisting of, in addition to the model itself, a meta-model (as described in Sect. 2.4.4) as well as training and certification as described in Example 1.2, and tool support, see Example 7.2.1.

Like other life cycle and process models discussed in this section, V-Model XT describes the overall life cycle, allowing different life cycle variants to support tailoring[12], plus the details of the processes included. These details include the individual activities, results and roles and their relationships, as well as templates for the results to be created. Furthermore, V-Model XT addresses the work to be done by the customer as well as the supplier, and therefore distinguishes three different project types: the "supplier" project type describes the work to be done by the supplier, i.e. the development and related work. the "customer" project type describes the work that needs to be done by the customer, such as defining requirements, selecting a supplier, monitoring the overall project, and integrating the results delivered by the supplier. Finally the "combined supplier and customer" project type essentially combines the two for the case where both roles are included in the same organisation, reducing the formality of the interfaces between the roles.

As a result, the V-Model XT overall consists of several hundred pages (available in HTML or PDF format).

Predecessors of V-Model XT. There were three predecessor models of V-Model XT, starting with a first prototype published in 1989 by the German armed forces to define the processes used for the development of software components in military systems. The later versions V-Model 92 and V-Model 97 were no longer specific to military systems but addressed software and (mainly in V-Model 97) systems development for all government agencies as well as other customer organisations. These three models had a common structure, consisting of four sub-models that describe the main topics relevant in software or systems development projects:

- Software development (in V-Model 97: systems development), represented in a V-shape
- Project management
- Quality assurance
- Configuration management

While these three initial versions had a fairly similar structure, their successor V-Model XT is a completely new model, with little similarity to the initial versions

---

[11] The model itself as well as various additional information are available from http://www.v-modell-xt.de (last access 2017-12-06).

[12] Actually, "XT" in the model name stands for "eXtreme Tailoring" because particular emphasis was put on tailoring support in the development of the model.

apart from purpose and name. Some of the main properties of V-Model XT that distinguish it from many other models are:

- Strong support for *tailoring*, e.g by structuring the overall model into *process modules* where individual modules may (to some extent) be selected or deselected depending on the kind of project (see Sect. 2.4.4). This approach is built on the concepts of *method engineering* as introduced in Sect. 4.4. The formal structure of the model additionally allows tool support for tailoring as described in Example 7.2.1.

  Furthermore, the sequence of the predefined *decision points* ("Entscheidungspunkte", similar to milestones) may be adapted as part of tailoring a project, which allows an iterative and incremental development life cycle as well as a V-shaped one. As a result, in spite of its name, the V-Model XT does not necessarily describe a V-shaped life cycle.
- Explicit consideration of both the *customer and the contractor processes* in a development effort, by defining different types of project: customer project, contractor project, and combined project where both roles are within the same organisation.[13]

Although it is generally accepted that the success of development work depends on the customer as well as the contractor, very few process models define the expectations on the customer explicitly.

3.4.3 Other Software Process Models

This section provides a short summary of some of the main process models applicable to software processes. However, the first two are not specific to software processes but have been created to describe project management in general.

The Project Management Body of Knowledge (PMBoK). The PMBoK, published by the *Project Management Institute* PMI in the PMBoK Guide [81], is a collection of guidelines and definitions of terminology regarding project management. The specific case of project management in software development is covered in a software extension (currently only available for fifth edition rather than the current sixth edition of the PMBoK Guide) to the guide, and an *Agile Practice Guide*, in partnership with the Agile Alliance, has been announced to support it.

An important part of PMBoK is the definition of the relevant project processes which are grouped into five project stages as shown in Fig. 3.14. Each of these stages contains a number of processes which are themselves defined in some detail as part of PMBoK.

---

[13] There was a fourth type of project which has however been removed from the model in its current version 2.1, which covered the process of introducing a software process model within an organisation.

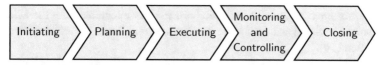

Fig. 3.14 The PMBoK project life cycle

Based on the PMBoK, the PMI has set up a multi-level qualification and certification scheme where knowledge about and experience with project management can be certified, including the well-known "Project Management Professional" (PMP).

PRINCE2®. PRINCE2 is a general project management method similar to PMBoK and claims to be "the world's most widely adopted project management method" [11]. The method consists of a set of principles, themes, and processes, where the processes are assigned to five different stages within the project life cycle

However, these stages are not identical to the stages of the PMBoK project life cycle, and, also different from PMBoK, several processes in PRINCE2 are assigned to multiple stages, for example the process "Directing a project" applies to all project stages from initiation to final stage.

PRINCE2 also acknowledges the importance of agile project management and therefore includes a guide on how to set up PRINCE2 when combining it with agile concepts, as well as a separate certification "PRINCE2 Agile Practitioner" in its certification scheme.

The Swiss standard model Hermes. Hermes [90, 89] is a project management method and standard that was developed by the federal administration of Switzerland and is used by many public and private organisations in Switzerland. It is published as an open standard (both online and for download) and included here as an example for the many national models that exist around the world. Its goal is to support projects in IT, services, products and business organisations.

Hermes includes different *scenarios*, such as "Standard IT application", "Customized IT application", and "Customized IT application (agile)" in order to support the different types of projects. These scenarios are implemented by selecting and tailoring the appropriate modules from the model. As a framework to structure the projects, Hermes uses a simple four-phase model similar to PMBOK, consisting of the phases Initiation, Concept, Implementation, and Deployment.

To support the application of Hermes, Switzerland has set up an entire infrastructure around it, including training courses and certification, user group meetings, and ongoing revision.

Microsoft Solutions Framework (MSF). The Microsoft Solutions Framework (MSF) provides a collection of software development process guidance and best practices, based on experience within Microsoft product development and consulting as well as external partners of Microsoft, and was first introduced in 1994 [103]. As described in [31] and [63], Microsoft already at that time used many concepts that would later be called "agile". The following description is based on the 2013 version of MSF as described in [69]. However, Microsoft no longer supports MSF itself but has since replaced it with the "process" as integrated with the Microsoft development tools Visual Studio Team Services and Team Foundation Server as described in [70].

MSF used two different process variants for agile software development and for CMMI process, which in [70] was further split into the three variants *Scrum*, *Agile* and *CMMI*. Even though this might look like the CMMI variant refers to a plan-driven process, the CMMI variant describes a process which combines agile practices with more formal project and change management.

Process models for individual processes. In addition to the process models discussed so far which each cover more or less the entire software (development) life cycle, there are a number of other process models that address individual processes or small groups of processes, such as ISO/IEC/IEEE 29119 for testing.

3.5 Agile and Lean Development Processes and Methodologies

In many cases, the plan- or requirements-driven approaches discussed so far showed their limitations which lead to the *agile* or *lean* approaches, two similar and overlapping but different approaches to software development each with a large number of different methodologies, techniques and practices. The focus of agile development lies on reacting fast to changes in the environment, such as changed requirements, in a combination of a suitable culture with practices supporting such reaction, and its core ideas are described in the agile manifesto, see below. To achieve this, agile approaches usually put a lot of emphasis on self-organisation of teams, which tends to make them fairly popular with developers but less so with managers. Lead development approaches, on the other hand, focus on the reduction and prevention of "waste" in its various forms, which in the case of software development in particular includes work in progress, i.e. work on which effort has been invested but which has not (yet) produced any benefit to the customer. This concept will be described in more detail in Sect. 3.5.6 below.

3.5.1 The Agile Manifesto

In 2001, representatives of a number of development approaches based on various ideas mostly called "light-weight" met to discuss these various approaches and search for a common basis. The result of this discussion was the "agile manifesto" [13], a collection of values and principles they shared and that introduced the name "agile" for these ideas, which was immediately accepted. The main part of the agile manifesto are its *values* as presented in Fig. 3.15.

> We are uncovering better ways of developing software by doing it and helping others do
> it. Through this work we have come to value:
>
> - *Individuals and interactions* over processes and tools
> - *Working software* over comprehensive documentation
> - *Customer collaboration* over contract negotiation
> - *Responding to change* over following a plan
>
> That is, while there is value in the items on the right, we value the items on the left more.

Fig. 3.15 The agile values as defined in the Agile Manifesto [13]

In addition to these agile values, the agile manifesto contains the *agile principles* which provide additional detail on agile development. Together, these values and principles define the basic concepts that are today known as agile development.

However, one of the difficulties about the agile manifesto is that it is often misinterpreted as *only* putting emphasis on the left hand side, which is clearly not what is stated in the manifesto.

For example, one of the main discussion points in this context is the second value, stating that working software has more value than comprehensive documentation. Of course, few if any proponents of plan-driven development will contradict this statement, and the discussions arise about how to interpret this value, and where to identify the right balance. Obviously, both extremes of not documenting anything or of documenting every detail before going starting to program are inadequate and will lead to failure (ignoring the few exceptions either way for now).

This leads to the third value, stating that customer collaboration is more valuable than contract negotiation. Again, most proponents of plan-driven development will agree, but the main challenge is that for various reasons, customer collaboration is not always possible as needed. Basic agreements therefore need to be explicitly stated and documented, e.g. taking the form of a contract (depending on the organisational relationship between customer and developer etc.). Otherwise, if problems occur in the project such as customer representatives being too busy to work on the project, or end users and customer management having different interests and expectations, there is no way to show what was agreed.

3.5.2 Scrum

Scrum is currently by far the most commonly used agile approach, as discussed in Sect. 3.13 below. The basic concept as well as the name "scrum" were introduced by H. Takeuchi and I. Nonaka who are well known for their work on knowledge management, in particular the SECI model. In their book [97] in 1986 they discussed product development from a knowledge management point of view and used the term "scrum" to describe a product development approach using concepts such as built-in instability, self-organising teams, and overlapping development phases. This approach was taken up and adapted to software development by Ken Schwaber and Jeff Sutherland in 1995 [86], and later refined and documented in the Scrum guide [95] which is the main reference on Scrum. While Schwaber and Sutherland jointly published the guide, they have started to compete on Scrum training and certifications, e.g. for Scrum masters, with separate organisations Scrum.org (Schwaber) and Scrum Alliance (Sutherland).

The core of the Scrum methodology as defined in the Scrum guide is shown in Fig. 3.16 (see also Table 2.1 for a summary of Scrum in SIPOC notation). Scrum consists of three roles (product owner, development team and Scrum master which together form the Scrum team), five events (sprint, sprint planning, daily Scrum, sprint review and sprint retrospective) and three artifacts (product backlog, sprint backlog and increment) plus the "definition of done" for backlog items and increments.

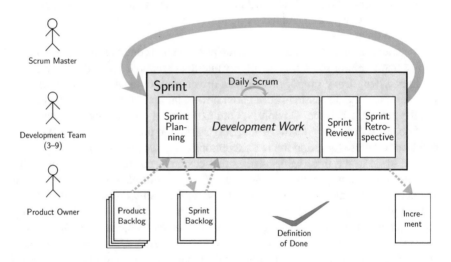

Fig. 3.16 The Scrum methodology

Scrum roles. The Scrum team consists of three roles: the Scrum master is responsible for ensuring that the Scrum methodology is understood and properly implemented by the development team and the product owner, and supports the team by helping everyone else to interact with the team according to the Scrum rules. The product owner is responsible "for maximizing the value of the product and the work of the Development Team" [95, p. 5], i.e. the product owner's task is to manage and help prioritise the requirements to be implemented as documented in the product backlog. The development team is responsible for developing the product, including all relevant tasks such as designing, coding, testing and documentation. According to the Scrum Guide, there are no separate roles or titles within the development team, all members are "developers" [95, p. 6]. Also quite surprising for many people coming across Scrum for the first time is the fact that there is no *project leader*, Scrum development teams are supposed to be self-organising as a team without any such leadership role. However, in practice many organisations do not follow these last two rules of Scrum and do define project leaders and other roles such as tester within the development team.

Sprints. The core entity of Scrum is the sprint, an iteration typically taking about two to four weeks. It is started with the *sprint planning* meeting where the Scrum team selects a number of items from the product backlog, the list of all work items that may be needed in the product, and transfers them into the sprint backlog, the list of work items that are to be addressed in the next sprint. The goal of the sprint is to deliver a new increment of working software ready for release. Whether it is actually released depends on the needs of the customer—not all customers want a new release of the software product every couple of weeks. During the sprint, the development team works on the increment, with short *daily Scrum* meetings (also called stand-up meeting) of the development team to synchronize work and address any problems that may arise.

At the end of a sprint, the increment is presented to the product owner and other stakeholders in a *sprint review*. After that, the *sprint retrospective* meeting is performed to inspect the way the sprint was performed, and identify and plan any improvements to be performed in the next sprint.

Time-boxes. In Scrum, sprints as well as most meetings are *time-boxed*, i.e. they last for a certain pre-defined time. If it turns out that it is not possible to achieve the goal within that time-frame, the goal is adapted rather than the time-frame. For example after a sprint, it is considered better value to deliver a new increment that only contains part of the planned functionality but is delivered on time, than to risk waiting for an indeterminate time to deliver the full functionality planned. Like most Scrum practices, time-boxing is not specific to Scrum but a widely used agile practice.

Scrum and empirical process control. Scrum is based on the concept of empirical process control as introduced in Sect. 3.1.1, with the three so-called pillars

- transparency, achieved by practices such as the product backlog, the daily Scrum meetings and sprint reviews, plus other practices that (according to the Scrum guide) are not part of Scrum itself but often used with Scrum, e.g. Scrum boards and burn-down charts (see Sect. 3.5.3 below for more information on these practices)
- inspection, achieved by applying the practices for transparency
- adaptation, as a reaction to the inspection results. Additionally, sprint retrospectives support the adaptation of the process to achieve better results.

Definition of done. A common discussion in software development regards the question when a certain development task is "done". Scrum tries to ensure that this definition is made explicit by requiring a "definition of done", where the development team defines for itself what it means for a backlog item to be done. Typical minimum requirements included in this "definition of done" that need to be satisfied before a certain work items is allowed to be integrated into the main branch include an adequate number of (unit and possibly other) test cases of the new functionality which have been defined and successfully performed, as well as checking the integration of the new code to ensure that it does not break the main development branch. Furthermore, the definition of done usually requires that the code has been documented adequately, where again the team defines for itself what "adequate" means in this context.

Similar to this "definition of done" for backlog items, a development team may define what it means to be done for other tasks, e.g. for a complete increment at the end of a sprint which may need additional testing, documentation etc.

Although not part of the Scrum guide, a variant of the definition of done that has become quite wide-spread over the last few years is the "definition of ready" which defines the requirements that a product backlog item needs to satisfy before it may be included into the sprint backlog. For example, it must be broken down into sufficiently small tasks so that it can be implemented within one sprint, or it must have an adequate number of acceptance criteria.

Both the "definition of done" and "definition of ready" are a form of quality gate in the sense that they define criteria that need to be satisfied before the next step of work. However, there is no separate quality assurance function that checks that these gates may be passed but the person responsible for the work also checks that it has been completed and the criteria are satisfied. Social pressure within the development team ensures that this is done properly, rather than some external mechanism.

Example 3.2. One of the fundamental concepts of Scrum is the release of a production-ready increment of the product at the end of each sprint. While this is very useful in many environments, it is not really feasible if the test of the product cannot be automated, e.g. because the product is a complex system covering several technical platforms or consisting of hard- and software.

This was the case in the company described in this example: the product developed consisted of software that was used to manage radar equipment and analyse data provided by this equipment. While part of the test of this software had been automated, considerable part of the test had to be performed manually, handling the collection of different, interacting hardware components appropriately.

Instead of standard sprints lasting two to four weeks and resulting in a releasable product, it was therefore decided to use sprints lasting six to ten weeks, consisting of two to four two-week development phases plus a final test phase. Each development phase is started by a planning meeting and results in a new version that is submitted to some basic, automated tests as well as some internal reviews, but is not sufficiently verified to be released to customers.

At the end of each sprint, a full (partly manual) test is performed as well as a sprint review including the product owner.

This approach uses some of the ideas that will be described as part of scaling agile methodologies, in particular SAFe® (see Sect. 3.5.9 below), but in this case not used to scale agile development but to adapt it to a different technical environment.

Adapting Scrum. Scrum is different from many other agile (and other) process models in that it has, in the *Scrum Guide*, a clearly defined core stating what exactly needs to be satisfied in order to follow Scrum: "Scrum's roles, artifacts, events, and rules are immutable and although implementing only parts of Scrum is possible, the result is not Scrum. Scrum exists only in its entirety and functions well as a container for other techniques, methodologies, and practices." [95, p. 16] While it is allowed and necessary to add additional practices such as those described below, leaving out any of the defined Scrum concepts leads to a approach that may no longer be called Scrum. As experience as well as various studies such as [34] show, many organisations or projects claim to use Scrum without doing so in its entirety, which should therefore not be called Scrum according to the Scrum Guide.

While the Scrum Guide explicitly states that leaving out parts of Scrum is possible, as long as it is no longer called Scrum, there are a number of purists in the agile community which emphasise a very rigid interpretation of Scrum and agile methods in general, calling whoever does not apply the agile approach in its entirety a *ScrumBut* (or even ScrumButt) and claiming that they are losing out on the benefits of agile development. It is surprising to see how rigid the agile methods are sometimes interpreted.

There are a number of ways why and how Scrum is commonly adapted: first of all and as mentioned before, Scrum alone is not sufficient in order to organise software development, and needs to be supplemented by a number of other practices, in particular regarding the technical aspects of software development. These will be discussed in more detail below.

Second, some development efforts just cannot be implemented by an individual Scrum team but need to scale up to agile approaches to larger teams. How to scale agile development to larger development efforts and teams will be discussed in Sect. 3.5.9.

Third, it is not always possible to have the entire development team in one location, as recommended by all agile methodologies, but sometimes distributed development is necessary, as for example discussed in [96] by Jeff Sutherland and his colleagues. In such a case, the Scrum events and other communication need to be adapted and for example performed via video conferencing.

3.5.3 Common Agile Practices

This and the following section describe a number of practices that are commonly used in agile development, often in combination with Scrum, but which are strictly speaking not part of the Scrum methodology since they are not defined in the Scrum guide [95]. Scrum on its own only provides a framework that concentrates on (project) management activities but leaves open many questions that may be answered by practices such as the ones described here.

User stories. User stories describe a format for describing user requirements as a "story". They should be short, typically just one sentence, and described from the *user* point of view. There are a number of different but similar templates to be used for describing a user story, a common template is

> As a <role>, I want <goal> so that <benefit>.

Example: "As a process engineer, I want to see the dependencies between different process steps so that I can easily verify and validate them."

Large user stories which are later broken down into smaller ones are often called *epics*. However, such epics do not necessarily follow the template given. The product backlog then mainly contains a collection of epics and user stories which may be broken down into smaller user stories and tasks as part of sprint planning.

Refactoring and reduction of technical debt. While the practices described so far are mainly concerned with managing development, refactoring is concerned with ensuring the technical quality of the software developed:

Definition 3.12 (Refactoring). *Refactoring is the process of changing a software system in such a way that it does not alter the external behaviour of the code yet improves its internal structure. [41]*

Refactoring has turned out to be an important practice in agile development since there is little focus on defining software architecture and design in advance, risking to spend a lot of effort on the design of code that may not be implemented. Instead, design is expected to emerge from the work of the team, but this does not happen on its own. It requires actively cleaning up the code, such as removing duplicated code or splitting up classes or methods that have grown too big, i.e. refactoring. If code is not refactored when such cleaning up becomes necessary this will lead to a gradual degradation of the code and higher cost for maintenance and for later changes. Such higher cost that will occur at a later stage if they are not "paid for" immediately are often described as *technical debt*. Apart from ill-structured code, technical debt can e.g. include missing documentation and missing test cases.

Note that although refactoring and the reduction of technical debt are mainly discussed in the context of agile development, the same gradual degradation of the code and its architecture happen in plan-driven development, and refactoring and the reduction of technical debt are therefore just as important in that context.

3.5.4 Planning and Tracking Work in Agile Development

Planning and tracking work is less important in agile development than it is in plan-driven development, as for example described in value 4 of the agile manifesto which states that responding to change is more important that following a plan. However, that does not mean that planning and tracking should not be done at all—just that they are less important.

An important reason for the need for planning and estimating the overall project, going beyond sprint planning, is that customers want to know what they will get for their money. "I'll tell you what you get two weeks before the end of the project" is not acceptable to customers. This is particularly true for public agencies as customers which have to satisfy legal requirements on acquisition.

The remainder of this section will therefore introduce some common practices for planning and tracking work in agile development.

Estimating effort. The size of user stories, i.e. the effort involved to implement it, is often estimated in a relative unit called *story points*. The idea is that, while a user story estimated at 2 story points will be roughly twice as much effort to implement as a user story estimated at 1 story point, these story points still do not directly translate into person-hours or some similar measure of effort. Since giving an exact estimate the effort involved in many cases is difficult to impossible anyway, story points do not even try but give a relative, rough estimate instead. Ideally, within one development group one story point should always denote more or less the same amount of effort, but a different development group may use very different numbers. In order to emphasise that an exact estimate is not possible anyway, most organisations restrict the allowed values to a rounded and adapted version of the Fibonacci series, typically allowing the numbers 0, $^1/_2$, 1, 2, 3, 5, 8, 13, 20, 40, and 100.

Alternative units used for estimating the effort involved in a user story or task are T-shirt sizes (XS, S, M, L, XL), which are however more difficult to use since there is no adequate way of adding them up to estimate the overall effort for a set of user stories or tasks, or the units person-days or person-hours as are common in plan-driven development.

To get to these numbers, a common estimation technique is the *planning poker*, also known as *planning game* or occasionally *Scrum poker*, where the development team tries to get consensus on the effort of a user story or task.

The *velocity* of a development team describes how much work the team can handle within a defined time frame such as a sprint, measured in the unit agreed for estimation such as story points. Considering the priorities set by the product owner, the estimates agreed by the team, and the expected velocity based on experience from previous sprints, the team can now define in the sprint planning session which and how many user stories to move from the product backlog to the sprint backlog.

Burn-down chart. Once the effort involved has been estimated and the tasks to be performed have been selected, these tasks are performed and progress needs to be tracked. In agile development, a common tool for progress is the burn-down chart as shown in Fig. 3.17.

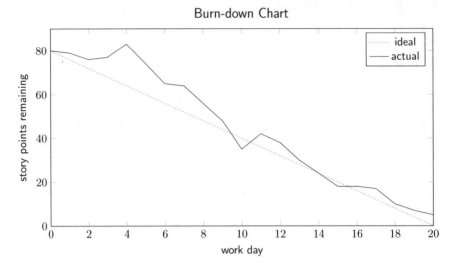

Fig. 3.17 A sample burn-down chart

It measures, usually in story points, the effort remaining in the current sprint, and as a result is quite similar to an upside-down earned value chart. Ideally, the effort remaining goes down in a straight line from the total number of story points planned for the sprint (80 in the example shown in Fig. 3.17) at the beginning, to zero at the end of the sprint. Obviously, the actual values rarely if ever follow this ideal, and occasionally the effort remaining will go up rather than down, for example because a task turns out to be more effort than planned, or an additional task had to be added, or because a task that was considered "done" turns out to be not done after all.

Scrum (task) board. Like the burn-down chart, the purpose of the Scrum board is to track progress within a sprint, and to make that progress visible for the entire team. Therefore, the Scrum board is often a physical board in or near the office(s) where the team works, but occasionally an electronic board is used instead.

The Scrum board consists of a number of columns such as "to do", "in progress", "in test", and "done", and of rows where one row usually contains one user story. For each user story, the relevant tasks are noted on cards which are then pinned into the appropriate column, gradually moving from left to right.

3.5.5 Extreme Programming (XP)

Extreme programming (XP) was one of the first agile methodologies, created by Kent Beck [12] and initially at least as widely used as Scrum but today has been largely replaced by Scrum. Nevertheless, since Scrum concentrates on the management aspects of development while XP (as the name indicates) emphasises the technical aspects, many principles of XP are useful add-ons to Scrum and therefore still quite widespread.

The core of XP are the twelve principles shown in Fig. 3.18, many of which are now considered standard agile practices independent of XP. One of the few excep-

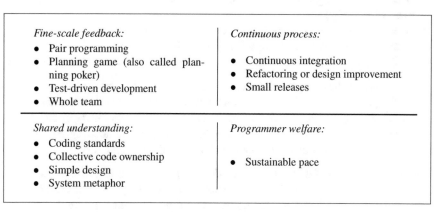

Fine-scale feedback:
- Pair programming
- Planning game (also called planning poker)
- Test-driven development
- Whole team

Continuous process:
- Continuous integration
- Refactoring or design improvement
- Small releases

Shared understanding:
- Coding standards
- Collective code ownership
- Simple design
- System metaphor

Programmer welfare:
- Sustainable pace

Fig. 3.18 The twelve principles of XP

tions is *pair programming* where developers work (at least part of the time) in pairs, where one of the developers actually writes code while the second takes the role of an observer, immediately reviewing the code produced, suggesting improvements etc. Within each pair, developers switch roles often. Although with this approach it obviously takes more effort to create code, the code will typically have better quality by bringing in different viewpoints, which according to the proponents may more than make up for the additional effort needed. Additionally, this can help to train programmers, in particular less experienced ones but pairs of experienced programmers may also gain from this approach. Nevertheless, pair programming is a well-known concept but, due to the additional effort involved, rarely used in practice.

3.5.6 Lean Development

The concept of "lean" work first was used in the Japanese automotive industry but following the publication of [105] these concepts spread to manufacturing worldwide. One of the core concepts of lean manufacturing is to reduce the amount of *waste*, where the term "waste" is interpreted very widely, often defining the following eight types of waste (with the mnemonic TIM WOODS):

- Transport: moving products or people
- Inventory: storage of products that are not needed yet, including work in process (WIP)

- Motion: people or equipment moving more than needed, for example bending, turning or lifting
- Waiting: waiting for parts or information before the next production step can be performed, including interruptions of work
- Over-production: producing more than is currently required (which will also lead to new inventory)
- Over-processing: producing higher quality than is needed
- Defects: effort involved in inspecting for and fixing defects
- Skills: under-utilizing capabilities and delegating tasks with inadequate training

A close look at these types of waste shows that most of them are not specific to industrial production but apply to product development as well, leading to the concept of *lean development*. In particular, the ideas of Goldratt's theory of constraints and Kanban are two sets of ideas that originate from manufacturing but are now commonly used for the development of software and other products:

Goldratt's theory of constraints. The *theory of constraints* is a lean management approach that was first introduced in the novel "The Goal" [43] by Eliyahu M. Goldratt. Like most similar approaches, it was first used in manufacturing, but today it is also applied in software processes, project management, services [83] and other application areas.

As the name suggests, the core concept of the theory of constraints is the *constraint*, defined as a limitation on the flow of a product or task through a process. The overall goal of the theory of constraints is to increase the overall throughput through a process.

Any process with such a flow must have at least one limiting constraint, since otherwise the throughput of the process would be unlimited and therefore infinite. To increase overall throughput, it is important to work on that constraint. Improving the capacity of any other process step will only lead to more idle time of this process step, but not increase the overall capacity of the process.

For example, assume we have a simple incremental life cycle model consisting of a pipeline containing the sequential steps requirements analysis, design, implementation, test, and delivery. Assume that the capacity of these steps is such that each step is able to complete ten story points per day, except for design which only manages nine story points per day, see Fig. 3.19.[14]

Fig. 3.19 Example for Theory of Constraints

---

[14] Of course, it is unlikely that any software development organisation or project will have such a stable capacity, but that does not change the principles described here. It only implies that one continuously needs to review any improvement activities introduced, since a solution that works perfectly today may no longer be so perfect tomorrow.

Assume furthermore that there is an unlimited amount of requirements available for analysis. What will happen in such a situation when everyone works full speed, trying to get as much work done as possible? Requirements that have been analysed will pile up because design is not able to handle them as fast as they come in, thus continually increasing the amount of work in progress. On the other hand, implementation, test and delivery will be idle 10% of the time because design cannot provide them with new work fast enough.

To improve this situation, it is important to deal with the constraint, in this case design, and to align the capacity of the different process steps, for example by moving personnel away from the process steps that are idle part of the time. A local optimisation at any other point in the process will not lead to a global improvement but on the contrary may damage the overall process by piling up more work in progress.

The general process for eliminating constraints consists of the following *five focussing steps*:

1. Identify the constraint.
   Any step with a large amount of work in progress or waiting to be processed is a likely candidate as a constraint.
2. Decide how to exploit the constraint.
   In particular, this involves ensuring that the process step with the constraint can work to full capacity, with no interruptions etc.
3. Subordinate and synchronize everything else to the above decisions.
4. Elevate the performance of the constraint.
   As described, this will directly influence the overall throughput of the process.
5. If in any of the above steps the constraint has shifted, go back to Step 1.
   Of course, this will eventually happen: if the capacity of the constraint is sufficiently improved, then another process step will become the new constraint.

The *critical chain project management* method applies these same concepts to project management. It has some similarity to the *critical path method* but goes beyond that by addressing the resources and resource limitations as well.

Kanban. Similar to the theory of constraints and most other lean methodologies, Kanban was originally introduced in industrial production in the early 1990s. Later, it was adapted to software development first by David Anderson [9] and then Mike Burrows [24]. It is based on the theory of constraints, and one of its main aims is to reduce processing times, mainly by restricting the number of tasks worked on in parallel. This way, the flow of individual tasks through all development stages can be accelerated and the amount of work in progress at any given time reduced.

Also like other lean development approaches, Kanban is quite similar to agile methodologies but has a somewhat different focus and there different opinions about whether Kanban should be counted as an agile methodology. An important difference to most agile methodologies is that Kanban does not use iterations but focusses on the flow of *individual* work items. In that sense, a sprint backlog containing more than the work items currently being worked on contains "waste" [56]. Nevertheless, it is quite possible to combine agile methodologies with Kanban (or other lean approaches), as for example done in *Scrumban*, see below.

Core principles of Kanban as defined by Anderson are to visualise the workflow and to limit the work in progress. This is usually done using a Kanban board as shown in Fig.3.20 which helps to visualise progress and is similar to the Scrum board introduced in Sect. 3.5.3 above. Then main difference is that the Kanban board usually distinguishes between work items that are currently in work ("doing"), and those that are waiting to be done ("to do"), in order to make waiting times more visible and thus speed up the flow of work from start to completion once it has been started. Additionally, a Kanban board usually defines a maximum number of work items that are allowed at any stage of the board. Since any work item on which work has already been invested is a form of inventory and therefore considered waste, Kanban tries to keep to keep this waste to a minimum.

Requirements Analysis		Design		Implementation		Test	
To do (5)	Doing (2)	To do (3)	Doing (3)	To do (4)	Doing (3)	To do (4)	Doing (3)

Fig. 3.20 A sample Kanban board

Kanban as a pull system. This form of reducing inventory is often described as a *pull system*, where work is only done if a "customer" asks for it. The customer, in this context, is not necessarily the customer of the overall product but may be the next step in the work flow. For example in the Kanban board shown in Fig. 3.20, the customer of requirements analysis is design, and if design has more work items to be done than they can currently cope with, requirements analysis should not deliver even more work items, thus increasing the inventory. Instead, requirements analysis workers might help design to reduce their backlog of work. In this example, only test has a customer in the conventional sense, and therefore no limit on the work they deliver to their customer.

Ideally, this customer now sets priorities by asking for a certain work item to be delivered. If available, test will now handle this work item first, otherwise it will push that request down to implementation, and eventually it will arrive at requirements analysis (if it is not already in work) which should therefore handle this work item next.

In [8], Anderson described different variants of Kanban for software development which are appropriate for different levels of organisational maturity. In contrast to many other proponents of agile development, he strongly argues for defining and using processes within development organisations, and for example was one of the authors of the study [42] analysing the relationship between agile development and CMMI (see Sect. 5.5.3), one of the first publications to show that both concepts can support each other.

While using Kanban and a Kanban board can be very helpful in many cases, there are a number of challenges that must be addressed in order for the flow of work items to continue: first, it is important that work items should have roughly the same size. Similarly, if one step in the process has problems, this may block the entire flow of work. To some extent, this is of course deliberate since in this case the focus should be put on resolving the blockade rather than just continuing work as before.

Another challenge is to set an adequate limit to the number of work items in any stage of the work-flow. Ideally, this number should be set to a very small value. However, if the number is too small then standard variations of the velocity of handling work items may lead to blocking the entire flow.

Furthermore, this approach works well for independent tasks but it is difficult to cope with dependencies.

Scrumban. The method Scrumban (Scrum-ban, ScrumBan) is a mixture of Scrum and Kanban that was originally created as a way to move from Scrum to Kanban [56] by gradually adding lean or Kanban features to Scrum, but now is often used as a methodology in its own right.

Basic Scrumban uses the standard components of Scrum, but additionally structures the work done within a sprint using a Kanban board with appropriate limits. In a more advanced form, sprint planning is reduced, moving towards on-demand planning, where only a small number of those work items with the highest priority is identified. Everything beyond that is not immediately needed and therefore considered "waste".

3.5.7 Other Common Agile and Lean Methodologies

In this section, we give a brief overview of some of the main agile and lean methodologies. Overall, there is a huge number of different such methodologies and we can therefore one present a few of these here.

Rapid Application Development (RAD) and Dynamic Systems Development Method (DSDM). The name RAD refers to two related but different development concepts that describe early forms of agile development:

- In a wider sense, RAD refers to a number of different approaches to software development which put a strong focus on using a sequence of prototypes for designing the user interface of a software system.
- RAD according to James Martin, introduced in the early 1990s, is an extension of his earlier work in *Information Engineering* and describes a well-defined methodology for the development of database-centered information systems

[64]. This is a mix of concepts from plan-driven development (e.g. initial requirements planning phase, use of CASE tools) and from agile development (e.g.
prototyping, strong user involvement, time-boxes), and also uses a sequence of
prototypes for user interface design.

Both types of RAD consist of a collection of best practices but do not define a full
development life cycle or software processes.

The *Dynamic systems development method* (DSDM) was created by the DSDM
Consortium, founded in 1994, and is based on the concepts of RAD but with the goal
to include more guidance on the processes to be used, while still applying the ideas
of agile development (even though that term was only coined a few years later).
The DSDM Consortium has since been renamed as the *Agile Business Consortium*
and continues to work on DSDM, the latest version being the "DSDM Agile Project
Framework" published in 2014. Compared to other agile methodologies, DSDM is
more formal, and has been explicitly defined such that it can be used in combination
with well-known project management approaches such as PRINCE2 or PMBoK.

Feature-Driven Development (FDD). In FDD, the functionality of a software system is described in terms of *features*, which are defined as short sentences of the
structure *<action> the <result> <by|for|of|to> a(n) <object>*, for example "Cal-
culate the total quantity sold by a Retail Outlet for an Item Description" [74].

The FDD process consists of five activities split into two phases, where the first
phase describes the preparatory work and therefore is only performed once, while
the second phase is iterated for each feature implemented, as shown in Fig. 3.21.

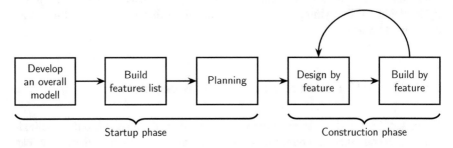

Fig. 3.21 The FDD process (based on [74])

Test-first and test-driven development (TDD). As the name indicates, the basic
idea of the test-first concept is that test cases are defined very early, in parallel with
the requirements or even replacing requirements in the usual form. Since these tests
are going to be repeated very often, it is important to automate them, or at least a
very large proportion. This way, a large collection of automated test cases testing all
relevant functionality is built up over time.

The implementation of a work item is only started once its test cases are available,
and it is considered complete once it passes all (new and old) tests successfully.

Scott Ambler describes the test-first process as the following loop, each time just implementing a very small change [4]:

1. *Add a test* based on the change required.
2. *Run the tests* to ensure that the new test fails but all previously existing ones pass.
3. *Make a little change* to implement the change required.
4. *Run the tests* to ensure that the new test as well as all previously existing ones pass.

Test-Driven Development, introduced as part of the Extreme Programming (XP) methodology, extends the test-first concept by adding refactoring, which again is performed as a sequence of very small changes, and after each change, the set of tests is run to ensure that no existing functionality has been broken by the change.

Behaviour-Driven Development (BDD). BDD builds on TDD, extending it by adding a strong focus on describing the expected behaviour of the system to be built. This is usually done by describing this behaviour in a domain-specific language, intended to be easily understandable for both domain experts and developers, and often using tools that automatically translate this description of behaviour into a test case. A common format of describing behaviour in BDD is the *Given–When–Then* structure.

Crystal. Crystal is not a single methodology but a whole family of agile methodologies applicable for different types of projects that was developed by Alistair Cockburn. Depending on the factors project size (number of people involved), criticality, and project priorities (productivity and cost vs. traceability and legal liability), one chooses the method that suits best [26]. *Crystal Clear* is an extremely light-weight methodology for small, non-critical projects, and for larger and more critical projects, the more complex methodologies Crystal Yellow, Orange, Orange Web, Red, Maroon and Sapphire are recommended, with darker colours referring to more complex methodologies.[15] The more complex methodologies differ for example by their higher documentation requirements and the number of roles defined.

3.5.8 Processes for Open Source Software Development

The development of open source software (OSS) has a number of specific properties that lead to somewhat different processes needed. These properties include the fact that development is usually decentralised, and often the different developers have never met in person. Little planning is possible since the development team usually is not able to commit to perform certain tasks within a given amount of time, and since developers are typically volunteers, they have strong influence on deciding which tasks they perform. As a result, OSS development is usually coordinated by

---

[15] The exact colours used vary in different publications, but yellow and orange are consistently used as the lightest colours, describing the methodologies applicable for small, less critical projects.

a small core team and performed in an iterative and incremental manner, taking on many agile concepts, but without being fully agile.

The cathedral and the bazaar. Probably the most common approach to OSS development was described by Eric S. Raymond in his essay [82], later also published as a book. In this essay, he investigated two different ways to develop open-source software which he called the cathedral model and the bazaar model.

In the cathedral model, a small group of developers builds the software, using top-design and releasing the software only when it is stable, usually taking months between releases. This is the approach that was common for the development of open-source software, used for example for the development of GNU Emacs and GCC, until Linus Torvalds started the Linux kernel development project where he used a rather different approach which Raymonds calls the bazaar model.

In the development of the Linux kernel, many ideas that we now call agile were taken up, in particular frequent releases and strong user involvement. However, in the context of open-source software, user involvement works somewhat different from the development of software in a commercial context, since here there is a large overlap between the user and the developer communities. If users find bugs or are missing certain features in open-source software, they can just correct or add them themselves rather than issue a change request which may take considerable time to decide, implement and release. One of the core concepts of the "bazaar" model therefore is to try to get a large proportion of development work done not by small core development team but to spread out the work to the users/developers, while the core team is mainly responsible for integrating the software and releasing it frequently.

Raymond summarised his observations from analysing the Linux kernel development approach as well as his own experience with open-source software development in a set of "lessons learned". The best-known of these is *Linus's Law* which states that "given enough eyeballs, all bugs are shallow", i.e. with a sufficiently large user base, there will always be someone to whom the cause of any bug is obvious.

3.5.9 Scaling Agile Development

Agile development methodologies usually address small development teams. For example, the Scrum Guide [95, p. 6] recommends a development team size of three to nine members. This of course raises the question what to do if the task at hand is too large and/or complex to be implemented with a team that size. This section gives an overview of the main approaches to scaling agile approaches.

There are two related but different factors involved which are addressed to varying degree by the different scaling approaches:

- development team size
- product and market complexity, in particular interfaces and dependencies

Most approaches for scaling agile are based on Scrum as the method to be used on the level of individual teams, plus an additional structure to coordinate these teams, adding more roles, coordination meetings etc.

The remainder of this section briefly introduces the best-known techniques and frameworks used for scaling agile development, except for the Scaled Agile Framework (SAFe) which will be described in the following section.

3.5.9.1 Techniques for scaling agile development

Scrum of Scrums is a technique used to scale Scrum to larger groups that was first introduced by Jeff Sutherland in [94]. At the bottom level, work is divided into individual Scrum teams. To coordinate these teams, an additional daily (according to [1]) or weekly (according to [94]) "Scrum of Scrums" meeting of team representatives is performed.

This is a fairly simple scaling technique that can work well for larger teams provided that the complexity of the task and therefore interdependencies and the need for cooperation is low. According to VersionOne's survey 2015 [101] (cf. Sect. 3.13), this is by far the preferred methodology for scaling agile, with 72% of respondents using it.

The agile release train extends the concept of a release train as described in Sect. 3.2.5.3 by including iterations, usually performed as Scrum sprints, as shown in Fig. 3.22. They are a core concept of the Scaled Agile Framework (SAFe®) as introduced in Sect. 3.5.10 below. Like the release train, the agile release train is used

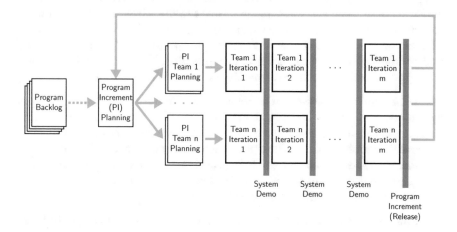

Fig. 3.22 Agile Release Train

as a metaphor for describing that various teams ("carriages") leave and arrive at stations at the same time, i.e. they start and end iterations at the same time. A program increment typically consists of about 4–5 iterations which each end with a system demo while a program increment is a new version of the system that at least could be deployed for production. This way, a full integration test—which may involve considerable effort—does not need to be performed after each iteration but at the end of a program increment.

3.5.9.2 Frameworks for scaling agile development

Apart from the specific techniques used for coordinating agile development teams, there are a number of entire frameworks with the same purpose.

Large-Scale Scrum (LeSS) is a framework for scaling Scrum with two variants:

- *LeSS* is the "classical" variant intended for up to eight teams of eight people each described in [57, 99].
- *LeSS Huge* is a new variant intended for larger environments of up to a few thousand people on one product described in [99].

LeSS is also based on Scrum teams, with a hierarchy of product owners to coordinate their activities.

Nexus is another framework for scaling Scrum and was developed by Ken Schwaber, one of the authors of Scrum [87]. Nexus is meant for teams consisting of three to nine Scrum teams, up to about 100 developers.

Nexus is described in the Nexus Guide [87], built on and in a similar format to the Scrum Guide [95]. It adds the role of *Nexus Integration Team*, accountable for the integration of the work done by individual Scrum teams, as well as events such as the Nexus sprint planning, where representatives from each Scrum team coordinate the activities of these teams for one sprint. Similarly, there is a Nexus Daily Scrum, a Nexus Sprint Review, and a Nexus Sprint Retrospective. Additionally, Nexus introduces the *Refinement* meeting where representatives from involved Scrum teams refine product backlog items to remove dependencies between teams.

Disciplined Agile, successor to Disciplined Agile Delivery (DAD), was developed by Scott Ambler and his colleague Mark Lines [61, 60]. One of its core concepts is the Agile Delivery Life Cycle, consisting of an inception phase, a construction phase, and a transition phase. The construction phase may consist of a sequence of iterations such as Scrum sprints, or of a lean, continuous flow approach. The focus of Disciplined Agile is less on scaling agile development than on adding some concepts from other methods to Scrum that the authors consider important.

The Spotify approach. The approach to scaling agile as used at Spotify is described in [52] and has become fairly popular over the last few years.[16] The basic

---

[16] The approach has since been revised and described in two videos available from `https://labs.spotify.com/2014/03/27/spotify-engineering-culture-part-1/` and `https://labs.spotify.com/2014/09/20/spotify-engineering-culture-part-2/` (last access 2017-10-08).

unit of the Spotify approach is the *squad* which is similar to a Scrum team. Squads are grouped into *tribes* based on their area of work, which may include up to about 100 people. To ensure that the different squads and tribes cooperate and work in a similar way, *chapters* and *guilds* are introduced where a chapter is a small group of people with similar skills, working on the same kind of tasks, e.g. testing or web development, and within the same tribe. There are regular chapter meetings to discuss their area of expertise and exchange experience. Each chapter has a chapter lead which is a line manager with the typical responsibilities of a line manager. Each team member therefore belongs to exactly one chapter. A guild, on the other hand, also acts as a community of interest which meets regularly to share ideas and experience, in that way similar to chapters but reaching across the entire organisation. Overall, the Spotify approach thus describes a variant of the standard matrix organisation which is specifically suited to large-scale agile development.

3.5.10 Scaled Agile Framework (SAFe®)

The Scaled Agile Framework (SAFe) [85, 106], developed by Dean Leffingwell and his company Scaled Agile, Inc., is probably most complex framework for agile development in-the-large, combining the closely related agile and lean development approaches. In this framework, the work is structured into four levels:

- *Portfolio* is the top-level, connecting engineering work with the business value to be created, addressing strategy, budget and governance issues. A portfolio includes one or more value streams.
- *Value Stream* is an optional level that was introduced with SAFe v4.0 and is intended for very large and complex systems but can be left out for systems not quite as large. A value stream is defined as a series of steps used to provide a continuous flow of value to a customer.
- *Program* is the level where different teams work together to create the results required. It is organised around the metaphor of the *Agile Release Train* (ART), a specific version of the agile release trained described above, defined as "a long-lived team of Agile Teams, typically consisting of 50–125 individuals" [85]. The ART delivers *Program Increments (PIs)* every eight to twelve weeks.

  At the beginning of each program increment, there is a two-day PI Planning meeting where all stakeholders (customer, developers, management etc.) come together to plan the work to be done during the PI, in particular to manage any dependencies between different teams. The meeting starts with presentations of the context of the PI, and continues with two cycles of team breakouts where the individual teams plan their work based on the context provided, and reviews of these plans by all participants.

  At the end of each program increment, the result is demonstrated and feedback collected at the "Inspect and Adapt" (I&A) meeting. Quantitative metrics are reviewed, and a retrospective on the PI level is performed, including a problem-solving workshop addressing any major problems identified.

- *Team* is the lowest level, similar to a sequence of sprints as performed in Scrum. Based on the plans agreed on the PI level, each team plans and executes a series of iterations, with one iteration typically lasting two weeks and delivering a system demo at the end.

While at the team level, work is performed in iterations lasting typically two weeks ("Develop on Cadence") and combined into Program Increments consisting of four to six iterations, releases may be performed following a very different pattern, depending mainly on business needs. At any time, parts of the system or the entire system may be released as appropriate ("Release Any Time"). This helps to separate the frequent delivery in development from business where frequent releases may or may not be useful.

While there is some criticism that the set of rules, guidelines, roles etc. in SAFe is considerably larger than in the other approaches to scaling agile described above, and that this may lead to less agility, SAFe seems to be quite successful for large and complex tasks. Approaches that are much simpler may not be able to cope with the complexity involved in such development tasks.

Example 3.3. A company developing tools to support the car development life cycle with about 300 developers in the past used a sequential development model but wanted to introduce to a more agile approach. The target was to achieve more flexibility and to move from push to pull principle—portfolio management prioritizes changes which are then implemented by product development according to their priority.

Since the different products developed by the company are closely integrated with a product portfolio consisting of three product families, a framework such as Scrum would not have been sufficient. Instead, the decision was taken to use SAFe.

The company therefore set up one portfolio of products, with a portfolio coordinator collecting and managing the major requirements on the product family. The new roles of enterprise architect—responsible for coordinating the overall architecture of the product portfolio—and systems architects—responsible for the architecture of a group of products—were introduced, in addition to the existing product architects.

At the time the company started to use SAFe, v2.5 was the current version of SAFe which did not contain value streams as a separate level—this was only introduced with version 4.0. Some changes that were introduced with later versions of SAFe were also introduced in the company's development approach, but a separate value stream level was not considered necessary. Therefore, work was split into three separate programs or ARTs (one per product family) where ARTs follow a joint 10-week-rhythm of program increments, each consisting of five 2-week-sprints. (The company does not always use the SAFe terminology and for example talks about "sprints" rather than "iterations".) At the beginning of each program increment, there is a major two-day release planning meeting with all involved stakeholders (business owners, customer project leads, architects, product managers, usability experts, documentation group etc.). Including all these roles in the meetings has helped to get them much more involved.

During these workshops, the next program increment is planned, with a focus on dependencies between teams, delivery milestones, team capacity etc. The individual sprints contained in the program increment are only planned on a rough level at this stage. Since the same teams also perform maintenance, a certain percentage of the time available (different for different products, based on historic data) is reserved for maintenance tasks, including both planned and ad-hoc maintenance.

Although a product release would in theory be possible after each program increment, customers do not want new releases that often and therefore new releases of the product family are performed at most twice a year. Bug fixes may be released in between full releases, according to a separate delivery plan which is agreed with customer service.

The last iteration or sprint within any product increment is usually an *innovation and planning sprint* which is used for a number of purposes such as preparing planning of the next program increment, act as a buffer for tasks that could not be completed according to plan, "Inspect and Adapt" activities etc.

Since system specifications are needed for maintenance, further development and overall testing as well as for legal reasons, such specifications are created as part of development work. However, while in the past these were created in the form of specification documents, the company is now in the process of implementing a tool set to manage and document all requirements levels. Using such a tool set makes it easier to maintain dependencies and other links between the different products and product components, and between the different levels of requirements.

In order to implement this new approach, an "agile coach" was employed early on and now guides the usage of the new process framework. Several employees participated in SAFe training, and additionally Scrum masters were trained and there now is Scrum master for each development team (with occasionally one Scrum master supporting two teams).

Regular meetings of the agile coach, Scrum masters and other stakeholders are held in order to further improve the development approach used.

A number of benefits of this new approach were identified by the company, including the following:

- The release planning meetings have helped to reduce the time needed for coordinating work to two days rather than weeks.
- Dependencies between different work items are much more transparent and well under control.

- There is common commitment of all people involved at the end of the release planning meeting.
- This approach allows high visibility of work progress from the highest level down to the level of individual tasks.
- There is one joint development work-flow across all teams.

3.6 Hybrid Approaches

In a wider sense, hybrid approaches are any approaches to software development that combine different types of models or methodologies, such as the process model VM-XT plus maturity model CMMI, or Scrumban as a combination of Scrum and Kanban. However, in most cases this term is used to describe hybrid approaches in a narrower sense of combining agile and plan-driven methodologies. As described e.g. by Boehm and Turner in [20], pure agile and pure plan-driven development are two ends of a scale with a lot of grey in between, and in many practical cases a combination is adequate. Even the assumption that there is anything like "pure agile" or "pure plan-driven" development in practice seems questionable.

The reasons for this need for hybrid models are that in many practical cases, neither agile nor plan-driven development addresses all issues at stake. A purely plan-driven model in many cases is too rigid and does not cope well with changes in the requirements or the environment, while a purely agile model does not cope well with complex systems containing many inter-dependent components.

On the other hand, hybrid development involves a number of risks. On the one hand, there is the risk that one tries to work both agile and plan-driven at the same time, leading to considerable overhead. On the other hand, there is a risk that by mixing two approaches, one will neither get the advantages of one nor of the other.

Combining practices from plan-driven and agile development. Depending on factors such as the changeability of requirements, the company culture, the size of the project, the criticality of its results and the qualification of the developers, an individual combination of agile and plan-driven practices is therefore often selected that in sum addresses all important development tasks. This selection is described in more detail in [20], cf. Sect. 4.4. As argued by Meyer in [67], several of the "agile" practices were actually already accepted as best practices in plan-driven develop-ment,even though not necessarily widely used. In that sense, the agile movement achieved to make these existing practices more popular but did not newly introduce them. For example, a development project using nightly builds, release cycles of a few months, allowing developers a lot of freedom for self-organisation, and putting a strong focus on collaboration with the customer would have been considered as using best practices but not as strange before the advent of agile development.[17] To-day, this might be called a hybrid approach because it is intermediate between very classical, plan-driven development, and agile development.

Water-Scrum-Fall. In many cases, software is developed in a context where it is necessary to agree early on on the basic project parameters such as high-level requirements, budget and schedule, and eventually deliver *one* release of the final product, with limited interaction between development and customer in between. On the other hand, development wants to apply agile development, typically Scrum, to address the risks involved.

This leads to the common combination of plan-driven and agile development that was for example described by Scott Ambler who wrote "... the reality for large-scale, mission-critical applications is that the OO development process is serial in the large and iterative in the small, delivering incremental releases over time" [3, p. xxiv]. This combination of early and late phases taken from a waterfall-type life cycle, and a sequence of Scrum-type sprints or iterations in between as shown in Fig. 3.23 has recently become known as the Water-Scrum-Fall life cycle. The term

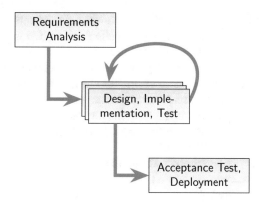

Fig. 3.23 The Water-Scrum-Fall life cycle

was originally introduced in [104], where it was, however, not presented as a de-liberate hybrid approach but as the reality in organisations that fail to use genuinely agile processes and as a "recipe for disaster" [104, p. 11]. However, today the Water-Scrum-Fall life cycle is often considered as a useful combination of the advantages of agile and plan-driven development, and probably the most commonly used hybrid life cycle model.

Project managers and agile development. When trying to apply an agile method-ology in the context of a classical company organisation, this will often lead to conflict. In such a case, a project manager will often be needed that acts as a "trans-lator" between the company organisation and the development team. While Scrum explicitly does not include the role of a project manager, this function of a translator

---

[17] Actually, the author saw all of these practices in development projects he was involved with in the 1990s, though not all in the same project.

between the worlds is often necessary and the role therefore introduced. Of course, introducing this role alone will not resolve all conflicts that will arise, and actually add some new ones, but overall it will often help to address them. The responsibilities of the project manager in such an environment will for example include the translation of project milestones into the planning of the sprints, the translation of a requirements specification document into a product backlog, and the translation of the results of sprint reviews into status reports.

3.7 (Capability) Maturity Models

(Capability) maturity models, discussed in more detail in Sect. 5.5, describe what it means for a development organisation and its processes to be "mature", and provide a framework for improving and evaluating processes and their maturity. The best-known examples of such maturity models are CMMI and SPICE, which each consist of a whole family of such models.

Since both CMMI and SPICE include requirements about performing the standard software development tasks requirements analysis, design, implementation and test (verification and validation), it is often mistakenly assumed that these models expect a waterfall-type life cycle model. A closer look however shows that this is not the case: although the models do contain some obvious requirements on the order of these tasks, stating for example that the implementation must conform to the design, this may well be done on the level of small pieces of functionality, using a highly iterative life cycle, and studies such as [25] show that indeed most of the organisations performing CMMI appraisals now use agile development in at least some of their projects.

In summary, maturity models do require that the life cycle models and processes used do contain all the usual development tasks (as well as the appropriate traceability between these tasks and their results), but do not require any particular such life cycle model or process.

3.8 IT Service Management and Operations

There are a number of different process models describing IT service management and operations, but today the *IT Infrastructure Library* (ITIL) is the only one that is widely used.

3.8.1 The IT Infrastructure Library (ITIL)

ITIL is a framework containing best practices for IT service management. It is called a "library" because it is defined as a collection of books which, in the current version ITIL 2011, each describe one of the five phases of the service life cycle that were introduced with ITIL v3 and are described in Sect. 3.1.3.

ITIL was first developed and published in the late 1980s by the UK Government's Central Computer and Telecommunications Agency (CCTA), and today is the standard reference model for IT service management world-wide.

ITIL certification. In order to prove their ITIL-compliance, to their customers or for internal purposes, many organisations would like to get certified accordingly. However, ITIL is not expressed in terms of verifiable requirements, and therefore the certification of ITIL-compliance is not possible. Instead, the standard ISO/IEC 20000-1 serves a very similar purpose and is therefore widely used, containing verifiable "service management system requirements" based on ITIL though not identical.

The related standard ISO/IEC 20000-4 contains a process reference model, but since there is no process assessment model available that is based on it, this cannot be used as a basis for a SPICE assessment as described in Sect. 5.5.4.

While there is no direct way to certify the ITIL-compliance of an organisation, there is a certification scheme regarding the ITIL qualification of personnel, starting with the *ITIL Foundation* certificate that confirms basic knowledge of ITIL and the underlying concepts. Increasingly higher levels of understanding of and experience with ITIL can be conformed by the certification levels *Intermediate*, *Expert* and *Master*.

3.8.2 Other Models for IT Service Management and Operations

There is a number of other process reference models for IT service management and operations, apart from ITIL. The best known of these models are products from various IT service providers, such as the Microsoft Operations Framework (MOF, not to be confused with the Meta Object Facility MOF), HP IT-Service-Management (ITSM), and IBM IT Process Model (ITPM). However, all of these models have more or less been replaced by ITIL which today is the only wide-spread model for this application area.

Slightly more general is the maturity model *CMMI for Services* (CMMI-SVC, described in more detail in Sect. 5.5.3) which addresses services in general, not only IT services. Nevertheless, it is well-suited to IT services, and in particular organisations that use *CMMI for Development* (CMMI-DEV) to improve their development processes often consider combining this with CMMI-SVC.

3.9 Integrating Software Development and Software Operations

A common difficulty is that both software development and software operations have set up their work systematically, each using suitable defined processes for their part of the overall software life cycle. However, the transition of software from development to operations is often rather difficult, partly due to the different cultures of the two groups. The main responsibility of development groups is to continually change the software infrastructure, and without such change, they would soon be out of work. Operations, on the other hand, needs to keep systems in working order, which leads to the mentality of "never change a running system". As a result, there is a natural conflict of interests, and usually there are different types of people working in the two groups.

Nevertheless, strong cooperation between both groups is needed, or neither of them will be able to deliver adequate service to their customer. One can distinguish three levels of cooperation in this context:

1. Development develops software with little or no contact with operations. When development is complete, the developed product is moved to operations which might be the first time they ever hear about this new system ("throwing the product over the fence"). Although this still happens regularly, it is obviously not a helpful form of (non-)cooperation.
2. Involvement of operations during development as a stakeholder from the start, including the identification of their requirements etc.
3. Continuous integration / deployment, based on automation of transition process, as described in Sect. 8.3.

For the following case studies, showing the move from the first to the second level of cooperation, it might be worth reminding the reader that these are real-world examples and not invented by the author. The good news is that this happened more than ten years ago, and the cooperation of the development and operations groups within this organisation have improved considerably by now.

Case Study 3.4. (CS Insurance InfoSys) As mentioned before, CS Insurance InfoSys is responsible both for the development and maintenance of software systems, and for their operation once they had been developed. However, cooperation between the two groups tended to be difficult, with both sides complaining about the other side making their life difficult.

One development project had a large proportion of database development, and realised that the new version of the DBMS they were using provided some new functions that would be very useful for the project. They therefore used this new version of the DBMS as the basis for development, which helped them to save considerable development effort.

The problem arose once development was completed and they wanted to pass the newly developed application on to the operation group. The operation group refused to accept this application because it did not use the standard DBMS version which was used for all other applications, since that different version would make life much more difficult for operations. After some lengthy discussions and pressure from the customer, the operation group finally had to accept the application and put it into operation, but they needed to charge about ten times the standard fee because the effort for them was so much larger. For the new application, more or less every standard DBMS maintenance task which was automated via scripts for all other applications needed to be performed manually, or at least the standard script adapted. As a result, the amount saved by using this version in development was spent several times over for operating the application, leading to far higher total cost of ownership over the life span of the application.

Case Study 3.5. (CS Insurance InfoSys) Some time after the project described in Case Study 3.4, a project leader who had heard about this kind of problems wanted to prevent them in his own project and tried to involve the operation group from the start. However, since the operation group had no clearly defined requirements on new projects, the feedback he got at first was that there was really no need to involve them at this early stage, but the operation group would perform an acceptance test on the completed software and would then let him know whether it was OK or what changes would be needed. It took many weeks of discussion and escalation to management to get any relevant requirements from operations before the start of design and implementation.

Case Study 3.6. (CS Insurance InfoSys) In order to resolve the problems described in Case Studies 3.4 and 3.5, management decided to introduce the ITIL role of a *service manager*, who is responsible for managing the end-to-end life cycle of one or more IT Services.

The main task of these service managers was to act as the main contact for development projects on the IT side, joining in development status meetings from an early stage of the project, clarifying the support from operations needed by development and ensuring that it was provided, as well as ensuring that any operations requirements were taken into account by the development project.

Not surprisingly, this turned out to be a rather challenging task, and service managers often felt like they were caught between a rock and a hard place.

Nevertheless, this eventually helped to improve cooperation between development project and the operations group considerably, and major problems like those described above at least became very rare.

3.10 Software Processes and Architecture

Even though architecture is not directly part of software processes, it has a strong influence on such processes, and IT architecture and software processes are related in several different ways:

- On the one hand, software processes across the entire life cycle need to incorporate the usage of an architecture, which may be defined in more or less detail, and may be defined for the individual project (or development effort), or it may go beyond that, covering an entire organisation or enterprise.
- On the other hand, processes are needed to create and define such an architecture, again both on the level of the project or of the entire organisation.

In this section, we will briefly discuss architecture as used in individual development efforts. The use of organisational or enterprise architectures and their relationship to IT governance will be discussed in Sect. 4.8.5.

Conway's Law. The influence of the organisational structure on the architecture or design of a system to be developed was for example stated in *Conway's Law* as first published in 1968:

> "Organizations which design systems (in the broad sense used here) are constrained to produce designs which are copies of the communication structures of these organizations." [29, p. 31]

In short, the argument behind this law is that system interfaces will only be possible where there is communication between the teams involved, and the closer the communication, the stronger the interface. Put differently, Conway's Law implies that (as explicitly stated in [29]) it is important to draft a high-level system design before setting up the design organisation, but to ensure that both system design and design organisation are sufficiently flexible to be adapted in parallel if needed.

Service-oriented architecture (SOA) and micro-services. Conway's Law is for example reflected in the recent trend to increase the emphasis on designs consisting of small, independent units such as services in a service-oriented architecture (SOA) or, going one step further, in architectures based on micro-services.[18] To achieve such independent (micro-)services, design and implementation are performed by

---

[18] Of course, this is not a completely new trend but an extension of the *high cohesion, loose coupling* dictum introduced with structured development in the 1970s.

small, independent teams, or, looking at the same concepts from a different viewpoint, the concept of small, independent services was introduced to allow work in small, independent teams.

Software architecture and agile development. In agile development, one usually tries to keep the definition of the architecture to a minimum, since—similar to software processes—the architecture definition does not provide any immediate benefit to the customer. If an explicit architecture is to be used, it should be defined by the team itself rather than some designated architect or a group outside the project. In the Agile Manifesto this is stated as the following principle: "The best architectures, requirements, and designs emerge from self-organizing teams" [14]. As a result, agile projects usually have little explicitly defined architecture but nevertheless try to base their product on a sound architecture by refactoring it as appropriate.

Software architecture as defined by the operations environment. Independent of whether a plan-based or an agile development approach is used, the software product under development is usually to be installed and operated in some environment that the development team cannot choose freely, e.g. as one application among many in a computing centre. The problems that can occur if the development team does not consider the resulting restrictions in time have been shown in Case Study 3.4.

Other types of restrictions on the software architecture can result from the environment that the software is to run on, e.g. the hardware environment, or a standard architecture such as the *AUTomotive Open System ARchitecture* (AUTOSAR) which aims to ensure, among other goals, the transferability and re-usability of functions in automotive systems [10].

3.11 Safety, Security and Privacy

Safety, security and privacy are related concepts of growing importance that do not immediately form part of the software process but that need to be addressed in software processes. As a result, relevant norms and standards regarding these topics, in particular safety and security of software systems, usually define a number of requirements on the development process.

3.11.1 Basic Concepts

To start off, we first need to define the relevant terminology:

Definition 3.13 (Safety). *The expectation that a system does not, under defined conditions, lead to a state in which human life, health, property, or the environment is endangered. (SEVOCAB)*

Definition 3.14 (Security). *Protection of information and data so that unauthorized persons or systems cannot read or modify them and authorized persons or systems are not denied access to them. (ISO/IEC/IEEE 12207:2017; SEVOCAB)*

Definition 3.15 (Privacy). *Protection of the fundamental rights and freedoms of natural persons and in particular their right to the protection of personal data. (Based on General Data Protection Regulation (GDPR) [30, Art. 1])*

Privacy is also often called *data protection*, e.g. in the GDPR. However, this sometimes leads to misunderstandings since its purpose is not the protection of data but the protection of individuals from misuse of their personal data. Therefore, the term *privacy* will be used here.

The three topics safety, security and privacy are closely related. For example, both safety of a system and privacy cannot be achieved without adequate security, since otherwise any mechanisms to mitigate safety or privacy risks may be switched off by unauthorized modifications.

Slightly over-simplified, security addresses the protection of a system from its environment, while both safety and privacy address the protection of the environment from the system. As a result, safety and privacy are commonly required by legislation, while security of a system—beyond what is needed in order to achieve safety—is mainly performed in the self-interest of the company.

On the other hand, security is relevant and needs to be considered in more or less all IT systems, since it is (with few exceptions) always important to protect a system against theft or accidental loss of data, against unauthorized modifications due to criminal intent or accidental user errors, and/or to ensure that the system is available when it is needed. Safety however only needs to be taken into account if the system actually does endanger "human life, health, property, or the environment". For example, safety is of course very relevant for the braking system of a car, while it can be ignored in the development of the multimedia system in the same car (assuming that the two systems are genuinely separated).

For simplicity, we talk mainly about the security of *systems*. Interpreted widely, this includes distributed systems such as *critical infrastructures* and *computing grids* which, by their nature, tend to be both very difficult and very important to secure. However, discussing these topics in detail would go too far in the current context.

Safety, security and privacy in software processes. Regarding safety, security and privacy, it is important to understand that all three are topics that—when relevant—need to be addressed across the entire software product life cycle, including development starting with requirements analysis but also including deployment and in particular operation of the software. Depending on the extent to which it was addressed in development, safety, security and privacy may be more or less difficult to achieve in operation, but in either case operation is where these properties need to be achieved above all.

In addition to this obvious aspect of addressing safety, security and privacy during development such that they can be achieved in operation, they are also relevant— though typically to a lesser extent—in development itself. For example, even a development prototype or a test version of a system must be safe to use for developers and testers. A development environment must be secure to prevent accidental loss or theft of data (e.g. industrial espionage), as well as malicious modification of development results. And even during development, personal data must be protected, for example in the case of data that are gathered by development tools (cf. Sect. 7.7), or test data taken from production that usually at least need to work with pseudonyms rather than actual data.

Controls. A core concept to implement safety, security and privacy as well as (IT) governance (cf. Sect. 4.8.1) is the control which usually forms part of a control system:

Definition 3.16 (Control). *The means of managing risk, including policies, procedures, guidelines, practices or organisational structures, which can be of an administrative, technical, management or legal nature. The term is also used as a synonym for safeguard or countermeasure. (COBIT 5 [47, Glossary])*

For example, a defined software development (or service) process may be a control, as may be a process audit. Controls usually also form part of (IT) governance, as discussed in Sect. 4.8.

Another control that is often used is the nomination of a person or group to take responsibility for a certain topic, often completely separate from the people who develop or operate the software, to prevent any conflict of interest. This is particularly applicable to safety and privacy where such a separate role is sometimes required by law, where an independent safety or privacy officer (or similar) may be needed to approve a certain system or software before it may go into operation.

Security. In the context of IT systems, security is usually broken down into the three properties mentioned in the definition:

- Confidentiality: no unauthorized person is able to read and use any information stored in the system, transmitted over any network, or currently being used. In an extended form, this may include meta-data, i.e. the information that a certain information has been stored or transmitted, by a certain person or at a certain time, without access to the information itself.
- Integrity: data stored, transmitted or used may not be modified in any unauthorised way, be it by an attacker or by some accidental modification such as a transmission error. Again, this may refer to the information itself or to meta-data, such as a modification of the sender of a message or the date when a certain information was stored or sent.
- Availability: authorized user are not prevented from accessing or modifying information, neither by a deliberate attack such as a denial-of-service attack, nor by accidents such as a disk or network failure.

Safety. An important difference between safety and security in the IT context is the fact that safety always refers to a technical, social, economic or other system going beyond software. Software can only endanger human life, health etc. if it is part of a larger system, while software on its own cannot do so. For example, running a certain software to control a robot in a test environment may be completely safe, but running the identical software in a factory environment may be very dangerous. For this reason, safety certifications usually refer to entire systems rather than individual components such as the software that are part of the system.

As a result, the first step to achieve safety is usually to analyse the overall system and the risks that arise from it, where "risk" is a core concept in the context of safety, security and privacy. Depending on the size of the possible damage involved, relevant standards usually define a maximum probability for this damage to occur, to keep the overall risk at an acceptable level. In general, it is not possible to achieve absolute safety, security or privacy, but only to reduce the risk to an acceptable level.

Some of these risks may then be addressed by specifying appropriate safety requirements on the software system, which feed into the development process. A difficulty in the context of software systems is that the usual statistical approaches to evaluating the probability of a risk occurring cannot be applied: in contrast to hardware systems, there is no degradation of the system by repeated use, and the same software run with the same data repeatedly will lead to the same results. Therefore, safety standards usually do not directly set requirements on the maximum probability of safety risks but define certain requirements on the software processes used to implement in software the functional requirements derived from the overall system. Typically, they require some kind of V-shaped model, as for example the model shown in Fig. 3.6 taken from the safety norm IEC 61508-3.

Due to the large amount of validation and verification that needs to be performed in each release cycle for software with high demands regarding safety, but to some extent also security and perhaps privacy, release cycles in this case are typically much longer than for software with low safety requirements, often lasting 1–2 years.

Privacy (data protection). Privacy is a concept derived from human rights and refers to the protection of individuals against misuse of their personal data, including the right to live one's everyday life without being observed, and to communicate with others in private (unless there is a special reason otherwise).

This is a topic that has very different importance and meaning in different cultures and for different people. For example, privacy tends to be fairly important in Europe, while e.g. in North America, freedom of speech is often considered more important, including the right to publish information about other people that would be considered unacceptable in Europe.

Another challenge is that privacy occasionally leads to a conflict with security: from a security point of view, it is often useful to log many activities in a system, but this may intrude on the privacy of the individuals involved, and an adequate compromise needs to be found.

As part of software process support, personal data are typically not in the focus but often collected, e.g. documenting the authors (possibly including contact data, date and time of access, etc.) of process documentation or of work products resulting from performing the process. Although these personal data are in general not critical, one still needs to ensure that they are handled properly. For example, even if the data are non-critical to be used within a company, this may be different if they are used outside and passed to other organisations such as customers or suppliers. Another example of a critical usage is to use personal data not just for process management and to know whom to ask about a certain topic, but to use it for other purposes as well such as performance evaluation of employees.

Privacy is sometimes seen as a burden on an organisation, some form of legal bureaucracy that organisations need to adhere to on top of their "real" work. However, organisations should remember that privacy is about protecting people. Their customers, their employees etc. have entrusted them with personal data, and expect that these data are handled properly, justifying the trust they have put into the organisation. Apart from the questions regarding ethical behaviour, organisations should realise that inadequate handling of the data can lose them a lot of good will with their customers, with strong effects on their financial success. Actually, implementing good privacy mechanisms can be a factor to increase business, since many users consider this an important criterion in selecting a supplier such as a service provider, either for intrinsic reasons or in order to satisfy relevant privacy regulations themselves.

3.11.2 Safety Standards and Software Processes

There is a large number of standards on (software) safety covering the large range of different systems and products where safety is relevant. Regarding software processes, these standards usually require (or at least expect) some variant of the V-model such as the one described in Fig. 3.6.[19]

Safety levels. All the standards below are based on an evaluation of the potential damage involved from which the required risk reduction is derived, categorized into different safety levels. These are e.g. called *performance levels* (PL) *a* describing small potential damage to *e* (high potential damage) in ISO 13849, *safety integrity levels* (SIL) *1* (low potential damage) to *4* (high potential damage) in IEC 61508 and IEC 62061[20], and *automotive safety integrity levels* (ASIL) in ISO 26262. DO-178B/C and ED-12B/C define *software levels* A (catastrophic) to E (no effect) for this purpose.

Depending on the safety level needed, these norms define a number of requirements, with some of these requirements referring to functionality to be provided by the system (or software), and some requirements referring to the quality of the implementation of this functionality.

IEC 61508. The standard IEC 61508 is applicable fairly widely (therefore called a type A standard) and provides basic guidelines and terminology for the design of (complex) electrical, electronic and programmable systems (E/E/PE). These systems may be part of machinery or be used in some other context.

---

[19] The discussion in this section regarding safety standards for machinery is mainly based on [92].

[20] Since IEC 62061 applies to individual machines, very high damage such as multiple fatalities is considered inapplicable, and the scale in this standard therefore only goes up to SIL 3.

IEC 61508 defines a general safety life cycle that applies to the development of the overall E/E/PE system. The development of software as part of this E/E/PE system is expected to use the V-shaped software safety life cycle shown in Fig. 3.6. Strictly speaking, this software safety life cycle only addresses the development of the safety functions and other safety-relevant parts of the software but in practice, it is usually difficult to strictly separate these components from the "normal" parts of the software.

ISO/IEC 13849 and IEC 62061. A somewhat more specific standard, called a type B standard, is ISO/IEC 13849 which provides safety requirements and guidance on the principles for the design and integration of safety-related parts of control systems (SRP/CS) which form part of machinery, including the design of software. Similarly, IEC 62061 addresses the safety of E/E/PE systems which form part of machinery. The latter standard is more applicable to complex systems with a high level of integrity, while the former is more applicable to common, less complex systems.[21]

ISO 26262. Yet another standard based on IEC 61508 is ISO 26262 which adapts the same principles not to machinery but to the development of E/E/PE systems within road vehicles. Part 6 of this standard specifically defines requirements on the development of software in such systems.

DO-178B/C and ED-12B/C. Quite a different application area is addressed in the *Software Considerations in Airborne Systems and Equipment Certification* which are used as the basis for the evaluation of software which is part of the certification of airworthiness of airborne systems and equipment, such as aircraft and aircraft engines. It is published jointly by the US-American *Radio Technical Commission for Aeronautics* (RTCA, Inc.) and the *European Organisation for Civil Aviation Equipment* (EUROCAE). The current version DO-178C (as denoted by RTCA) or ED-12C (as denoted by EUROCAE) was published in 2012, but due to the long product life of aircraft the previous version DO-178B / ED-12B (published in 1992) is still in common use [38].[22]

DO-178B/ED-12B and DO178C/ED-12C do not prescribe any specific software development processes but define a set of objectives that need to be satisfied, which does of course influence the processes allowed to be used. In particular, a requirements-driven process is required, with different levels of requirements, an emphasis on traceability of requirements and requirements-based testing in various forms, which implicitly states that agile processes are not allowed to be used. The software life cycle processes need to interact with the system life cycle processes, in particular via system requirements that are allocated to software, and software levels identified by the system processes that need to be implemented in the software processes.

---

[21] Since these two standards are closely related, there is discussion about combining them into one.

[22] Earlier versions of this document were DO-178/ED-12, published in 1982, and DO-178A/ED-12A, published in 1985.

While the technical requirements in DO-178B/ED-12B essentially assumed the use of an imperative programming language, one of the main goals of DO-178C/ED-12C was to allow other, more modern software development approaches, in particular model-based development, object-oriented development and formal methods. The target here was not to introduce any new requirements on the software life cycle but to clarify the existing requirements, in particular in the context of these new development methods [38, 66].

Good Manufacturing Practice (GMP). GMP is a generic term that describes various regulations set by different national and international regulatory bodies regarding the manufacture of drug and pharmaceutical products and food. These regulations are mostly based on the GMP published by the World Health Organization, for example those published by the U.S. Food and Drug Administration (FDA), or by the European Union. As the name indicates, the focus of GMP lies on the *manufacture* of the relevant products, but this includes regulations such as [39] regarding the development of relevant software, e.g. for packaging of these products. Since there are a number of similar regulations such as the *Good Laboratory Practice* (GLP), these are often described by the joint abbreviation GxP.

As for the contents of these regulations, they expect a systematic quality system, with particular emphasis on the validation of the resulting software, plus thorough documentation of the development and in particular the validation performed.[23] As the basis, *standard operating procedures* (SOPs) are expected for most relevant processes.

3.11.3 Security Standards and Software Processes

Again, there is a large number of security standards that contain requirements on software processes, and in the following some of them will be described, starting with the ISO/IEC 270xx family of standards. The Common Criteria consist of evaluation criteria for security products, which include different levels of requirements on the development process. Finally, the Payment Card Industry Security Standards provide an example of an industry-specific security standard. An example of a standard that goes beyond the issues discussed here, addressing the security of critical infrastructure, is the *NIST Cybersecurity Framework*[24].

ISO/IEC 270xx. Probably the most important and best known standard in the context of IT security is ISO/IEC 27001, or strictly speaking the entire family of standards ISO/IEC 270xx. This family of standards defines the set-up of an Information

---

[23] Even though documentation of software development is in general not one of the favourite tasks of development projects, this is understandably very important for this application area. Just imagine you are seriously ill and get the wrong medicine because it has been incorrectly labelled due to a software bug.

[24] See https://www.nist.gov/cyberframework for more information about the NIST Cybersecurity Framework.

Security Management System (ISMS), starting with an overview of the topic and the relevant vocabulary in ISO/IEC 27000. The requirements on such an ISMS, to be used for internal purposes or for certification, are defined in ISO/IEC 27001. This standard defines how to set up a management system for information security, using the common *High-Level Structure* (HLS) that was defined by ISO to be used for all management system standards, such as the quality management system standard ISO 9001 (see Sect. 5.4.3) [98]. The HLS can be seen as a extended version of the Plan-Do-Check-Act-Cycle (PDCA) (see Sect.5.4.2 for more details), starting with requirements regarding the understanding of the context of the organisation (Clause 4), and continuing with topics such as leadership (Clause 5), planning (Clause 6), support (Clause 7), operation (Clause 8), performance evaluation (Clause 9), and improvement (Clause 10).

In a fairly large appendix amounting to roughly half the entire document, ISO/IEC 27001 defines a list of 114 information security controls, structured into 14 groups with 35 control objectives. In this context, the most relevant groups of controls are

- A.12: Operations security, with controls regarding the establishment of procedures and responsibilities, malware protection, use of backups and logs, etc.
- A.13: Communications security, with controls regarding the protection of networks and of information transferred.
- A.14: System acquisition, development and maintenance, with controls requiring that security is made an inherent part of information systems, that system development activities are protected and controlled adequately, and that test data are protected.

Overall, ISO/IEC 27001 thus defines the ISMS as a framework for the relevant security processes, and many of the controls defined in the appendix form requirements to be integrated into the relevant software processes.

In addition to ISO/IEC 27001 which describes the requirements on a IT security system, as may be used as the basis for a certification, there are many more standards in this series, including in particular ISO/IEC 27002 which contains guidelines (as opposed to requirements) on how to set up an IT security system, and ISO/IEC 27005 which describes risk management, one of the basic tasks in a IT security system, in more detail.

Common Criteria (ISO/IEC 15408). ISO/IEC 15408, also known as Common Criteria because they were jointly described by several national agencies, defines criteria for the evaluation of IT security products. In contrast to the safety norms described above, ISO/IEC 15408-3:2008 explicitly distinguishes between requirements on the functionality, and requirements on the quality of the implementation. For this purpose it defines different *functionality classes* such "FIA Identification and Authentication" and "FCS Cryptographic Support", and a hierarchy of *evaluation assurance levels (EAL)* for the evaluation of the IT security of IT products "implemented in hardware, firmware or software". These EALs put requirements on the scope, depth and rigour of the evaluation and therefore on the software processes used to develop the product as shown in Fig. 3.24.

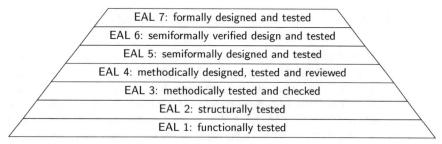

Fig. 3.24 Evaluation assurance levels according to ISO/IEC 15408-3 (Common Criteria).

Payment Card Industry (PCI) Security Standards. This set of standards was developed to define the requirements set by the major credit card companies on the security of credit cards and credit card transactions. It consists of a set of security standards addressing different stakeholders in this context [80]:

- PCI PTS (PIN Transaction Security) covers the security of PIN entry devices and therefore mainly addresses the manufacturers of such devices.
- PCI PA-DSS (Payment Applications—Data Security Standard) [79] covers the security of payment applications and therefore mainly addresses software developers and software vendors.
  PCI PA-DSS requirements consist of functional requirements for applications that handle credit card payment data, and requirements on the development processes used to create such applications. The functional requirements refer e.g. to the data that are (not) allowed to be stored by an application, while the process requirements mainly refer to the verification and testing procedures used.
- PCI DSS (Data Security Standard) [78], finally, is the best known in this series of standards and covers the security of the environments in which payment data are handled and stored. It therefore mainly addresses merchants and service providers, or generally all organisations that handle credit cards and credit card data from any of the major credit card brands.
  PCI DSS requirements therefore mainly refer to software operations processes, including requirements such as the building and maintenance of a secure network and systems.
  PCI DSS is also sometimes used to refer to the entire set of standards, including all the other PCI standards mentioned.

Additionally, there are a number of more detailed standards and technical documents.[25]

Apart from the security requirements themselves, these standards also include requirements on assessments that need to be performed to confirm compliance.

---

[25] All these documents can be downloaded from the PCI SSC Document Library at `https://www.pcisecuritystandards.org/document_library`.

3.11.4 Privacy Standards and Software Processes

There are a number of different standards and frameworks covering privacy, looking at the topic from different angles. These include for example the "Privacy Engineer's Manifesto" [33] covering privacy from the engineer's viewpoint, the NIST standard NISTIR 8062 [22] that mainly looks at privacy in the context of federal systems, and the "Standard Data Protection Model" [28] published by the German data protection authorities which puts the emphasis on auditing software systems for compliance to privacy legislation.

Below, some other relevant standards and regulations will be covered in somewhat more detail.

Data protection and the General Data Protection Regulation (GDPR). The GDPR was adopted in the European Union (EU) in 2016 and has become applicable in May 2018. Note that this regulation does not only apply in European countries but also elsewhere if personal data of EU citizens are handled.

The GDPR explains the need for data protection as follows: "The protection of natural persons in relation to the processing of personal data is a fundamental right. ... " [30, Recital 1] "The principles of, and rules on the protection of natural persons with regard to the processing of their personal data should, whatever their nationality or residence, respect their fundamental rights and freedoms, in particular their right to the protection of personal data ...." [30, Recital 2]

Data protection refers to *personal data* which GDPR defines as "any information relating to an identified or identifiable natural person ('data subject') ... " [30, Art. 4 (1)].

GDPR data protection principles and software processes. A core principle of data protection according to GDPR is that the collection and processing of personal data in general is *forbidden* unless the data subject has explicitly agreed or there is an explicit basis in law for such collection and/or processing [30, Art. 6].

In addition to that, the GDPR defines a number of data protection principles [30, Art. 5], including the following which are especially relevant for software processes:

- *data minimisation*: personal data should only be documented if they are really needed. E.g. if there is write access to the process documentation for many or all users, there is a need to document changes in order to trace changes, in particular questionable changes. It is unlikely, however, that there is any need to log read access to the process access, and not doing so will therefore both help to work more efficiently and to satisfy data protection requirements.
- *purpose limitation*: personal data should only be used for the purpose that they were collected for. It would be inadequate for the people concerned if they agree to their data being collected for one purpose, and their data are then used for other purposes as well, which they might not agree with.
- *transparency*: users need to know what personal data about them is collected and used. For example, using personal data collected in a process management tool

for performance evaluation without the employees knowing about it in advance would be very unfair and therefore in general illegal.

- *accuracy*: when personal data are collected and used, it is necessary to ensure that they are accurate and up-to-date. Again using the example of performance evaluation, it is obvious that personal data used for this purpose must be accurate and up-to-date—not just to satisfy their purpose but also because otherwise the rights of the employees would be infringed.

Furthermore, the "controller", i.e. the person or organisation that determines how personal data are processed, is not just required to *implement* the principles described above (and the more detailed regulations refining them) but "shall ... be able to demonstrate compliance with" these principles and regulations [30, Art. 5, item 2]. This requirement was added in the GDPR compared to most previous legislation and implies a need for more documentation than was needed previously.

Privacy by design/by default. In order to ensure that privacy does not need to be incorporated into a system after is has been built, possibly by organisational rules and guidelines that may or may not be adhered to in the everyday use of the system, privacy needs to be built into systems from the start (privacy by design, privacy by default), e.g. by only collecting personal data that are genuinely needed, and by working with anonymised or pseudomised data where possible [30, Art. 25].

ISO/IEC 29100. This document is not legally binding as GDPR above, but an international standard that describes how to achieve privacy in information technology, with an emphasis on the early phases of ensuring privacy within an organisation. The first main step consists of the identification of privacy safeguarding requirements, based on the (legal and regulatory, contractual, business, and other) factors that influence management of privacy risks. Based on these requirements, the standard covers the definition of privacy policies and controls.

Furthermore, ISO/IEC defines a set of privacy principles such as "purpose legitimacy and specification" and "openness, transparency and notice", where these privacy principles "should be used to guide the design, development, and implementation of privacy policies and privacy controls." (ISO/IEC 29100, Sect. 5.1)

The OASIS Privacy Management Reference Model and Methodology (PMRM). The PMRM was published by OASIS, a non-profit open standards consortium, in 2016 [36]. Its goal is to start from the privacy principles and policies as e.g. defined based on ISO/IEC 29100, and help to identify and select suitable services and functions that will help to implement these principles and policies. To achieve this, PMRM contains a total of 20 tasks, structured into six phases, where the sixth phase initiates the iteration of the previous phases.

3.11.5 Safety, Security and Privacy in the Development Life Cycle

To ensure safety, security and/or privacy in a software product, e.g. by conformance to any of the relevant standards mentioned, it is quite obvious that these properties need to be addressed in the development life cycle more or less from the start, and it is difficult, if not impossible, to "build in" these properties into an existing software product.

The basic approach to integrate safety, security and/or privacy into a software process, as required by most of the standards mentioned above, involves the following steps:

- Perform a risk analysis, including the identification, categorisation and evaluation of relevant risks, e.g. assigning an appropriate risk level. In the case of safety, this may for example take the form of a *Hazard and Operability Study (HAZOP)*, in IT security it may be a threat analysis.
- Define safety, security and/or privacy requirements, based on these risks and risk levels. There is usually a combination of requirements, with some referring to the life cycle process, requiring e.g. the use of a certain life cycle model such as a V-model, and other requirements referring to the development results themselves.

  Again taking the example of safety, such requirements on development results may lead to so-called *safety functions* which are functions built into a system in order to mitigate certain risks. For example, a safety function for an industrial robot may be to stop all movement if, at any time, there is no (or inconsistent) feedback from the position sensors.

  Similarly, security requirements may involve the use of coding guidelines that prevent certain attacks such as SQL injection or XSS.
- Define measures to implement these requirements, to a large proportion defined in the relevant norms. Examples of such measures are redundant architectures, encryption of data or coding standards. Depending on the relevant standards and the safety or security level required, there will typically be a specified set of methods to be applied and measures to be implemented.
- Ensure traceability to ensure that these requirements are indeed satisfied.
- Thorough verification of the resulting software and system, both regarding the proper implementation of the requirements and the technical quality of the code, e.g. by automated analysis. For software with very high safety or security requirements, this may go as far as using formal methods for the verification.

This starts with the development process, but to achieve safety and/or security, these properties need to be continued in the configuration of the system and in usage / operation, starting with such obvious activities as the administration of users and their permissions—implementing the relevant functionality is necessary but not sufficient to ensure safety, security and/or privacy of the overall system. In many cases, a systematic process to update or patch the systems is also needed to cope with any new attacks, weaknesses or defects that become known.

The MS Security Development Lifecycle (SDL). An example of integrating the above sequence of steps into a development life cycle is the MS Security Development Lifecycle.

SDL was created as a consequence of the Microsoft trustworthy computing initiative that was started in 2002, and extends a standard life cycle by specific practices aimed at improving security and privacy of their products. A variant of this SDL with references to internal resources removed was published as [68, 71].

To achieve its goals, the SDL contains a standard linear life cycle, plus an initial *Training* providing "core security training", and a final *Response* phase that involves the execution of an incident response plan after the product is released. In each of these phases, a set of security-specific tasks are defined, such as "Use threat modelling" in the *Design* phase.

Fig. 3.25 MS Security Development Lifecycle (SDL) [71]

Of course, Microsoft also uses agile development and still wants to ensure the security and privacy of the systems developed. Therefore, [68] also covers the mapping of the SDL practices to agile development, defining e.g. which requirements are to be addressed for each sprint, which need to be addressed regularly (the so-called "bucket requirements"), and which only need to be addressed once.

The Open Web Application Security Project (OWASP). As the name suggests, OWASP was originally initiated to improve the security of web applications, but today it covers other applications as well. It is an online-community that collects information on different aspects of software security and makes it publicly available on its web site [76].

Among many other documents, OWASP has published guides on development, testing and code review, where these guides concentrate on a collection of important practices for creating secure software, with little consideration of the overall development process.

Additionally, OWASP has published the Software Assurance Maturity Model (OpenSAMM) [75] intended to help organisations "formulate and implement a strategy for software security that is tailored to the specific risks facing the organization" [75, p. 3] across the business functions governance, construction, verification and deployment.

Case Study 3.7. (CS AutoSystems) Since some of the products developed by CS AutoSystems are safety-relevant, they need to be developed according to the relevant norms and standards.

In one such project, the product developed by CS AutoSystems was an instrument that was to be integrated into a machine. The customer had analysed the safety required for this machine and come to the conclusion that certain functions within the instrument had to satisfy performance level C according to ISO 13849-1. This was therefore stated as a requirement in the specification provided by the customer.

The development team initially created a rather superficial system specification and started to design the system, following the V-shaped model as described in Case Study 3.2, with three separate branches for housing, PCB and software development. As part of the design and with support by an external consultant, an FMEA (Failure Mode and Effects Analysis: a method to systematically identify and prioritize risks, and to define measures to reduce these risks as needed) was performed on the system to identify the safety risks involved. This resulted in a number of requirements for each of the three components, in particular a number of safety functions to be provided by the software component.

Although it would have been advisable, CS AutoSystems did not usually document and explicitly trace the requirements across the project. In this case, it was therefore decided to do so only for the safety requirements and safety functions—as required by ISO 13849.

Regarding the safety requirements and safety functions, these were designed and implemented following the defined process model, with appropriate documentation of the results. These results then had to be thoroughly validated and verified, which following ISO 13849 involved reviews of all major documents, code reviews and various levels of testing. Since the relevant verification and validation requirements look at the system under development from very different viewpoints, and therefore are spread across the standard, a separate validation plan was created to ensure all these aspects are addressed adequately, plus a validation report summarizing the main results of verification and validation.

3.12 Application-Specific Life Cycle Models

For some types of application or project, specific life cycle models are available that take the particular properties of that application or project type into account. The following sections provide a short overview of some of the main properties of such specific models.

3.12.1 Life Cycle Models for the Development of Cyber-Physical Systems

In the context of developing cyber-physical systems, also known as *smart factory*, prototyping is very important, because it usually is difficult or impossible to know in advance exactly how the different components of such a cyber-physical system, for example sensors, will behave in their physical environment such as a factory.

Nevertheless, genuine agile development is usually not adequate in this context because of the many hardware components involved. While it is comparatively easy to modify the software involved in such a system, changes to the electronic and mechanical components—even if they can be bought off-the-shelf—typically take far more effort and time.

The life cycle used for developing cyber-physical systems therefore usually involved separate but synchronised life cycles for the different types of products developed (software, mechanics, electronics, integrated system) where the software life cycle may be agile, but the other life cycles include several but not a large number of prototypes.

3.12.2 Life Cycle Models for Customisation, Configuration and Integration Projects

A different type of software development that has gained in importance in recent years is the creation of software systems based on existing software systems which are then customised, configured and integrated as needed. Examples for this type of development are the customisation of a single COTS[26] software package such as an ERP system, and the configuration and integration of multiple web services or micro-services.

As is to be expected, there are many different life cycle models used for such projects, with some basic common properties [73, 23]:

- Independent of the specific details, the basic requirement are usually needed and identified at the start. In general, the identification of high-level requirements is sufficient at this stage because the details of the system to be developed will largely depend on the software or services selected.
- Next, the software or services to be used as a basis for the system are selected. The selection usually includes some initial customisation, configuration and integration to validate the decision.
- The approach to customisation, configuration and integration is designed. For example, integration may be performed via some integration platform, or by directly calling one software or service from the previous one. Customisation may

---

[26] COTS = Commercial-off-the-shelf

need some high-level mapping between software entities and organisation entities, before customisation proper is started.
- After that, the selected customisation, configuration and integration are performed. In the case where several software systems or (micro-)services are integrated into one overall system, steps two to four may be iterated many times.

3.12.3 Life Cycle Models for Artificial Intelligence Systems

Another type of development concerns systems based on artificial intelligence (AI). Since the development of such systems includes a lot of experimentation, the relevant life cycle models usually put a lot of emphasis on iteration.

In the past, the development of AI systems usually included a large proportion of individual development. With the advances in machine learning over the last few years, many off-the-shelf libraries, services and products have become available so that development now involves mainly training and configuration of the system, similar to the approach described in the previous section.

The main stages of AI systems development typically include

- requirements analysis
- design, fixing the algorithms to be used and their main parameters
- training of the system: in the case of supervised learning, this includes the creation of training data to distinguish between good and bad solutions to the task to be implemented. In the case of unsupervised learning, an evaluation function is needed that provides feedback on the quality of a solution.
- validation of the system, based on experimenting with different input data and evaluating the results.

In particular the last two or three steps are usually performed highly iteratively, until a solution of acceptable quality has been found.

3.12.4 Life Cycle Models for Big Data Projects

Big data projects often go beyond the development of an individual system but start with the identification of relevant data available, and an analysis of what could or should be done to use these data effectively. As an example, the life cycle model prepared by the German digital association *Bitkom* will be presented here. This model is intended to help move from the current to a future "data and systems landscape", and consists of the following stages [32]:

- *Assessment:* identify the potential of using big data and plan a suitable strategy to achieve this potential
- *Readiness:* set up a suitable hardware and software infrastructure, and develop the necessary skills.

- *Implementation and integration:* design, implement and introduce the big data applications.
- *Consolidation and migration:* integrate the new data sources and consolidate them.
- *Usage of new data:* in this step, the data provided by the new applications are used, and the organisation learns from it to achieve the best benefit.
- *Reporting and predictive analytics:* the new data are used to optimise existing reporting processes, and to predict new trends.
- *End-to-end processing:* step by step, the usage of data is extended to monitor and improve processes from end to end, as well as to develop new business processes.
- *Optimisation:* once the big data landscape has been set up, the permanent task of monitoring and optimising this landscape starts.

3.13 Estimating the Dissemination of Software Life Cycle Models

When discussing software process models, an important question concerns the actual dissemination of these models in development projects. There are a number of studies investigating this question, but of course they all find it difficult to get reliable input data[27]: getting feedback from different organisations across different communities is quite a challenge, but without that there is a built-in bias in the results. For this reason, the agile management tool vendor company VersionOne decided to only ask about *agile methodologies* in the first place when studying this question, so that their study (described below) provides a reasonably reliable understanding of the relative distribution of the various agile methodologies, but no information about the use of agile methodologies compared to plan-driven approaches.

A second difficulty is due to the fact that few projects use any standard software process model in a pure form, but usually only some close or not so close approximation. For example, today many projects state they use Scrum when they use some core concepts of Scrum such as sprints, product backlogs and sprint backlogs but without using the full methodology as described in Sect. 3.5.2. Similarly, as Fig. 3.29 shows many projects in Germany state that they use the process model V-Model XT (described in Sect. 3.4.2 above) but this author's personal experience indicates that in most cases these projects actually use some self-defined variant of a V-shaped model (cf. Sect. 3.2.2), with only a very superficial similarity to V-Model XT.

Once we look at entire development organisations, we get even more variance, and it is quite common in large organisations to perform some projects using a plan-driven approach, while at the same time other projects use some agile methodology such as Scrum.

Figure 3.26 shows the results of a study that has attempted to get an overview of the software development methodologies used. As the individual entries add up

---

[27] This is the reason why this section talks about "estimating" the dissemination of software process models.

to about 200%, one can see that on average about two different methodologies are used in each of the projects that responded. In many cases, this leads to a hybrid methodology consisting of plan-driven (here called "traditional") and agile components as shown in Fig. 3.27. [100] comes to a very similar conclusion, describing various combinations of plan-driven and agile approaches that are in common use.

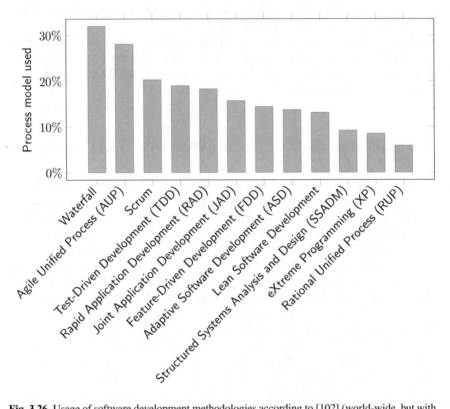

Fig. 3.26 Usage of software development methodologies according to [102] (world-wide, but with 86,9% in the United States)

A series of studies similar to [102] was performed in Germany, with about 80% of participants in Germany, Austria or Switzerland, see [53]. This study came to very similar results as [102], as shown in Fig. 3.28. "Selective" in this study refers to organisations deciding per project which approach is to be used.

This study also confirmed that Scrum is clearly the most widely used agile methodology, with more than 60% of participants describing Scrum as their main methodology, plus another 25% stating that Scrum is used among others. The only other methodology that reaches at least 50% (sum of main importance or usage among others) in this study was Kanban. The study also asked about the various agile techniques used, and even among participants that described themselves as using Scrum, the only agile technique used by more than 90% was the daily scrum.

Fig. 3.27 Software development approach clusters according to [102]

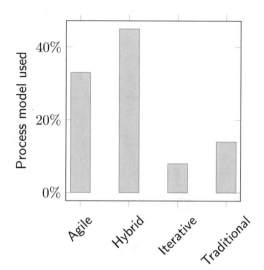

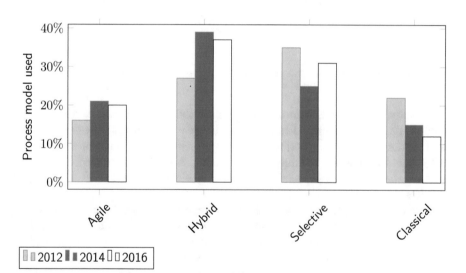

Fig. 3.28 Software development approaches used in Germany according to [53, p. 18]

Other techniques defined as part of Scrum, such as product or sprint backlog, spring review and sprint retrospective, are used by 80% to 90% of participants.

The results of another study in Germany (see [55]) analysing the dissemination of different software process models are summarised in Fig. 3.29.

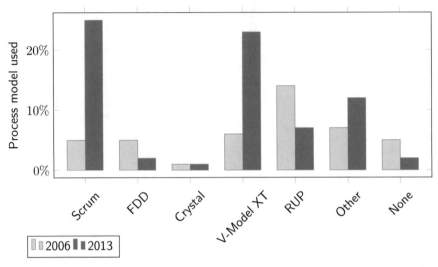

Fig. 3.29 Dissemination of software process models in Germany according to [55]

When we look at the dissemination of agile software processes, a well-known study is the above-mentioned annual *State of Agile^{TM}* report [101] by the software tool vendor VersionOne, based on a web survey. Among other questions, this study asks about the agile methodologies used, see Fig. 3.30. As can be seen, Scrum has become the standard agile methodology, either alone or as a hybrid with XP or Kanban (Scrumban).

However, a comparison between the results reported in Fig. 3.26 and Fig. 3.30 (of course only taking into account agile methodologies) gives an indication of the difficulties involved in investigating the dissemination of the different methodologies and process models. While the VersionOne report in 2015 reports the Agile Unified Process (AUP) being used in less than 1% of the organisations, AUP is clearly leading the (agile) field according to [102] with a usage of 28.1%.

In conclusion of all these studies, one may say that there continues to be a large variation of life cycle and process models in use. Among the many different agile methods, Scrum is becoming the favoured approach, while among the plan-driven approaches, V-shaped models are becoming the standard to use, with shortening times taken per release. Agile approaches are becoming more wide-spread, but often as a hybrid model with plan-driven approaches.

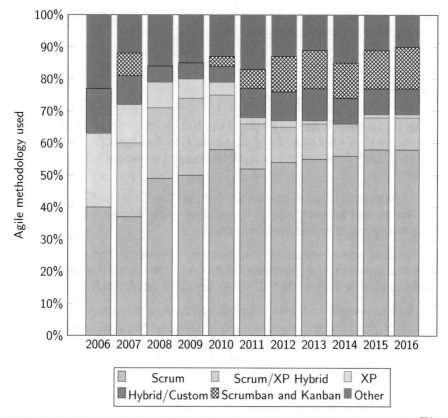

Fig. 3.30 Trend in use of agile methodologies used according to VersionOne "State of Agile^{TM}" reports [101]

Further Reading

Good overview of of the main life cycle models, even though a few years old by now, can be found in [65, Chap. 7]. Similarly, [27] (not quite as old) provides a good overview of the main agile methodologies.

While many publications on plan-driven development and even more so on agile development describe "their" approach in a rather positive, uncritical way, there are a few publications that provide a critical analysis and discuss the question of when to use which approach, and how and when to combine them. Recommended reading here is the book by Boehm and Turner [20], as well as Meyer's critical analysis of agile development in [67].

Scaling agile methods has become an important topic and [2] provides a review of the methods available to do so.

The Open Web Application Security Project (OWASP) [76] is a platform that contains a large collection of information on the security of application development. As the name indicates, its original focus was on web applications but it now covers application security in general.

Exercises

3.1. In your country, is there any national standard model to be used for IT projects? If so, create a half-page summary of this model. How does it compare to the models described here? To what extent is agile development allowed or supported by this model?

3.2. In your country and/or industry, are there any studies of the dissemination of software process models? How do they compare with the results reported here? What reasons might explain the differences?

3.3. Ignoring, for the moment, any relevant safety standards: to what extent is it possible to achieve safety of software-based systems or products using agile methodologies, and when is it necessary to apply plan-driven approaches?

3.4. Assume that you work for an organisation that often contracts out development projects to various suppliers that use very different development approaches. The organisation wants to ensure that the suppliers are able to deliver what is agreed, and therefore plans to review the suppliers and their development processes before a contract is agreed.

You were now given the task to identify adequate criteria to judge the quality of the processes used, accepting that the suppliers use very different approaches, some of them plan-driven and others agile or hybrid.

References

1. Agile Alliance. Scrum of Scrums. http://guide.agilealliance.org/guide/scrumofscrums.html (last access 2017-01-08).
2. M. Alqudah and R. Razali. A review of scaling agile methods in large software development. *International Journal on Advanced Science Engineering Information Technology*, 6(6):828–837, Dec. 2016.
3. S. W. Ambler. *Process Patterns. Building Large-Scale Systems Using Object Technology.* Cambridge University Press, 1998.
4. S. W. Ambler. Introduction to Test Driven Development (TDD). http://www.agiledata.org/essays/tdd.html (last access 2018-01-03), 2002–2013.
5. S. W. Ambler. Enterprise Unified Process (EUP): Strategies for enterprise agile. http://www.enterpriseunifiedprocess.com/ (last access 2018-01-08), 2002–2015.
6. S. W. Ambler. The Agile Unified Process (AUP). http://www.ambysoft.com/unifiedprocess/agileUP.html (last access 2018-01-08), 2005–2014.
7. S. W. Ambler. The Discipline of Agile. *Dr. Dobbs Journal*, Sept. 2007.
8. D. Anderson. Driving evolutionary change with the Kanban method. http://anderson.leankanban.com/driving-evolutionary-change-with-the-kanban-method/ (last access 2017-11-16), 2016.

9. D. J. Anderson. *Kanban: Successful Evolutionary Change for Your Technology Business.* Blue Hole Press, 2010.

10. AUTOSAR development cooperation. AUTOSAR. Technical overview. http://www.autosar.org/about/technical-overview/ (last access 2017-07-12), 2016.

11. AXELOS. What is PRINCE2? https://www.axelos.com/best-practice-solutions/prince2/what-is-prince2 (last access 2018-02-01).

12. K. Beck. *Extreme Programming Explained—Embrace Change.* Addison-Wesley, 1999.

13. K. Beck, M. Beedle, A. v. Bennekum, A. Cockburn, W. Cunningham, M. Fowler, J. Grenning, J. Highsmith, A. Hunt, R. Jeffries, J. Kern, B. Marick, R. C. Martin, S. Mellor, K. Schwaber, J. Sutherland, and D. Thomas. Manifesto for agile software development. Available online at http://agilemanifesto.org (last access 2017-07-19), October 2001.

14. K. Beck, M. Beedle, A. v. Bennekum, A. Cockburn, W. Cunningham, M. Fowler, J. Grenning, J. Highsmith, A. Hunt, R. Jeffries, J. Kern, B. Marick, R. C. Martin, S. Mellor, K. Schwaber, J. Sutherland, and D. Thomas. Principles behind the agile manifesto. Available online at http://agilemanifesto.org/principles.html (last access 2017-07-19), October 2001.

15. B. W. Boehm. Guidelines for verifying and validating software requirements and design specifications. In *Euro IFIP 79*, 1979.

16. B. W. Boehm. A spiral model of software development and enhancement. *ACM SIGSOFT Software Engineering Notes*, 11(4):14–24, 1986.

17. B. W. Boehm. A spiral model of software development and enhancement. *IEEE Computer*, 21(5):61–72, 1988.

18. B. W. Boehm. Spiral development: Experience, principles, and refinements. Special Report CMU/SEI-2000-SR-008, Carnegie Mellon, Software Engineering Institute, 2000.

19. B. W. Boehm. Some future software engineering opportunities and challenges. In S. Nanz, editor, *The Future of Software Engineering*, pages 1–32. Springer, 2011.

20. B. W. Boehm and R. Turner. *Balancing Agility and Discipline: A Guide for the Perplexed.* Addison-Wesley Professional, Aug. 2003.

21. F. B. Brooks. *The Mythical Man-Month.* Addison-Wesley Publ. Company, 1975.

22. S. Brooks, M. Garcia, N. Lefkovitz, S. Lightman, and E. Nadeau. An introduction to privacy engineering and risk management in federal systems. Internal Report NISTIR 8062, National Institute of Standards and Technology (NIST), January 2017. Available online at https://doi.org/10.6028/NIST.IR.8062 (last access 2017-03-12).

23. T. Brückmann, V. Gruhn, W. Koop, J. Ollesch, L. Pradel, F. Wessling, and M. Benner-Wickner. Codeless engineering of service mashups—an experience report. In *Proceedings of the Fourteenth IEEE International Conference on Services Computing 2017 (SCC 2017)*, 2017.

24. M. Burrows. *Kanban from the Inside.* Blue Hole Press, 2014.

25. CMMI Institute. A guide to Scrum and CMMI: Improving agile performance with CMMI. Available online at http://cmmiinstitute.com/cmmi-and-agile (last access 2017-03-14).

26. A. Cockburn. Methodology per project. http://alistair.cockburn.us/Methodology+per+project (last access 2018-02-16), December 1999.

27. R. Coffin and D. Lane. A practical guide to seven agile methodologies. Part 1 available online at http://www.devx.com/architect/Article/32761; part 2 available online at http://www.devx.com/architect/Article/32836 (last access 2017-01-18), 2006.

28. Conference of the Independent Data Protection Authorities of the Bund and the Länder. The Standard Data Protection Model. A concept for inspection and consultation on the basis of unified protection goals. Available online at https://www.datenschutzzentrum.de/uploads/sdm/SDM-Methodology_V1.0.pdf (last access 2018-02-28), November 2016.

29. M. E. Conway. How do committees invent? *Datamation*, 14(5):28–31, May 1968.

30. Council of the European Union. Regulation (EU) 2016/679 of the European Parliament and of the Council of 27 April 2016 on the protection of natural persons with regard to the processing of personal data and on the free movement of such data, and repealing Directive 95/46/EC (General Data Protection Regulation). Official Journal of the European Union, Vol. 59, 4 May 2016. Available online at `http://eur-lex.europa.eu/legal-content/EN/TXT/?uri=CELEX:32016R0679` (last access 2018-02-28).

31. M. A. Cusumano and R. W. Selby. *Microsoft Secrets*. Touchstone, 1995.

32. B.-A. B. Data. Management von big-data-projekten. leitfaden. Technical report, BITKOM, 2013. Available from `https://www.bitkom.org/Bitkom/Publikationen/Management-von-Big-Data-Projekten.html` (last access 2018-02-06).

33. M. F. Dennedy, J. Fox, and T. R. Finneran. *The Privacy Engineer's Manifesto*. APress Open, 2014. Available online at `http://link.springer.com/book/10.1007%2F978-1-4302-6356-2` (last access 2017-03-12).

34. P. Diebold, J.-P. Ostberg, S. Wagner, and U. Zendler. What do practitioners vary in using Scrum? In *International Conference XP*, pages 40–51. Springer, 2015.

35. E. W. Dijkstra. *A Discipline of Programming*. Prentice Hall, 1976.

36. M. Drgon, G. Magnuson, and J. Sabo. Privacy management reference model and methodology (PMRM) version 1.0, committee specification 02. Technical report, OASIS, May 2016. Available online at `http://docs.oasis-open.org/pmrm/PMRM/v1.0/cs02/PMRM-v1.0-cs02.html` (last access 2017-03-12).

37. Eclipse Foundation. OpenUP. `http://epf.eclipse.org/wikis/openup/` (last access 2018-01-07), 2012.

38. M. R. Elliott. DO-332/ED-217. Using modern software practice in airborne systems. *CrossTalk*, 30(2):11–16, March/April 2017. Available online at `http://www.crosstalkonline.org` (last access 2017-03-04).

39. H. European Commission and C. Directorate-General. Eudralex. the rules governing medicinal products in the european union. volume 4, good manufacturing practice, medicinal products for human and veterinary use, annex 11: Computerised systems. `https://ec.europa.eu/health/sites/health/files/files/eudralex/vol-4/annex11_01-2011_en.pdf` (last access 2017-07-31), 2010.

40. C. Floyd. A systematic look at prototyping. In R. Budde, K. Kuhlenkamp, L. Mathiassen, and H. Züllighoven, editors, *Approaches to Prototyping; Proc. Namur*, pages 1–18. Springer, 1984.

41. M. Fowler. *Refactoring: Improving the Design of Existing Code*. Addison-Wesley, 1999.

42. H. Glazer, J. Dalton, D. Anderson, M. D. Konrad, and S. Shrum. CMMI or agile: Why not embrace both! Technical note CMU/SEI-2008-TN-003, Software Engineering Institute, 2008. Available online at `https://resources.sei.cmu.edu/library/asset-view.cfm?assetid=8533` (last access 2017-11-29).

43. E. M. Goldratt and J. Cox. *The Goal: A Process of Ongoing Improvement*. North River Pr Inc, 3rd revised edition, 2014.

44. F. Harmsen, S. Brinkkemper, and H. Oei. Situational method engineering for information system project approaches. In A. Verrijn-Stuart and T. Olle, editors, *Methods and Associated Tools for the Information Systems Life Cycle. Proceedings of the IFIP WG 8.1 Working Conference, Maastricht, Netherlands, September 1994*, number A-55 in IFIP Transactions, pages 169–194. North-Holland, 1994.

45. W. S. Humphrey. *Managing the Software Process*. SEI Series in Software Engineering. Addison-Wesley Professional, 1989.

46. Institute of Design at Stanford. bootcamp bootleg. `https://dschool.stanford.edu/s/METHODCARDS-v3-slim.pdf` (last access 2017-07-16).

47. ISACA. *COBIT® 5. A Business Framework for the Governance and Management of Enterprise IT*, 2012.

48. I. Jacobson, G. Booch, and J. Rumbaugh. *The Unified Software Development Process*. Addison-Wesley, 1999.

49. C. B. Jones. *Systematic Software Development Using VDM*. Prentice-Hall Int., 1986.

50. C. B. Jones, K. D. Jones, P. A. Lindsay, and R. Moore. *mural. A Formal Development Support System*. Springer, 1991.

51. R. Kneuper. Limits of formal methods. *Formal Aspects of Computing*, pages 379–394, 1997.

52. H. Kniberg and A. Ivarsson. Scaling Agile @ Spotify. http://blog.crisp. se/wp-content/uploads/2012/11/SpotifyScaling.pdf (last access 2017-10-08), October 2012.

53. A. Komus. Abschlussbericht: Status quo agile 2016/2017. http://www.status-quo-agile.net/ (last access 2018-01-07), 2017.

54. P. Kruchten. *The Rational Unified Process: An Introduction*. Addison-Wesley, 1998.

55. M. Kuhrmann and O. Linssen. Welche Vorgehensmodelle nutzt Deutschland? In M. Engstler, E. Hanser, M. Mikusz, and G. Herzwurm, editors, *Projektmanagement + Vorgehensmodelle 2014 (PVM2014)*, number P-236 in Lecture Notes in Informatics (LNI), pages 17–33. Gesellschaft für Informatik (GI), 2014.

56. C. Ladas. Scrum-ban. http://leansoftwareengineering.com/ksse/scrum-ban/ (last access 2018-01-02), 2008.

57. C. Larmann and B. Vodde. *Scaling Lean and Agile Development*. Addison Wesley, 2008.

58. M. Lehman. On understanding laws, evolution, and conservation in the large-program life cycle. *The Journal of Systems and Software*, pages 213–221, 1980.

59. M. Lehman. Laws of software evolution revisited. In C. Montangero, editor, *Software Process Technology. EWSPT 1996*, volume 1149 of *LNCS*, pages 108–124. Springer, 1996.

60. M. Lines and S. W. Ambler. Disciplined Agile 2.0. http://www. disciplinedagiledelivery.com (last access 2018-01-07).

61. M. Lines and S. W. Ambler. *Introduction to Disciplined Agile Delivery*. CreateSpace Independent Publishing Platform, 2015.

62. R. C. Linger and C. J. Trammell. Cleanroom software engineering. Reference model version 1.0. Technical Report CMU/SEI-96-TR-022, Software Engineering Institute, Carnegie Mellon University, November 1996.

63. S. Maguire. *Debugging the Development Process*. Microsoft Press, 1994.

64. J. Martin. *Rapid Application Development*. Macmillan, 1991.

65. S. McConnell. *Rapid Development. Taming Wild Software Schedules*. Microsoft Press, 1996.

66. J. McHale. Upgrade to DO-178B certification—DO-178C—to address modern avionics software trends. Avionics Intelligence, available online at http: //www.intelligent-aerospace.com/articles/2009/10/upgrade-to-do-178b-certification-do-178c-to-address-modern-avionics-software-trends.html, October 2009.

67. B. Meyer. *Agile! The Good, the Hype and the Ugly*. Springer, 2014.

68. Microsoft. *Security Development Lifecycle. SDL Process Guidance Version 5.2*. Microsoft Corporation, 2012. available online at https://www.microsoft.com/en-us/download/details.aspx?id=29884 (last access 2017-11-25).

69. Microsoft. Microsoft Solutions Framework (MSF) Overview. https://msdn. microsoft.com/en-us/library/jj161047(v=vs.120).aspx (last access 2017-11-25), 2013.

70. Microsoft. Choose a process. https://docs.microsoft.com/de-de/vsts/work/work-items/guidance/choose-process (last access 2017-11-25), 2017.

71. Microsoft. What is the security development lifecycle? https://www.microsoft.com/en-us/sdl/ (last access 2017-07-03), 2017.

72. H. D. Mills, M. Dyer, and R. C. Linger. Cleanroom software engineering. *IEEE Software*, 4(5):19–25, 1987.

73. M. Mosisio, C. Seaman, V. Basili, A. Parra, S. Kraft, and S. Condon. COTS-based software development: Processes and open issues. *The Journal of Systems and Software*, 61:189–199, 2002.

74. Nebulon Pty. Ltd. Feature driven development. Overview. Available from http://www.featuredrivendevelopment.com/node/967 (last access 2018-01-11), 2005.

75. Open Web Application Security Project (OWASP). *Software Assurance Maturity Model. A guide to building security into software development. Version 1.0.* http://www. opensamm.org/ (last access 2017-07-04).
76. Open Web Application Security Project (OWASP). Available online at https://www. owasp.org (last access 2017-07-04).
77. M. C. Paulk. Surviving the quagmire of process models, integrated models, and standards. In *Proceedings of the ASQ Annual Quality Congress, 24-27 May 2004, Toronto, Canada.* American Society for Quality, 2004. Available online at http://citeseerx.ist.psu. edu/viewdoc/download?doi=10.1.1.644.9865&rep=rep1&type=pdf (last access 2017-03-05).
78. Payment Card Industry (PCI). Data Security Standard. Requirements and Security Assessment Procedures. Version 3.2. Online available at https://www. pcisecuritystandards.org/document_library (last access 2017-03-16)., April 2016.
79. Payment Card Industry (PCI). Payment Application Data Security Standard. Requirements and Security Assessment Procedures. Version 3.2. Online available at https: //www.pcisecuritystandards.org/document_library (last access 2017-03-16)., May 2016.
80. PCI Security Standards Council. PCI DSS Quick Reference Guide. Available online at https://www.pcisecuritystandards.org/documents/PCIDSS_ QRGv3_2.pdf?agreement=true&time=1488666033089 (last access 2017-03-04), 2016.
81. Project Management Institute. *A guide to the project management body of knowledge (PMBOK® guide).* Sixth edition, 2017.
82. E. S. Raymond. The cathedral and the bazaar. Version 3. Available online at http://www.catb.org/~esr/writings/cathedral-bazaar/cathedral-bazaar/index.html (last access 2017-03-18), 2002.
83. J. A. Ricketts. Theory of constraints for services: Past, present, and future. In H. Demirkan, J. C. Spohrer, and V. Krishna, editors, *Service Systems Implementation*, pages 113–131. Springer, 2011.
84. J. Rothman. Not ready for agile? Start your journey with release trains. https://www.jrothman.com/articles/2011/01/not-ready-for-agile-start-your-journey-with-release-trains/ (last access 2017-05-28), Jan. 2011.
85. Scaled Agile, Inc. SAFe® 4.0 for Lean Software and Systems Engineering. http:// scaledagileframework.com/ (last access 2018-01-07).
86. K. Schwaber. SCRUM Development Process. In *OOPSLA '95 Workshop Proceedings 16 October 1995, Austin, Texas.* Springer, 1997.
87. K. Schwaber. Nexus guide. the definitive guide to Nexus: The exosceleton of scaled Scrum development. Available online at https://www.scrum.org/Resources/The-Nexus-Guide (last access 2018-02-28), 2015.
88. K. Schwaber and M. Beedle. *Agile Software Development with Scrum.* Prentice Hall, 2002.
89. Schweizerische Eidgenossenschaft. Hermes 5. Method overview. http://www.hermes. admin.ch/onlinepublikation/index.xhtml (last access 2018-02-28).
90. Schweizerische Eidgenossenschaft. Hermes 5.1. http://www.hermes.admin.ch/ index.xhtml (last access 2018-02-28).
91. S. A. Sheard. Evolution of the frameworks quagmire. *IEEE Computer*, pages 96–98, July 2001.
92. S. Sogus. Achieving machinery functional safety according to IEC 61508, ISO 13849 and IEC 62061. White paper, Programming Research PRQA, November 2015.
93. A. Spillner. The W-Model—strengthening the bond between development and test. In *Proc. STAREAST, 10th International Conf. on Software Testing, Analysis & Review, Orlando, FL, USA,* 2002.
94. J. Sutherland. Agile can scale: Inventing and reinventing SCRUM in five companies. *Cutter IT journal*, 14(12):5–11, December 2001.

95. J. Sutherland and K. Schwaber. The Scrum Guide™. The Definitive Guide to Scrum: The Rules of the Game. http://www.scrumguides.org/ (last access 2018-02-28), July 2013.

96. J. Sutherland, A. Viktorov, J. Blount, and N. Puntikov. Distributed Scrum: Agile project management with outsourced development teams. In *Proceedings of the 40th Hawaii International Conference on System Sciences (HICSS'07*, 2007.

97. H. Takeuchi and I. Nonaka. The New New Product Development Game. *Harvard Business Review*, Jan. 1986.

98. S. Tangen and A.-M. Warris. Management makeover—new format for future ISO management system standards. Available online at https://www.iso.org/news/2012/07/Ref1621.html (last access 2017-03-16), July 2012.

99. The LeSS Company. LeSS Framework. http://less.works/less/framework/index.html (last access 2018-02-28), 2014.

100. G. Theocharis, M. Kuhrmann, J. Münch, and P. Diebold. Is water-scrum-fall reality? On the use of agile and traditional development practices. In P. Abrahamsson, L. Corral, M. Oivo, and B. Russo, editors, *Product-Focused Software Process Improvement, 16th International Conference, PROFES 2015*, pages 149–166. Springer, 2015.

101. VersionOne. State of agile survey. Available online at http://stateofagile.versionone.com/ (last access 2018-03-19), 2006–2016.

102. L. R. Vijayasarathy and C. W. Butler. Choice of software development methodologies—do project, team and organizational characteristics matter? *IEEE Software*, 33(5):86–94, 2015.

103. Visual Studio Team System, Microsoft Corporation. Visual Studio 2005 Team System: Microsoft Solutions Framework. https://msdn.microsoft.com/en-us/library/aa302179.aspx (last access 2017-11-25), May 2004.

104. D. West. Water-scrum-fall is the reality of agile for most organizations today. Technical report, Forrester Research Inc., July 2011.

105. J. P. Womack, D. T. Jones, and D. Roos. *The Machine That Changed the World : The Story of Lean Production*. Harper Perennial, Nov. 1991.

106. A. Yakyma. *Pacific Express*. Scaled Agile, Inc., 2014.

107. F. W. Zurcher and B. Randell. Iterative multi-level modeling—a methodology for computer system design. In *Proc. IFIP Congress 68*, pages 138–142. IEEE CS Press, 1968.

Chapter 4
Governance and Management of Software Processes

Abstract In order to provide work teams with adequate software processes, organisations face the challenge to manage the processes, including the set-up of a suitable infrastructure, the selection of appropriate approaches and their tailoring to the individual situation. Once they have been selected and tailored, processes need to be deployed and the resulting changes need to be managed. These are demanding tasks, as various context and project attributes have to be taken into account. In this chapter, we introduce different approaches to these process governance and management tasks, including an overview of the role of processes in IT governance and the framework COBIT.

4.1 Introduction

While in the previous chapters the focus was first on different aspects of *the definition format* of software processes and then on the contents of these processes, we now move closer to *using* them within an organisation and its software development.

Similar to the meta-models that define a notation for defining models, *meta-processes* define processes that operate on other processes, such as the selection, tailoring, deployment and governance of processes in an organisation or project as discussed in the current chapter. The following chapters will cover some further meta-processes, in particular the assessment and improvement of processes (see Chap. 5) and the measurement of (software) processes as well as their results, see Chap. 6.

First, we define the concept of process management. The closely related concept of process governance will be addressed as part of IT governance in Sect. 4.8.

Definition 4.1 (Process management). *Process management is the direction, control, and coordination of work performed to develop a product or perform a service. (SEVOCAB)*

© Springer Nature Switzerland AG 2018
R. Kneuper, *Software Processes and Life Cycle Models*,
https://doi.org/10.1007/978-3-319-98845-0_4

In software processes, process management needs to be performed on two different level, the level of the overall organisation and the level of individual projects (or teams).

All of the steps of this value chain will be covered in more detail in the remainder of this chapter, with the exception of process assessment and improvement which will be covered in Chap. 5, and process measurement, which will be covered in Chap.6.

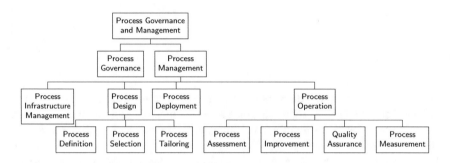

Fig. 4.1 Process governance and management taxonomy

Process management is not only needed in a classical, plan-driven environment, as is sometimes believed, but also in an agile environment. In this case, the task of process management may involve setting up an environment such that Scrum can be used, and ensuring that it is indeed used.

4.2 Process Infrastructure

One of the first steps in managing (software) processes within any organisation is to set up a suitable infrastructure. This includes the definition of the relevant process management roles (who is going to decide on the processes to be used; who is going to write them down, etc.), selecting a suitable process notation, as well as selecting the processes and tools to be used for managing and controlling the resulting documents and other artefacts.

4.2.1 Process Roles

An important part of the infrastructure needed to define and manage processes are the different people involved and their roles. A common tool to describe such roles and their responsibilities is the RACI chart. This section therefore first introduces the RACI chart and then the main roles involved in processes and process management.

RACI chart. A RACI chart illustrates the relationship between a set of roles or organisational units and a set of activities. This relationship can take one of the following forms [16]:

- *Responsible:* "The individual, group or entity that is ultimately responsible for a subject matter, process or scope."

  - Answers the question: who is getting the activity done?
  - At least one individual, group or entity should be responsible for any activity.

- *Accountable:* "Refers to the person who must ensure that activities are completed successfully."

  - Answers the question: who accounts for the success of the activity?
  - Exactly one person should be accountable for any activity.
  - The same person may also be responsible for the same activity.

- *Consulted:* "Refers to those people whose opinions are sought on an activity (two-way communication)"

  - Answers the question: who is providing input?
  - Any number of person, including zero, may be consulted for any activity.

- *Informed:* "Refers to those people who are kept up to date on the progress of an activity (one-way communication)."

  - Answers the question: who is receiving information?
  - Any number of person, including zero, may be informed about any activity.

An example of a RACI chart summarizing the main process management roles described in more detail below is contained in Table 4.1.

Table 4.1 Process management roles

	Process owner	Process engineer	Process tailor	Process performer	Process assurance
Ensure performance of process	A	C	R	R	R
Improve process	A	R	C	C	C
Analyse, define and maintain process	A	R	C	C	C
Perform process on day-to-day basis	I	C	C	A,R	C

Process owner A central role in process management is that of the process owner, also called process champion or process sponsor, who takes the main responsibility for a process. The following definition taken from COBIT defines the role of the process owner as the person accountable for the process:

Definition 4.2 (Process owner). *An individual accountable for the performance of a process in realising its objectives, driving process improvement and approving process changes." (COBIT 5 [16, p. 76]*[1]*) (SEVOCAB)*

The role of the process owner is usually a part-time role that line managers responsible or accountable for the operational performance of the process take on in addition to their other tasks.

Definitions of this role vary considerably, in particular regarding the distinction between responsibility and accountability. For example, ITIL describes the role of the process owner similar to COBIT but defines the process owner to be responsible rather than accountable, even though the distinction between responsibility and accountability is introduced in ITIL as well.

SEVOCAB defines the role of the process owner as a "person or team responsible for defining and maintaining a process". According to this definition, the process owner is quite a different role from the one defined here, but similar to the role of the process engineer below.

ITIL additionally introduces the role of the *process manager* that may be separated from the process owner in larger organisations. In this case, the process manager takes responsibility for the operational management of a process, while the process owner puts the focus on the sponsorship and guidance of the process management activities.[2]

In order to coordinate the process management activities for different processes, in particular if there is an improvement project that aims to improve several processes in parallel, a *process steering group* is often formed that consists of the affected process owners and/or process managers, plus other process stakeholders as needed.

Process engineer While process owners take overall accountability/responsibility for their processes, they rarely create the process definitions and documentation themselves. This is the task of the process engineers:

Definition 4.3 (Process engineer). *Person or group responsible for analysing, defining, modelling and maintaining life cycle and process descriptions.*

Very similar roles are the process architect (SEVOCAB), the process analyst ([12, p. 24]), and the method engineer (ISO/IEC 24744:2014, SEVOCAB)

In large software organisations, process engineers often work together as a group with responsibility for the overall software development life cycle and its processes. This group is often called a *Software Engineering Process Group (SEPG)* or, in systems development, *Engineering Process Group (EPG)*.

The role of a process engineer may be a full-time role, or it may be a part-time role, usually for people whose main role is to perform the process, and who are therefore specially qualified to describe it as it is actually performed, and to identify

---

[1] COBIT 5 actually calls this role *business* process owner, but the definition can be adapted without change to other processes such as software processes.

[2] The difference between both roles is only hinted at in ITIL itself, but quite common in the ITIL community, see e.g. [1].

any improvements needed. A common combination in large organisations is that of a small core of full-time process engineers who bring in process management know-how, plus a larger group of part-time process engineers who each bring in know-how about a few specific processes. Working only with full-time process engineers, without involvement of process performers, will often lead to process definitions that do not adequately address the real-life problems involved, or at least complaints that they do not do so.

Smaller organisations in general will not have any full-time process engineers but do all the process definition and improvement work with small teams of process performers.

Process tailor. The "process tailor" is a role that is needed whenever a standard process is to be applied in a specific situation, but is not commonly defined separately from that of the process engineer and therefore has no widely used name. As the suggested name indicates, the process tailor is responsible for tailoring a standard process, which may for example be performed by a project leader as part of project planning, as an extension of the role of the process engineer, or in cooperation between the two.

Definition 4.4 (Process tailor). *Person or group responsible for tailoring the standard process to a specific situation such as a project.*

This role is similar to that of the *Scrum master* who "is responsible for ensuring Scrum is understood and enacted. Scrum Masters do this by ensuring that the Scrum Team adheres to Scrum theory, practices, and rules" [30, p. 6].

Process performer The role that in the end has most effect on the process and how it is performed is that of the person performing it:

Definition 4.5 (Process performer). *Person or group responsible for performing the activities of a process on a day-to-day basis.*
(Based on the definition of "process participants" in [12, p. 24])

This role includes line management and is also called process participant (e.g. [12, p. 24]) or process agent (e.g. [22, Glossary]).

Process assurance. In order to verify that the defined process is performed correctly, the role of process assurance is needed, also called process quality assurance. The work involved is described in more detail in Sect. 4.7.

Definition 4.6 (Process assurance). *Person or group that verifies that the process is performed correctly according to the process definition.*

Case Study 4.1. (CS AutoSystems) Since the development department of CS AutoSystems is very small, there is no full-time process engineer for development. The company has a quality manager who is responsible for the company quality system based on ISO 9001, with a focus on production. As part of this task, the quality manager has taken on the role of process engineer for all processes and created, as part of the company quality management system, a procedure defining the development process based on the V-Model as described in Case Study 3.2. As happens often in such a case, this procedure is fairly superficial and not considered helpful by the development engineers.

Initiated and led by the head of development, a more detailed life cycle model and process description was therefore created by a group of developers, see Case Study 4.3, thus filling the role of process engineers as well as that of process performers.

Case Study 4.2. (CS Insurance InfoSys) When CS Insurance InfoSys decided to manage its processes on a systematic basis, the IT operations department selected ITIL as the reference model while the development department selected CMMI-DEV. This also influenced the process roles that were defined:

The IT operations department followed the ITIL tradition and nominated, for each of the ITIL processes, a process owner from higher-level management, plus a process manager responsible for the operational management of the processes, in particular the day-to-day management of the process definition and improvement activities. Both were part-time activities, and each process manager reports, in this role, to the relevant process owner. In most cases, the process managers are at the same time line managers responsible for the performance of "their" processes, for example the process manager for *Incident Management* is the head of the service desk team that deals, among other tasks, with incidents. To implement the process management tasks, each process manager has a team of several part-time process engineers, usually from the line organisation led by this process manager.

The process engineers are responsible for creating and later maintaining the definitions of the ITIL processes, setting up measurements on these processes and evaluating the measurement results, and implementing improvement activities. One of the main tasks of process owners is to jointly define the general approach to managing the processes, and to coordinate the definitions of and improvement activities for the individual processes.

The development department, on the other hand, decided to set up an SEPG, consisting of a core team of two people working as full-time process engineers plus extended teams consisting of representatives from development projects. The core team is responsible for the coordinating the process definition and improvement activities, helping with the documentation of defined processes, and training and coaching project managers, developers and other process performers. The extended teams are each responsible for defining and improving a group of related processes, supported by the core team.

After some time, it was decided to move the ways of working of both departments closer together, for example introducing the roles of process owner and process manager in the development department as well.

4.2.2 Selecting a Process Notation

An important step in managing the software processes is the selection of a suitable notation. This selection will usually be performed on the organisational level, in particular if the processes to be described are to be applicable for the entire organisation. If the process description is to only apply for an individual project or team, then the notation may be selected on that level as well, but of course this makes any exchange of tools or description much more difficult.

Typical criteria to be used for selecting a process notation are:

- Usage of the process descriptions: are the process descriptions mainly used to provide process performers with an overview of the processes to be used? In this case, one of the less formal notations with only basic structure is quite appropriate. The more tool support is intended, however, the more formality will be needed in the process notation.
- If applicable, external requirements from customers, regulatory bodies etc. of course also need to be taken into account.
- Who will use the process notation and create the descriptions? Full-time process engineers will be able to deal with a fairly complex notation, while process performers who only occasionally work on process descriptions will need a rather easy-to-use notation.
- How much explicit tailoring is expected to be performed on the process descriptions, and what relevance will different process variants have? Of course, if tailoring and different process variants are important, then the process notation should help to make this easy while at the same time to keep control over the different variants.

In addition to these criteria, of course all the properties of process notations and meta-models as described in Section 2.1.2 are relevant for this selection as well.

4.2.3 Process Asset Management and Control

Apart from the process definition or model itself, there are usually a number of other artefacts that help in working with the processes, such as training material, templates, examples and measurement data. These artefacts are often called (organisational) process assets, and they are collected in an (organisational) process asset library:

Definition 4.7 ((Organisational) Process assets). *Artefacts that relate to describing, implementing, and improving processes, such as policies, measurements, process descriptions, and process implementation support tools.*
(SEVOCAB)

A common structure for process documentation and the relevant process assets was described by [5], see Fig. 4.2.

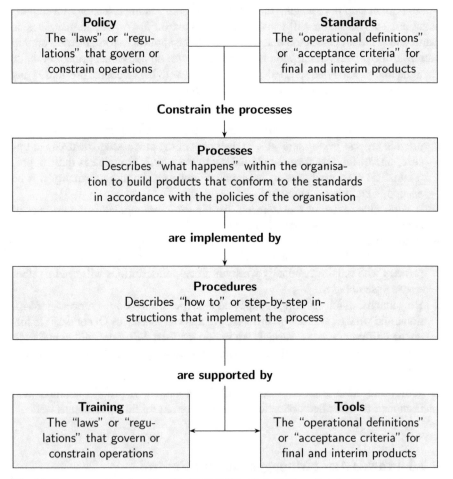

Fig. 4.2 Process asset relationships [5]. © CMMI Institute 2007, reprinted with permission.

Alternatively, this structure is also sometimes presented as a pyramid, indicating that the number and size of the documents grows from top to bottom.

Once the process assets have been created, a key challenge is to ensure that they are available to all stakeholders as needed, and these stakeholders are able to find them when needed. This is the main purpose of the process asset library:

Definition 4.8 ((Organisational) Process asset library). *Collection of information that can be useful to those who are defining, implementing, and managing processes in the organisation. (SEVOCAB)*

Process asset release process. Another important part of the process infrastructure is the release process to be used for process assets. While a minor modification of the process assets (such as an improvement of wording or adding an example) may be released by the responsible process owner alone, any major modification that affects how the process is performed should be reviewed and released jointly by the relevant stakeholders and roles. Of course, the main stakeholder in this context is the relevant process owner, but in many cases, the owners of other processes interfacing with the process to be released need to be involved as well. Process performers know from personal experience what works well and what does not, and therefore also need to be involved. Finally, process engineers are needed to verify that the process notation is correctly used, and also usually have a good overview of the integration of the different processes which allows them to identify any potential problems or conflicts.

Tool support. In order to manage process assets adequately, tool support is usually needed. This topic will be discussed in more detail in Sect. 7.2.2.

Languages used for process assets. The selection of the (natural) language to be used for the process asset library might seem just a minor issue, but can be quite a challenge if developers, customers and possibly other relevant stakeholders do not speak the same language. In many such cases, English is selected as a common language, but even this is not always sufficient. Depending on the qualification of the stakeholders involved, the size and industry branch of the organisation, and the country and region where they live, one may not always assume that everybody speaks English sufficiently well to cope with English-language process definitions, and perhaps to add to them as necessary.

Example 4.1. A large automotive supplier decided to introduce standardised development processes for its software development groups spread around the world. One of the challenges was to decide on the language to be used for the process assets. Initially, the plan was to use English language process assets consistently, but it soon turned out that this was not possible for two main reasons: while in some locations, developers were well able to at least read and understand English, in other locations that was not the case. Additionally, there was a considerably number of documents that had to be submitted to various regulatory bodies in order to get the relevant safety certifications, and these usually had to be submitted in the relevant local language.

Eventually, it was therefore decided to translate the core documents into the relevant languages. Overall, 35 core documents were identified which each needed to be published in 12 different languages.

To manage these documents, a set of tools and processes was set up to ensure that these 12 language versions of the 35 documents were always synchronised, ensuring that every change was incorporated into each language version. Creating and maintaining the translations required close cooperation between professional translators and subject specialists, since neither of them was able to create high-quality translations on their own.

Additionally, several hundred supporting documents were in use, some of them relevant for all languages and regions, some of them only relevant in specific cases, but because of the effort involved, it was decided that these would not be needed to be available and synchronised in all languages, but should be added to the document management tool if available.

4.3 Process Definition

4.3.1 Basic Concepts

In defining processes, it is important to start off with identifying both the goals of the process and the goals of its description or model. If we do not really know what the process is expected to achieve, it is more or less impossible to define the process such that our goals will be achieved. The process quality model *Gokyo Ri* (described in Sect. 6.5) therefore defines the "process objectives and requirements" as the first quality characteristic, and Appendix B.1 contains a check-list to evaluate this characteristic.

Once the process goals as well as the goals of the process description have been defined, the next step is to ensure that these goals are addressed by the process, and also that there are no unwanted side effects. For example, [29] describes how a restrictive change control process can lead to bad design, in this case by making refactoring too arduous. In that example, the organisation later relaxed the rules on change control but added a design quality gate to eventually improve the design quality considerably.

So far, the discussion assumed that the process to be defined has not been modelled before. In some organisation, there is a tendency to start developing a new process model if the current model is not accepted by process performers and therefore not used. However, if the underlying reasons for not accepting the process are not addressed, this will not resolve the problem but just add to it. If a process is not accepted, it is important to start by understanding why this is the case. Is the process too difficult to use? Then it probably should be simplified, rather than just replaced by another process which might be just as difficult to use. If it has not been deployed properly, with tool support, training, quality assurance and so on, creating a new process description will not change anything, at least not for the better.

Customer viewpoint. Considering the definition of processes as a service to the organisation, there are different types of customers whose viewpoints should be taken into account:

- Every process has (or should have) a primary customer who benefits from the *process*. In many cases, this will be an internal customer.
- Most processes support the delivery (more or less directly) of products or services to a customer of the *organisation*.
- Finally, there are the customers of the process definition who will *perform* the process.

Important in designing a process is to identify these different kinds of customers, and to identify the value created by the process (definition) for these customers. This can be difficult in some cases, in particular in the case where the service to the organisational customer is only indirect; for example, the salary payment process is obviously important but it is difficult to identify the *customer* value created.

Process definitions for different levels of experience. If we want to address the customer viewpoint in process definitions, we have to take into account that different customers or users of the process definition will have varying levels of experience with the process. Therefore, they will need different types of support by the documentation, for example using the following three levels [23]:

- *Expert level*: an expert needs a concise description of the process, for example as a check-list or flow-chart. This is particularly important if the process is only performed occasionally, for example a task that only needs to be done once per year or per project. Where relevant, this check-list or flow-chart defines the mandatory and auditable part of the process.
- *Intermediate level*: process performers with some experience additionally need some guidance on how to perform the process and how to interpret the concise, expert-level description. The expert-level description is therefore expanded by some optional, intermediate-level guidance.
- *Beginner level*: beginners additionally need training material on the process. This is not part of the process description itself but should be available from there, e.g. via hyper-links.

4.3.2 Software Process Development

The major steps needed to define a software process include the preparation, the agreement on the process, its documentation, and—integrated into the previous steps—its validation. Of course, after that work is not completed yet, but the topic of process deployment will be discussed in Sect. 4.6 below.

Preparation. To prepare for the development of software processes, the properties as described in Sect. 3.1.1 need to be defined, though not necessarily in that order. In most cases, preparation will be performed iteratively, including revision while work on the process definition is going on.

Additional tasks in preparing process development include:

- Identify external requirements on process, such as standards, legal requirements, interfaces to other processes.
- Identify process stakeholders, in particular roles involved in the process. Who are the process customers, and what is the experience level of the process performers?
- Ensure that the main process stakeholders, in particular process performers and top management, are involved in the definition of the process, and try to continually get their commitment.
- Clarify how the process model is going to be validated and deployed. A common mistake is to concentrate too much on the development of the new process model, and only start thinking about its validation and deployment once the model is completed. Without proper validation, there is a high risk that some important aspects will be left out, and, even more important, without proper deployment, even the best process model will be of little or no use.

The main responsibility for these preparatory tasks lies with the process owner, supported by process engineers and possibly process performers.

Agreement on the process. Once the relevant preparatory information has been collected, the next step is to involve the main stakeholders, for example by setting up a joint workshop, and develop the (new or revised) process on a high level. Similar to the process of requirements identification and process modelling, the main sequence of actions should be identified first, and later the special cases and deviations from the main sequence of events are added, with multiple iterations through these steps.

In order to ensure that the resulting process definition is realistic and accepted, it is important that this process of process definition should mainly be driven by the process performers, with process engineers moderating and supporting it.

Documentation. Once there is agreement on the overall process, it needs to be documented in the appropriate notation, including the relevant process assets. Obviously, there will be some going back and forth between agreement and documentation, with documentation throwing up new questions for which answers need to be agreed upon.

While agreement on the process usually involves a larger group of stakeholders, the documentation of the agreed process will be easier to perform if only a few individuals are involved, such as process engineers with sufficient skills regarding the process notation used.

Validation of the process. As an intermediate step between documenting the process and deploying it, the process should be validated to ensure that the process itself as well as its documentation are adequate for practical use and help to achieve the goals defined. Additionally, this may help to identify missing components of the process documentation such as a template to be used for a new process deliverable.

To some extent, validation is integrated into the previous steps by involving the relevant stakeholders. In addition to that, major process changes should be piloted, for example by just using the new or revised process within one project.

Case Study 4.3. (CS AutoSystems) In order to define the variant of the V-Model as described in Case Study 3.2, a one-day workshop was performed. Participants included almost the complete development team, the head of development who also had the role of process owner for the development processes, the CEO of the company, plus an external consultant to facilitate the workshop.

By collecting and structuring input from the participants on how the process was currently performed, including the identification of gaps in the process, a graphical model similar to that shown in Case Study 3.2 was created jointly on drawing board, with some additional notes such as who performed which step and what products were expected to be created.

Once this overall process had been agreed, the external consultant documented it as a ten-page structured text document, identifying a number of open issues while doing so. Emphasis was put on the fact that the external consultant did not himself *define* the process, but documented what had been agreed in the workshop, to ensure that the result was the team's process and not the consultant's process. Initially, it had been suggested that the documentation of the process should also be performed by the team itself, but this was rejected because of lack of time and insufficient experience in documenting such a process.

The draft process document was then distributed to the participants for review, together with the open issues identified. In a second, shorter workshop feedback was collected and open issues were clarified or decided. Based on the results of this second workshop, the process document was revised and eventually released.

An important advantage of this approach was that very little deployment was needed because the process performers already knew the new process from the two workshops, and the process was well accepted since they had been actively involved in developing it.

4.4 Process Selection

The selection of software processes is typically relevant on two different levels: first, an organisation selects a process or set of processes to be used within the organisation. For example, it may select a standard reference model such as V-Model XT, or a framework such as Scrum, and then tailor the selected model by refining and adapting the general description to the specific organisational environment. As an example, the European Commission selected the RUP as the standard reference model for development projects, and tailored this model in two alternative ways to define *RUP@EC* and *Agile RUP@EC*.

Second, within the limits of the first selection (if relevant), each instantiation selects its own processes, for example each specific development project. Again, this selection will fix the general frame which may then have to be tailored and adapted to the specific context.

Experience shows that in practice, there are three common ways of selecting the processes to be used in any specific context such as a development effort: first, there may be an organisational decision that a certain process is to be used, which is then implemented. Second, the processes may be "historically grown", meaning that the processes are used because they were used in the past, with little or no reflection of whether they are (still) adequate. Third, it may be an individual decision, for example by the project leader, based on personal experience with the approach selected.

Why—What—How? The following three-step approach to the selection of an IT reference model or process standard, slightly more general than just a process model, was described in [2] and aims to help in focussing the use of the reference models on the relevant environment, without introducing any unnecessary overhead:

- *Why?* Before selecting any specific reference model, it is important clearly understand why one wants to do so. What is the benefit to be achieved?
- *What?* Next, the appropriate reference model(s) are selected, based on the answer to the previous question. In this step, it is important to set priorities and decide which parts of any selected model are really important to achieve the objectives identified, and which may not be relevant in the current context and should therefore only be addressed very superficially if at all. In many cases, there will not be a single reference model to be considered but several such models.
- *How?* Finally, the selected (parts of the) reference model(s) have to be tailored and implemented in a way that genuinely helps the organisation. The target is not to do a certain step in just any way as long as the reference model is satisfied, but to perform it in a way that is genuinely helpful to achieve the identified objectives.

Selection based on multi-attribute utility models. Multi-attribute utility models provide a formalised way to evaluate different options, such as software process or life cycle models, consisting of the following steps (not necessarily exactly in that order):

- Identify the different options available. While this is an obvious pre-requisite for selecting an option, it is often far more difficult than it seems at first sight, since apart from the large number of different models available, there is an even larger number of combinations of parts of such models that might be selected.

- Identify the relevant attributes of the different options which may make one model "better" in some sense than another in a given context. Examples for such relevant attributes are requirements stability, the size of the project, or previous experience with the model.

  Depending on the importance of each attribute in the current context, each attribute is given a "weight" for the evaluation.

  In a formalised, quantitative approach, these weights are numerical values, as are the values assigned to a certain model for a certain attribute. However, in doing so there is a risk of providing pseudo-exact values to entities that in truth can only be estimated roughly. Therefore, it may be more useful to restrict oneself to a small number of ordinal values such as high, medium and low importance, or even nominal values if there is no useful ordering of the values.[3]

  A property may be defined as a must-attribute, or assigned a minimum value required. Any option that does not satisfy the must-attribute or achieve the minimum value will then be disqualified from selection, independent of its other properties. For example, if requirements stability is known or at least expected to be low, then any model requiring high requirements stability does not need to be analysed any further.

- Once the options as well as the relevant attributes and their weights are defined, each option is evaluated, i.e. values are assigned to the attributes.

- Finally, each option is evaluated based on the combination of values and weights for each attribute. If a formalised, quantitative approach is used, the overall utility of a option is calculated as the sum of the weighted attribute evaluations, while in a less formal approach, an approximation of this overall utility is estimated.

  Based on the results, the option that provides the highest overall utility is selected.

Although this approach can be very useful for selecting a software process or life cycle model, one should not expect too much from it. As mentioned above, trying to be too formal and using quantitative values and weights will provide an apparent exactitude that is not truly possible. While the evaluation of the different attributes for the options available usually involves a lot of work but is not too difficult, a lot of discussion may arise around the weights assigned to the different attributes. At first, this may seem to be a major disadvantage of the method, but it actually is very useful because it pinpoints the disagreements between stakeholders about the relevant importance of the different attributes, and thus helps to resolve such conflict.

A second challenge that again is not caused by the method but made visible by it is the relevance of "soft" factors or attributes, such as the extent to which a process fits with company philosophy, or the extent to which it supports trust and cooperation within the organisation. Of course, these attributes are important in the selection, but very difficult to define and evaluate.

Plan-driven, agile or hybrid? In many practical cases, neither agile nor plan-driven development addresses all issues at stake. A purely plan-driven model in

---

[3] See Sect. 6.1.3 for more explanation on these different types of scales.

many cases is too rigid and does not cope adequately with changes in the requirements or the environment. Furthermore, the risks involved in integrating and validating a software system late in the life cycle are fairly high. Agile development, on the other hand, is for example difficult to use for systems where it is important to prove in some way what the system does, for example systems where safety or security play an important role, or other legal requirements such as in finance or accounting.

In the following, we discuss a number of factors to be taken into account in this decision.

"Five critical factors" by Boehm and Turner. In [6, Chap. 2], Boehm and Turner describe the combination of practices from agile and plan-driven development, and define "five critical factors" for selecting the right mix of both:

- *Size* refers to the fact that agile methods are more suitable for smaller teams, while plan-driven methods are more suitable for larger teams. The importance of this factor has since decreased with the introduction of different approaches for scaling agile, but a close look shows that this is mostly done at the expense of losing some agility in the process.
- *Criticality* is a similarly well-known factor, with plan-driven methods more suitable for ensuring that non-visible properties such as safety and other non-functional requirements are satisfied, while agile development tends to put more focus on visible properties such as functionality and ease of use.

  This may go as far as legal and other regulations that need to be adhered to, and which may prescribe a certain development approach in order to verify that relevant properties such as safety or conformance to accounting standards are not just satisfied but can be proved to be satisfied.

  On the other hand, there has been some work on how to use certain agile practices in the context of critical systems, see for example [9]. Of course, it is not possible to be "completely agile" in this context, but practices such as a strong focus on short iterations, or test-driven development and strong test automation, may actually be very helpful.
- *Dynamism*: dealing with a very dynamic environment and fast-changing requirements was one of the reasons for introducing agile development and calling it by this name. Plan-driven development, on the other hand, is more suitable for a stable environment where requirements do not change too often.
- *Personnel* is a factor less well-known, but still very important. Since agile development puts more emphasis on self-organisation and on joint responsibility rather than specialisation, personnel needs a higher skill-level regarding the development methods used. Larry Constantine stated this as follows (cited here after [6, p. 46]): "There are only so many Kent Becks in the world to lead a team. All of the agile methods put a premium on having premium people …".
- *Culture*, finally, also has a large impact on the best mix of methods in any given context. In a culture where people feel empowered by many degrees of freedom (and the responsibility that goes with it), agile development tends to be more

successful, while plan-driven development tends to be better suited to a structured culture with clear policies and procedures.

Proponents of agile development sometimes ignore this factor, leading to the situation that the project eventually fails because "there was insufficient management support for agile development" or due to "resistance to cultural change". If a project development approach was selected where there is strong organisational resistance, i.e. that does not fit the organisational culture, this is a project problem rather than an organisational problem.[4]

Of course, few development efforts will be clearly only agile or only plan-driven according to these factors, and the task in any given context therefore is to find the right mixture of both, based on the values of the factors in that context.

Further selection criteria. In addition to the criteria listed by Boehm and Turner, additional criteria that affect the selection of development methods are:

- *Customer availability*: in plan-driven development, it is difficult if customers (or, to be more precise, stakeholders) are not involved continuously in the development effort, answering open questions as needed and so on. However, within certain limits this customer involvement may be concentrated within the analysis phase early on, with little involvement later. In agile development, less customer involvement is needed in the early phases, but continuous involvement across the entire development effort is needed instead.

  Depending on when and to what extent customers are available during the development effort, agile or plan-driven development may be better suited.

- *Complexity*: another selection criterion might be the complexity of the work to be done, in particular of the architecture of the resulting system. However, in this case there are differing opinions about whether agile development is more suited, since it supports iteration and feedback on bad architectural decisions, or whether plan-driven development is more suited, since it puts more emphasis on defining, documenting and reviewing the architecture.

  This can even be seen by different statements by Ken Schwaber himself at different times. In the original paper on Scrum, he stated:

  > Scrum is concerned with the management, enhancement and maintenance of an existing product, ... Scrum is not concerned with new or re-engineered systems development efforts. [28]

  Later, however, he changed his mind, and the current Scrum guide states more or less the opposite:

  > Scrum is a framework for developing and sustaining complex products. [30]

- *Legal and other regulatory requirements.* In addition to the requirements based on criticality of the system to be built there are a number of other regulatory requirements to be taken into account, for example regarding acquisition by public

---

[4] Of course, this does not only apply to agile development but this seems to be where this problem is most common.

bodies who are often required to base their contracts on competitive bidding and pre-defined requirements. Both requirements are difficult to satisfy with agile development.

Method engineering. In the 1990s, a multitude of different development methods was published, in particular in the context of object-oriented development which became very popular at the time. This led to the creation of *method engineering* as an approach to build new development methods and processes from components of existing methods,. The new method may then be applied in a certain context such as a new technology, or a specific project [8]. This, of course, requires that the methods are described in a modular fashion, such that the modules can be combined as needed in a new context, as for example used for tailoring in the V-Model XT. While the term "method engineering" is no longer in fashion, the underlying task remains important and today is usually discussed under the name of "hybrid approaches".

4.5 Process Tailoring

Once the process to be used has been selected, it usually has to be adapted to the specific circumstances of the task, project or team concerned. This adaptation of a general process (description) to a specific instance or group of instances is called tailoring (see Def. 1.28) and may involve deleting parts of the process definition that are not relevant in the current context, modifying parts that do not fit, or adding to it, for example by defining how to perform a certain task which is not usually relevant and therefore not part of the standard process.

Tailoring does not only apply to plan-driven development but also to agile development, even though in agile development it rarely is called by that name. Nevertheless, a "self-organising team" that decides how to adapt Scrum to its specific project is tailoring standard Scrum.

4.5.1 Overview of Process Tailoring

Practical implementation of tailoring involves the following major challenges:

- Tailoring should lead to the "best process" for the specific instance(s), which is not always an obvious choice. Identifying which process components may be left out without loss, which ones need to be adapted, and what needs to be added is a challenging task.
- While adapting the process, tailoring should at the same time respect the core of the process, ensuring that the process is not tailored "beyond recognition". This implies that this core of the process must be defined in some way, without being too restrictive. Depending on context, this core may be defined by some external regulatory standard that has to be satisfied.

- Tailoring should conserve the consistency of the process model, ensuring that no components are deleted that are referred to elsewhere in the process, and that relevant cross-references are added as needed. For example, if a new product is added, then some activity is needed that will produce this product, and some role will need to be responsible for it.
- When the original standard process is modified, the tailored process usually needs to be adapted as well. This is for example relevant if a industry standard process definition is used as the starting point for tailoring, and a new version of this industry standard is published. Ideally, one would want to re-use the same tailoring as far as possible, rather than re-do the tailoring from scratch.

To address at least some of these challenges, organisations often define a tailoring guideline defining limits on what may be adapted in tailoring:

Definition 4.9 (Tailoring guideline). *Instructions that enable an organization to adapt standard processes appropriately to meet specific needs.*
(ISO 33001:2015, SEVOCAB)

Tailoring and the degree of obligation of the standard process. Depending on context, such tailoring guidelines may be very restrictive, as is typically the case in a regulated environment (e.g. banking, pharmacy) where the organisation may later have to prove that they used the "correct" process. In an agile context, on the other side, tailoring guidelines may not explicitly be defined at all, implicitly stating that any tailoring that the team agrees on is allowed.

An important aspect to consider in tailoring therefore is the degree of obligation (such as required, recommended or suggested) of the original standard process. In particular, this affects the documentation of the tailoring performed, since any modification of a required or recommended standard process will probably need to be documented in order to be traceable.

Documenting the tailoring performed. Depending on the the formality of the process description, the tailoring performed may need to be documented appropriately. If the process itself is documented informally, there is little chance to document the tailoring formally, beyond noting in (structured) natural language who changed what, when and why. While the rationale for performing certain tailoring may sometimes be quite obvious ("we left out database modelling because we do not have a database"), this is not always the case, and if traceability of the process used in needed, then this rationale must be documented as well. Even if traceability is not required from the outside, it will be very helpful once the standard process is changed and the question arises what effect that has on the tailored process.

One approach to document the changes performed by tailoring is to use an extension model, i.e. to leave the original standard process unchanged but add a model explicitly defining the tailoring performed. This is the approach taken for tailoring the V-Model XT and has the advantage that, once a new version of the V-Model XT is released, the extension model can be re-used and only needs to be adapted in those cases where the tailoring is genuinely affected by the new version.

Levels of tailoring. If an general industry standard process such as RUP or V-Model XT is used, then multiple levels of tailoring may be adequate, such as tailoring the industry standard process to become an organisational standard process, which in turn is tailored to become a project or team process, as shown in Sect. 1.4.5.2, in particular Fig. 1.6. A different way to view these two levels of tailoring is their representation in the process cube as shown in Fig. 4.3.

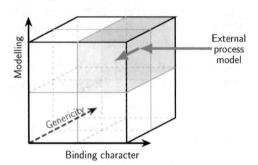

Fig. 4.3 Process tailoring represented in the process cube

Steps needed for tailoring. Tailoring itself may be seen as a process, including a number of process steps needed. First of all, tailoring must be prepared, by defining tailoring guidelines that define how to perform tailoring, and what kind of tailoring is allowed or supported.

Next, performing tailoring itself for a certain project may be split into the following steps [33]:

1. Evaluate project goals and environment
2. Assess challenges
3. Determine tailoring strategies for the various process elements
4. Tailor software process (including different forms of checking the tailored process)

4.5.2 Tailoring Strategies

Different strategies may be used to perform tailoring. Probably the best-known and certainly easiest strategy is the interpretation of tailoring as "cutting off" those parts of the process that are not needed in the certain context, which may refer to individual parts of a process component such as a product, or an entire component, in this case deleting the entire product. This is mainly adequate if the process model used as a starting point is fairly extensive and covers all or most aspects needed in the tailored process.

However, this is not the only form of tailoring needed, and adding of parts of the process definition may be needed if important non-standard tasks are relevant for the work. This for example often applies to agile processes where the standard process does not provide much detail, which will then have to be filled in by each project individually (whether explicitly documented or not).

Finally, tailoring a process may involve the modification of some part of the process, by redefining an existing component, such as renaming a role as a very simple example, or replacing some (part of a) component, in this case replacing the role with a similar role.

In practice, tailoring will often be performed as a mix of these different strategies listed, with different emphasis depending on how generic and how complete the standard model is.

4.5.3 Tailoring Criteria

Whether explicitly defined in the form of tailoring guidelines or implicitly used, there are many different criteria that affect what tailoring is performed or is allowed to be performed in a specific context. Kalus and Kuhrmann in [17] collected 49 different tailoring criteria via a systematic literature review, grouping these criteria as follows:

- *Team*: criteria such as the team size, its distribution (all in one room or on different continents, to name the extremes), and the knowledge domain and processes will of course affect the tailoring of a standard process.
- *Internal environment*: this group includes criteria such as the project duration and type, as well as availability of and support by management, and tool infrastructure.
- *External environment* includes criteria such as number, availability and background of stakeholders, and the type of contract.
- *Objectives* refers to the tailoring criteria that are based on the objectives of the development effort, such as the domain and complexity of the system to be developed, and the relevance of safety and security.

Of course, no one will apply all 49 criteria for tailoring, but this list gives an impression of the aspects to consider for the tailoring of a process.

To some extent, process tailoring can be automated based on such criteria. For example, the *V-Model XT Assistant* allows the user, typically the project manager, to tailor the model based on a set of pre-defined criteria, starting with the project type and adding properties such as the importance of safety and security, and the inclusion of off-the-shelf products. Once this information has been entered, the initial tailoring of the model is performed automatically. After that, more specific tailoring may be performed manually.

4.6 Process Deployment

Process deployment can be considered as possibly the most important task in process management, since this is the step of moving from a process definition, essentially a piece of paper, to changing the way work is actually performed in an organisation. This task, sometimes called the last-mile problem in process management, is a challenging task and will be covered in more detail in the current section.

4.6.1 Challenges in Process Deployment

In spite of its importance, process deployment is a commonly underestimated task, and many organisations expect that once a new set of processes has been developed and published, they have completed their work (cf. Fig. 4.4) while actually, the real work usually only then starts.

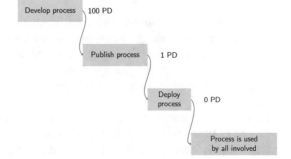

Fig. 4.4 Process deployment as it is often tried but never works

Process deployment in the process cube. Process deployment is concerned with turning a prescriptive process model into an actually performed process. In the process cube, this can be represented as shown in Fig. 4.5.

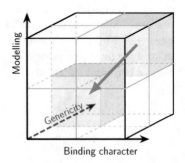

Fig. 4.5 Process deployment in the process cube

Typical challenges. One of the main challenges in process deployment is that many people are hesitant to work according to a given set of rules set by someone else, in particular if it involves extra effort and they do not themselves get any benefit from this extra effort, at least not in the short term. For example, the main benefit of documenting software will be gained in maintenance, which at the time of development seems are long way away, and may not even be done by the same people.

There are a number of common challenges to software process deployment, for example:

- Inertia: "I'll do it as soon as I have time"
- Resistance: "this is how we always did it"
- Cost: "if we use the new process now, it will be more expensive since we have to re-learn"

To some extent, the relevance of these challenges is also a question of national or organisational culture. To look at the extreme cases: in some cultures, rules set by the organisation and its management will be accepted more or less without questioning, even if they obviously are not useful. In other cultures, the first reaction to any such rules will be to ignore or resist them, independent of their actual content. As so often, the ideal solution lies somewhere in between, but changing an organisational or even national culture is very difficult at best.

In the following, we will discuss a number of methods and models that help to overcome these challenges.

4.6.2 State–Enable–Verify–Reward.

Four basic steps can be identified that are necessary to deploy any processes (or process changes) in an organisation:

- *State expectations clearly*: if members of the organisation are expected to work to certain processes, this must be stated very clearly (by management or, in a self-organising team, by the team itself). Furthermore, it is important to explain *why* this change is introduced so that process performers do not only see it as another bureaucratic burden. If the expectations are not clear, there is little chance that it will be fulfilled.
- *Enable implementation*: once everybody knows what they are expected to do, they must be enabled to do so. This involves providing the necessary resources (time, tools etc.) and appropriate training so that they know how to do.
- *Verify implementation*: even when everybody knows what to do, how to do it, and has the necessary resources, there still remains the natural tendency to continue working as before. Most changes involve additional effort at first, even if they make work easier in the long-term. To ensure that not just a few willing team members comply to the new way of working but all or at least the large majority, one additionally needs to verify that this is done, by implementing suitable quality assurance checks (cf. Sect. 4.7).

- *Reward*: of course, knowing who follows the new rules and who does not in itself does not help as long as there is no adequate reaction. This does not necessarily require a financial reward but following the defined process needs to be visibly appreciated. Similarly, there must be a reaction to not doing so. If management plays non-conformance down and does not react on it, it sends (deliberately or not) a clear signal that conformance is not important, and employees will act accordingly.

These steps are independent of the specific process or change to be deployed. Readers that know CMMI or SPICE may recognize them as a (much) simplified version of the generic practices included in those models (see Chap. 5.5 for more information on generic practices). Extended versions of this list of steps can be found in the process management check-list in Table B.3 in the appendix, or in the *process deployment checklist* in [20, App. B].

> **Case Study 4.4. (CS AutoSystems)** As described in Case Study 4.1, the development life cycle model was defined by a group of developers. It was then agreed by the team that this model is to be used for all projects, i.e. the step *state expectations clearly* was performed by the development team itself. The configuration management tool Git was selected and installed to support the work, and a half-day workshop was performed so that all developers knew the life cycle model and the expected use of Git.
>
> Since the team itself has decided to use this life cycle model, verification of the implementation of this model is essentially done via social control within the team and any developer who does not follow the agreed process is told off by his or her colleagues. Additionally, the quality manager performs internal audits as part of the ISO 9001 quality management systems, but these audits are fairly superficial and only performed once per year.

4.6.3 Change Management

Change management is the discipline concerned with managing changes within an organisation, and therefore has a large overlap with process deployment which manages the change of deploying processes within organisations.

Different meanings of the term "change management". Note that the term change management can mean very different things in different contexts, since there are very different things that one might want to change in a managed way:

- Change of requirements, which is dealt with as part of requirements management.
- Change of work products within a project: this form of change management is part of configuration management and tries to keep changes to individual work

products or sets of work products (baselines) under control, e.g. using versioning. This may be necessary as a consequence of a change to requirements.

- Change of an organisation due to the introduction of a new or modification of an existing IT system: this form of change management involves tasks such as training and roll-out, but also more technical tasks such as installing the new system and keeping the changes to the work products and their versions under control. This form of change management is for example addressed by the process "Change Management" in ITIL.
- Change of organisation due to process modification or improvement: this is the form of change management relevant in the context of process deployment and will be discussed in more detail in the remainder of this section.

Big bang vs. phased or iterative deployment. In software development, we have learned by experience that in most cases it is more effective and efficient to work iteratively, in order to get fast feedback and to put results into production early on. The same is true in change management: changes and improvements should not be planned and implemented over a long period of time, and then rolled out in a big bang, but implemented in short increments, for example using Scrum as described in the Case Study 5.1.

Closely related, changes should start from existing best practices, identifying them and deploying them across the entire organisation, and build on them rather than trying to reinvent processes from scratch. Even assuming that the newly invented processes are very good, process performers will not easily accept them.

The Pickerill triangle. A common mistake in change management it for management to try and delegate the responsibility for change to a staff function such as the EPG (or quality management or ...), rather than taking on that responsibility themselves. However, the process performers in general will focus on what management expects from them, rather what the EPG expects from them, even if it has the nominal support of management. Management therefore personally needs to set appropriate priorities in day-to-day work, actively communicating the changes and asking process performers about their implementation, and acting on the replies. Otherwise, process performers will focus on those issues management asks about and consider everything else low priority.

The main role of the EPG therefore should not be to try and enforce a change (which they in general cannot) but to support the process performers in implementing the management's expectations.

Moore's revised technology adoption life cycle. Although this life cycle was originally created to describe the adoption of new technology, it also applies to the deployment of processes and will here be presented in this context. This life cycle looks at the different groups of users that adopt a new or revised process, their motivation and how long it takes for them to do so. This has important implications on what to do in order to deploy a process within these different groups.

Moore's life cycle distinguishes the following groups of users of a new process:

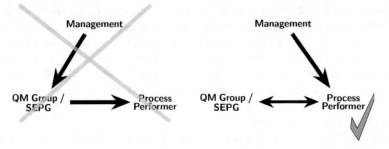

Fig. 4.6 The Pickerill triangle (based on [25])

- *Innovators* are the first to accept any new way of working, always keen to try out new things. To convince them to use any new or modified process, it is important to ensure (and convince them) that it really is an innovative and modern approach. The difficulty is that innovators are fairly easy to convince to use a new process, but they are also easy to lose as soon as the next innovative process becomes available. From a process deployment perspective, this will be the main challenge for this group.
- *Early adopters* are not quite as eager to try out any new process, but once there is positive feedback from the innovators, they will also be very willing to try out this new way of working.
- *Early majority* describes the group of process performers that do not rush to try out any new approach, but that are open to take up any such approach once there is genuine positive feedback and a clear statement from management that this is the way to go.
  In many cases, this is where the real challenge starts, as the larger gap in the life cycle between early adopters and early majority shows. This gap is called the *chasm* by Moore, leading to the title of book "Crossing the Chasm" [21]. The chasm represents the insight that it is considerably more difficult to reach the early majority, since this group needs to be genuinely convinced that the new process is better than the old one.
- *Late majority* refers to the process performers which are rather reluctant to use any new process but prefer to continue working "like we always did". This is where the State–Enable–Verify–Reward paradigm becomes important: the late majority will need a clear statement from management in order to look seriously into the new process, and will be rather critical whether it really is better than the old one and whether the appropriate resources and support are available. Even then, they may need several reminders (via quality assurance) before they really move to the new process.
- *Laggards*, finally, are almost impossible to convince and will need a certain amount of pressure in order to move to the new process and leave the established way of working. As it was put be the CEO of an IT company that the author was involved with when some important changes to the project management processes were announced at a large meeting with all company employees:

"You are free to continue working in any way you wand or are used to"—getting the members of the process management group frightened, but then he continued "...but not in this company".

It is easy to be very critical about the early and in particular the late majority because they are so reluctant to take on any new way of working and thus make life so difficult for the people responsible for process deployment. While this criticism may be adequate for laggards, it is important to understand that early and late majority have an important role to play in process deployment: Since not every claimed process improvement does indeed constitute an improvement, it is important to validate any process changes. It is the role of the early and late majority to challenge this assumption and validate the improvement before it is widely used, and process management groups should support this validation and listen to it rather than trying to ignore it and introduce process changes solely based on pressure on the process performers.

In (national or organisational) cultures where this does not usually happen and process changes are implemented because management says so, experience shows that there is a high risk that claimed improvements are indeed not as good as they seem, or might at least be implemented in a better way, but are implemented as planned anyway.

Change curve. A common model to describe how the acceptance and (visible) benefits of major changes vary over time is the change curve shown in Fig. 4.7, also known as the "Valley of Despair". According to this model, major organisational or technological changes typically go through the following phases which have a certain similarity to Moore's model above:

- *Excitement* describes the initial phase when mainly the benefits of the change are seen, when innovators and then early adopters use it and are excited about it.
- *Disillusion* starts when users experience the limitations and problems of the change: not all existing problems are solved, but some new ones arise. Tools and other support are not (yet) available. The benefits of the new approach take time to materialise, and it takes time and effort just to learn to use the new solution.
- *Despair* is the result when acceptance and visible benefits reach their low points. This is when management needs to take the difficult decision whether they believe that this the "normal" disillusionment one has to go through before a change becomes successful and benefits can be reached, or whether this shows that the change is not as good as expected and should be rolled back.
  In Moore's model above, this is the "chasm" going from the early adopters to the early majority.
- *Benefits* is of course the phase one eventually wants to reach. If the change indeed is an improvement (in whatever way may be relevant), and the change was not interrupted in the valley of despair, the benefits of the change can now be realised, and a higher level has been achieved compared to before the change.

Of course, at the end the next change may be just around the corner, and the change curve may re-start from the beginning.

Some organisations do not have the stamina to go through the valley of despair but always stop the change there. This leads to frustration in the work force and a high risk that for future similar changes, everybody will follow the "bend and wait" principle, bending back while a change is in progress and waiting for it to go away.

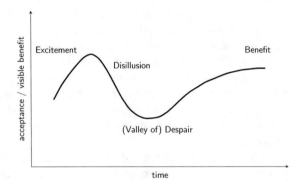

Fig. 4.7 Change curve

Kruse's eight rules for total gridlock in the organisation. Peter Kruse, change consultant and professor of organisational psychology, gave some sarcastic advice on managing change by defining a set of "rules for total gridlock in the organisation". Based on personal experience, it is amazing to see how many organisations seem to apply these rules shown in Fig. 4.8, in particular the last two.[5] In particular

1. *Alternate total control with total freedom*: management should either keep out completely, along the lines "Guys, you will do it," or have everything under control.
2. *Discuss change only at the informal level*: discussions about the goals and content of possible change should be consistently held only at the informal level.
3. *Maximize the number of new activities*: ensure constant work overload.
4. *Competition and survival of the fittest*: there should always be intense competition.
5. *Always find the guilty one*: there should always be a persistent and unrelenting quest to find the person responsible for the problems.
6. *Do not question existing rules*: there should be under no circumstances any public discussion about the sense and nonsense of existing rules.
7. *Fast formal decision making followed by questioning on the informal level*: decisions should reach a consensus as fast as possible on the formal level, and then be extensively questioned on the casual level.
8. *Maximize decision-making speed and minimize implementation abilities*: the rate of change on the decision-making level should always be greater than on the implementation level.

Fig. 4.8 Kruse's "eight rules for total gridlock in the organisation"

---

[5] The original rules are available as a video under https://www.youtube.com/watch?v= ZAWCWz1QPL4. The list in this figure is based on the transcript and translation available from http://www.allaboutlean.com/eight-rules-peter-kruse/.

the last rule can be seen applied quite often when organisations keep changing direction, for example because, whenever they reach the bottom of the change curve, they give up rather than waiting for the change to start taking effect. Process performers then "learn" that it is best to ignore such changes because they will not last anyway, described by Kruse as the "bend-and-wait" strategy.

4.7 Quality Assurance

Quality assurance (QA) is concerned with providing confidence that quality requirements are satisfied. QA may be performed on different objects, mainly the products and services that are created by the software processes, and the processes themselves, the main task in this context. There is a large variety of process QA activities, the most important ones are process audits (which will be introduced in Def. 5.3) and assessments (see Def. 5.2).

There are two main goal of process QA: first, the goal is to ensure that the process achieves its goals, delivering high-quality results (products and services) on time and in budget, and does so consistently and reliably. Secondly, but eventually supporting the same goal, process QA tries to ensure that the process is performed according to its definition, starting as the "verify" step in the state–enable–verify–reward approach of process deployment, and continuing as a permanent task, though usually with a lower coverage.

This checking of process conformance is needed on several different levels, as can be seen in the process cube in Fig. 4.9. The main purpose of process conformance checking is to ensure that the different components of the process cube are consistent, in particular that the left-hand side (the "process-as-is") conforms to the right-hand side (the "process-to-be"): the performed process-as-is instance is expected to conform to the process-to-be model for this instance (arrow 1), as defined in the project plan, project manual or similar. Possibly, no such project plan, project manual or similar exists but the process instance is expected to conform to a general process model (arrow 2). Looking at processes with a large number of instances such as incident management, QA will usually not investigate the individual instances but the general process performance across all incidents (arrow 3).

Once a non-conformance has been identified, it needs to be resolved, usually by adapting the performed process. However, this is not always the case: non-compliances may point to problems in the process rather than developers just not doing their job, and occasionally the better solution to correct a non-conformance therefore is to adapt the defined process.

Apart from this main goal of ensuring conformance, process QA is also responsible for assuring other process quality characteristics, as e.g. defined in the process quality model *Gokyo Ri* (see Sect. 6.5). As indicated above, assuring quality is relevant on both the level of the individual instance or project, and the level of the overall organisation, aggregating and evaluating the results of QA on the level of individual instances. This is where the step from quality assurance to quality man-

Fig. 4.9 Process conformance

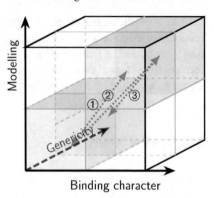

agement and improvement becomes particularly important, learning from what went wrong in one project or team to improve this topic across the entire organisation, see Sect. 5.4.

As explained e.g. in [4], the way QA (or, to be precise, software quality assurance SQA) should be performed depends a lot on the current status or maturity of the organisation. In an organisation with rather weak processes, SQA should concentrate on "policing" processes in order to introduce the necessary process discipline. Once this process discipline is instilled in the organisation, the task of SQA should move to collecting and analysing process data for improvement, and conformance checking takes the form of periodic random checks.

Stage containment. An approach to improve the quality of products and processes, and in particular to reduce the cost of quality defects, is the integration of stage containment[6] in the definition of the software development life cycle.

Stage containment starts from the ideal that all defects should be found within the stage in which they were caused. For each defect found, no matter whether during review, test, operation, or other, the stage when this defect was introduced is identified and documented, together with the stage when it was found. Presenting these data in a matrix then shows how close one has come to the ideal—in that case all non-zero entries would lie in the diagonal of the matrix. The further away any entry in the matrix lies from the diagonal, the more expensive it will typically be to correct it. This matrix representation will then help to identify those stages in the life cycle where many defects where introduced but only found (much) later, i.e. which stages cause high repair cost and should be improved.

A difficulty with this approach is that it is not always easy to identify the stage that caused the defect. However, in general this can be identified by looking at the results that need to be corrected in order to correct the defect, and when they were created.

---

[6] Stage containment is better known as *phase* containment, but that term is not quite correct according to definitions 1.18 and 1.19.

4.8 IT Governance and Process Governance

So far, we have mainly talked about the software (development) life cycles themselves. The current section moves the focus on how to embed these processes into the overall organisation, and how to ensure that these processes support the overall objectives of the organisation. This leads us to the topic of IT governance or, somewhat more general, of (corporate) governance which has the objective to clearly define in which direction an organisation is to go, and to ensure that this direction is indeed taken.

The growing importance of governance, and therefore also of IT governance, was triggered by two major issues: on the one hand, it is a tool for senior management to know and influence what is really happening in a large organisation, as opposed to what middle management tells them. On the other hand, there is a need from society and governments to prevent large-scale fraud and mitigate major risks in large organisations, which after some scandals led to the US-American Sarbanes-Oxley Act (SOX) and similar legislation in many other countries, requiring the affected companies—among other requirements—to introduce strict governance of all aspects that influence the financial statements of the company, and to set up risk management systems. Both requirements of course have major effects on the IT and the IT processes of the companies.

As a result of the growing importance of IT governance, a number of relevant standards have recently been published, including in particular ISO 21505:2017 covering governance of projects, programmes and portfolios, and ISO/IEC 38500: 2008 on IT governance.

4.8.1 Basic Concepts

First of all, we need to define the terms governance and IT governance:

Definition 4.10 (Governance). *Governance ensures that stakeholder needs, conditions and options are evaluated to determine balanced, agreed-on enterprise objectives to be achieved; setting direction through prioritisation and decision making; and monitoring performance and compliance against agreed-on direction and objectives. (COBIT 5 [16, Glossary])*

An important tool to implement governance in an organisation is the *control* (see Def. 3.16). Since individual controls do not typically get very far, they are usually combined into an internal control system. For example, an organisation might combine the definition of a process with the assignment of the individuals to the relevant process roles, and include checks that the process is performed correctly as the third control.

IT governance is the part of governance that applies these concepts to the IT of an organisation, and aims to ensure that IT supports the overall working of the organisation:

Definition 4.11 (IT governance). *System by which the current and future use of IT is directed and controlled. (ISO/IEC 38500:2008)*[7]

A governance view that ensures that information and related technology support and enable the enterprise strategy and the achievement of enterprise objectives. It also includes the functional governance of IT, i.e., ensuring that IT capabilities are provided efficiently and effectively. (COBIT 5 [16, Glossary])[8]

The standard model used for IT governance is COBIT[9] (currently in version 5, see [16]), published by the *Information Systems Audit and Control Association* (ISACA). The first version of COBIT was published in 1996 as a tool for IT auditors but now COBIT has grown into a model for governing the use of IT as an integrated part of corporate governance.

Another model used for "corporate governance of information technology" is described by ISO/IEC 38500:2008. As shown in [16, Appendix E], implementation of this standard can be supported by using COBIT v5. However, in the following we will focus on the use of COBIT for IT governance, since this model is far more widely known and used.

The third level of governance relevant in this context is process governance, which applies the same concepts to processes.[10]

Definition 4.12 (Process governance). *A governance view that ensures that processes support and enable the enterprise strategy and the achievement of enterprise objectives. It also includes the functional governance of processes, i.e., ensuring that processes are performed efficiently and effectively.*

Closely related to (IT) governance and sometimes confused with it is (IT) compliance:

Definition 4.13 (Compliance). *A general concept of conforming to a rule, standard, law, or requirement such that the assessment of compliance results in a binomial result stated as "compliant" or "noncompliant" (PMBOK® Guide)*

Rules etc. where compliance may be relevant can be grouped as follows:

- legal regulations and contracts, referring e.g. to safety, privacy, or financial regulations
- industry standards and requirements, e.g. including ISO and similar standards
- internal standards and requirements, e.g. a software process model defined to be mandatory within the organisation

---

[7] In ISO/IEC 38500:2008, this is the definition of "governance of IT".

[8] In COBIT 5, this is the definition of "Governance of Enterprise IT".

[9] COBIT originally was defined as an acronym for *Control Objectives for Information and related Technology* but since COBIT has moved beyond being a collection of control objectives, this full title is no longer used in COBIT 5.

[10] Neither ISO/IEC 38500:2008 nor [16] include a definition of process governance. However, since this is the most important aspect of governance in this context, we adapt the above definition of IT governance to processes.

It is the task of governance and (executive) management to define the rules etc. for which conformance is expected within an organisation. In theory, legal regulations should of course always be binding but practice shows that this is not always the case. Figure 4.10 shows an overview of typical sources of standards relevant for compliance.

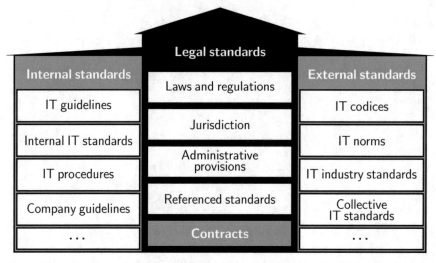

Fig. 4.10 The "house of IT-compliance" (based on [18]); original version ©Klotz, adapted and printed by permission

Governance–Compliance–Risk (GCR). A third topic that is often combined with governance and compliance is risk, leading to the commonly used term Governance–Compliance–Risk (GCR). There are a number of requirements on the processes that result from these three topics and usually overlap considerably.

Applying an adequate level of GCR. While it is obviously important to govern the IT of an organisation including its processes, to ensure compliance, and to manage risks, it is also very important not to overdo it: there is a considerable risk that IT governance leads to IT bureaucracy, stifling innovation and creativity by introducing rules, guidelines and processes that—focusing only on the risks involved—also reduce the opportunities as well as the motivation of the employees involved. It therefore is equally important not to confuse IT governance with strict compliance to rules such as process definitions, but to focus on the objectives one tries to achieve using IT governance, such as effectiveness and efficiency as well as risk mitigation. If that is kept in mind, IT governance supports rather than prevents the use of agile development approaches, as discussed in more detail in Sect. 4.8.4 below.

Case Study 4.5. (CS Insurance InfoSys) Some years ago, a small team was working on the creation and deployment of a set of software process descriptions to be used in the development projects. Since IT security started to become an important topic, there was also a team, installed by the board of CS Insurance InfoSys, that was responsible for ensuring the security of the applications developed and run, and therefore also had defined a set of process descriptions to be implemented by the development and operations group.

The process team realised that there was a certain overlap between their process documents and those created by the IT security team, and on closer analysis, that these documents were actually in some cases inconsistent. Their process definitions did not always handle security issues adequately, while the IT security documents required that some security questions be handled in a certain way which was inappropriate from the development process point of view.

To resolve these inconsistencies, the process team contacted the IT security team and started discussion about how to align both sets of process documentation. However, the IT security team argued that *they* had been assigned the task of defining standards to ensure IT security by the board, and the development teams had to adhere to these standards. Therefore, they were not willing to adapt their process descriptions.

It turned out that many projects already considered these IT security standards unhelpful and therefore ignored them, and eventually the process team decided to do the same. Their refusal to cooperate and search for a joint solution led to the situation that the IT security team was ignored completely, and IT security was only implemented as each project team saw fit.

Some comments on this case study: even though in this case the IT security team could be considered the "bad guys", while the process team were the "good guys", process teams should always ensure that they do not end up in the same situation by insisting on their process standards even if these are not helpful or at least not accepted by process users. Of course, from a governance and compliance point of view, just ignoring company standards is unacceptable, but fortunately, this is still what will happen if the standards are not helpful. If, via management pressure, even those standards are deployed, it will be a very short-sighted success for the process (or IT security, or ...) team. Note that the likelihood of developers following such standards even if they consider them as hindering their work will depend considerably on the company culture, the branch of industry, and the national culture involved. There are countries, industry branches and companies where even helpful standards stand a good chance of being ignored, and there are others where internal standards and procedures will be implemented more or less without thinking.

Compliance with multiple reference models (multi-model compliance). In many cases, an organisations needs to be compliant not with just one model, but with multiple models at the same time, for example in order to get certain certifications or to satisfy legal or other regulatory requirements. In this case, it is important that the resulting process should not just add the requirements from multiple models and thus become too complex or even inconsistent.

A better way to achieve multi-model compliance is to define a single set of processes in such a way that both reference models are satisfied. The process performers then do not have to know the reference models but "only" their process, and it is the responsibility of the process engineers to ensure that these process definitions satisfy the required reference models. To do so, it will often be useful to set up a compliance mapping which lists the requirements from the different reference models, and documents how these requirements are satisfied by the defined processes (or elsewhere, as the case may be).

Example 4.2. A software development company had decided to work according to CMMI-DEV, but at the same time needed to preserve its ISO 9001-certification. To achieve both, two separate process manuals were created, one defining the relevant processes from a CMMI point of view, and one defining the same processes from the ISO 9001 point of view. The development teams were thus expected to adhere to two separate sets of processes at the same time, which at best described the same processes differently, and occasionally even were inconsistent. The obvious result was that the development teams just ignored at least one of the process manuals, often both.

Case Study 4.6. (CS Insurance InfoSys) A major challenge for the company was the multitude of different regulations from different sources that it needed to adhere to, often due to legislation addressing large financial institutions.

Different organisational units within the company involved with compliance therefore set up check lists of controls that each development project had to implement, adding up to many hundreds of controls that each project needed to check. However, it usually turned out the about two thirds of these controls were not relevant for any given project, but each project had to analyse all controls first to identify which ones were not relevant. Furthermore, there were often several very similar but not identical controls from different sources that needed to be implemented. An additional problem was that the sources of the different controls were not well documented, and it became very difficult to keep them up-to-date once the underlying (internal or external) regulations were changed.

To address these problems and reduce the effort involved for the projects, it was therefore agreed to set up a systematic catalogue of controls, explicitly documenting the source of each control and the conditions under which it was applicable. It turned out that—different from what was expected—the total number of controls could not be reduced this way even though some controls from different sources could be combined since they essentially required the same thing. However, this systematic analysis showed that some controls had not been included properly when regulations had changed, and these controls had to be added to the catalogue.

However, projects were now able to quickly identify which controls that actually applied to them and which did not, which saved days or weeks of effort for each project. Additionally, the better documentation also helped to understand the control better, and define standard ways of implementing them which again reduced the effort involved considerably.

Overall, even though of course the projects typically still each had to implement several hundred controls, they could do so far more efficiently than in the past, and acceptance for the regulations within the company also improved considerably.

4.8.2 The COBIT Framework

In COBIT, processes are defined as an *enabler* that helps to realise effective governance. Other enablers defined in COBIT are "Principles, policies and frameworks", "Organisational Structures", "Culture, Ethics and Behaviour", "Information", "Services, Infrastructure and Applications", and "People, Skills and Competencies" [16, p. 27]. In this context, we will however focus on the enabler "Processes".

In order to govern an enterprise IT, in particular its processes and other enablers, COBIT contains a number of different mechanisms:

- Goals cascade
- Enabler dimensions
- Measurement of enabler dimensions
- Process reference model and process assessment model
- Internal control systems

Each of these mechanisms will be described briefly below.

One of the goals of COBIT is to provide a framework that is aligned to "other relevant standards and frameworks, such as ITIL, TOGAF and ISO standards" [16, p. 26]. While most of these other standards and frameworks only address certain parts of IT, COBIT and its process reference model (as shown in Fig. 4.12 below) provides an overall framework in which to position them, and includes information about how to map standards such as ISO/IEC 38500 or ITIL with COBIT.

COBIT goals cascade. COBIT puts particular value on a strong connection between company goals and strategy on the one hand, and processes and other enablers on the other hand. To achieve this, COBIT contains a goals cascade, see Fig. 4.11, where stakeholder drivers and stakeholder needs are broken down into so-called enabler goals, with (IT) processes as one of the main enablers. COBIT includes predefined lists of enterprise goals and IT-related goals, called *generic* enterprise / IT-related goals.

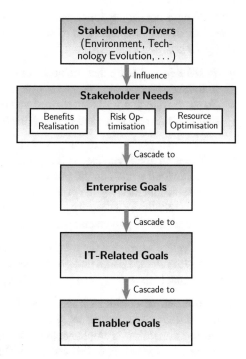

Fig. 4.11 COBIT goals cascade [16, Fig. 4]. COBIT 5 ©2012. ISACA. All rights reserved. Used by permission.

Example 4.3. Note that this example is special in that it describes how an organisation may use the goals cascade, rather than describing a real-world example of using it.

Assume that for some organisation, cost pressure is an important stakeholder driver which leads to the stakeholder need of optimising resources and their usage. This stakeholder need cascades to the enterprise goals

- 10. *Optimisation of service delivery costs*
- 12. *Optimisation of business process costs*

On the next level, these enterprise goals cascade to the IT-related goals, including only goals with a primary relationship to the enterprise goals above [16, Fig. 22]:

- 04. *Managed IT-related business risk*

- 05. *Realised benefits from IT-enabled investments and services portfolio*
- 06. *Transparency of IT costs, benefits and risk*
- 11. *Optimisation of IT assets, resources and capabilities*

COBIT enabler dimensions. For each enabler including processes, COBIT defines four dimensions that need to be addressed in order to govern the enabler, see [16, p. 69]:

- *Stakeholders:* Ensure that the needs of all internal and external stakeholders are addressed.
- *Goals:* Ensure that goals are defined and implemented. Process goals are further split into three categories, describing the quality of the processes:

  - "Intrinsic goals—Does the process have intrinsic quality? Is it accurate and in line with good practice? Is it compliant with internal and external rules?
  - Contextual goals—Is the process customised and adapted to the enterprise's specific situation? Is the process relevant, understandable, easy to apply?
  - Accessibility and security goals—The process remains confidential, when required, and is known and accessible to those who need it." [16, p. 69]

- *Life Cycle:* Ensure that the life cycle and its processes are managed adequately.
- *Good Practices:* Ensure that good practices are used, based on the process reference model (see below) that is defined as part of COBIT.

Measurement of enabler dimensions. For each of the four enabler dimensions described above, measurements need to be defined that provide feedback to what extent the dimension is implemented. This aspect is called *Enabler Performance Management* in COBIT. In this context, COBIT distinguishes *lag indicators* (also called *lagging* or *trailing* indicators) that refer to the dimensions "stakeholders" and "goals" and describe the actual outcomes of the enabler, and *lead indicators* that refer to the dimensions "life cycle" and "good practices" and describe how well it is currently governed and what actual outcomes of the enabler are expected in the future.

COBIT process reference model and process assessment model. A core aspect of IT governance is to evaluate or assess an organisation's IT processes regularly in order to identify weaknesses and improvement opportunities or needs.

In the previous version 4.1, COBIT defined a process maturity model as the basis for assessing IT processes and their maturity, using the structure of CMMI (see Sect. 5.5.3). In the current version COBIT 5, it was decided to follow the concepts introduced by ISO/IEC 15504 and define a process reference model (PRM) and a process assessment model (PAM) for that purpose instead (see Sect. 5.5.1). Figure 4.12 provides a top-level view of the COBIT PRM. It defines five groups of processes, called domains, for the governance and management of IT, where each domain consists of three to thirteen processes, including those mentioned in Example 4.3.

Fig. 4.12 Top level view of the COBIT process reference model (based on [16, Fig. 16]) COBIT 5 ©2012. ISACA. All rights reserved. Used by permission.

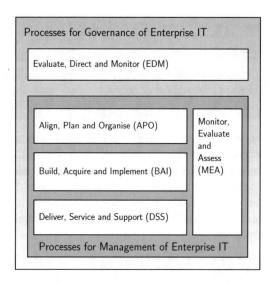

Based on this PRM, the COBIT PAM defines the criteria to be used for assessing the maturity of its processes (cf. Sect. 5.5.4).

Distinction between governance and management. One of the principles of CO-BIT 5 is to separate governance from management: governance is concerned with setting direction, based on stakeholder needs etc., and monitoring performance and compliance against this direction. Typically, this is the responsibility of the board of directors or some similar body. Management, on the other hand, is concerned with implementing the direction set by the governance body, and typically the responsibility of the executive management.

This distinction is reflected in the PRM shown in Fig. 4.12: the domain *Evaluate, Direct and Monitor* (EDM) is concerned with the governance processes, while the four other domains shown in Fig. 4.12 contain the management processes. These four domains are structured according to the Plan–Build–Run–Monitor structure as described in Sect. 3.1.2.

Example 4.4. (Continued from Example 4.3)
The IT-related goals can now be mapped to processes from the COBIT process reference model (see below). In this context, the last IT-related goal (11.) of the list is the most important one. It is mapped to the following processes (again only including processes with a primary relationship):

- EDM04 *Ensure Resource Optimisation*
- APO01 *Manage the IT Management Framework*
- APO03 *Manage Enterprise Architecture*

- APO04 *Manage Innovation*
- APO07 *Manage Human Resources*

In conclusion, the first priority in governing this specific organisation should be put on these five processes.

Internal control system. An internal control system is a systematic structure that brings together the various controls (cf. Def. 3.16) in order to achieve defined objectives. The COBIT process *MEA02 Monitor, evaluate and assess the system of internal control* describes the setup of such a system. Examples of controls that may form part of an internal control system are the definition of accountability and responsibility, use of the four-eye-principle, process reviews and audits, and automation of processes.

Example 4.5. (Continued from Example 4.4) To implement the five processes identified, the next step is to set up the relevant internal control system with appropriate controls. For this step, there are no pre-defined goals as for the higher levels in the goals cascade. Instead, the task now is to implement the selected processes based on the COBIT process reference model, including appropriate controls to achieve the identified goals.

COBIT helps with this task by providing, for each of the selected processes, detailed descriptions including practices with inputs and outputs (linking these practices to other processes and practices that generate the inputs or consume the outputs), responsibilities (using a RACI chart), and activities detailing the practice. For example, the selected process *EDM04 Ensure Resource Optimisation* is broken down into the practices

- EDM04.01 *Evaluate resource management.*
- EDM04.02 *Direct resource management.*
- EDM04.03 *Monitor resource management.*

Although this is still somewhat abstract, it provides a good starting point for identifying what exactly needs to be done.

4.8.3 Software Process Governance

The most important part of (IT) governance in the current context is of course the governance of software processes. This starts off with the definition of the process goals, as derived from the COBIT goals cascade (or some similar approach), as well as setting up an infrastructure to support these process goals.

Next, the relevant software processes need to be defined at an adequate level of detail where, depending on the process goals, the "adequate level of detail" may vary between leaving a lot of freedom for self-organising teams, and quite rigidly defining what needs to be done and how.

Once the processes are defined, the next step of process governance is to ensure that they are used, following the steps *state–enable–verify–reward* as introduced above.

This leads to the final step of software process governance, the continuous supervision of the processes to ensure that they continue to be used as expected, and to ensure their quality and improve them as adequate. This is often includes the use of a suitable system of metrics, e.g. based on the process quality model Gokyo Ri (as introduced in Sect. 6.5).

4.8.4 IT Governance and Agile Development

At first sight, IT governance requires a plan-driven approach, with detailed definitions of processes, which would be in conflict with agile development. However, looking back at Def. 4.11, one can see that the main focus of IT governance is to achieve the IT objectives, as e.g. derived from the stakeholder needs according to the COBIT goals cascade.

Depending on these objectives and stakeholder needs, IT governance may therefore not only *allow* but even require an agile approach to development, for example if a fast response to a changing environment is of high priority. In such a case, IT governance is not implemented by guidelines, process definitions and similar means, but by providing an environment supporting self-management of development teams, ensuring that these teams get the feedback from customers and other support they need to be successful.

Since in such an environment, agility may be an important objective of the entire company, not just within software development, the concept of *agile governance* has started to come into discussion [11].

4.8.5 Governance of IT Architecture

In Sect. 3.10, the difference between the architecture used within an individual development effort and an enterprise architecture was introduced. In this section, we will look at some aspects of the enterprise architecture and its relationship to IT governance. Enterprise architecture has a strong influence on the overall effectiveness and efficiency of an enterprise, and it is therefore an important task to ensure adequate governance of the enterprise architecture. A defined technology architecture will for example help to improve the cooperation between development and operation, helping to ensure that development activities are based on the technical infrastructure that will later be used to run the developed system.

The best-known framework for this purpose is TOGAF:

The Open Group Architecture Framework (TOGAF). TOGAF [32] is a framework that addresses the definition and use of enterprise architectures. It distinguishes four different types of (enterprise) architecture, namely business architecture, application architecture, data architecture, and technology architecture.

The *business architecture* describes the overall structure of the business and is often represented as a process landscape, such as the one shown in Fig. 2.5. The application describes the structure and interaction of the applications used in the enterprise. Similarly, the data data architecture describes the structure and interaction of the enterprise's major types and sources of data. Together, they form the *information systems architecture*. Finally, the technology architecture describes the different technology components and their interaction.

In order to define these different types of architecture, TOGAF includes the *Architecture Development Method* (ADM) as one of its main components, see Fig. 4.13.

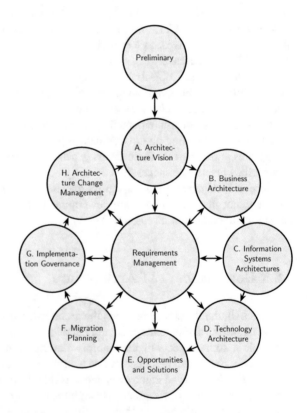

Fig. 4.13 The TOGAF Architecture Development Method (ADM) [32]. ©1999-2011, The Open Group, reprinted with permission.

Example 4.6. In order to ensure that the exchange of jointly used data between different applications is possible, a railway company decided to introduce an *enterprise data model* that defined the meaning and data types for the main objects used.

The company quickly identified several major challenges:

- The same object was used in multiple applications, under a different name and with different data types. For example, application A needed a certain attribute for the object which application B did not provide.
- Far more difficult to resolve were cases were the same object or attribute was used, but with a slightly different meaning. For example, one application assumed that the passenger was the person who travelled, while another application assumed that the passenger was the person who bought the ticket. Although in most cases, this amounts to the same person, there are some exceptions which made it very difficult to exchange passenger data between these two applications. One of the tasks of the enterprise data model was therefore to find an adequate solution for any such conflicts.
- A third challenge were the apparent synonyms which turned out to be quite different objects. A typical example here was the object "train", which depending on the application considered could mean very different things. For example, a train could be a physical object, consisting of a locomotive and a number of carriages, or it could mean a timetable object (the train going at 10:00 from A to B), etc.

Although the term "data architecture" was not used in this context, the aim of the enterprise data model was to define a data architecture. Since the individual projects initially had little direct benefit from supporting this activity (until they wanted to use data collected by some other application), it turned out to be rather difficult to ensure that projects did indeed use the data structures as defined by the enterprise data model. Its use was mainly for the benefit of the company, and as such that use was first of all a governance task for the company.

COBIT and enterprise architecture. COBIT contains similar requirements on the management of the enterprise architecture, defined in the process "APO03 Manage Enterprise Architecture", though of course on a much more abstract level. Similar to TOGAF, COBIT defines different architecture layers, namely business process, information, data, application and technology architecture layers. This overlap is no coincidence since the creators of COBIT explicitly aimed at aligning the model with other relevant models such as TOGAF.

4.9 Software Processes as a Form of Knowledge Management

Software processes involve the usage and creation of knowledge, and therefore many ideas and concepts from knowledge management can be usefully applied here. In this section presents, we will present some of these ideas and concepts. Closely related is the concept of the *experience factory* which will be introduced in Sect. 5.7.

4.9.1 Codification vs. Personalisation of Knowledge

Hansen et al. defined the following different knowledge management strategies depending on the type of knowledge to be managed [14]:

- *The codification strategy* puts the main emphasis on making tacit organisational knowledge explicit, for example by describing it in a process model.
- *The personalisation strategy* puts the emphasis on transferring knowledge directly between individuals, without making it explicit. Examples of this strategy are regular meetings between individuals with similar skills or roles to exchange experience, the use of peer programming, or setting up "yellow pages" of experts for different topics within an organisation.

In the context of software processes, both strategies can be useful. The codification strategy is mainly applicable for structured knowledge, such as how to deal with routine tasks, while the personalisation strategy is more applicable for creative, problem-solving tasks. Although not 100% true, one may say that as a trend, plan-driven development tends more towards the codification strategy, while agile development tends more towards the personalisation strategy (remember the first agile value in the agile manifesto: "Individuals and interactions over processes and tools").

4.9.2 Probst's Building Blocks of Knowledge Management

A common structure used to manage knowledge is described by the "building blocks of knowledge management" introduced by Gilbert J.B. Probst [26, 27], as shown in Fig. 4.14.

In the following, we give a summary of the meaning of these building blocks in the context of software process knowledge.

- *Knowledge goals* are to support development teams in their task to produce high-quality results efficiently. Similarly for IT service management processes, the knowledge goals are to efficiently provide a high-quality service to customers.
- *Knowledge identification* is concerned with identifying the knowledge needed for software processes, including both a high-level description of the process and

Fig. 4.14 Probst's building blocks of knowledge management (based on [26]). ©1998 Wiley, reprinted with permission.

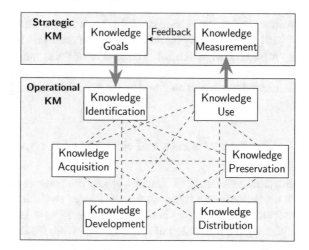

a more detailed level description of process steps, artefacts produced, and roles involved, as described in Sect. 2.1.

- *Knowledge acquisition:* one approach to get the needed knowledge as identified, an organisation may acquire it, for example by using a standard reference model such as RUP or Scrum for software development, or ITIL for IT service management.

  However, knowledge needed does not necessarily have to be acquired from the outside. In many cases, there are internal experts for many relevant topics, and the challenge is to ensure that these internal experts share their knowledge, for example contributing to the process descriptions or by advising other projects as needed. Davenport and Prusak in [10] describe three "currencies" or potential benefits that can convince employees to share their knowledge: reciprocity, repute and altruism. Each of these may work (within limits in the case of altruism), but needs to be actively managed in order to do so.

- *Knowledge development:* if needed knowledge does not exist yet, it needs to be developed, for example by setting up a process improvement initiative to find a solution to a certain process problem.

- *Knowledge distribution:* once knowledge has been developed, it needs to be distributed in order to be useful. Depending on the type of knowledge concerned, this should be done using the codification or the personalisation strategy.

- *Knowledge preservation* deals with the fact that knowledge tends to disappear if nothing is done about it, because people forget or leave the company, or the knowledge gets outdated. This of course also applies to process knowledge. To some extent, this will be resolved by documenting the processes, but additionally, activities like continuous training, regular review and revision of the processes, and quality assurance are needed.

- *Knowledge use* is the core of these activities, because only by using it (process) knowledge becomes relevant. To achieve this, the processes must be deployed as described in Sect. 4.6.

- *Knowledge measurement*, finally, leads back to strategic knowledge management and refers to applying measurement on processes including their quality, deployment and improvement. The results of these measurements then help to adapt the (process) knowledge goals, for example identifying that more knowledge is needed to support and implement agile development in large projects.

4.9.3 Armour's Laws of Software Process

According to Philip G. Armour in [3], the true product of software development is not the software itself but the *knowledge* contained in the software. As a result, software development should be considered as a knowledge acquisition activity, including the translation of this knowledge into the language of code.

Put differently, software processes are concerned with reducing ignorance, and depending on the "order of ignorance", different types of processes will be necessary.

- *The First Law of Software Process:* "Process only allows us to do things we already know how to do." [3, p. 11]

  - This implies that processes for new tasks or tasks that are not well understood can only be defined on a fairly superficial level. In the context of software processes, this explains why the main development processes are difficult or impossible to define in any detail, while other processes such as standard version management, or IT service management processes such as incident management, can be described in much more detail.

- *The Second Law of Software Process:* "We can only define software processes at two levels: too vague or too confining." [3, p. 13]

  - While this law is expressed in a "tongue-in-cheek" form, it actually points to the difficulty that process definitions need to address different levels of ignorance at the same time. For someone who basically knows how to do a certain task, a high-level definition will be "too vague" and not really helpful. He requires a detailed description to learn anything new, which however has to fit exactly to the problem at hand, since it will be "too confining" otherwise. At the same time, for someone who does not know yet how to do the same task, a high-level definition is exactly what is needed to start with.

- *The Third Law of Software Process:* "The very last type of knowledge to be considered as a candidate for implementation into an executable software system is the knowledge about how to implement knowledge into an executable software system." [3, p. 15]

  - This third law is rather difficult to understand (one might also say: not stated very clearly) but the concepts expressed are very convincing: there is a need in software development to distinguish between processes that address the application of knowledge, which includes the routine and repetitive work and can be defined in some detail, and processes that address the discovery of new knowledge, which includes the creative aspects of software development and cannot be defined in detail. This distinction is similar though not the same as the distinction between the codification strategy and the personalisation strategy as described above.

4.10 (Globally) Distributed Software Processes

A challenge that has been growing in importance for many years is the global distribution of software processes, both development and IT service processes. The main reason for such distribution of processes is the expected reduction in cost, even though there are many hidden costs involved and this cost reduction is not always achieved. Other reasons include the need for skilled resources that may not be locally available.

There are a number of challenges involved in globally distributed processes which need to be addressed. In general, the main challenge is communication [15], which is made difficult by a number of factors, starting with the fact that one can't just "walk down the hall" to discuss and resolve any problems. Lack of awareness of what other teams are doing as well as different cultures, languages (cf. Sect. 4.2.3), time zones, and sometimes technical challenges such as slow internet access additionally make communication difficult. Apart from communication, James D. Herbsleb in his survey paper [15] mentions the software architecture, requirements, environments and tools, and orchestrating global development as the main challenges making global software engineering difficult.

Splitting up the work for distribution. In order to distribute work between different teams, it needs to be split up in some way, independent of whether the different teams work in the same building or on different continents. However, if the teams are distributed globally, communication between them becomes far more difficult and therefore it is more important to reduce the dependencies between the teams, even though in general this is only possible to a limited extent.

Different forms to do so include splitting up the final product into separate components which are then developed by separate teams, or splitting up along the work flow, for example having one development team and one testing team. Another form of distribution that works quite well if the work to be done can be split into many small, independent tasks, as is often the case in maintenance or for incident management, is to consider the distributed groups as one large team, where team members work independently on different tasks from a common requirements management or ticket system.

The software processes used of course depend on the form of splitting work between locations selected: if the different teams work on separate components, they may use different processes as long as the interfaces between these components are clearly defined, as well as their schedules synchronised. Put differently, the teams may used different but cooperating processes. In this case, the different components should be reasonably large in order to reduce the synchronisation effort required [13].

If the work is split along the work-flow, it is important to have clearly defined interfaces between the different process steps, with a joint overall life cycle and high-level process, but again each team may work according to its own detailed processes. In either case, using the same processes across the different teams is more difficult to implement, but will allow more freedom to move work between different teams and locations. On the other hand, the different teams and locations usually each have their own separate history and background, which makes it difficult to implement the same processes.

Finally, in the third case of setting up the different teams as one large team, use of the same processes is of course necessary for successful cooperation.

Distributed processes and agile development. Agile development processes were originally designed for co-located teams. While this worked well for small teams such as individual Scrum teams, larger projects often had to be distributed geographically, in some cases globally, and many of the processes and techniques introduced for scaling agile development as described in Sect. 3.5.9 also address this geographical distribution [24, 31]. On the one hand, global distribution of work makes it far more difficult to implement the different communication mechanisms considered important in agile development. On the other hand, it may be argued that exactly this emphasis on communication makes agile development better suited to resolve the core challenge of inadequate communication in globally distributed development [24, p. 111].

4.11 Software Processes for Software Acquisition

While most software process descriptions look at the work done by the suppliers, the customers of course also need to do their part in order for a development effort to be successful. The most obvious reason for this is that the customer usually needs to define the requirements, whether in the form of an initial requirements document in plan- or requirements-driven development, or in the form of continuous feedback on the current results in agile development (or, probably most common, some mix between the two).

This is the reason why some models explicitly address the customer processes in the overall life cycle, for example the V-Model XT in the project type "customer project". Similarly, the *CMMI for Acquisition* (CMMI-ACQ), as described in Sect. 5.5.3.1, also addresses the same issue, but on the more abstract level of a maturity model rather than a process model. The main tasks addressed in these models, in addition to standard project management tasks like project initiation, include

- the identification of requirements

- the creation of call for proposals
- the selection of suppliers and setting up agreements or contracts with them, including the definition of the on-going cooperation and reporting
- continuous cooperation, for example providing feedback or making decisions within a reasonable time frame
- the monitoring of the project, in particular of the work of the supplier
- acceptance testing of the delivered result
- and eventually integrating the delivered product into the customer's own environment.

Defining the supplier processes. An important question in this context is whether or to what extent the customer should define the processes to be used by the supplier. On the one hand, requiring a supplier to use a process he is not used to will in most cases make the supplier less efficient, losing some of his strengths and know-how and thus resulting in higher costs and lower quality of the results. On the other hand, the processes used are to some extent reflected in the product and its architecture. Furthermore quality management standards, e.g. ISO 9001 and IATF 16949, as well as legal regulations in relevant industries, require the qualification first of direct suppliers but also down the supply chain, including their processes used. In these cases, organisations do not necessarily have to prescribe a certain process but to ensure that adequate processes are used.

Even if the supplier processes themselves are not defined by the customer organisation, it is of course important to agree on the process interfaces between the customer and the supplier, to ensure that cooperation and the different tasks described above can be performed effectively.

Further Reading

Change Management. There is a large amount of literature on change management and process deployment. Two classics well worth reading are Moore's "Crossing the Chasm" [21] that introduced the *technology adoption life cycle* discussed above, and Bridges' "Managing Transitions" [7].

IT governance and COBIT. The main reference on COBIT is [16] which is the core document of this model and describes its structure and basic concepts.

Agile governance. Reference [11] does provide an overview of the literature on agile governance, including but going beyond the relationship between governance and agile development. While it does not cover much detail of the topic itself, it contains a large overview of the relevant literature.

Knowledge management. A survey of the relationship between software processes and knowledge management can be found in [19].

Exercises

4.1. For the application S-Sec, stakeholders put strong emphasis on IT security, in particular the integrity of the data stored which should under no circumstances be modified without appropriate permissions and verification.

Following the approach defined by the COBIT goals cascade and using [16], identify the appropriate goals for the enabler "processes" in this context.

4.2. Summarise the main properties of the national culture you live in regarding software engineering. How does it differ from other national cultures?

4.3. Based on what you have learned about the company CS AutoSystems from the case study descriptions, suggest a high-level enterprise architecture consisting of the four architecture types as defined by TOGAF. What interaction is there between this enterprise architecture and the software processes used in CS AutoSystems?

References

1. S. Alexander. Process owner, process manager or process engineer. http://www.theitsmreview.com/2013/03/process/ (last access 2018-03-08), March 2013.
2. U. Andelfinger and R. Kneuper. Governance und Compliance von Anfang an wirksam umsetzen. In M. Knoll and S. Strahringer, editors, *IT-GRC-Management—Governance, Risk und Compliance*, Edition HMD, chapter 2, pages 25–36. Springer Vieweg, 2017.
3. P. G. Armour. *The Laws of Software Process. A New Model for the Production and Management of Software*. Auerbach Publications, 2003.
4. E. R. Baker. Which way, SQA? *IEEE Software*, pages 16–18, January/February 2001.
5. M. Bandor. Process and procedure definition: A primer. Presentation at SEPG 2007 conference, March 2007. Available online at https://resources.sei.cmu.edu/library/asset-view.cfm?assetID=21160 (last access 2018-03-08).
6. B. W. Boehm and R. Turner. *Balancing Agility and Discipline: A Guide for the Perplexed*. Addison-Wesley Professional, Aug. 2003.
7. W. Bridges. *Managing Transitions. Making the Most of Change*. Addison -Wesley Publishing Company, 1991.
8. S. Brinkkemper. Method engineering: Engineering of information systems development methods and tools. *Information and Software Technology*, 38:275–280, 1996.
9. R. Chapman, N. White, and J. Woodcock. What can agile methods bring to high-integrity software development? *Commun. ACM*, 60(10):38–41, Sept. 2017.
10. T. H. Davenport and L. Prusak. *Working Knowledge. How Organizations Manage What They Know*. Harvard Business Review Press, 1998.
11. A. J. H. de O. Luna, P. Kruchten, M. L. G. do E. Pedrosa, H. R. de Almeida Neto, and H. P. de Moura. State of the art of agile governance: A systematic review. *International Journal of Computer Science & Information Technology (IJCSIT)*, 6(5), October 2014.
12. M. Dumas, J. Mendling, M. La Rosa, and H. A. Reijers. *Fundamentals of Business Process Management*. Springer, 2013.
13. C. Ebert, M. Kuhrmann, and R. Prikladnicki. Global software engineering. An industry perspective. *IEEE Software*, 33(1):105–108, 2016.
14. M. T. Hansen, N. Nohria, and T. Tierney. What's your strategy for managing knowledge? *Harvard Business Review*, pages 106–116, March–April 1999.

15. J. D. Herbsleb. Global software engineering: The future of socio-technical coordination. In *2007 Future of Software Engineering*, FOSE '07, pages 188–198, Washington, DC, USA, 2007. IEEE Computer Society.
16. ISACA. *COBIT® 5. A Business Framework for the Governance and Management of Enterprise IT*, 2012.
17. G. Kalus and M. Kuhrmann. Criteria for software process tailoring—a systematic review. In *Proceedings of International Conference on Software & Systems Process (ICSSP)*, 2013.
18. M. Klotz. IT-Compliance: Begrifflichkeit und Grundlagen. SIMAT Arbeitspapiere, SIMAT Stralsund Information Management Team, Fachhochschule Stralsund No. 06-14-028, Stralsund, 2014. http://hdl.handle.net/10419/102710 (last access 2017-10-09).
19. R. Kneuper. Supporting software processes using knowledge management. In S. Chang, editor, *Handbook of Software Engineering and Knowledge Engineering*, volume 2, pages 579–608. World Scientific Publishing Co., 2002.
20. R. Kneuper. *CMMI. Improving Software and Systems Development Processes Using Capability Maturity Model Integration (CMMI-DEV)*. Rocky Nook, 2009.
21. G. A. Moore. *Crossing the Chasm*. Collins Business, 2002.
22. J. Münch, O. Armbrust, M. Kowalczyk, and M. Sotó. *Software Process Definition and Management*. Springer, 2012.
23. T. G. Olson. Defining short and usable processes. *Crosstalk*, 19(6):24–28, June 2006.
24. M. Paasivaara and C. Lassenius. Could global software development benefit from agile methods? In *2006 IEEE International Conference on Global Software Engineering (ICGSE '06)*, pages 109–112, 2006.
25. J. Pickerill. What is this "thing" called management commitment? In R. Kneuper and M. Verlage, editors, *Vorgehensmodelle, Prozeßverbesserung und Qualitätsmanagement. 6. Workshop der GI-Fachgruppe 5.1.1 Vorgehensmodelle für die betriebliche Anwendungsentwicklung*. Fraunhofer IRB Verlag, 1999.
26. G. J. B. Probst. Practical knowledge management: A model that works. *Prism (Arthur D. Little)*, (2nd quarter):17–29, 1998. genevaknowledgeforum.ch/downloads/prismartikel.pdf (last access 2018-02-25).
27. Probst, Gilbert J.B., S. Raub, and K. Romhardt. *Managing Knowledge: Building Blocks for Success*. Wiley, 1999.
28. K. Schwaber. SCRUM Development Process. In *OOPSLA '95 Workshop Proceedings 16 October 1995, Austin, Texas*. Springer, 1997.
29. G. Suryanarayana, T. Sharma, and G. Samarthyam. Software process versus design quality. Tug of war? *IEEE Software*, 32(4):7–11, July/August 2015.
30. J. Sutherland and K. Schwaber. The Scrum Guide™. The Definitive Guide to Scrum: The Rules of the Game. http://www.scrumguides.org/ (last access 2018-02-28), July 2013.
31. J. Sutherland, A. Viktorov, J. Blount, and N. Puntikov. Distributed Scrum: Agile project management with outsourced development teams. In *Proceedings of the 40th Hawaii International Conference on System Sciences (HICSS'07*, 2007.
32. The Open Group. TOGAF version 9.1. http://pubs.opengroup.org/architecture/togaf9-doc/arch/ (last access 2017-07-12), 2011.
33. P. Xu and B. Ramesh. Using process tailoring to manage software development challenges. *IT Professional*, 10(4):39–45, 2008.

Chapter 5
Software Process Assessment and Improvement

Abstract In order to use software processes successfully, they need to be assessed regularly, and the assessment results need to be used to improve these processes. To support these steps, Software Process Improvement (SPI) initiatives use various standards and methods that help companies to assess their process quality and maturity, and to set up improvement and measurement programs. This chapter provides an overview of software process assessment and improvement, introducing the basic concepts of quality management, with a special emphasis on relevant standards. Furthermore, we introduce the Capability Maturity Model Integration (CMMI) and SPICE as the two major assessment and improvement models. We conclude this chapter with an overview of some alternative approaches.

5.1 Introduction

Based on the topics discussed in the previous chapter, we now cover the topic of process assessment and improvement in more depth. Once processes have been defined and deployed, it is to be expected that as the technical and organisational environment changes, the processes will have to change as well. Additionally, parts of the processes will turn out to be less than ideal for achieving the purposes of the process, new ideas will come up how the process could be improved further, and possibly it turns out that the process is not performed as expected.

All these issues show the importance of assessing the processes regularly, in order to check that they provide the expected results and to identify any improvement opportunities. The current chapter therefore addresses the question of how to examine and improve the processes used within an organisation to ensure that they are adequate to achieve their relevant goals, such as projects which are performed in time, in budget and delivering the needed quality of results, and to continually improve these processes.

In spite of all the methods and activities to assess and improve quality as described in this chapter, one should realise that there is no way to *ensure* the quality

© Springer Nature Switzerland AG 2018

R. Kneuper, *Software Processes and Life Cycle Models*,

https://doi.org/10.1007/978-3-319-98845-0_5

of the process results. If all goes well, these methods and activities will increase the *probability* of getting quality results as expected, but on the other hand, factors like the complexity and size of the task at hand reduce this probability. Hopefully, one will achieve a high likelihood of getting the expected results in the expected quality, but there never is a guarantee.

5.2 Quality of Software Processes and Software Process Models

When talking about the quality of processes, we need to distinguish between the quality of the overall process and the quality of process models. As discussed in the context of the process cube, a process consists of a process model and a performed process, where ideally the performed process conforms to the process model. The quality of the overall process includes all three aspects.

The quality of the overall processes is briefly discussed below. An extensive quality model for processes, including different aspects of the performed process and the process model, as well as their relationship, is *Gokyo Ri*, which will be described in Sect. 6.5 in the context of measuring process quality.

Regarding the quality of process models, there are a number of frameworks, mainly in the context of business processes:

- *SIQ Framework*
- *Guidelines of modelling*
- *Seven Process Modelling Guidelines*

The first two will be described below, while the Seven Process Modelling Guidelines only address modelling using graphical notations for business processes, such as BPMN, and will therefore not be discussed her any further [32].

The SIQ framework. The SIQ framework distinguishes three subcategories of the quality of process models [33]:

- *syntactic* quality describes whether the model conforms to the relevant rules of the meta-model or notation used.
- *semantic* quality describes whether the model correctly and completely describes the relevant aspects of the real world (as-is or to-be). Of course, as the reduction property of models shows, a model never completely describes the real world but should ideally describe the relevant part of it.
- *pragmatic* quality describes whether the model can be understood by the people involved

To ensure quality in each of these three subcategories, two "walls" are introduced: the "wall of checking" defines that quality assurance or checking is required for each subcategory to identify whether quality has been achieved. However, as an analytical approach, this helps to find out afterwards whether one has done a good job in setting up the process. What is also needed is the constructive approach, ensuring that process quality is achieved *by design*, and this is defined as the second wall, the "wall of ensuring".

Guidelines of modelling. The "guidelines of modelling" describe a set of guidelines to consider in process modelling which in effect define a set of quality criteria for process models [35, 5]. Like the SIQ framework, they were developed for business processes but are similarly applicable for software processes as well. In [5], the following guidelines are listed which are similar but not quite identical to those in the earlier [35]:

- correctness, referring to both syntactic and semantic correctness
- relevance
- economic efficiency
- clarity
- comparability
- systematic design

The first three of these guidelines are defined as "basic" guidelines, while the second three are defined as "optional".

These guidelines of modelling are also integrated into the process quality model Gokyo Ri (see Sect. 6.5) to evaluate the quality of process models as part of the overall process quality.

Process quality in business process management In business process management, one usually uses the following three process performance dimensions (see e.g. [16]):

- time, in particular cycle (or throughput) time, which can be broken down into *processing time* and *waiting time*
- cost
- quality, sometimes broken down further into

  - *external quality*, addressing the client's satisfaction with the process or the product
  - *internal quality*, from the viewpoint of the process participants, which addresses aspects such as the feeling of control and the level of variation of the process.

Instead of quality, *scope* of the project is sometimes used as the third dimension of the project triangle.

Occasionally, flexibility is added as a fourth dimension of process performance.

The three dimensions of process performance are often represented as a triangle known under different names, e.g. the project triangle or (in the context of quality management) the quality triangle, see Fig. 5.1. It is often used to represent the aspect that it is possible to improve one of the three dimensions, e.g. time, but delivering a project result in shorter time will usually come at the expense of lower quality and higher cost. One of the challenges addressed by quality improvement therefore is

Fig. 5.1 The project triangle

to improve the processes in such a way that the triangle overall becomes larger, not just one of its dimensions.

Note that the definition of process quality as used in this book, following ISO 9000 terminology (see Def. 1.39), is equivalent to what [16] describes as process performance, which goes beyond the definition of process quality used in [16].

5.3 Software Process Improvement

Even assuming that an organisation has achieved "perfect" software processes at some point in time, these would not stay perfect for long because since the technical and organisational environment, the customer's requirements, and many other topics keep changing. In practice, perfection is of course never achieved and organisations need to continually improve their software (as well as any other) processes. This concept of continual improvement is the basis of more or less all approaches to process improvement, often using the PDCA-Cycle as described in Sect. 5.4.2.

Starting from organisational goals and strategy. An apparently easy question regards the meaning if "improvement" in this context. Since most changes to a process affect different parameters, including the type and number of problems in the delivered software but also the speed of delivery and the development cost, most changes at the same time improve certain parameters but change other parameters for the worse. Even if an improvement is a genuine according to all parameters, it may only affect minor parameters with low priority.

To ensure that any software process improvement activities move in the right direction, focussing on those aspects with high priority, it is therefore important to start from the organisational goals and strategy, as defined e.g. by the COBIT goals cascade. Any improvement initiative should start with a clarification of what is really considered important for the organisation, identify the resulting process objectives, and then think seriously about achieving those objectives and improving the processes.

Quality and improvement culture. The main foundation for achieving consistent improvement is to install a quality and improvement culture, where it is considered important to perform one's work correctly the first time rather than performing it some way or other and correcting it later on. Nevertheless, it should be accepted and expected that things will occasionally go wrong, and also that employees have ideas for how to perform work in a better way, which are then taken seriously and implemented whenever adequate.

The approach used to achieve a quality and improvement culture and implement improvement activities usually reflects the approach used for software (development) processes. Organisations with a focus on agile processes tend to use these for improvement as well, for example in the form of sprint retrospectives. Organisations that tend to use a plan-driven development approach will also tend to use a plan-driven approach to improvement, leading to longer improvement cycles e.g. based on "lessons learnt" sessions at the end of a project or a major project stage, and setting up separate, longer-term improvement initiatives.

A culture very different from such a quality and improvement culture but nevertheless widely spread culture was described by Jochen Ludewig in one of this author's favourite quotes: "Very few people really want HQS[1]. They appreciate high quality in the same way they appreciate a warm day in May: It is something sent from heaven, and free. But as soon as they are asked to pay for it, high quality is hardly on the shopping list." [29, p. 12]

This seems true in many organisations even though the "payment" Ludewig talks about is mainly in terms of *initial effort*, not in terms of long-term financial cost. If an organisation manages to install a quality and improvement culture where getting feedback fast and doing work correctly the first time round becomes the default way of working rather than taking short-cuts, then this will involve little additional effort, and this additional effort will pay for itself because there is less need for correction of problems later on. Philip B. Crosby, in his classic [15], therefore even argued that "quality is free".

5.3.1 Collection, Analysis and Handling of Improvement Ideas

A core task of any improvement program is the systematic collection, analysis and handling of improvement ideas, which may come from several different sources: process performers as well as other stakeholders in a process continually see what could be improved in a process, or what possibly goes wrong. Similarly, customers may complain about the products or services they get. Although not every single complaint will point to a need for improvement, some of them will do, in particular if there are repeated complaints about the same issues.

To identify improvement needs and opportunities more systematically, an organisation may perform various forms of checking the processes, such as assessments, appraisals and audits. Alternatively, it may use measurements of the processes and their results, helping e.g. to identify inefficiencies and bottlenecks, or it may analyse

---

[1] HQS=High Quality Software

the results of other quality assurance tasks and of problems and bugs reported from the field.

Collection of improvement ideas. A task that seems very obvious but still is often performed inadequately is the systematic collection of these improvement ideas, which in practice requires suitable tools. Depending on the tool set used for the collection of process description, the collection of improvement ideas might directly be integrated into that tool set, for example using the discussion functionality of a wiki.

Dedicated tools for representing software process sometimes include a feedback button or similar which allows process performers to immediately provide feedback on the process definition when they read it. This feedback automatically includes the part of the process definition affected, and may result in a mail to the process engineering group, or it may directly end up in a suitable ticket system or similar tool. Experience shows that it is important to make it easy for process performers to give such feedback, because otherwise they will not bother to do so, and the information will be lost.

Process for handling improvement ideas. Just as important to motivate process performers to provide their improvement ideas on the processes they perform is that this feedback is handled and analysed appropriately, and the get regular feedback on what happens to their ideas. Of course, not every improvement idea will be implemented, but at least process performers have to see that their ideas are taken seriously.

While it is important to ensure that these ideas are collected and managed properly, it is just as important to ensure that this task does not get to bureaucratic. Some companies introduce a very structured process for handling improvement suggestions, including bonus payments for the employees suggesting such improvements. At first, this sounds like a very good idea in order to motivate employees to think about possible improvements and submit their ideas, but in practice this tends to lead to a very bureaucratic system for handling improvement suggestions, with more discussion about bonus payments than about the improvements themselves.

Once improvement ideas have been identified and collected, the next step is their analysis and evaluation. Not all improvement ideas lead to a genuine improvement, and others lead to a minor improvement which may not (currently) be worth the effort. Even improvement ideas that are worth implementing will not all be implemented immediately, but will need to be integrated into some form of improvement plan, based on their benefits, cost and dependencies. Like in software development, it is often not a good idea to create a long-term plan including the work to be done, but a more agile, Scrum-like approach is often much more useful, as for example shown in Case Study 5.1.

In one form or another, an improvement plan incorporating the accepted improvement ideas needs to be created and implemented. Finally, one should verify that the process modification indeed was an improvement and has achieved the expected improvement results.

Case Study 5.1. (CS Insurance InfoSys) A few years after agile development and Scrum became popular for software development projects, CS Insurance InfoSys started a major improvement initiative. Since it quite difficult to plan such an initiative in advance, it was agreed to use an agile approach, similar to Scrum.

It was considered important to involve the process performers in the initiative, and the main definitions on process changes and improvements were to be prepared by several working groups. There was one working group on project management, a second one on requirements and configuration management, and a third group on quality assurance and measurement. (The reader may notice that this covers the CMMI-DEV process areas on maturity level 2. Indeed, this was an improvement project based on CMMI-DEV which will be introduced in more detail later in this chapter.)

Each of these groups then started a cycle of four steps each lasting one month:

- The first step involved the preparation and planning of the improvement: deciding on the improvements to address, getting the necessary resources, identifying pilot projects etc.
- Next, the improvement was implemented, including the definition or adaptation of the relevant process descriptions, creation of templates etc.
- To validate the improvement, the next step was the piloting of the change in one or two project. This turned out to be much more difficult than expected since most improvements could only be performed at a certain stage within the project life cycle, and therefore only few projects were able to pilot the change at the time planned. As a result, the piloting step sometimes had to be extended.

  In parallel with the piloting, the necessary preparations for the deployment of the process were performed, such as creation of training material.

  As far as possible, minor changes that piloting showed to be necessary were performed immediately.
- Finally, the improvement was deployed, including release of the revised or new process documentation and templates, performance of training etc.

5.3.2 Assessments, Appraisals and Audits

An important step in order to improve processes is to check them systematically. In the following, we will introduce a number of methods for doing so.

Assessing processes. A major challenge for any assessment of software processes is the difficulty to identify suitable criteria. How can we distinguish a "good" process from one that is not so good? Even if process A leads to better results faster than process B, do we really know that this is due to a genuinely better process? Maybe process *A* was just performed in a more advantageous environment, with better tools and more qualified personnel. Or perhaps the statistical variance that is inherent in software processes just happened to work in favour of process *A*? This is made even more difficult by the fact that the environment and type of project (more or less stable environment; duration and size of project; safety-relevant or not; etc.) has a large influence on what is the "best" process.

The sad answer is that in many cases we do not really know, and this explains some of the large variation of processes we find in different projects. There are some approaches that are obviously bad, and experience from many projects shows that some processes, methods etc. work better than others. Such experience is often collected as "best practices". Nevertheless, one has to admit that there is a considerable amount of belief involved to decide whether which process is the best in any given situation, with the obvious example that some people will be absolutely certain that agile methodologies are best for many or most projects, while others are just as certain that plan-driven development is needed for the same projects.

In this chapter we present some of the commonly used methods to assess and improve software processes. These methods are based on collections of best practices, but they usually stay on a somewhat abstract level, stating *what* needs to be done but not specifying *how* it is to be done. This allows very different development methodologies to be used, and helps to identify gaps in these methodologies and their use.

The model Gokyo Ri contains a definition of quality criteria for processes, including effectiveness and efficiency of the process as two important quality characteristics (see Sect. 6.5). This models helps to define suitable assessment criteria for software processes, but needs to be refined to contain sufficient detail to assess a process.

One important aspect contained in most approaches to assessing processes is the question of consistency of the different process cube components as introduced in Sect. 1.4.5.1, in particular between the process as-is and the process to-be, but also e.g. between different instances of the same process.

Process assessments. A basic mechanisms to analyse a process is a process assessment, which needs some form of assessment model as a basis:

Definition 5.1 (Process assessment). *Disciplined evaluation of an organisational unit's processes against a process assessment model (ISO/IEC 33001:2015, SEVO-CAB)*

The main objective of an assessment is to identify the strengths and weaknesses of the processes, to identify the extent to which they achieve their goals, and what could be done to achieve these goals even better.

Instead of process assessments, CMMI (see Sect. 5.5.3) uses the term *appraisal*, with a very similar meaning:

Definition 5.2 (Appraisal). *An examination of one or more processes by a trained team of professionals using an appraisal reference model as the basis for determining, as a minimum, strengths and weaknesses. (SCAMPI MDD v1.3b [14])*

Distinguishing assessments according to sponsor. Assessments can be performed internally, initiated by the assessed organisation itself, or they can be performed by external stakeholders such as customers. This so some extent influences the goals of the assessment and the way it is performed. Therefore, SWEBOK [6, Chap. 8, Sect. 3] distinguished different kinds of assessments depending on who performs or sponsors them, leading to a different terminology:

- An *appraisal* is an assessment which is performed by or on behalf of the assessed organisation itself, with the main goal of identifying improvement opportunities.
- A *capability evaluation*, also called capability determination, is an assessment which is performed by a (potential) acquirer or on his behalf, with the main goal of providing input on which to base a decision about whether the supplier's processes are considered acceptable.

CMM, the predecessor of CMMI, used the same distinction but with appraisal as the general term and assessment as the special case where an appraisal is performed by the organisation, i.e. with the interpretations of assessment and appraisal switched compared to the definition in SWEBOK.

To hopefully reduce confusion, in the current book we will in general follow SEVOCAB and use the term (process) assessment, except when talking specifically about CMMI-based assessments which will be called appraisals.

Assessments are related to but different from process audits which analyse a process to determine the compliance of the process with relevant standards, regulations etc.:

Definition 5.3 (Audit). *Systematic, independent and documented process for obtaining objective evidence and evaluating it objectively to determine the extent to which the audit criteria are fulfilled. (ISO 9000:2015)*

Although an audit by definition is required to be *independent*, this does not necessarily mean that it is performed by a separate organisation. It is often quite helpful (and therefore required by process improvement standards such as ISO 9001) to perform *internal audits* by some internal quality assurance organisation which often has far more previous knowledge about where to look for problems.

Such *first-party audits* are then supplemented as needed by *second-party audits*, performed by a customer, and/or *third-party audits*, performed by some other party such as a certification agency.

Example 5.1. In the European automotive industry, the car manufacturers (often called the Original Equipment Manufacturers, OEM) put strong emphasis on auditing and assessing the development processes of their software suppliers to ensure that they get products in the expected quality. They therefore perform many second-party audits and assessments on these suppliers.

From the stand-point of the suppliers, this involves a lot of effort, with a different customer wanting to see the software processes every couple of weeks or months, with the additional challenge of always having to ensure that the customer only sees the results of "his" project and not results from a competitor's project which may be performed by the same supplier. The suppliers therefore look to third-party audits and assessments performed by some neutral certification body, hoping that the OEMs will accept the results and thus reduce the number of second-party audits and assessments.

In either case, to improve their processes and to prepare for such second- or third-party audits, the suppliers have to perform regular internal, first-party audits to find and correct problems before the customer or external certification body does, and it is usually a requirement of the relevant models and standards (e.g. ISO 9001 or CMMI) that regular first-party audits are performed.

5.3.3 The SPI Manifesto

Starting at the EuroSPI conference 2009 in Spain, a group of experts described the core values and principles of software process improvement in the form of a manifesto which was published as the *SPI Manifesto* [36] in 2010, summarized in Fig. 5.2. With this manifesto, they wanted to address some of the difficulties they saw in process improvement, and identify the success factors relevant for improving software processes.

The manifesto values refer to the following topics:

- *People*: To genuinely improve processes, it is important that the people who perform the processes are involved in analysing and defining the processes, and this is not done by a group of process experts alone who may be too distant from the actual work. This is important both to get a better understanding of the processes and better motivation of the process performers as a result. This is closely related to continually learning about what works well and what does not, both on the level of the individuals and the organisation.
- *Business*: Process improvement activities should focus on better support for the business and its objectives. Process models and improvement models are tools to achieve this but should not become a goal of their own.
- *Change*: Any improvement can only be achieved by change, which may concern the individual, the project and/or the organisation. Although it is obvious that improvement is not possible without change, the importance of managing such change is not always sufficiently understood.

Values:
We truly believe that SPI

- must involve people actively and affect their daily activities (People)
- is what you do to make business successful (Business)
- is inherently connected with change (Change)

Principles:

People:	*Business:*	*Change*
- Know the culture and focus on needs - Motivate all people involved - Base improvement on experience and measurements - Create a learning organisation	- Support the organisation's vision and objectives - Use dynamic and adaptable models as needed - Apply risk management	- Manage the organisational change in your improvement effort - Ensure all parties understand and agree on process - Do not lose focus

Fig. 5.2 The SPI Manifesto [36]

The SPI Manifesto does not only resemble the Agile Manifesto in name and in structure, but also the values and principles in the SPI Manifesto are based on the same underlying philosophy. To a large extent, the SPI Manifesto, with its emphasis on people, business success and change, tries to apply the agile ideas to the task of software process improvement.

5.4 Quality Management

Assessing and improving software processes is closely related to quality management, using many general quality management concepts and adapting them to this specific domain. In the following, we will look at this relationship in some more detail.

5.4.1 Foundations of Quality Management

Quality management is a management discipline that deals with the activities implemented to ensure quality of the products, services and processes. ISO 9000:2005 defines quality management as "coordinated activities to direct and control an organisation with regard to quality". As a discipline, it started in the 1930s with the application of statistical methods in industrial production (statistical quality control, later also called statistical process control (SPC)). At that time, quality management focused on testing the final products rather than controlling the processes used to create these products. Similarly, in the early years of software development one mainly tried to ensure quality of the final software product by testing it, although statistical methods in this context were rarely applied since they would require large numbers of similar products to test and analyse. More recently, there were some attempts to use statistical methods in software development as well, see Sect. 8.2.

This changed in the 1980s when first in industrial production but soon also in software engineering processes started to be seen as an important lever to ensure the quality of the products created (cf. Sect. 1.3.2). As a result, almost all relevant approaches to quality management today are based on managing *p*rocess quality, sometimes with additional product-focused activities. The best-known and most widely used description of process-based quality management is contained in the ISO 9000 series of standards, see below.

There are two main goals that organisations usually try to achieve using quality management:

- improving the processes in order to get better results, better insight into the current state of the relevant activities, and based on that insight better control of where it is heading.
- certification in order to prove to customers and sometimes other bodies that the organisations can be relied upon to deliver adequate quality of their work products.

Ideally, organisations should focus on the first goal and collect the relevant certification as a by-product, but in practice, it is often the other way round. Organisations sometimes spend considerable effort to get a certificate, "proving" that they work to a certain set of standard processes, while doing their best to evade these standards in their day-to-day work. The challenge to any organisation needing any certification is to take the relevant standards as a framework that needs to be implemented in such a way that it provides genuine benefit beyond the certification itself.

5.4.2 The Plan-Do-Check-Act-Cycle (PDCA)

The Plan-Do-Check-Act-Cycle (see Fig. 5.3) is the most commonly used approach to describe improvement activities and the basis of continuous improvement. In this cycle, you plan what you intend to do and what you want to achieve; you do it; you check whether you achieved your goals; and you act on the results and adapt your approach, leading back to planning:

It describes the basic idea of improvement as a cycle where the implementation of a change leads to a better understanding and is followed by further improvement. The PDCA-Cycle or a variation of it is used in almost all improvement methods, e.g. ISO 9001, ITIL, the EFQM RADAR model, or Kaizen, as a basis for continuous improvement. Although it is not specific to software processes, it is commonly used in this context.

Fig. 5.3 The Plan-Do-Check-Act-Cycle

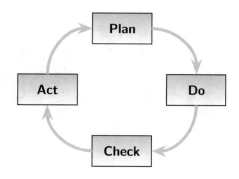

The PDCA-Cycle is also called Shewhart-Cycle, after Walter A. Shewhart, an American statistician who pioneered statistical process control as a quality management technique, or Deming-Cycle after W. Edwards Deming, an American engineer and management consultant who had a major role in spreading (total) quality management in Japan and the USA.

The four phases of the PDCA-Cycle are:

- *Plan* what to improve and how to go about it.
- *Do* implement the improvement according to the plan, perhaps initially as a pilot, for example just implementing it within a single project.
- *Check* whether the implementation was successful and has actually achieved the intended benefit, e.g. resolved the underlying problem.
- *Act* on the result of the check and learn from it, by adapting or revising the improvement if needed, by rolling out the improvement to the entire organisation if it ws piloted first, and by identifying further improvements leading back to the planning phase.

A frequent mistake in this context is an incomplete "check" step in the PDCA-Cycle, putting the focus on selected aspects of process quality and forgetting about other, possibly more important aspects. This way, local optimisation of some factors may lead to overall decrease in process quality.

Example 5.2. As part of its process improvement activities, a systems development organisation within a large enterprise identified that its projects were putting a lot of effort into reviews, but these reviews only identified a limited number of problems.

It was therefore decided to save on this effort and reduce the number of reviews as defined in the engineering process description performed considerably.

The "check" was performed by estimating the reduction in the number of reviews and the resulting effort saved, and these data were reported as benefits from this modification of the process.

However, this check only addressed one aspect of the process, namely the effort caused by these reviews, but did not compare it against the benefit that was lost by identifying any problems in the work products later or not at all. Since this effect was not measured or analysed, the organisation did not really know whether or not the modification of the process, the reduction of the number of reviews performed, was in fact an improvement or not.

5.4.3 The ISO 9000 Series of Standards

ISO 9000 is a series of standards that describes the set-up of process-oriented quality management systems and consists at its core of the following standards:

- *ISO 9000:2015 Quality management systems—Fundamentals and vocabulary* is the introductory standard which describes the basic ideas and the terminology used in the series.
- *ISO 9001:2015 Quality management systems—Requirements* is the normative standard that describes requirements on quality management systems such that they can be verified in an audit. It is commonly used for certification of an organisation's quality management system.
- *ISO 9004:2009 Managing for the sustained success of an organisation—A quality management approach* provides guidelines on using ISO 9001, and for improving beyond the requirements of that standard.

In practice, ISO 9001 is by far the best-known and most commonly used ISO standard, in general and in software engineering in particular, although there is considerably criticism about it. The main concern is the observation that ISO 9001 certification has become an entry requirement on many markets, but auditing and certification have themselves become a competitive market with some certification organisations handing out certificates after minimal checking of documentation, with little genuine benefit to the customer. One should point out here that this is not a problem of the standard itself but of the way it is commonly used—as an obstacle one needs to get out of one's way rather than a tool to improve and manage one's processes.

One major criticism regarding the ISO 9000 series is that it is very general, covering every business from running a bakery or an industrial production unit to software development, and therefore cannot provide any specific guidance for any of these businesses.

This is one of the reasons why, since its first release in 1989, the ISO 9000 series has developed considerably, moving from specific requirements on processes such as sales, production or development to a more generic approach, setting requirements on how to manage the processes and the resulting product quality. As a result, difficult questions such as how to interpret the requirements on the production processes in the context of a software development organisation are no longer relevant.

ISO 9001 and software processes. As an additional help on applying ISO 9001 to specific industries, various industry-specific interpretation guides have been produced, e.g. for software development:

- ISO/IEC 90003:2014 *Software engineering—Guidelines for the application of ISO 9001:2008 to computer software* contains exactly what the title states— guidelines for applying ISO 9001 to software. Note, however, that it still refers to the previous version of ISO 9001 issued in 2008. It is not meant to be used as a basis for certification itself but as optional support in certifying a software development organisation according to ISO 9001. Alternatively, software development organisations are free to
- *TickIT* (expired) and its successor *TickITplus* which were both created by British government organisations. They are based on the requirements stated in ISO 9001 and support the certification of software development organisations but interpreting these requirements for and adapting them to software development.

  The new TickITplus scheme actually goes beyond software development and additionally addresses IT service management (ISO/IEC 20000-1), IT security (ISO/IEC 27001), reporting different capability levels based on the approach defined in ISO/IEC 15504 Part 2 (also known as SPICE, see Sect. 5.5.4).

While TickITplus is quite successful in the UK, outside the UK most software development organisations work with ISO 9001 itself, in spite of the difficulties of interpretation.

Similarly, there are industry-specific interpretations of ISO 9001 for various other industries which sometimes have a strong impact on software processes as well, for example IATF 16949 (formerly ISO/TS 16949) for the automotive industry, and ISO/TS 22163 for the railway industry, in the past known as *International Railway Industry Standard* (IRIS).

ISO 9001:2015. The recent new edition ISO 9001:2015 of this standard continued the development from specific requirements on processes to requirements on managing one's processes and the resulting product quality. To achieve this, a new structure of the norm was introduced that is based on the PDCA-Cycle. This so-called *High-Level Structure* (HLS) is to be used for most or all ISO/IEC standards describing management systems, including ISO/IEC 27001 as described in Sect. 3.11.3.

This common structure is intended to help companies to combine different management systems into one common system that supports the different goals such as quality and IT security in parallel.

5.4.4 Responsibility for Quality, Quality Management and Quality Assurance

In this section, we discuss some aspects of the responsibility of the various functions involved in quality.

Responsibility for quality. Who is responsible for the quality of the software developed (or other products produced)? This is a common cause for discussion between quality management and development. Contrary to what is often stated, the quality management or quality assurance function can only take responsibility for making the quality of the software visible, e.g. as a basis for correcting problems found and of decisions on the release of the product. The responsibility for the quality of development results needs to lie with those that produce these results.

Of course, it is easier for the process performers to pass the responsibility for the quality of their results, as well as for the processes used to create these results, on to the quality management function, rather than accepting it themselves. However, without performing the process, quality management has only very indirect influence on how the process is performed and what results from it.

Example 5.3. In a software development project several years ago, one developer was responsible for implementing a fairly complex function. Additionally, there was a separate quality assurance group responsible for testing the resulting software.

The developer implemented the function and passed it on to QA for testing, who quickly found some bugs. The developer corrected these bugs, passed the new version to QA for testing, and again they did find bugs in the code. This cycle was repeated more than forty (!) times before the code was in a state ready for release.

When the developer was asked about this, he did not see any problem: he had developed the code, quality assurance did their part to test it and assure the quality of the code—everything OK and according to the role model. QA, on the other hand, strongly complained that the developer was not taking his responsibility of delivering quality code seriously, did not sufficiently think through the solution he was providing, and did not properly test the software himself before passing it on to QA.

Independence of the quality assurance function. Another common cause for discussion is the independence of the QA function. On the one hand, QA should be independent in order to reduce the risk that it does not (want to) see or report any relevant problems. On the other hand, an independent QA function is more distant from the product or process checked and will find it more difficult to understand the product and its environment, which often tends to lead to a rather formal QA, with insufficient regard for the contents of the product or process.

There are two major approaches to address this difficulty: first, in most cases it is useful to include both types of QA. This includes setting up a more contents-oriented QA that might not be independent of the development team but that works closely with the team, is able to provide valuable feedback and therefore gets accepted as helping the team to create quality software. Additionally, it includes setting up an independent QA that might not have quite as much understanding of the software to be built but provides objective feedback on the work performed and the resulting work products. The adequate importance and size of this independent QA will mainly depend on the risks involved and on the relevant legal and regulatory requirements.

The second approach—which to some extent should be combined with the first one—is to ensure that the independent QA nevertheless puts its focus on providing valuable feedback that helps to improve the overall quality of the results, rather than on minor formalities as occasionally happens.

Separation of powers. While it is obvious that at least some independence of the quality assurance function from development is needed, this is not quite as clear for the separation of the definition and management of processes on the one side, and process quality assurance on the other. If there is no such separation, and both functions are perhaps even performed by the same people, then this has the advantage that the process engineers see what is needed in the processes from first hand, and which parts of the processes ought to be improved. On the other hand, there is the risk of a conflict of interest between both roles, e.g. when a problem is found, QA should think about whether this is perhaps not a problem of how the process is performed but how it is defined. However, it the same person has also defined the process, QA may be less willing to accept that this is the case.

5.4.5 Certification

When an organisation wants to confirm that it satisfies certain a certain set of requirements such as those defined by ISO 9001, the usual approach is to get an appropriate certification:

Definition 5.4 (Certification). *Formal demonstration that a system or component complies with its specified requirements and is acceptable for operational use. (SE-VOCAB)*

A certification may be related to

- products: in this context, we are interested in the certification of software products. Certification of (software) products usually refers to their quality or their safety, but occasionally other properties are considered relevant and therefore certified.
  In the past, the certification of a software product was mainly based on testing it after development was completed, but more recently the increasing complexity

of such products has led to a need to analyse the development processes as part of the certification review.

- processes: by certifying that adequate processes were used to develop the software product (or sometimes to operate it), companies try to indirectly confirm properties such as the quality or safety of the product itself.
- management systems: going beyond the individual processes, a management system may be certified, such as a quality management systems that may be certified as conforming to ISO 9001. Two other management system certifications that have become quite wide-spread in IT are based on ISO/IEC 20000-1 for IT service management (cf. Sect. 3.8.1), and on ISO/IEC 27001 for IT security management (cf. Sect. 3.11.3). Since both the structure and the content of these three standards have been streamlined, following the common *High-Level Structure* for management system standards mentioned in Sect. 3.11.3, IT service providers have started to combine the three certifications, talking about the "56k" certification.
- persons: a certification of a person usually confirms certain qualifications or skills, for example as Scrum master, CMMI lead appraiser or "certified solution designer Rational Unified Process".

A certification may be useful for internal purposes, as a confirmation that a certain objective has indeed be achieved, or—more often—it is used for external purposes, proving conformance to certain requirements to a customer, some other external entity, or the entire customer base as part of marketing. In some environments, certain certifications are required by law, typically when the safety of a product or system is important.

Accreditation. Since in theory everybody may "certify" any property or qualification they want, not every certificate is really worth the paper it was written on. Therefore, the concept of *accreditation* was introduced to confirm that a certification such as one confirming that a certain organisation satisfies the requirements of ISO 9001 itself satisfies the relevant requirements for issuing such a certificate and therefore may be "believed".[2] The accreditation of a certification agency is usually performed by some state-sponsored entity and confirms that the certification agency follows the relevant rules and the certificates it issues are therefore considered acceptable. For example, in the European Union it was agreed that every state sets up exactly one accreditation body which may then accredit different "conformity assessment bodies".

---

[2] This is what the term accreditation originally means (*accredere*, Latin for "to believe", "to trust"), and it is also used, with a similar meaning, in other contexts, such as in higher education and in diplomacy.

[3] This number refers to the number of SCAMPI A appraisals performed. Strictly speaking, there are no "certificates" for CMMI since for legal reasons, this term is not used here.

Table 5.1 Number of certificates awarded in 2016 [25, 13]

Standard	Number of certificates
ISO 9001	1 106 356
ISO/IEC 27001	33 290
ISO/TS 16949	67 358
ISO 20000-1	4 537
CMMI[3]	2 235

5.4.6 Total Quality Management (TQM)

An extension of quality management is the concept of total quality management which tries to take a total, holistic view of quality management, based on a very quality-oriented culture from top management downwards and going far beyond the processes as discussed so far.

Definition 5.5 (Total quality management (TQM)). *A holistic approach to quality improvement in all life cycle phases. (SEVOCAB)*

Unfortunately, this definition from SEVOCAB is rather vague and does not really help to understand the concepts of TQM. In practice, organisations who want to move towards TQM often use the evaluation criteria of one of the major quality awards as their guideline, with the Japanese *Deming Price*, the US-American *Malcolm Baldrige National Quality Award* (based on the Baldrige Excellence Framework), and the *European Quality Award* (based on the EFQM Excellence Model developed by the *European Foundation for Quality Management*) being the best-known examples.

The model includes nine main criteria in total, grouped into

- enablers, i.e. things that enable an organisation to achieve excellent results. Processes are part of one such enabler, further examples include "leadership" and "people".
- results, which refer to measuring whether implementing the enablers actually achieves the expected results. For example, it is not sufficient to implement best practices in an organisation's processes but the organisation needs to set up measurements

Even when not moving towards genuine TQM, these concepts should serve as a reminder that processes are one out of several important tools (enablers) for achieving good results rather than a goal on its own. Furthermore, to validate their processes organisations should measure the results in different dimensions, and adapt the processes if needed.

5.5 (Capability) Maturity Models

Capability maturity models, often just called maturity models, are useful tools to assess one's development processes and their "maturity", which organisations may want to do for a variety of reasons—or sometimes they do not really want to but have to because their customer asks for it.

To help assess process maturity, these models collect best practices and use them as criteria to judge whether an organisation or project is sufficiently mature to deliver promised results. These best practices used in maturity models should not be confused with the activities that form part of a process model. They stay on a more abstract level and essentially identify topics that need to be addressed in a development process, without stating how this is to be done. For example, the maturity model CMMI-DEV states that every project needs to define a project life cycle[4] but does not prescribe any fixed life cycle—this is for the project to decide. As a result, the processes used by organisations achieving high maturity levels nevertheless are very different, including both plan-driven and agile development. Since maturity models originally come from an environment of large, plan-driven defence projects, this comes as a surprise to many people but some of the organisations reaching the highest maturity levels actually use development methodologies based on Scrum.

To do so, maturity models collect best practices and group them into different levels to suggest an improvement path for the organisation or project to follow.

There are three main purposes to use such a maturity model:

- prove capability to external stakeholder, in particular customers: this was the original trigger to create and use maturity models. Customers use maturity models to evaluate suppliers in the selection process, sometimes even requiring a certain maturity level, and to monitor the supplier once the contract has been signed. This happens for example in the US defence industry (mainly based on CMMI, see Sect. 5.5.3) and in the European automotive industry (mainly based on Automotive SPICE, see Sect. 5.5.4.4).

  Even if the customer does not explicitly ask for a certain maturity level, suppliers use maturity models and the maturity levels achieved as a marketing tool, in particular if they are geographically far away from their customer base. This is one of the reasons why use of CMMI has become very popular in the Indian and Chinese software industries, as shown by the recent CMMI process maturity profiles [13].
- process improvement: since maturity models are based on collections of best practices, they provide a useful tool for internal process improvement. To improve, an organisation usually first assesses its processes based on the selected model. The assessment results provide feedback on what should be improved, including priorities based on the levels.
- IT governance: a more recent usage of maturity models is to support governance of IT processes. Since maturity models put strong emphasis on clearly stating

---

[4] Process area "Project Planning", specific practice SP 1.3: "Define project lifecycle phases on which to scope the planning effort."

the goals of the processes, to set up the activities such that they support these goals, and to make the status and results very transparent, they provide the tools leadership needs to direct and govern an organisation in the direction intended.

So why should an organisation use a maturity model, perhaps in addition to a process model? The main reason is that a maturity model helps to deploy and to improve the process model, mainly with the help of the generic practices described below.

5.5.1 Basic Concepts of Capability Maturity Models

Before discussing individual capability maturity models, in particular the CMMI and the SPICE families of models, we first introduce some of the basic concepts and give a short overview of their history.

Definition 5.6 (Capability maturity model). *Model that contains the essential elements of effective processes for one or more disciplines and describes an evolutionary improvement path from ad hoc, immature processes to disciplined, mature processes with improved quality and effectiveness. (SEVOCAB).*

This concept was first introduced by Philip B. Crosby as "Quality Management Maturity Grid" in his classic "Quality is Free" [15].

The idea was taken up some years later by Watts Humphrey when he was working at the *Software Engineering Institute* (SEI), looking for a solution to the problem that many suppliers were unable to deliver to the US-American Dept. of Defense (DoD) what they had promised [23]. This resulted in the *Software Capability Maturity Model* (SW-CMM), with the pilot version 1.0 published in 1991, and version 1.1 two years later.

Note that "capability maturity model", as defined above, is a generic term, referring to a whole class of models, while it is also often used as the name of this individual model, leaving out the qualifier "Software". The generic term is often abbreviated to just "maturity model".

Around the same time or soon after, several similar models were developed, such as the European *Bootstrap*, the *Trillium* model at Bell Canada, and several variants of the SW-CMM, e.g. for systems development.

In order to create a common standard model that would replace these different models, a project called *Software Process Improvement and Capability Determination (SPICE)*[5] was started in 1992 with support from ISO. In 1998, such a model was published as an ISO/IEC Technical Report. However, the feedback on this version led to a complete revision of the approach since a new process reference model had been defined and used even though such a model already existed in ISO/IEC 12207.

Although "SPICE" originally was only the name of the project started to develop the process maturity model, it soon was also used as a synonym for the resulting

---

[5] Actually, the project was initially called *Software Process Improvement and Capability Evaluation* which explains the acronym SPICE. However, to simplify translation into French it was soon renamed.

model, and today is used to refer to the entire family of norms and related standards as described below.

While work on the initial version of SPICE was ongoing, the SW-CMM became quite successful and there were several similar models using the same concepts, mainly for systems development in different industries. This led to the decision to *integrate* these different CMMs into the new model *Capability Maturity Model Integration* (CMMI) rather than join the SPICE effort. CMMI version 1.1 was published in 2002, which was not specific to software development but covered systems development as well.

Today, there are two families of capability maturity models that have practical importance and will be discussed below, CMMI and SPICE. Both started from software development but by now include a number of different application areas which will be discussed below.

Apart from these two model families, there are dozens if not hundreds of different maturity models, typically defined by individual consultancies, research projects or Ph.D. students, but rarely used by anyone else than the respective authors. The only exception is the *Business Process Maturity Model* (BPMM) [8] which is based on CMMI and was published as a standard by the OMG. As the name suggests, BPMM refers to the maturity of business processes and will therefore not be covered any further.

Process capability and process maturity. The improvement path mentioned in the definition of capability maturity models is achieved using different levels of process capability that build on each other:

Definition 5.7 (Process capability). *Characterization of the ability of a process to meet current or projected business goals. (ISO/IEC 33020:2015, SEVOCAB)*

Definition 5.8 (Process capability level). *Characterization of a process on an ordinal measurement scale[6] of process capability. (ISO/IEC 33020:2015, SEVOCAB)*

Actually, SEVOCAB defines that a six-point scale ordinal scale for process capability levels is to be used, but the definition was adapted here since there is no fundamental reason why this should be the case other than that it is the tradition as implemented by SPICE.[7] An alternative representation of the same contents, used in CMMI but not in SPICE, is based on the concept of maturity levels which do not refer to an individual process but to a whole set of processes:

Definition 5.9 (Maturity level). *Point on an ordinal scale of organizational process maturity that characterizes the maturity of the organisational unit assessed in the scope of the maturity model used (ISO/IEC 33001:2015, SEVOCAB).*

---

[6] An ordinal scale is characterized by the fact that the values on the scale are in a defined order, but there is no concept of difference or distance between any two values.

[7] For example, the current version 1.3 of CMMI only contains *four* capability levels, in contrast to previous versions which contained six capability levels as well. The interpretation of capability levels 0 to 3 has been kept the same, but the higher level 4 and 5 were removed.

This results in two different representations that can be used in a capability maturity model: the *continuous representation* defines capability levels of individual processes, while the *staged representation* additionally defines the improvement path by assigning defined sets of processes to each maturity level. To achieve a certain maturity level, all processes that belong to this maturity level need to achieve the associated capability level; to achieve a higher level, both the set of processes and the required capability level may be increased.

Definition 5.10 (Continuous representation). *Capability maturity model structure wherein capability levels provide a recommended order for approaching process improvement within each specified process area. (SEVOCAB)*

Definition 5.11 (Staged representation). *Structure wherein attaining the goals of a set of process areas establishes a maturity level; each level builds a foundation for subsequent levels. (SEVOCAB)*

As stated above, CMMI uses both the staged and the continuous representation, with (almost) the same contents structured in two different ways, while SPICE only uses the continuous representation. From level two upwards, capability and maturity levels are based on the same philosophy, as shown in Fig. 5.4.[8]

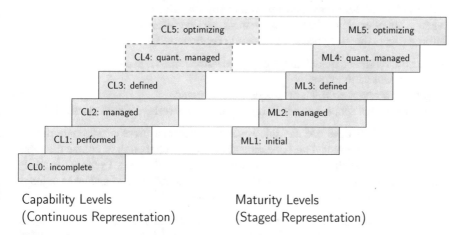

Fig. 5.4 Capability vs. maturity levels

Process reference models and process assessment models. Regarding the reference model used as a basis for an assessment, SPICE introduced an explicit distinction between the concepts of a process reference model which defines the process(es) to be assessed, including its main properties such as process goals, results etc., and a process assessment model which defined the criteria used in assessing the process(es) defined in the process reference model.

---

[8] Ignoring for the moment the fact that CMMI in its current version only goes up to capability level 3, and SPICE does not include a staged representation.

Definition 5.12 (Process Reference Model (PRM)). *Model comprising definitions of processes in a domain of application described in terms of process purpose and outcomes, together with an architecture describing the relationships between the processes. (ISO/IEC 33001:2015; SEVOCAB)*

Definition 5.13 (Process Assessment Model (PAM)). *Model suitable for the purpose of assessing a specified process quality characteristic, based on one or more process reference models. (ISO/IEC 33001:2015; SEVOCAB)*

For example, ISO/IEC 15504-5 contains a process assessment model that defines practices and results that are expected to be delivered by an organisation that develops software, and an assessment using this PAM checks whether the defined practices are performed and the defined results created and used. This PAM is based on the process reference model ISO/IEC/IEEE 12207 *Systems and software engineering—Software life cycle processes* described in Sect. 3.1.5.

Similarly for systems development, ISO/IEC 15504-6 contains a PAM based on the PRM ISO/IEC/IEEE 15288 *Systems and software engineering—System life cycle processes*. A third example is COBIT v5 as described in Sect. 4.8 , which includes a process reference model for governance and management of enterprise IT, as well as a process assessment model for these processes.

To judge the relevance and importance of any given assessment, for example when a supplier states that an assessment was performed, at least the following information is therefore needed and should be requested if relevant:

- process reference model and process assessment model used
- assessment method used
- process scope, i.e. which processes were assessed
- organisational scope, i.e. which organisation or part thereof was assessed

However, CMMI does not use this separation between process reference model, process assessment model and assessment method, even though of course the same information is available. In this case, one needs to know the CMMI variant (correctly called "constellation", see Sect. 5.5.3 below) used instead of PRM and PAM to judge the relevance of an assessment for a certain context.

Process and process quality dimension. An important concept in the continuous representation is the two-dimensional structure, with the *process dimension* referring to the processes assessed, and the *process quality dimension* (called the capability dimension in ISO/IEC 15504-1:2004 and in CMMI) referring to the quality of implementation of these processes, leading to two-dimensional capability profiles as shown in Fig. 5.5.

Definition 5.14 (Process dimension). *Set of process elements in a process assessment model explicitly related to the processes defined in the relevant process reference model(s). (ISO/IEC 33001:2015, SEVOCAB)*

Definition 5.15 (Process quality dimension). *Set of elements in a process assessment model explicitly related to the process measurement framework for the specified process quality characteristic. (ISO/IEC 33001:2015, SEVOCAB)*

Fig. 5.5 Sample capability profile of an organisation

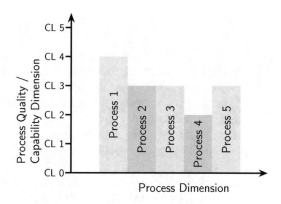

Section 5.5.4.2 describes the usage of these dimensions in SPICE.

Generic practices. In Sect. 4.6.2, the steps *State–Enable–Verify–Reward* were introduced as a tool for deploying processes or process changes. Generic practices as used in maturity models extend and refine this concept by defining steps needed to ensure that a certain process is used as the standard way of working within an organisation. In CMMI, this concept is called the "institutionalisation" of the process. The following definition contains the basic idea of generic practices as used in CMMI and SPICE.[9]

Definition 5.16 (Generic practice). *Activity that helps to introduce and perform a process routinely within an organisation.*

Generic practices are *generic* in the sense that they are applicable to any process, both within the particular model and beyond it. An example of such a generic practice from CMMI is "GP 2.2 Establish and maintain the plan for performing the process", with a very similar practice contained as GP 2.1.2 in SPICE. As a generic practice, this practice is applicable to any process, requiring (somewhat simplified) that the process activities are planned.

Specific or base practices. Apart from the generic practices that describe how to ensure that a process is indeed performed, maturity models of course also need to describe the process itself. This is mainly done using specific (in CMMI) or base (in SPICE) practices:

Definition 5.17 (Specific or base practice). *Activity that describes what needs to be done as part of a particular process to achieve its purpose.*

Obviously, while the generic practices are the same for any process, the specific or base must be defined individually for each process.

---

[9] The definitions of "generic practices" in CMMI and SPICE describe the same basic concept but unfortunately each in a way that it is not applicable to the other model.

Case Study 5.2. (CS Insurance InfoSys) As described in Case Study 4.2, CS Insurance InfoSys decided to use CMMI-DEV for managing and improving development, and ITIL for managing and improving operations.

In order to ensure that the defined development processes were actually used, and to continually improve these processes, regular small CMMI assessments were performed. This included quarterly one-day assessments for each development department, typically consisting of 100–200 developers, always selecting one project from the department to assess. For this task, an internal assessment team was built up including project leaders and quality managers from all departments who then performed the assessments on different departments. This helped to increase the acceptance of the assessment results as well as improve communication and flow of ideas between projects and departments. Additionally, a larger but still "inofficial" assessment was performed once per year with an external lead appraiser to get an external view.

When the company tried to move the process management approaches used for development and operations closer together, it was decided to introduce some form of assessment for operations as well. However, operations was based on ITIL which is not expressed in a way to be used as the basis for assessments (cf. Sect. 3.8.1), and neither CMMI for Services (CMMI-SVC, see below) nor ISO/IEC 20000 had been published yet. It was therefore decided to follow the approach described in [21] and create an internal process assessment model, using the contents of ITIL but the structure of CMMI. In this model, the ITIL statements were translated into CMMI-type specific practices, and the generic practices from CMMI were applied to the ITIL processes.

5.5.2 Capability and Maturity Levels

This section provides a short overview of the thinking behind the different levels in the major capability maturity models.

Maturity levels. Maturity levels describe the overall maturity of processes within an organisation. This is usually described using the following scale:

- Maturity level 1 ("initial"): no requirements; this is the starting maturity level.
- Maturity level 2 ("managed"): basic project or work management is implemented, but different projects or teams may still work rather differently.
- Maturity level 3 ("defined"): the work processes are defined and standardised, work is performed according to this definition, and processes are managed.
- Maturity level 4 ("quantitatively managed"): once processes are standardised, quantitative models based on experience data are used to predict and manage

them. For example, based on the type of project and the amount of testing done, one may predict the number of defects remaining and use this prediction for release decisions.

- Maturity level 5 ("optimising"): using the quantitative models developed on the previous level, processes are continuously and systematically optimised. While on the previous levels, the focus was on improving the various technical and management processes, the improvement processes themselves are now improved systematically.

Capability levels. In contrast to maturity levels, capability levels describe the capability of an individual process within an organisation but, at least in the case of capability level 2 upwards, the core concepts behind the level are the same as for maturity levels:

- Capability level 0 ("incomplete"): no requirements; this is the starting capability level.
- Capability level 1 ("performed"): the process is performed, but without any systematic management yet. This capability level is achieved if the specific practices are implemented but not the generic or management practices. (In SPICE, specific practices are occasionally assigned to higher capability levels.)
- Capability level 2 ("managed"): the process under consideration is managed, i.e. the generic practices for managing the process are implemented.
- Capability level 3 ("defined"): the process is defined and standardised.
- Capability level 4 ("quantitatively managed"): quantitative models are used to predict and manage the process.
- Capability level 5 ("optimising"): using the quantitative models developed on the previous level, the process is continuously and systematically optimised.

5.5.3 Capability Maturity Model Integration (CMMI®)

Capability Maturity Model Integration (CMMI) [11, 27] is a family of models for process improvement and process governance which was originally developed for systems and software development. Like its predecessor CMM, it was created at the Software Engineering Institute (SEI), Carnegie Mellon University, in Pittsburgh, USA, but at the end of 2012 responsibility for CMMI was transferred to the newly founded CMMI Institute, also at Carnegie Mellon University. In March 2016, the CMMI Institute was acquired by ISACA®, the organisation that also publishes COBIT.

5.5.3.1 CMMI constellations

There are three different so-called constellations of CMMI, covering different application areas, with a large common core.

- *CMMI for Development* (CMMI-DEV) addresses the development of systems and software.
- *CMMI for Acquisition* (CMMI-ACQ) addresses the acquisition of products and services, typically products that are developed specifically for the acquiring organisation. In the context of software processes, this constellation covers the practices that the customer has to perform in order for the development (project) to be successful.
- *CMMI for Services* (CMMI-SVC) addresses the provision of services. This model has some similarity with ITIL but explicitly covers services in general, not just IT services.

Although rarely used in this combination, these three constellations support each other in the joint business model shown in Fig. 5.6.

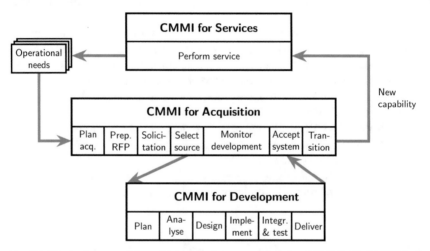

Fig. 5.6 The business model combining the three constellations of CMMI. © CMMI Institute 2007, reprinted with permission.

In this context, the main focus will be on CMMI-DEV, which was the initial constellation of CMMI, based on its predecessor SW-CMM. The current version of all three constellations is v1.3, which will be used as the reference in the following description. Work on a new version (working title: *CMMI Next Generation*) is under way but so far no publication date has been announced.

Case Study 5.3. (CS Insurance InfoSys) Once CMMI-SVC was first published in 2009, the question arose whether to continue with the assessment model created by CS Insurance InfoSys itself which was based on a mixture of CMMI and ITIL (as described in Case Study 5.2), or to move to CMMI-SVC.

After some discussion, it was decided to stick with the current internal model since on the market, adherence to ITIL was considered far more relevant than CMMI-SVC. However, since in the meantime ITIL-based certification model ISO/IEC 20000 had been published (cf. Sect. 3.8.1), the internal model was revised using concepts and requirements from ISO/IEC 20000. A few years later, the company decided to go for a certification based on ISO/IEC 20000.

5.5.3.2 Structure of CMMI

In CMMI, the same contents can be represented in two different ways, either in a staged representation or in a continuous representation (as introduced in Def. 5.11 and Def. 5.11 above). The continuous representation uses the same structure as SPICE as described in Sect. 5.5.4.2 below.

The basic structure of the staged representation is shown in Fig. 5.7 and consists of five maturity levels, where each maturity level consists of a number of process areas. The process areas, in turn, consist of specific and generic goals, which are further broken down into specific and generic practices.

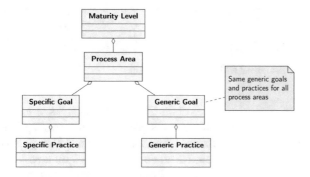

Fig. 5.7 Class model of the CMMI staged representation

CMMI does not distinguish between a process reference model and a process assessment model but integrates both into one model, consisting of the goals and practices that both describe the process and form the criteria for assessing the process.

In addition to the model itself, there is a family of assessment methods called SCAMPI which will be described below.

As Fig. 5.8 shows, the process areas of CMMI-DEV are arranged in four categories (the four columns of the table) which help to understand what these process areas are about even though they do no affect their meaning. The rows show which maturity level these process areas belong to, starting with maturity level 2 since there are no requirements on level 1.

CMMI-DEV v1.3	Process Mgmt.	Project Mgmt.	Engineering	Support
2		Project Planning (PP)		Configuration Management (CM)
		Project Monitoring and Control (PMC)		Process & Product Quality Assurance (PPQA)
		Supplier Agreement Management (SAM)		Measurement and Analysis (MA)
		Requirement Management (REQM)		
3	Organizational Process Focus (OPF)	Integrated Project Management (IPM)	Requirements Development (RD)	Decision Analysis and Resolution (DAR)
	Organizational Process Definition (OPD)	Risk Management (RSKM)	Technical Solution (TS)	
	Organizational Training (OT)		Product Integration (PI)	
			Verification (VER)	
			Validation (VAL)	
4	Organizational Process Performance (OPP)	Quantitative Project Mgmt.(QPM)		
5	Organizational Performance Mgmt. (OPM)			Causal Analysis and Resolution (CAR)

Fig. 5.8 The process areas of CMMI for Development

The specific goals and practices of the CMMI process areas essentially define the basic steps needed to perform the process properly. When reading these goals and practices, one will find few surprises if any, and the main challenge in general is not performing the practices as such, but to do this consistently across all projects all the time, which leads us to the basic philosophy of CMMI as described below.

Before that, some examples of specific practices in CMMI will help to understand these concepts:

- The specific practice SP 1.2 in the process area *Organizational Process Focus* (OPF) summarises an important topic of the current chapter by stating "Appraise the organization's processes periodically and as needed to maintain an understanding of their strengths and weaknesses". In other practices of this process area, the results of such appraisals (as well as other improvements) are then turned into process action plans and implemented.
- Looking at the process area *Product Integration*, the specific practice SP 1.3 states "Establish and maintain procedures and criteria for integration of the product components". Again, these procedures and criteria are later used to perform

the integration of the product components into larger components and eventually the final product.

In Sect. 6.2.3, the process area *Measurement and Analysis* will be described in some detail, providing an additional example. As these examples show, CMMI addresses both technical tasks and management tasks, as well as work performed on the level of the individual project or the overall organisation.

5.5.3.3 Basic philosophy of CMMI

CMMI is based on a few fundamental concepts that are implemented in various ways:

Adequacy. To ensure that processes provide business value, CMMI puts strong emphasis on adequacy of all activities, but this sometimes makes life difficult for beginners to the model. There are few strict rules in CMMI stating that work has to be performed in a certain ways, and beginner's question about how to perform a certain process almost always get the answer "it depends ... do it as adequate". CMMI states, in the various practices, that certain topics such as training people for the work they do must be performed, but almost always explicitly stating "as adequate". In the training example, this allows the organisation to decide that maybe in one case, a full-blown training programme lasting several weeks may be adequate, whether in another case a short email informing everybody about a change in the process may be sufficient.

This way, CMMI ensures that all important questions of how to perform the work are addressed, but the answer should always be based on what provides most business value, and therefore may be very different for different projects and organisations.

In particular, the emphasis on adequacy helps to ensure that CMMI is not specific to any one development approach, and it can be used (and is used) by organisations working with both plan-driven and agile development, as shown for example in [12].

Consistency. Building on adequacy, consistency is concerned with making sure that the adequate way of working is actually performed. Consistency therefore is expected in various ways, starting with the obvious consistency between process definitions and their implementation. As just described, process definition should be adequate regarding their contents and level of detail, but whatever is defined as a mandatory part of the processes should be treated as such, with exceptions only in genuinely exceptional cases. Implementation of defined process standards should be checked by quality assurance, with more or less coverage as adequate, and deviations should be addressed.

Another aspect of consistency regards the handling of process policies and similar documents: many organisations define nice policies or quality manuals stating the importance of quality, customer satisfaction etc. but then do not even set up any form of measurement or tracking of this allegedly important values. However, the purpose of such policies is to guide the daily work in the organisation, and state what is considered important by high-level management. Therefore, whatever is stated as important in the policies and similar documents needs to be reflected in quality assurance priorities, measurements and other aspects of day–to–day work. Without that, the policy is worthless and just a piece of paper.

Visibility. Finally, visibility is a tool helping to implement whatever was agreed, and to support consistency. Using mechanisms such as measurements, reporting, reviews and other QA activities, an organisation can identify to what extent objectives are indeed achieved, or whether a project is progressing as planned.

With these fundamental concepts, CMMI supports the governance of an organisation. On the other hand, this implies that using and adhering to CMMI is not a task that can be delegated to the quality management or development groups but higher-level management itself has to play an active part.

5.5.3.4 Generic goals and practices

CMMI uses the concept of generic practices as defined in Def. 5.16 but additionally groups them using *generic goals*, see Table 5.2. Generic goals and practices describe needs to be done to integrate a process in the culture of an organisation, or to "institutionalise" it as it is usually called in the CMMI community.

Table 5.2 CMMI Generic goals and practices

GG 1	Achieve Specific Goals
GP 1.1	Perform Specific Practices
GG 2	**Institutionalize a Managed Process**
GP 2.1	Establish an Organizational Policy
GP 2.2	Plan the Process
GP 2.3	Provide Resources
GP 2.4	Assign Responsibility
GP 2.5	Train People
GP 2.6	Manage Configurations
GP 2.7	Identify and Involve Relevant Stakeholders
GP 2.8	Monitor and Control the Process
GP 2.9	Objectively Evaluate Adherence
GP 2.10	Review Status with Higher Level Management
GG 3	**Institutionalize a Defined Process**
GP 3.1	Establish a Defined Process
GP 3.2	Collect Improvement Information

These generic goals and practices are therefore very useful for process improvement and deployment. At the same time, the large number of practices that needs to be checked for each process area in an CMMI appraisal causes a lot of work for such appraisals. This is the main reason why generic goals and practices in this form will probably be no longer part of the forthcoming Version CMMI 2.0, see Sect. 5.5.3.7.

5.5.3.5 CMMI (SCAMPI) appraisals

Appraisals based on CMMI usually follow the *Standard CMMI Appraisal Method for Process Improvement* (SCAMPI) as defined in [14]. These appraisals use a combination of different types of documents (including both documents defining the processes appraised, and documents resulting from performing these processes) and interviews with the personnel involved in the processes, on different levels ranging from developer/tester etc. to senior management.

Although in practice it does not always work out like that, the main goal of SCAMPI appraisals is to identify process improvement opportunities and needs. The secondary goal is to provide objective feedback on the maturity or capability of the processes used in the organisation appraised for internal (management) or external (customer) use.[10]

There are three different classes of SCAMPI appraisal are distinguished based on their required thoroughness, the amount of data to be collected and the resulting effort, and the results provided:

- SCAMPI A appraisals are the most thorough and the only ones that are allowed to report a maturity or capability level of the organisation appraised. A SCAMPI A is performed by a team of at least four members including the lead appraiser, and will typically include an on-site period of about one week or more for a medium-sized organisation and maturity level 3. SCAMPI A is the only method that is allowed to provide a "rating", i.e. a statement about whether or not certain CMMI goals have been satisfied, and whether a certain maturity or capability level has been achieved as a result.
- SCAMPI B appraisals are less thorough, therefore involve less effort but also not quite as reliable as a SCAMPI A. Their main result is a presentation of the strengths and weaknesses of the organisation and a so-called characterisation of the individual CMMI practices in the scope of the appraisal on a red/yellow/green scale. SCAMPI B appraisals are mainly performed for internal process improvement or as an intermediate step towards performing a SCAMPI C to reach a certain maturity level of capability level profile.
- SCAMPI C, finally, are the appraisals with the least effort and typically last a few days, with a team consisting of one or two members. Although these appraisals involve the least effort and therefore are considered the least reliable, they can still be very useful for internal process improvement where there is hopefully little motivation to hide problems.

SCAMPI appraisals must be led by a *certified lead appraiser* (SCAMPI A) or a *certified team lead* (SCAMPI B or C), and team members must have taken the "of-

---

[10] This emphasis is sometimes summarised by stating that "performing a SCAMPI without process improvement results in a scam".

ficial" CMMI Introduction training. The results of a SCAMPI appraisal must be reported to the CMMI Institute, which reviews the reports to ensure the SCAMPI method was applied correctly, and analyses them for statistical reports. If requested by the appraised organisation, the results of a SCAMPI A will be published on the CMMI Institute's web site[11]. Many organisations that perform the appraisal for internal purposes therefore decide not to use the SCAMPI methods but some similar but self-defined appraisal methods based on the *Appraisal Requirements for CMMI* (ARC) instead, performing an ARC B or ARC C appraisal rather than a SCAMPI B or C.[12]

5.5.3.6 A small example of using CMMI for improvement

Example 5.4. The company TechSys develops large technical systems consisting of hardware and software, with safety as an important requirement. Therefore, quality and safety of the products are treated with high priority. These products and their on-time delivery also has a certain public visibility, so on-time delivery is TechSys' main concern apart from safety.

Nevertheless, there were a number of projects in the past that could not be delivered on time, which caused the company serious problems and negative publicity. Therefore, it was decided to improve the development processes, and CMMI-DEV was selected as the reference model for the improvement project. To support these activities, an external consultant was engaged.

After about a year, TechSys considered that it was getting close to reach at least maturity level 2, and decided to perform an initial SCAMPI appraisal. To start, a small (SCAMPI C) appraisal was performed which showed however that there were still considerable gaps before reaching maturity level 2. It turned out that the consultant came from a SPICE background rather than a CMMI background, which in many ways is very similar but there are a few important differences. In particular, TechSys had put the focus on improving the processes in some selected projects, rather than addressing the processes as used in the entire organisation, including *all* projects.

After some initial discussion, the company understood that including all projects in the improvement effort would bring far more benefit, in particular in the long-term, compared to the current approach. As a result, the improvement project was restarted, this time addressing all projects (excluding just one or two small, non-typical projects).

In order to ensure that projects are delivered on time, particular emphasis was initially put on project estimation (part of the process area Project Plan-

---

[11] https://sas.cmmiinstitute.com/pars/pars.aspx

[12] Since many people do not understand the difference between a SCAMPI B/C and an ARC B/C appraisal, they often still use the better-known term SCAMPI rather than ARC.

ning) and on monitoring project progress (which is part of the process area Project Monitoring and Control). This involved identifying the cost drivers of the development work, and to collect data to quantify these cost drivers. Furthermore, TechSys put strong emphasis on standardising the development processes, with the goal to learn from each other and to make it easier to prepare the documentation necessary for release of the products by the relevant regulatory bodies (which was important because most products had high safety requirements). Before, there was little contact between different development teams, and each team essentially interpreted the process definitions in the quality manual in very different ways.

It also turned out that the QA group—which was strongly separated from the development teams, as required by most safety standards—was insufficiently staffed and not able to perform QA adequately, leading to bugs found late in the process and therefore to delays. As a result, additional staff was moved to the QA group.

Implementing these changes involved considerable cultural change and took some time, but after a bit more than two more years TechSys was able to perform an appraisal to confirm maturity level 3. Apart from this, rather formal, achievement, the main achievement was that projects were almost always able to keep to their schedules, and if they started to run late this could be identified early on so that the project leaders could react. An unexpected but welcome side effect was that the standardised development processes helped developers to find their way in a different project fairly quickly. As a result, it was still effective to move additional people to a project fairly late in the project, reducing the effect of *Brooks's Law "Adding manpower to a late software project makes it later"* [7, Ch. 2].

Overall, it was agreed that this initiative had considerably improved the company, in particular the risks involved had been strongly reduced and most projects after that were performed at least close to plan.

5.5.3.7 The way ahead: CMMI v2.0

At the time of writing, work on CMMI v2.0 (initially called CMMI Next Generation) is under way, expected to be released in 2018. Of course, it is not possible to predict exactly the changes that will be incorporated, but the following changes are currently expected:

- Increased emphasis on performance and performance measurement / benchmarking
- More methodology-specific guidance, in particular for using CMMI in combination with Scrum: so far, CMMI has tried to leave out any methodology-specific contents, which has led to the strange situation where most of the organisations using CMMI for improvement are using Scrum in at least a considerable propor-

tion of their projects, while at the same time many people see CMMI as focussing on plan-based development and disallowing agile methodologies.

- Easier language: for all its useful contents, CMMI currently certainly is no easy reading, using a lot of specific terminology that is difficult to understand for non-specialists. It will therefore certainly be very helpful if this issue is now addressed.
- The distinction between specific and generic practices will be removed. From the author's point of view, this is rather unfortunate, since the generic practices and the resulting emphasis on "institutionalising" the processes are one of the strong points of the CMMI.

In contrast to previous versions, it currently seems that the model will no longer be available for free download but must be purchased based on a subscription model.[13]

5.5.3.8 Close relatives: Team Software Process (TSP) and Personal Software Process (PSP)

The Team Software Process (TSP) [24] and the Personal Software Process (PSP) [22] were mainly developed by Watts S. Humphrey at the Software Engineering Institute (SEI) who also created the predecessor version of CMM, and apply the same ideas to the level of the project team or individual that CMMI-DEV applies to the level of the development organisation. As a result, they can easily be used in combination, and support each other, as for example the case study [38] shows.

With PSP, the individual developers collect data about the any mistakes made, and the effort invested in certain tasks, in order to learn from these data to create higher-quality software and to increase the accuracy of estimates. TPS builds on that by using these data for project management.

TSP and PSP are very disciplined processes and need a lot of initial training. As a result, start-up cost are fairly high but the benefit as reported in [20] and [40, Chap. 5] well makes up for that. Of course, since the main concepts of PSP and TSP are published, it is also possible to implement them without any formal training as provided by the SEI, but this is unlikely to work for small, self-motivated teams.

5.5.4 SPICE (ISO/IEC 15504 and ISO/IEC 330xx)

One of the core concepts of SPICE which distinguishes it from e.g. CMMI is the distinction between process reference models (PRM) and process assessment models (PAM), as introduced in Sect. 5.5.1. As a reminder, a PRM describes the processes involved, including purpose, main results and main steps of the process as well as

---

[13] See https://cmmiinstitute.com/products/cmmi/cmmi-v2-products, last access 2018-03-30.

the separation between different processes. A PAM builds on the PRM and adds criteria for assessing the capability of the process.

5.5.4.1 The SPICE Family of Norms

Eventually, the feedback mentioned led to a completely new structure of the norm, including the following main parts of the ISO/IEC 15504 series:

- ISO/IEC 15504-2 was defined as the *normative* part of the norm, while all other parts are defined as *informative*. Part 2 describes the general approach, the conceot of PRM and PAM, the two-dimensional structure of the results with capability dimension and process dimension (see below), the required competency of an assessor, and other basic concepts.
- ISO/IEC 15504-5 describes a PAM for software development based on the PRM given in ISO/IEC 12207 (cf. Sect. 3.1.5). This is the model most people think of when talking about "SPICE".
- Similarly, ISO/IEC 15504-6 describes a PAM for systems development based on ISO/IEC/IEEE 15288 as the underlying PRM
- Later, a PAM for IT service management was added in ISO/IEC 15504-8, based on the new PRM ISO/IEC TR 20000-4, which itself is based to some extent on ITIL.

Currently, a move is underway to revise the ISO/IEC 15504 family of norms and replace it by the new ISO/IEC 330xx family.

5.5.4.2 Capability and Process Dimension in SPICE

In the continuous representation as used in both SPICE and CMMI, one is free to select a set of processes to be assessed (the process dimension, based on the PRM), and to assign an individual (target or actual) capability level to each process (the capability dimension, based on the PAM), which leads to a *capability profile* of the form shown in Fig. 5.5 above. An important step in planning an assessment therefore is the definition of the target profile, i.e. the processes and their respective capability levels to be assessed.

As shown in Fig. 5.9, each capability level is assigned a number of process attributes which are defined as follows:

Definition 5.18 (Process attribute). *Measurable property of a process quality characteristic. (ISO/IEC 33001:2015, SEVOCAB)*

The capability levels defined in SPICE and the assigned process attributes are shown in Table 5.3.

To evaluate these process attributes in an assessment, assessment indicators are defined as part of the process assessment model which tell the assessor what information to look for.

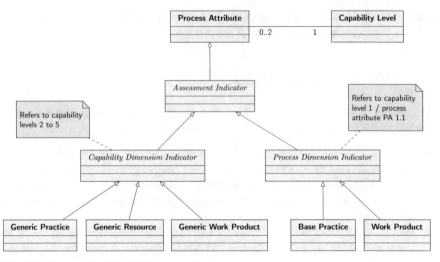

Fig. 5.9 Class model of the SPICE process attributes

Table 5.3 SPICE process attributes and capability levels

Level 5	**Optimizing**	The process changes and adapts to meet business goals effectively
PA 5.1 PA 5.2	Process Innovation Continuous Improvement	
Level 4	**Predictable**	The process performs consistently within defined limits
PA 4.1 PA 4.2	Process Measurement Process Control	
Level 3	**Established**	The process uses a defined process based upon software engineering principles
PA 3.1 PA 3.2	Process Definition Process Deployment	
Level 2	**Managed**	The process is managed; work products are established, controlled and maintained
PA 2.1 PA 2.2	Performance Management Work Product Management	
Level 1	**Performed**	The implemented process achieves its process outcomes
PA 1.1	Process Performance	
Level 0	**Incomplete**	The process is not implemented, or fails to achieve its process outcomes

Definition 5.19 (Assessment indicator). *Sources of objective evidence used to support the assessors' judgment in rating process attributes. (ISO/IEC 33001:2015, SEVOCAB)*

In order to assess the capability level of an organisation or project, the assessment indicators are rated (in both capability and process dimension), and the result is aggregated into a rating of the process attributes, and these in turn lead to the rating of the capability level.

The rating of assessment indicators and process attributes is performed on the scale shown in Table 5.4.

Table 5.4 SPICE process attribute rating scale

N	Not achieved	0–15%	Little or no evidence of achievement
P	Partially achieved	16–50%	Some evidence of a sound systematic approach. Some aspects of achievement can be unpredictable
L	Largely achieved	51–85%	Evidence of a sound systematic approach. Some performance variation
F	Fully achieved	86–100%	Evidence of complete and systematic approach. No significant weaknesses

However, the apparently very exact definition of the different rating levels based on percentages are in fact much less exact since no underlying measurements are defined.

The capability dimension. This dimension defines the possible values (capability levels) that an assessment can assign to a process, with SPICE using a scale from 0 to 5. The capability levels form a hierarchy, and for a process to achieve a certain capability level the criteria for all lower levels must be fulfilled.

The philosophy behind the individual capability levels is the same as for the equivalent capability and maturity levels in CMMI, even though the details of their definitions are of course different.

The main type of indicator in the capability dimension is the *generic practice*, which is based on the same ideas as the generic practice in CMMI, even though the detailed wording is of course different. In contrast to CMMI, SPICE additionally defines generic resources and generic work products as indicators.

The process dimension. SPICE can be used with different processes based on different reference and assessment models. This possibility to select the processes to be assessed is described as the process dimension.

In the process dimension, indicators are the process-specific *base practices*, similar to the specific practices in CMMI, and work products describing the results to be produced by the process.

We have already mentioned several pairs of PRM and PAM that can be used in this context, some of them included in the ISO/IEC 15504 or ISO/IEC 330xx family of norms, see Sect. 5.5.4.1, while others use that same structure without being part of that family of norms, such as the COBIT PRM and PAM and some other models listed in Sect. 5.5.4.4 below.

5.5.4.3 SPICE assessments

Like CMMI appraisals, SPICE assessments use data collected from interviews and documents to provide feedback for process improvement and about the capability of the processes assessed. However, for SPICE there is no defined institution responsible for ensuring the quality of assessments and the correct application of the assessment method. The requirements on SPICE assessments are defined in ISO/IEC 33002 (which in 2015 replaced the original ISO/IEC 15504-2), but does not go as far as defining any specific assessment method, or any minimum criteria regarding the information to be collected as the basis for assigning a certain capability level.[14] As a result, there is no distinction between different classes of assessments, and different SPICE users and assessors have defined their own assessment methods with varying degrees of thoroughness. The value of SPICE assessments and their results can therefore vary widely.

Another difference between CMMI appraisals and SPICE assessments is that SPICE is usually applied to individual projects, while CMMI puts a strong emphasis on appraising an entire organisation.[15] This is partly due to the fact that SPICE is often used to monitor projects from the customer point of view, while CMMI tends to be used either internally, to identify weaknesses to be addressed, or as a tool for selecting a contractor, before a contract has actually been agreed. In particular if a customer (rather than a third-party assessor) performs the assessment, he will of course in general not be allowed to see any projects performed by the same supplier for different customers, possibly his competitors. This is a situation that is particularly common for Automotive SPICE.

SPICE assessor qualification An important part of any maturity model-based assessment is to ensure the qualification of the assessment team, in particular the assessment team leader. For CMMI, this is ensured by the CMMI Institute which certifies *lead appraisers* that have proven that they are adequately qualified. Since the CMMI Institute also owns the relevant intellectual property rights, it is the only organisation that is entitled to certify assessment leaders. ISO/IEC 33002 does define minimum requirements on the qualification of assessors, but since for SPICE there is no organisation comparable to the CMMI Institute, in theory everybody could self-certify his or her qualification. However, this is of course not a practical situation, and over time two generally accepted organisations have been founded to certify SPICE assessment leaders:

---

[14] This statement is not true for all variants of SPICE, for example Automotive SPICE described below does define an assessment method, a common qualification scheme for assessors, and some more infrastructure for assessments.

[15] Of course, in some cases a large and long-running project might be seen as an organisation, so the difference is not quite as clear-cut as it might seem at first.

- The *International Assessor Certification Scheme* (INTACS[16]) was founded in 2003, when work on the ISO/IEC 15504 standards was nearing completion.
- The *International Registration Scheme for Assessors* (IntRSA[17]) grew out of a split of INTACS in 2006.

Both schemes work in a very similar way, with a three-level certification scheme for assessors: after passing the training plus exam, applicants become *provisional assessors* which entitles them to participate on assessment teams. Once they have gained sufficient assessment experience, they may become *assessors* which entitles them to lead small assessments or, with extensive assessment experience, they become *principal assessors* and are entitled to lead larger assessments and assessment teams.

Using assessment results for process improvement. One of the main goals of performing process assessments is to use the results for process improvement. From the improvement point of view, the "real work" only starts once the assessment has been completed. In SPICE, such improvement is addressed by the norm ISO/IEC TR 33014 *Guide to process improvement*. This norm looks at improvement from three different perspectives:

- process perspective: process improvement is a process in itself which should be managed adequately.
- organisational perspective: from this perspective, the task of process improvement is to improve the organisational standard processes and provide adequate support for the projects implementing these standard processes.
- project perspective: improve the processes as performed in the organisation's projects.

5.5.4.4 Variants of SPICE

There are a number of variants of SPICE that adapt the general concept to a specific application area. This subsection describes some of the main such variants. All of these variants were developed by various initiatives of SPICE users and consultants from the relevant application area, often under the umbrella of the SPICE User Group, but were not published as official standards in the ISO/IEC 15504 (or now ISO/IEC 330xx) series.

Automotive SPICE. Automotive SPICE is in practice by far the most relevant variant of SPICE, being widely used in the European automotive industry. In the 1990, the large car manufacturers realized that software formed a growing part of their product and its value, but they did not have sufficient control of this part.

Spice for Space (S4S). The development of SPICE for Space was sponsored by the European Space Agency (ESA) to support the improvement of development

---

[16] http://intacs.info

[17] http://intrsa.org

processes for space software [17, 18, 10]. Like Automotive SPICE, it uses the basic SPICE framework but includes a PRM and PAM adapted in this case to the development of space software. This was mainly done by integrating the requirements from several standards on space software development into SPICE, which resulted in several additional processes, many additional notes on how to interpret a certain practice in the context of space software. Furthermore, an assessment method is described as part of S4S.

To address the selection of processes to be assessed, [17] contains an appendix with four example target profiles based on four software criticality classes.

SPICE Medical Devices (MediSpice). This variant applies the concepts of SPICE to the development of medical devices [9]. Since safety is a high priority and there are many legal guidelines and other standards that need to be addressed in such development, MediSPICE is working on integrating these other requirements into the PRM and PAM.

COBIT. The IT Governance model COBIT (cf. Sect. 4.8.2) also supports the assessment of the processes described. While the assessment approach included with COBIT 4 was based on CMMI, the current version COBIT 5 moved to an assessment approach based on SPICE and therefore includes a PRM and a PAM.

Since ISACA, the organisation that is responsible for COBIT, has acquired the CMMI Institute in 2016, it remains to be seen what influence this has on assessments for future versions of COBIT.

Enterprise SPICE. While most SPICE variants put their focus on individual projects or organisations, Enterprise SPICE, although also based on the concepts of SPICE, puts its focus on the entire enterprise and its processes.

5.5.5 Capability Maturity Models from the Customer's Point of View

Apart from using capability maturity models for internal process improvement, there are two other common usages:

- for marketing purposes: by achieving a certain maturity level or capability profile and publishing this, development organisations hope to get a better standing on the market and to increase their (potential) customers' trust that they will be able to deliver what they promise. This is an approach particularly popular in Indian software houses, where in most cases the customers are geographically very distant which makes communication more difficult and such trust therefore is particularly important.
- for supplier selection: in contrast to the previous usage, this usage type is driven by the customer who performs or initiates assessments on one or more potential suppliers as a basis for selecting a supplier for a certain project. This is for exam-

ple common in US-American defence projects (typically based on CMMI), or in the European automotive industry (typically based on Automotive SPICE).

Example 5.5. An enterprise needed a supplier to deliver the software and hardware for a advanced radar system, to be part of a large (civilian) systems product the enterprise was planning to offer to its customers.

A first selection process narrowed the number of potential suppliers down to two. In the next step, SCAMPI C appraisals were performed on both these potential suppliers, as well as some other technical reviews. To get an objective picture, an external SCAMPI lead appraiser was contracted to perform these appraisals on behalf of the enterprise. In this case, it was particularly important to clarify the flow of information: the lead appraiser had to sign standard non-disclosure statements for the two potential suppliers, with explicit exceptions defined as needed for the appraisal. Of course, the presentation of appraisal results, containing the strengths, weaknesses and improvement recommendations as well as the characterisation of the CMMI practices assessed, needed to go to the enterprise.

Furthermore, there was some discussion about whether to perform these appraisals as "official" SCAMPI C appraisals, which implied that the results plus certain administrative information was to be delivered to the CMMI Institute, or to perform the appraisals as in-official appraisals, without involving the CMMI Institute. It was eventually decided to perform an official SCAMPI C in order to ensure that the relevant rules about such an appraisal would be followed correctly, but to ensure that the administrative information to be provided to the CMMI Institute would be on a very high level, for example without names of persons involved or of projects appraised.

5.6 Assessment and Improvement in Agile and Lean Development

While assessments are not wide-spread in agile and lean development, improvement is considered important and for example integrated in the Scrum methodology as the sprint retrospective at the end of every sprint, identifying what went well and what should be improved in the next sprint.

Even assessments based the standard maturity models such as SPICE and CMMI, however, are applicable in agile development as well as plan-driven development, and, contrary to what is occasionally stated, there is no conflict between agile development and maturity models [19, 12].

Looking at it the other way round, process improvement itself can be based on an agile approach, for example by using Scrum and its concept of short sprints to organise the improvement activities. A different way of applying agile concepts to software process improvement is described by the SPI Manifesto described in the next section.

David Anderson, who introduced Kanban into the world of IT (cf. Sect. 3.5.6), in [1] described this in more detail, showing how maturity levels and different forms of implementing Kanban relate to and support each other.

Using katas for improvement. An improvement technique that become quite well-known in the agile community over the last few years is the use of *katas*. The Japanese term "kata" originally described a training form in martial arts where a certain predefined movement pattern is practised repeatedly so that it becomes the natural way for the individual to react, without thinking about what to do next. The same concept has more recently been adapted to process improvement and to coding:

- *Code katas* were introduced by Dave Thomas, one of the authors of the Agile Manifesto, as exercises to perform in order to practice one's coding skills where it is OK to try out different approaches, without causing problems in a project environment [37]. So far, Thomas has defined 21 katas, taking about 30 to 60 minutes, that can be solved in very different ways.
- Quite a different approach, but with the same underlying kata principle, are the *Toyota katas* [34], consisting of the *improvement kata* and the *coaching kata*. The basic idea here is to get into a habit of continual improvement by regularly performing the improvement kata consisting of the following four steps:
  - – Understand the direction / challenge
  - – Grasp the current condition
  - – Establish the next target condition
  - – Experiment toward the target condition

  To ensure learning from these improvement katas, they should be supported by coaches who practice their skills by the coaching kata.

5.7 The TAME Project and Related Work

The TAME (*Tailoring A Measurement Environment*) project was performed by Victor R. Basili's group at the Univ. of Maryland, USA, with the main purpose to develop methods and tools for software process improvement, with a strong focus on using metrics and empirical data [4]. This group developed a surprising number of different but related concepts that became very well-known, some of which existed before but were revised and improved by TAME:

- *MVP-L* is a notation for the formal description of processes and their interaction, and was introduced in Sect. 2.2.2 above.
- The *Quality Improvement Paradigm (QIP)* is a variant of the PDCA improvement cycle as described below.

- The *Experience Factory* extends the concepts of QIP and will also be described below.
- The *Goal-Question-Metric Paradigm (GQM)* describes an approach to the systematic definition and use of measurements, see Sect. 6.2.2, and thus helps to collect the data needed in an experience factory.
- The *TAME system* is a software engineering environment with the purpose to automate, based on the MVP-L notation, a considerable part of the software processes.

The Quality Improvement Paradigm (QIP). The Quality Improvement Paradigm (QIP) describes an improvement cycle, but in contrast to models such as the PDCA cycle the QIP cycle is performed on two interacting levels, the level of the individual project and the corporate level [2, 3]. Experience is collected by the individual projects, evaluated and packaged on the corporate level, and the packaged experience is then used by other projects to improve.

The Experience Factory. The concept of the Experience Factory extends and formalizes the QIP, making the two levels even more explicit by distinguishing between the project organisation which runs and improves the project, and the "Experience Factory" on the corporate level which has the task to collect, analyse and package the projects' experience in an experience base which is then used to support the projects, see Fig. 5.10.

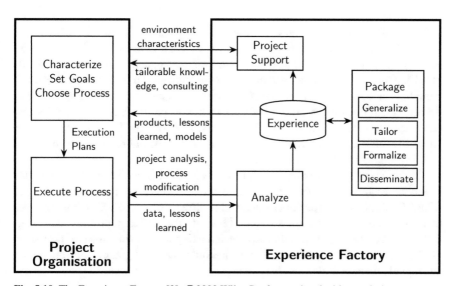

Fig. 5.10 The Experience Factory [3]. ©2002 Wiley Books, reprinted with permission.

5.8 Further Assessment and Improvement Approaches

This section gives a short overview of some other well-known approaches to assessing and improving software processes.

IDEAL^{SM}. The IDEAL improvement method was developed at the Software Engineering Institute [31] and is therefore best known in the context of CMM(I), but actually it is a variation of the PDCA cycle and independent of CMMI.

IDEAL stands for the five phases of this improvement method:

- **I**nitiating phase is different from the other phases, as well as from the phases of the PDCA and similar cycles, in that it is only performed once to establish the general improvement infrastructure.
- **D**iagnosing phase starts the improvement cycle with some form of assessment of the existing processes.
- **E**stablishing phase addresses the identification of the improvement goals, setting up metrics to monitor progress, etc.
- **A**cting phase refers to the actual implementation of the selected improvements, including creation of the solution, piloting, and deployment across the entire organisation.
- **L**everaging phase, also called Learning phase, looks at the improvements and how they were performed, with the goal of improving the improvement cycle itself.

ISO/IEC TR 29110 "Lifecycle profiles for Very Small Entities (VSEs)". is a family of standards that addresses VSEs where a VSE is defined as an "enterprise, an organization, a department or a project having up to 25 people" (ISO/IEC TR 29110-1:2016, Sect. 3.75). The goal is to provide VSEs with a set of processes and process definitions adequate for these entities, and with an opportunity to get their adequate definition and implementation of software processes certified, as often required by customers, based on certification requirements adequate for VSEs rather than for larger organisations. According to [28] many VSEs have already achieved such a certification based on ISO/IEC TR 29110.

The core concept of this family of standards is to define a set of so-called *profiles* which each consist of a collection of practices extracted from standards such as ISO/IEC 12207 but are specifically adapted to different types of VSEs. For example, there is a set of software engineering profiles with four different profiles addressing different levels (entry, basic, intermediate and advanced). A similar set of profiles is available for systems engineering. For each profile, there is a specification document and a guide document.[18]

TPI, TPI NEXT and TMMi. As the name suggests, Test Process Improvement (TPI) as well as its successor TPI NEXT and the Test Maturity Model integration

---

[18] In order to genuinely support VSEs and unusual for ISO/IEC standards, several of these standards, in particular the profile guides, are available for free while usually such standards are fairly expensive.

(TMMi) are models for assessing and improving the test processes. Similar to the capability maturity models discussed above, they do not define the processes as such but defines a number of practices that are needed for mature test processes. All three models interpret the term "test" rather widely, beyond the standard definition where tests are based on execution of the system tests (see e.g. Def. 1.33) to include further analysis activities such as reviews.

Benchmarking. Not a specific improvement model but a more general approach is benchmarking which aims to evaluate and measure certain aspects of the performance of an organisation or project, and to compare it with other, similar organisations and projects. For example, an organisation developing commercial may have its productivity measured in terms of function points implemented per developer-day, and compared with other organisations in order to get feedback beyond its own experience. Such feedback can then be used as a guide for internal improvements, or as a basis about outsourcing decisions such as deciding whether or not to hand certain tasks to an external service provider.

To get comparable data from other organisations, this usually requires support from a suitable consultancy which collects measurement data from different customers. To some extent, published data are also available, for example in [26].

Although standardisation of processes is not strictly speaking necessary for benchmarking them, it makes the benchmarking results far more reliable since they lead to less variation between different instances of the same process.

Further Reading

A very good introduction to software quality management can be found in [39]. Since this book concentrates on basic concepts of "systems thinking" rather than specific technologies and methods, it still is very much up to date. despite having been published in 1992.

Similarly old but still very relevant is [30] which describes hands-on experience in improving development processes at Microsoft in the early 1990s.

To understand the capability maturity models in depth, one needs to read, or better work through, the models themselves. While CMMI is available for download from the CMMI Institute's web site[19], SPICE consists of ISO/IEC norms which are fairly expensive to buy.

Exercises

5.1. The company CS Insurance InfoSys as described in our case study plans a new project to develop a large commercial web application. However, because of lack of

---

[19] http://cmmiinstitute.com/cmmi-models, registration needed

resources it will not be able to perform the project itself but intends to use a software development company as a supplier. Nevertheless, CS Insurance InfoSys intends to do its best to ensure that the project will be successful, and considers to use one of the reference models discussed in this chapter to structure its own part of the project work.

1. What are the main challenges that the customer organisation needs to address in a large software development project?
2. Which of the models described are suitable to support this work?
3. Which criteria should CS Insurance InfoSys use to select one of the models, or possibly to decide against using any of them?

5.2. For each of the three values *People*, *Business*, and *Change* of the SPI Manifesto, describe one example of an SPI activity where this value was not adequately taken into account. What happened as a result? (If you do not know any actual example, think about what could typically happen in such a case.)

References

1. D. Anderson.   Driving evolutionary change with the Kanban method.   `http://anderson.leankanban.com/driving-evolutionary-change-with-the-kanban-method/` (last access 2017-11-16), 2016.
2. V. R. Basili. The experience factory and its relationship to other improvement paradigms. In I. Sommerville and M. Paul, editors, *Software Engineering—ESEC '93. 4th European Software Engineering Conference, Garmisch-Partenkirchen, Germany, September 13–17, 1993. Proceedings*, number 717 in LNCS, pages 68–83. Springer, 1993.
3. V. R. Basili, G. Caldiera, and H. D. Rombach. Experience factory. In J. J. Marciniak, editor, *Encyclopedia of Software Engineering*. John Wiley and Sons, Inc., second edition, 2002.
4. V. R. Basili and H. D. Rombach. The TAME project: Towards improvement-oriented software environments. *IEEE Transactions on Software Engineering*, 14(6):758–773, June 1988.
5. J. Becker, M. Rosemann, and C. v. Uthmann. Guidelines of business process modeling. In W. v. d. Aalst, J. Desel, and A. Oberweis, editors, *Business Process Management*, number 1806 in LNCS, pages 30–49. Springer, 2000.
6. P. Bourque and R. Fairley, editors. *Guide to the Software Engineering Body of Knowledge (SWEBOK®), Version 3.0.* IEEE Computer Society, 2014. Available online at `http://www.swebok.org` (last access 2018-01-07).
7. F. B. Brooks. *The Mythical Man-Month.* Addison-Wesley Publ. Company, 1975.
8. Business Process Maturity Model (BPMM), version 1.0. Technical report, OMG Group, 2008. Available online at `http://www.omg.org/spec/BPMM/1.0/PDF` (last access 2017-03-14).
9. V. Casey and F. McCaffery.   The development and current status of Medi SPICE.   In T. Woronowicz, T. Rout, R. V. O'Connor, and A. Dorling, editors, *Software Process Improvement and Capability Determination. 13th International Conference, SPICE 2013, Bremen, Germany, June 4-6, 2013. Proceedings*, CCIS, pages 49–60. Springer, 2013.
10. A. Cass, C. Völcker, L. Winzer, J. Carranza, and A. Dorling. SPiCE for SPACE: A process assessment and improvement method for space software development. *ESA Bulletin*, pages 112–119, August 2001. Available online at `http://www.esa.int/esapub/bulletin/bullet107/bul107_14.pdf` (last access 2017-03-14).
11. M. B. Chrissis, M. Konrad, and S. Shrum. *CMMI for Development: Guidelines for Process Integration and Product Improvement.* Addison Wesley, 3rd revised edition, 2011.

12. CMMI Institute. A guide to Scrum and CMMI: Improving agile performance with CMMI. Available online at `http://cmmiinstitute.com/cmmi-and-agile` (last access 2017-03-14).

13. CMMI Institute. Process maturity profiles. Available online at `http://partners.clearmodel.com/cmmi-appraisals/process-maturity-profiles/` (last access 2017-03-14).

14. CMMI Institute. Standard CMMI® Appraisal Method for Process Improvement (SCAMPI^SM). Version 1.3b: Method Definition Document for SCAMPI A, B and C. Handbook CMMI-Institute-2014-HB-001, December 2014.

15. P. B. Crosby. *Quality is Free. The Art of Making Quality Certain*. Penguin Books Ltd, 1979.

16. M. Dumas, J. Mendling, M. La Rosa, and H. A. Reijers. *Fundamentals of Business Process Management*. Springer, 2013.

17. ECSS Secretariat. Space product assurance. software process assessment and improvement—part 1: Framework. Technical Report ECSS-Q-HB-80-02 Part 1A, European Cooperation for Space Standardization, 2010. Available online at `http://ecss.nl/hbstms/ecss-q-hb-80-02-part-1a-software-process-assessment-and-improvement-part-1-framework/` (last access 2017-03-14).

18. ECSS Secretariat. Space product assurance. software process assessment and improvement—part 2: Assessor instrument. Technical Report ECSS-Q-HB-80-02 Part 2A, European Cooperation for Space Standardization, 2010. Available online at `http://ecss.nl/hbstms/ecss-q-hb-80-02-part-2a-software-process-assessment-and-improvement-part-2-assessor-instrument/` (last access 2017-03-14).

19. H. Glazer, J. Dalton, D. Anderson, M. D. Konrad, and S. Shrum. CMMI or agile: Why not embrace both! Technical note CMU/SEI-2008-TN-003, Software Engineering Institute, 2008. Available online at `https://resources.sei.cmu.edu/library/asset-view.cfm?assetid=8533` (last access 2017-11-29).

20. G. Goth. The Team Software Process: A quiet quality revolution. *IEEE Software*, pages 125–127, November/December 2000.

21. T. Greb, R. Kneuper, and J. Stender. Nutzung der CMMI-Assessmentmethode für ITIL-Prozesse. *it Service Management*, 2(3):10–15, 2007.

22. W. S. Humphrey. *Introduction to the Personal Software Process^SM*. SEI Series in Software Engineering. Addison-Wesley Professional, 1989.

23. W. S. Humphrey. *Managing the Software Process*. SEI Series in Software Engineering. Addison-Wesley Professional, 1989.

24. W. S. Humphrey. The Team Software Process^SM (TSP^SM). Technical Report CMU/SEI-2000-TR-023, Carnegie Mellon University, Software Engineering Institute, November 2000. Available online at `http://resources.sei.cmu.edu/library/asset-view.cfm?assetid=5287` (last access 2017-08-11).

25. ISO. The ISO survey of management system standard certifications 2016—executive summary. Available online at `https://www.iso.org/the-iso-survey.html` (last access 2018-01-22).

26. C. Jones. *Applied Software Measurement*. McGraw Hill, 3rd edition, 2008.

27. R. Kneuper. *CMMI. Improving Software and Systems Development Processes Using Capability Maturity Model Integration (CMMI-DEV)*. Rocky Nook, 2009.

28. C. Y. Laporte and R. V. O'Connor. Software process improvement standards and guides for very small organizations. an overview of eight implementations. *Crosstalk*, 30(3):23–27, May/June 2017.

29. J. Ludewig. People make quality happen (or don't). In Swiss Association for the Promotion of Quality (SQA) and European Organization for Quality—Software Committee (EOQ-SC), editors, *Software Quality. Concern for People. Fourth European Conference on Software Quality*, pages 11–21. vdf Hochschulverlag AG an der ETH Zürich, 1994.

30. S. Maguire. *Debugging the Development Process*. Microsoft Press, 1994.

31. B. McFeeley. Ideal[SM]: A user's guide for software process improvement. Handbook CMU/SEI-96-HB-001, Software Engineering Institute, Carnegie Mellon University, February 1996.

32. J. Mendling, H. Reijers, and W. van der Aalst. Seven process modeling guidelines (7PMG). *Information and Software Technology*, 52(2):127–136, 2010.

33. H. A. Reijers, J. Mendling, and J. Recker. Business process quality management. In J. vom Brocke and M. Rosemann, editors, *Handbook on Business Process Management 1, International Handbooks on Information Systems*, pages 167–185. Springer, 2nd edition, 2015.

34. M. Rother. Improvement kata and coaching kata practice guide. http://www-personal. umich.edu/~mrother/Handbook/Practice_Guide.pdf (last access 2017-06-27, 2015.

35. R. Schuette and T. Rotthowe. The guidelines of modeling—an approach to enhance the quality in information models. In T.-W. Ling, S. Ram, and M. L. Lee, editors, *Conceptual Modeling— ER '98. 17th International Conference on Conceptual Modeling, Singapore, November 16-19, 1998. Proceedings*, number 1507 in Lecture Notes in Computer Science (LNCS), 1998.

36. SPI Manifesto. http://2017.eurospi.net/images/Documents/spi_manifesto.pdf (last access 2017-01-08), 2010. Chief editors: Jan Pries-Heje and Jørn Johansen.

37. D. Thomas. Codekata. http://codekata.com/ (last access 2017-06-27), 2016.

38. D. S. Wall, J. McHale, and M. Pomeroy-Hff. Case study: Accelerating process improvement integrating the TSP and CMMI. Special Report CMU/SEI-2005-SR-012, Carnegie Mellon, Software Engineering Institute, December 2005. Available online at http://resources. sei.cmu.edu/library/asset-view.cfm?assetID=7347 (last access 2017-08-11).

39. G. M. Weinberg. *Quality Software Management. Vol. 1: Systems Thinking*. Dorset House Publishing, 1992.

40. E. Yourdon. *Rise & Resurrection of the American Programmer*. Yourdon Press, PTR Prentice Hall, 1996.

Chapter 6
Software and Software Process Measurement

Abstract To investigate whether a (deployed) software process achieves its goals, some form of validation is needed. In many cases, a measurement program can provide a useful basis for such validation, providing information about performance and quality of software and software processes, and thus helping to find gap and identify improvement opportunities or needs. In this chapter, we lay the foundation for such measurement programs. We discuss the measurement basics and provide an overview of different measurement approaches such as the Goal Question Metric (GQM) paradigm. In particular, the measurement of processes and their quality is introduced, using the process quality model Gokyo Ri. Additional information about software processes can be gained from measuring related objects such as the software created or the service provided.

6.1 Introduction

6.1.1 Why measure?

One of the first to argue for the use of metrics in software development was Tom Gilb who compared the software development process to a ship navigating at sea where the ship's captain needs a number of instruments to succeed. Similarly, "the captains of the software ships will be more likely to succeed in meeting their specifications if the instruments for measuring the development process are sufficiently detailed and accurate, and used at a sufficiently early point in the work process" [7, p. 50].

If you can't measure it, you can't manage it. This common saying (alternatively stating "... can't improve it") is variously attributed to a number of famous people such as management guru Peter Drucker or W. Edwards Deming. Nevertheless, it over-simplifies the topic since there are many properties and objects that are important but cannot be measured and still must be managed or improved. On the contrary, there are good reasons to state that "if you don't understand it, you should not mea-

© Springer Nature Switzerland AG 2018
R. Kneuper, *Software Processes and Life Cycle Models*,
https://doi.org/10.1007/978-3-319-98845-0_6

sure it" because otherwise one will measure the easy-to-measure properties rather than the important ones.

Put differently, it is important to analyse what information can really be gained from measurement and measurement data. Some organisations have a tendency to over-interpret measurement data because they provide objective information about the object measured. While this is in general true, it is not always true, and even if the information is objective, it rarely includes *all* relevant information.

Reasons for using measurements. For a variety of reasons, measurements are commonly used in the context of software processes. Two of the main reasons for measuring software processes are:

- monitoring and control of the process: regarding software processes, this may refer to an individual instance of the process such as a specific project. In this case, one usually starts with planning, i.e. setting target values, and then regularly comparing actual values against these targets. In this case, the main purpose of measurement is to provide the information needed to manage the project or, more general, the development effort. On the other hand, the resulting measurement data can then feed into the planning and estimating future work.

  Regarding processes in the early stages of the software life cycle, measurements usually provide limited benefit and are therefore rarely used.

  At a late stage of the software life cycle, operations and service management are also commonly monitored and measured in order to manage and control the process, for example by measuring the number of open incident tickets and reacting if this number moves outside the target range.

  Since operations and service management processes tend to be fairly standardised, defining meaningful measurements for these processes is easier than e.g. for development, and therefore more widespread.

- process improvement: measurements can also help to identify weaknesses in the process, both the process model and the performed process. For example, such weaknesses may consist of process steps that are inefficient or lead to many problems. Once such weaknesses have been identified, they can be addressed and the process improved.

The combined use of measurement data for process improvement and for managing projects is for example described in the Experience Factory concept, see Sect. 5.7, where data are collected to improve processes and to plan and support future work.

6.1.2 Measurement Terminology

Before discussing measurement in more detail, we first introduce the relevant terminology. Two important and closely related terms are measure and measurement:

Definition 6.1 (Measure).

1. Variable to which a value is assigned as the result of measurement.
2. Make a measurement.

(ISO/IEC 25000:2014, SEVOCAB)

Definition 6.2 (Measurement). *Set of operations having the object of determining a value of a measure.*
(ISO/IEC 25000:2014, SEVOCAB)

Unfortunately, these two definitions reference each other, leading to an infinite circle, something the author learned as a maths student not to do.

The following definitions relate measures (which may or may not include relevant information) to information needs or relevant attributes of the object measured.

Definition 6.3 (Indicator). *Measure that provides an estimate or evaluation of specified attributes derived from a model with respect to defined information needs.*
(ISO/IEC 25000:2014, SEVOCAB)

An indicator that is considered particularly important is often called a *Key Performance Indicator* (KPI). In practice, however, nearly all indicators are called KPI, independent of their importance.

Definition 6.4 (Metric). *Quantitative measure of the degree to which a system, component, or process possesses a given attribute. (SEVOCAB)*

In the following, we will therefore mainly discuss indicators and metrics, while measures that are not at the same time a metric or indicator are not really of interest.

6.1.3 Measurement Foundations

Measurement scales. According to the definition of a measure, measurement assigns "a value" to a measure without stating the type of value. In the case of the metric, this must be a quantitative value, while in the case of other measurements this is not required. The following different types of measurement scales are commonly distinguished, for example in ISO/IEC/IEEE 15939:2017:

- A *nominal scale* contains named values, which do not allow any form of computation or comparison other than for equality. An example is the measure which assigns the affected product component to the bugs found. In many cases, measures using a nominal scale are not directly considered as measures but are used as the starting point for measuring the frequencies of the different nominal values as described below.

- A *ordinal scale* also contains named values which do not allow any form of computation but which are ordered. An example for a simple ordinal scale consists of the values "major", "medium" and "minor" for measuring the severity of bugs found, or the maturity or capability level 1 to 5 as used in CMMI and SPICE.
- An *interval scale* (cardinal scale without meaningful zero) is a quantitative scale where differences between two values are a meaningful concept but not their ratio (e.g. value *a* is twice as large as value *b*) or, put differently, there is no meaningful zero value in the scale. An example of a interval scale measure is the point in time when a certain event happened, such as the opening or closing of a ticket in a ticket system.
- A *ratio scale*, finally, also is a quantitative scale but one which contains a meaningful zero value, and as a result computing the ratio between different values also becomes a meaningful concept.

  Examples of ratio scale measures are the average time taken for a certain task, the percentage of planned functions that have already been implemented, and the percentage of tickets that had to be re-opened due to customer complaints.

The first three types of scales are often used as base measures since they can be directly measured, but from these, a ratio-scale measure is then derived which is easier to handle and provides more information about the property measured. For example, by counting the appropriate frequency of values in a nominal or ordinal scale such as the number of "major" bugs found in testing a certain product, we can derive a new, ratio scale measure. Looking closely, the examples of ratio scale measures given above are all not measured directly but derived from other, base measures, as the difference between two interval scale measurement values, or the ratio (percentage) between two measurement values.

This leads us to the common distinction between base measures and derived measures:

Definition 6.5 (Base measure, derived measure).
Base measure: measure defined in terms of an attribute and the method for quantifying it.
Derived measure: measure that is defined as a function of two or more values of base measures.
(ISO/IEC/IEEE 15939:2017, SEVOCAB)

Lag and lead indicators. While the distinctions between different measurement scales as well as between base and derived measures are mainly of theoretical interest with little practical relevance, the following distinction between lag and lead indicators is very important for practical usage of indicators.[1] Most obvious indicators provide information about work done in the past, for example the number of bugs found in testing, the memory needed by a certain software package, or the number of requirements in status "implemented". Although in most cases this is the information one is most interested in, it does not help to manage work because the

---

[1] Note that this distinction only is relevant for indicators and not for measures in general.

work was already done in the past. In addition to these "lag indicators" that lag behind and describe what happened in the past, one therefore needs "lead indicators" that give an indication of what will happen in the future and can therefore be used to manage work. This is a distinction that is for example emphasised in COBIT 5 which distinguishes between "metrics for achievement of goals" (lag indicators) and "metrics for application of practice" (lead indicators) [8].

6.1.4 Metrics

While the definition of metrics strictly speaking talks about measuring "system, component, or process" attributes, in the context of software processes one commonly distinguishes between

- product metrics, in this case mainly software metrics, which provide information about the quality and other important properties of (software) products. In many cases, product metrics are lag indicators since measurements on products tend only to be possible fairly late in the life cycle.
- project and service metrics
- process metrics which provide information about how well or how efficient a process is defined, and performed. To get early feedback on the quality of products, in many cases process metrics are required as lead indicators.

Each of these types of metrics will be discussed in more detail below. However, even though the distinction as described seems very clear, in practice it is often far less clear which of these groups a certain metric belongs to. For example, the number of bugs found in a certain product may of course be considered a product metric, but it may also be considered a project metric, providing information about the state of the project, or as a process metric, providing information about the quality of the process used to create the product.

6.2 Implementing and Deploying Measures and Measurement Systems

When setting up measures on an object such as a process, a common approach is to start with the measures themselves, collecting the measures that come to mind and that possibly are supported by the tools available. The problem with this approach is that the measures that first come to mind rarely provide the information needed, or at best only part of the information needed. A better solution therefore is to start with the goals that one wants to achieve by using the measures, and derive the measures from these goals. Below, two approaches to defining measurements starting from the goals or information needs are the Goal–Question–Metric–Paradigm (GQM) and the CMMI process area "Measurement and Analysis", both described in more detail below.

6.2.1 Basic Concepts

A fairly high-level measurement process is described in ISO/IEC 15939:2017, see Fig. 6.1. This process emphasises the fact that any measurement activities should

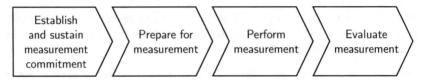

Fig. 6.1 The measurement process according to ISO/IEC 15939:2017

start with establishing commitment on such activities, and then to prepare for measurement by systematically selecting and defining the measures to be used, as described above. After the obvious step of performing measurement, the real benefit of any measurement activities is gained from evaluating and analysing the measurement results.

Measure definition. The definition of measures needs to include a number of attributes in order to be useful. As a minimum, the following attributes should be included:

- identifier, name
- description
- goal supported
- data sources and data collection
- allowed/possible values, scale
- definition, calculation of measure
- analysis and interpretation
- reporting format / visualisation / presentation
- frequency of collecting and reporting

Example 6.1. An IT service provider wanted to speed up the handling of customer requests that were handled by its service desk. As a first step towards that goal, the obvious choice was to start measuring the time it took the service desk to handle tickets received.

The result was that soon after such measurement started, handling times for tickets handled by the service desk really was reduced. However, at the same time the number of tickets passed on to second-line support grew consider-ably, and an analysis showed that many tickets that were slightly complex that would have been handled by the service desk in the past now were passed on to second-level support.

So even though the original goal was achieved, it turned out that the overall process in fact had deteriorated because second-level support now got many tickets to handle that should have been handled by the service desk.

In order to prevent problems such as those described in Example 6.1, it is usually recommended to introduce an entire *measurement system*, ideally including measures of all relevant aspects of the object to be measured, rather than just individual measures. Supported by concepts such as GQM and the CMMI process area "Measurement and Analysis", models such as ISO/IEC 25010 or Gokyo Ri as described below provide a basis for such measurement systems.

Example 6.2. Several years ago, a software company that developed various off-the-shelf software products started to work on improving its software processes.

Soon after that, a new release of one of its main products was prepared, and the results at first seemed devastating: the number of problems found in testing and in beta release had nearly doubled compared to the previous release that had had roughly the same amount of new functionality.

However, a more detailed analysis soon showed that this was not a problem but a sign of genuine progress. While in the past, many defects found in testing or beta had never made it into the bug tracking tool, this was the first release where (almost) all defects found were reported in that tool. So the number of defects itself actually had not increased at all, but only the number of defects that were visible and documented in the tool. In fact, this helped the company to correct nearly all the defects found, while in the past there always was a considerable number of defects found but then "lost" before they were corrected, and eventually customers were quite pleased with the new product version and its quality.

Metrics systems based on a quality model. Using a certain metric in general will lead to an improvement of the property measured just by pointing the emphasis to that property. As seen in Example 6.1 above, this may however be a local improvement leading to a global deterioration because other, possibly even more important aspects are ignored. This may get even worse if bonus payments or similar benefits depend on the metric. To prevent this, it is therefore important to work with an entire system of metrics that helps to ensure that *all* important properties are taken into account rather than just a few, one-sided ones. A useful basis for such a metrics system may be a quality model for the object to be measured. Two examples of such quality models are the software product quality model contained in ISO/IEC 250xx (see Sect. 6.3.2), or the process quality model Gokyo Ri (see Sect. 6.5). Both these models break down the concept of quality of the product or process into a set of quality characteristics and sub-characteristics which together aim to provide a full picture of this quality.

Balanced Score Card. A related approach that addresses an entire organisation rather than an individual process or product and its quality is the *Balanced Score Card* (BSC). It is called "balanced" because it aims to provide a balanced picture of where an organisation stands, and can be used as a tool for (strategic) management of an organisation [9]. The concept was developed by Robert S. Kaplan and David P. Norton to emphasise that financial data are not sufficient to lead an organisation because these data tend to be lag indicators, missing out on feedback that helps to identify problems early on. Today, there is a large number of variants of the perspectives or dimensions used in a BSC, but the original perspectives introduced by Kaplan and Norton were

- Financial
- Customer
- Internal business process
- Learning and growth.

In the current context, the internal business process perspective is the main important one, and most of what is described in this chapter feeds into that perspective.

The concept of the BSC can be applied on an individual level such as an IT service or software development department. In a more advanced form, Kaplan and Norton in [9] described it as a tool for strategic management using a top-down approach: at the top level, management defines goals for each of the perspectives, and sets up suitable measures to monitor the achievement of these goals. These goals and measures are then broken down step by step, for example starting from enterprise business goals and eventually defining and monitoring suitable metrics on the level of an individual software project.

Measures based on number of defects. Measurements are often based on the number of defects found in a certain context. This often needs some classification of these defects as a basis, for example describing when the defects was introduced or found in order to improve stage containment. A well-known defect classification system is the *orthogonal defect classification* (ODC) which classifies defects by defect type and defect trigger [6].

6.2.2 The Goal-Question-Metric Paradigm: GQM and GQM$^+$

GQM, closely related to the Quality Improvement Paradigm QIP and the Experience Factory (see Sect. 5.7), is the standard method to systematically identify appropriate metrics for a given purpose, and most other methods for the same purpose use some variation of GQM. Although developed for measurement systems in the context of software development, this paradigm is actually quite independent of software and applicable in other environments as well.

GQM emphasises the importance of defining metrics using a top-down approach, starting from *measurement goals* describing what one wants to achieve with the measurement programme. In the next step, questions are identified that characterise the attainment of these goals. Finally, metrics are associated with questions in order to answer them in a quantitative way [2]. These metrics are not necessarily associated with exactly one question but may be used to answer multiple questions, as shown in Fig. 6.2.

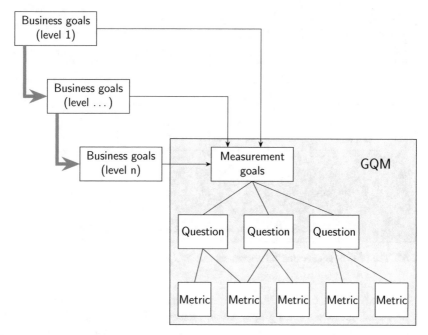

Fig. 6.2 GQM and GQM+

Since GQM starts with *measurement* goals, it does not include a direct link to the *business* goals of the organisation. To address this short-coming, the extension GQM$^+$ was developed in which business goals are explicitly included on different levels, and measurement goals link to these business goals, i.e. the focus of the measurement goals is to support achievement of the business goals, or provide feedback on the extent to which the business goals are being achieved [1, 3].

6.2.3 Measurement and Analysis in CMMI

The maturity model CMMI contains a process area "Measurement and Analysis" (MA) that is based on ideas similar to the measurement process defined in ISO/IEC 15939 and to GQM. SWEBOK [5, Chap.6, Sect. 6] also describes a very similar approach. As all process areas in CMMI, it includes a number of specific (SG) and generic (GG) goals, which are then detailed into specific (SP) and generic (SP) practices, where in the current context only specific goals and practices are relevant (see Sect. 5.5.3.2 for more detail on the structure of CMMI).

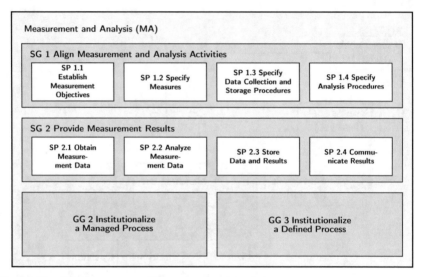

Fig. 6.3 The CMMI process area "Measurement and Analysis"

As shown in Fig. 6.3, the MA process area contains two specific goals, where the first goal addresses setting up suitable measures: based on the relevant information needs, measurement objectives are identified and measures to satisfy these objectives are specified, including procedures to collect and store the data and thus ensure that the data collected are comparable. Also included is the important specifying how to analyse the data collected. In far too many cases, organisations collect data which seem "interesting" but without any clead understanding what to do with these data, and how to analyse them. What is a "good" measurement value, and when is there any need for action or at least further analysis?

Once the measures have been defined, the next step is of course to collect the measurement data, and this aspect is addressed in the second specific goal. Although this essentially only requires that measurement data are collected, analysed and the results communicated as defined, this nevertheless is quite a challenge for many organisations, mainly because of the requirement "as defined".

Measurement and Process Maturity. CMMI (and, similarly, SPICE) does not cover measurement only in this process area "Measurement and Analysis" on maturity level 2, but extends this topic on higher maturity levels.

On maturity level 2, processes usually still vary considerably between different projects or teams, making measurement values difficult to compare. However, the main objective of maturity level 3 is to standardise processes and their enactment, which allows more meaningful process measurement. This provides a useful basis for quantitative management on maturity level 4, using measurement data from previous work for planning and managing future work.

6.2.4 Aggregating Different Metrics For Reporting

Management is usually flooded with information of various kinds, which it needs to interpret quickly. A common challenge in using measurement therefore is to evaluate and aggregate different indicators so that it is easy to identify at first sight where there is any need for action. The following algorithm for aggregating different metrics was developed as part of the project described in Example 6.3 below. Among other aspects, it addresses the challenge that different indicators need different ranges for their target value. For example, while for some indicator a measured value of 95% might be a great success, for some other indicator it might be inacceptably low.

Assume there are n indicators $M_1, \ldots, M_n$ with measured values $m_1, \ldots, m_n$. To make these values comparable, target ranges are defined that are used to transform the m_i into characterisations $c_1, \ldots, c_n$. The characterisations c_i take values from $\{\text{red}, \text{yellow}, \text{green}, \text{white}\}$ with the interpretation

- green: value is OK, no action needed
- yellow: value is not quite OK, values must be monitored
- red: value is not OK, analysis and possibly corrective action needed
- white: value is not available, or should only be monitored since no target ranges have been defined (yet). Values with this characterisation are excluded from further aggregation of values.

Take for example the indicator "average solution time" for tickets in a ticket system. It is now a business decision to decide on suitable target values (and in this case, an organisation may decide to additionally distinguish between tickets of different priorities). The organisation may decide that all tickets that are solved within 24 hours are characterised as green, tickets taking more than 24 hours but solved within 48 hours are characterised as yellow, and tickets taking longer than 48 hours are characterised as red. Similar, a second indicator "average response time" might use target values of 6 and 12 hours.

This way, different indicators deliver characterisations that are comparable and can now be aggregated. To aggregate them, they are converted into numerical characterisations $d_1, \ldots, d_n$ as follows: green is converted into 100%, yellow is converted into 50%, and red is converted into 0%. Now it is easy to compute the mean of the numerical characterisations of a set of indicators, and thus get an aggregated value which is a percentage in the range from 0% to 100%. To make it easy to evaluate these aggregated percentage values, it is suggested to convert aggregated values > 85% into green, values ≥ 50% but ≤ 85% into yellow, and values < 50% into red.

An alternative and stricter algorithm to aggregate the characterisation in this last step is to take the "worst" value as aggregate, i.e. if at least one of the aggregated values is evaluated as red, then the aggregate is red; if none is red but at least one is yellow, the aggregate is yellow as well; only if all values are green, the aggregate is green as well.

Example calculation. As an example of this multiple conversion of values, assume that an organisation has defined the indicators "average solution time" and "average response time" and its target values as described above. Assume the measured average solution time is 33 hours, which is characterised as "yellow" and converted to the numerical characterisation 50%. Similarly, assume the measured average response time is 5 hours which is "green" and converted to 100%. The mean of these two values is 75%, which in turn is characterised as "yellow".

So overall, the aggregated value for these two indicators that might get reported is 75%, characterised as yellow, and a manager will see at first sight that this is a value that needs closer monitoring.

6.3 Product Metrics

Product metrics provide information about the product developed or produced, and since this is usually delivered to the customer, it is in some sense the most important type of metrics. The main difficulty is that product metrics are usually lag metrics that can only be measured once the product is more or less complete, which makes it more difficult to react if they show any problems. In the following, we look at various kinds of metrics for software, in particular the software quality model defined in ISO/IEC 250xx.

6.3.1 Software Metrics

Over time, a large number of different kinds of software metrics has been developed, and the following description will cover some of the most important such metrics, without going into detailed definitions of the metrics covered.

Software size metrics. The size of software in itself in general is not very relevant, but it is relevant in order to make other metrics comparable. For example, the development effort as well as the number of bugs to be found grow more or less linearly with the size of the software under consideration, and the size is therefore an important factor for calculating derived measures. Unfortunately, there is no measure of software size that is widely usable and helpful; measures typically used are different variants of the code size measured in lines of code, or of function points which are mainly appropriate for commercial information systems.

Software complexity. There are many different measures for the complexity of software which help to estimate the effort needed for a certain software component, or to identify software components that need more thorough quality assurance because they are more likely to contain defects due to their high complexity. Two well-known metrics used for this purpose are McCabe's cyclomatic complexity, and Halstead's complexity measures.

6.3.2 Software Quality Metrics

In order to measure the overall quality of software, several models of software quality have been defined. Such a model may be used for defining the requirements on software, helping to address all relevant properties of the software to be developed. Once it has been developed, it helps to ensure that quality assurance addresses these relevant properties, and of course to set up a measurement programme for software quality.

A fairly old software quality model is FURPS, which is an acronym of the following properties that together define software quality according to this model:

- Functionality
- Usability
- Reliability
- Performance
- Supportability

The quality model described in the standard ISO/IEC 9126 was developed later with the same purpose, which has since been replaced by the ISO/IEC 250xx series, in particular ISO/IEC 25010. In this model, the quality of software is broken down into a number of quality characteristics (similar to FURPS), which in turn are further broken down into sub-characteristics. Figure 6.4 shows these characteristics and sub-characteristics of software quality, as defined in ISO/IEC 25010.

6.4 Project and Service Metrics

Measurement of projects and services performed is probably the most widely used form of measurement used in software processes. Some variant of measurement of the budget or effort spent and/or the work performed (earned value, burn-down

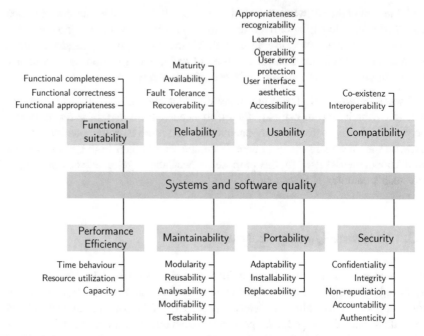

Fig. 6.4 Software quality characteristics according to ISO/IEC 25010:2011

chart, etc.) is used more or less in every development effort, as well as in every software services provided.

Project and service metrics refer to the middle ground between products and processes, and there is some overlap with product and process metrics. For example, the number of defects reported within a project provides information about the project and its current status, but also about the quality of the product developed and the processes used to do so. The main difference lies in the point of view. From the project point of view, one is mainly interested in the number of open defects and the effort involved. From the product point of view, one is mainly interested in the number of defects remaining, including the open defects found as well as the predicted number of defects not found yet. Finally, from the process point of view one is interested in questions such as during which process these defects were introduced and during which they were found, to help improve these processes.

IT service metrics. Since IT service processes often have a high number of instances and therefore highly structured, measurement of these processes is far more widely used than for development processes. For example, ITIL contains a set of metrics for each process, e.g. for incident management including the metrics "Total numbers of Incidents (as a control measure)", "Breakdown of incidents at each stage (e.g. logged, work in progress, closed etc)", "Size of current incident backlog" and "Number and percentage of major incidents".

The main purpose of using metrics in IT service management is to monitor and control the work, similar to project management. This often includes service quality metrics since the quality of the services is usually agreed upon with the customer in a Service Level Agreement (SLA) and the service provider needs to both track that this SLA is satisfied, and report this to the customer. Quality goals set in an SLA typically address various aspects of performance of the systems serviced (such as response times of the systems or applications), or of the service desk services provided (such as response and solution times for incidents reported).

6.5 Process Metrics: Measuring Process Quality Using Gokyo Ri

There are many different properties of processes that may be worth measuring. Most of them address some aspect of process quality and can therefore be subsumed under that topic. In this section, we will therefore discuss process quality and the characteristics that form part of it.

As described in Chap. 5, there is a large number of models to assess and improve the quality of processes. However, none of these models explicitly defines what is meant by "process quality", beyond the very high-level definition given in Def. 1.40. Therefore, the model *Gokyo Ri* was developed that provides a more detailed definition of process quality by identifying the different characteristics that together constitute process quality, not only for software processes but for processes in general [10].

Fig. 6.5 shows how in this model the quality of processes is broken down into characteristics and sub-characteristics, using the same structure as used to define software quality in ISO/IEC 25010 as described above.

Two of these process quality characteristics address the process to-be, two of them address the process as-is, and the remaining three address the combination or relationship of the two.

In the following, the process quality characteristics and sub-characteristics as defined in Gokyo Ri will be described in some more detail. Similar to other quality models, Gokyo Ri provides a foundation for defining requirements on the process, for process quality assurance, and for measuring the quality of the process by defining suitable measures for the sub-characteristics. While the sub-characteristics are still sufficiently abstract to apply to all processes and environments, the measures need to be defined specifically for each process and environment.

Process objectives and requirements. For a process to be of high quality its objectives and requirements must be defined, including clear agreements on what the process is to achieve.

Since there are no metrics that directly allow to measure this characteristic, suitable check-lists are provided in Appendix B.1 that help to evaluate its sub-characteristics.

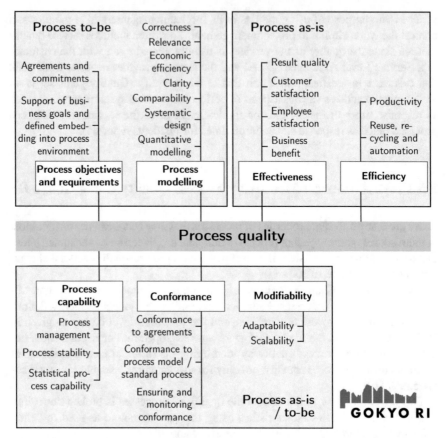

Fig. 6.5 Process quality according to Gokyo Ri

Agreements and commitments. This sub-characteristic addresses the question whether there are clearly defined agreements and commitments about the process and its
objectives, e.g. how the process is to be performed and what it is to achieve. Is
clearly defined what others, not directly involved in the process, may expect from
it?

Looking at software development processes, this may for example involve agreements with customers regarding a certain process (model) to be used, or working
on a certain CMMI maturity level. Agreements and commitments may also define
specific intermediate and final results to be delivered by the process. In IT Service
Management, such agreements are often documented in a Service Level Agreement
(SLA).

Support of business goals and defined embedding into process environment. A related aspect is the embedding of the process into its environment, e.g. as part of a
process landscape with agreed interfaces to other processes. This sub-characteristic
therefore looks at the interfaces between different processes and whether they are

suitably defined. A process scores highly if it fits well into the overall process landscape, with defined interfaces.

As a high-level example, the Plan-Build-Run process architecture used by some companies describes the cooperation between the business processes including the resulting requirements on the software used to support them ("Plan"), the software development processes ("Build"), and the operations processes used to run the software and provide the relevant services to the business ("Run"). For the software development process to run smoothly in this environment, it needs agreed interfaces to the "Plan" stage to define and agree on the relevant requirements, and to the "Run" stage to agree on the delivery of the software developed as well as the maintenance process that follows.

Process modelling. This characteristic refers to the quality of the model of the process: assuming some form of process model exists, is this model adequate and built up systematically; does it describe the relevant aspects of the process; is it easy to understand for the users of the model, etc.?

As described in Chap. 2, process modelling can be performed on very different levels of formality. The formality of the process model as such, however, is not part of the process (modelling) quality since no general statement is possible about which level of formalisation is best for modelling a process—other than to say that it must be adequate.

Therefore, the general "Guidelines of (Business Process) Modelling" as introduced in [13, 4] are used as criteria to evaluate the quality of process models, cf. Sect. 5.2. Even though they are stated as guidelines for business process modelling, they are equally applicable to other processes. These criteria are described in [4] and therefore only listed listed in Fig. 6.5 as the sub-characteristics of process modelling, apart from "quantitative modelling" which has been added and will be described below.

Quantitative modelling. A quality sub-characteristic that was added to the guidelines for modelling is the use of *quantitative modelling*. To satisfy this sub-characteristic, there should be a quantitative process model that defines an explicit relationship between input parameters that can be influenced by the organization performing the process, and output parameters that result from this input. For example, such a model could describe the relationship between the amount of testing done and the expected number of bugs remaining, as input to a decision about whether or not to release the product.

Such quantitative modelling is a very common approach in industrial production but less common and more difficult to use in software development. The reason for this is that such a quantitative model can only be created if the process is performed sufficiently often, with little variation, to get meaningful data as the basis for such a model. In CMMI, such models (called "process performance models") are therefore first required on maturity level 4.

Effectiveness. Does the process achieve its objectives, as seen by the quality of its results, the satisfaction of the customers and employees involved, or the business benefit?

Result quality. As mentioned before, the quality of the results of a process also is an important part of the quality of the process itself. In software development, the result quality can for example be seen and measured by the results of testing the software, or by feedback and bug reports from customers. A more general definition of software quality is provided by ISO/IEC 25010 as described above, and product quality can be evaluated based on these definitions.

Customer satisfaction. If a process is truly effective, this is reflected by the satisfaction of its customers. Note that this sub-characteristic refers to the satisfaction of the customers of the *process*, who are not necessarily the same as the customers of the organization but may for example be a different unit within the same organization. The customers of the process are those people who ask for and/or receive the process resuts.

Employee satisfaction. For an organization and its processes to be successful, not only the customers must be satisfied but also the employees. If developers are not satisfied with their work processes, they will be less productive and may try to circumvent the processes.

Employee satisfaction with a process can be measured using the usual tools such as an employee survey or, to some extent, the conformance to the defined process.

Business benefit. One of the sub-characteristics that are most important but at the same time most difficult to measure is the business benefit of a process. In the case of software development, this may for example be measured as the value of the process results as compared to the value of the process input and the cost incurred.

Efficiency. Does the process make good use of its resources to achieve its objectives? This characteristic includes for example the productivity of the process and the reuse (and not just reusability!) of its results.

Productivity. The productivity of a process is defined as the results in relationship to the resources put in. In processes such as IT service management, this is easier to measure, for example as the number of incidents handled per person-day. Much more difficult is the measurement of productivity in software development, since this involves the need for an adequate measure of the results created within a certain timeframe. Typical measures used are the number of lines of code or the number of function points implemented, which both may or may not be a suitable measure of the amount of results created depending among other aspects on the kind of software developed.

Another important factor that influences the measurement of productivity are the resources put in to create a certain result. These are typically measured either in terms of the effort involved (person-hours) or cost. When working with more or less fixed hourly rates, this leads to easily comparable results. If, however, the rates vary a lot, productivity can be very different between the two approaches, as is typically the case in off-shoring. In off-shoring, a typcal goal may be to increase the cost efficiency while accepting that the effort efficiency may be reduced.

Reuse, recycling and automation. This sub-characteristic brings together several approaches to re-using work of resources. While recycling is of little or no relevance in the context of software processes, reuse has been discussed a lot during the last twenty years or so. It is now mainly achieved using libraries and frameworks and has contributed a lot to the increased productivity of software developers.

Finally, automation looks at what part of the development process has been automated, for example using generators, build or testing tools.

Process capability. The capability of a process describes it ability to deliver the expected results reliably and in adequate quality.

Process management. This sub-characteristic describes to what extent the process is managed, both performing the essential steps of the process and process management steps such as setting a process policy, defining the process, training people and verifying the process. Appendix B.2 contains a check-list for evaluating this characteristic. Alternatively, it can be measured using the capability level from either of the models CMMI-DEV or SPICE.

Process stability. The stability of a process is a concept taken from statistics and therefore mainly applicable for processes that are repeated often. While this is often the case for some IT service management processes, process stability is less applicable to development processes.

A process is defined as stable (in the sense of statistical process control) if its main features are measured regularly and the statistical parameters, mean value μ and standard deviation σ in the case of a Gaussian distribution, stay constant for these features.

Statistical process capability. Statistical process capability assumes a stable process and therefore is of little relevance for development processes in most organizations.

It compares the interval $[\mu - 3\sigma : \mu + 3\sigma]$ which contains all measurement values apart from few exceptions, with the range of tolerance for the metric. The better the interval lies within the range of tolerance, and therefore the higher the confidence that all measurement values lie within the range of tolerance, the higher the statistical process capability. (Some more background on this concept will be provided in Sect. 8.2.1.)

Conformance. Conformance to relevant standards and agreements can be of very high or of little importance, depending on the environment. It involves the conformance to external required standards as well as to internal agreements on the process such as process definitions and models. In addition to the positive results of checking for conformance of the process (ex post), conformance also involves ensuring conformance in the way the process is set up (ex ante).

Conformance to agreements. The conformance to agreements refers to the agreements as discussed above and will usually be measured using some kinds of audits or reviews.

As far as the agreements define some process model or standard process to be used, this is not included here but covered in the following separate sub-characteristic.

Conformance to process model / standard process. This sub-characteristic is very similar to the conformance to agreements above but refers to relevant process models or standard processes that are to be used.

A process model or standard process may be relevant because of some agreement with the customer or an internal requirement by management. In some cases, for example when developing safety-critical software, it may also be required by law or some regulatory body.

Ensuring and monitoring conformance. In most cases, conformance alone is not sufficient if one cannot in some way show or prove it. An important part of conformance therefore is to evaluate the extent to which the organisation actively ensures and monitors conformance to agreements, process models and standard processes. In practice, this will usually be a prerequisite for reliably achieving conformance.

A simple measurement of this of this sub-characteristic could for example be the percentage of process requirements from agreements, process models and standards that have some activity assigned to ensure and monitor conformance, out of all such process requirements. This would then be measured based on some form of review or audit.

Modifiability. Finally, modifiability addresses how easy (or difficult) it is to modify the process or to adapt it to a different size of input, such as smaller or larger projects.

Adaptability. A process is highly adaptable if it can easily be adapted to changes of the environment. Such an adaptation of the process may need to include both the process definition and the way the process is actually performed. In the case of software development, this may involve adapting the process to a change in technology or a new tool.

Scalability. Closely related to adaptability is the scalability of a process which evaluates how easy it is to scale the process up or down to a change in volume. While this is more difficult in software development and will typically mainly be achieved by scaling the resources, i.e. the number of developers, it is fairly common in IT service management. In particular for cloud services which have recently become more and more important, scalability is a central success factor.

Example 6.3. This example has been published as a case study in [11], and led to the development of the process quality model Gokyo Ri described above.

As one step in the introduction of globally consistent processes for IT service management, the IT department of a large enterprise decided to set up a system of indicators providing feedback on the quality of the IT service management processes in the different units or regions. The following design decisions were taken early on:

- To make indicators for different processes comparable, on a high level the same indicators were to be used for all processes, addressing their differences only on a more detailed level.
- Since a DWH including a reporting structure for other topics was already in use, the new system of indicators was to be integrated into this structure.
- Since absolute numbers are difficult to interpret, indicators were to be set in relation to the size of the relevant group or similar, where appropriate. This also allowed to compare measurement values for organisational units of different sizes.
- To ease interpretation, wherever possible the indicators were to be defined as percentages, with 100% being a perfect value and 0% being an extremely bad value. In some cases, this implied that indicators had to be defined in a non-intuitive way, for example measuring the percentage of non-problems rather than of problems.

Based on these decisions and using a variant of the GQM paradigm, the following four KPIs were defined for each process, where each KPI was calculated as an aggregation of a set of process-specific measures:

- degree of implementation: is the process implemented according to the relevant guidelines and agreements?
- process performance: how efficiently is the process performed?
- process output quality: how good are the process results, and do they satisfy the process customer requirements?
- process management: is the process managed adequately?

For each of the main ITIL processes, a suitable set of metrics was defined using this structure. For example, for the process *Incident Management* the following metrics were defined:

- degree of implementation: all the following metrics address implementation problems that the organisation tried to resolve
  - non-long-term incidents
  - level resolution rates (measuring the distribution of incidents across the three support levels used)
  - percentage of incidents related to a SLA (i.e. with the relevant SLA documented in the ticket system)
  - percentage of incidents correctly assigned (i.e. with a low number of re-assignments to different support groups)

- percentage of incidents correctly classified (i.e. without re-classification)
- percentage of (closed) incidents with documented solution
- process performance
  - incident backlog (calculated as the number of open incidents in relation to the monthly workload of the unit)
  - average solution time
- process output quality
  - first call resolution rate
  - percentage of incidents without reopen and without complaints
  - percentage of incidents handled according to SLA (including only SLA statements on reaction and solution times)
- process management: measured using a questionnaire based on the CMMI generic practices

For the other ITIL processes considered, similar metrics were defined. Each of these metrics was defined in detail, using a standard template which included an identifier, definition, data source and formula for calculation, an SQL script where appropriate, and so on.

For each of the four KPIs described, the relevant metrics were aggregated as described in Sect. 6.2.4, and the resulting aggregated values were collected into a dashboard containing these four values for each ITIL process reported, allowing management to see at first sight where action was needed. At the same time, the process managers were able to drill down on these aggregated data as needed, to analyse why any of the KPIs was reported as needing monitoring or corrective action.

In setting up this measurement scheme, it turned out that there were two major challenges apart from identifying suitable metrics. The definition of suitable target values is not a technical but a business decision, and it turned out to be quite difficult to define adequate values. In particular, different process owners had different expectations about the quality of their process, and some of them tended to set very ambitious targets while others set very generous targets, so that initially, processes where the process owners had low expectations seemed to work very well (all metrics were reported as "green") while other processes that might have higher quality were reported as "yellow" or even "red" because they did not achieve the ambitious targets of the process owners.

The second challenge in defining the metrics was rather unexpected but turned out to be really difficult to solve: the goal was to be able to report the metrics separately for different units or regions. However, this required that each ticket had to be assigned to one of these units or regions, but this assignment turned out to be far from obvious. A ticket might have been reported by the customer in one region, worked on within a second region, and finally resolved within at third region. This in particular was likely to happen for high-priority tickets where a "follow-the-sun" mode had been introduced, but also happened in other cases for a variety of reasons. An assignment scheme was finally agreed upon even though everyone agreed that this was far from perfect.

6.6 Measurement and Agile Methods

In agile development, metrics usually have far less importance than in plan-driven development. Nevertheless, there are a number of metrics needed in agile development as well, mainly for estimation and tracking progress. According to the eight principle of the agile manifesto, the primary measure of progress is defined by working software, and any progress metric therefore ought to be based on the amount of working software produced. The most common tool to do so is the burn-down chart (see Sect. 3.5.4) that represents the amount of working software still to be produced, usually measured in terms of *story points*, the same measure also often used for estimating the effort involved in producing the software. Two other, related metrics that are fairly common in agile and lean development are lead time and cycle time (see e.g. [12, Sect. "Level 2 Scrumban"]).

Apart from that, metrics are of limited importance in agile development, and if metrics are needed there is a trend towards subjective metrics as shown in Example 6.4.

Example 6.4. A software development company used an agile development process for its projects, derived from Scrum. When the company wanted to introduce measurements to evaluate this process, is started off trying to define some suitable objective metrics to measure. However, all the measurements it tried were difficult to interpret since there were very different possible reasons for any changes in the measurement results, and there was a risk that developers would change their way of working to improve the measurement results without improving the process itself.

Therefore, it was decided to use a set of subjective measurements, based on school marks (using the marking scheme 1 = *very good* down to 5 = *failed* similar to what is used at German schools). At regular intervals, e.g. at the end of each sprint, process metrics are taken by asking for subjective feedback from the developers, covering topics such as estimation accuracy, incorrect commits to the configuration management system, and the results of unit testing. Although all three of these metrics could be replaced by objective measurements such as the number of incorrect commits, the decision was that this number on its own would not really help because the number and complexity of the commits had to be taken into account as well.

So what to think about this kind of measurement? Although it is certainly a good idea to include subjective measures in order to measure properties that are difficult or impossible to measure objectively, it seems very questionable whether it is a good idea to extend such subjective measures to properties that could just as well be measured using objective measures. It is important not to over-interpret measured values if there are different possible reasons for changes, but working only with subjective measures can (and did, to some extent) lead to a atmosphere where developers always gave good marks in order to make things easy for themselves—there was no reason to change anything, as the measurement values showed.

Further Reading

A very systematic approach to using measurement in software processes, without going into the details of defining any specific metrics, is described in [14].

The web site http://psmsc.com/ sponsored by the US Department of Defense and the US Army provides a lot of information about "Practical Software and Systems Measurement", including templates and a selection of metrics definitions. These descriptions are partly based on the standard ISO/IEC 15939.

Exercises

6.1. Provide one example each of a) a measure that is not an indicator, and b) an indicator that is not a metric.

6.2. Choose two (very) different software systems that you work with. For each of the eight software quality characteristics according to ISO/IEC 25010, define the main requirements of these two software systems, and identify one metric that can be used to provide information about how well these requirements have been implemented. Compare the results for the two software systems.

6.3. Consider the process of product backlog maintenance as defined in Scrum. For each of the process quality characteristics according to Gokyo Ri, define the main requirements of this process, and identify one metric that can be used to provide information about how well these requirements have been implemented.

References

1. V. Basili, A. Trendowicz, M. Kowalczyk, J. Heidrich, C. Seaman, J. Münch, and D. Rombach. *Aligning Organizations Through Measurement: The GQM+Strategies Approach.* Springer, 2014.
2. V. R. Basili, G. Caldiera, and H. D. Rombach. The goal question metric approach. In J. J. Marciniak, editor, *Encyclopedia of Software Engineering.* John Wiley and Sons, Inc., 1994.
3. V. R. Basili, J. Heidrich, M. Lindvall, J. Münch, M. Regardie, and A. Trendowicz. GQM$^+$ strategies—aligning business strategies with software measurement. *First International Symposium on Empirical Software Engineering and Measurement (ESEM 2007)*, pages 488–490, 2007.
4. J. Becker, M. Rosemann, and C. v. Uthmann. Guidelines of business process modeling. In W. v. d. Aalst, J. Desel, and A. Oberweis, editors, *Business Process Management,* number 1806 in LNCS, pages 30–49. Springer, 2000.
5. P. Bourque and R. Fairley, editors. *Guide to the Software Engineering Body of Knowledge (SWEBOK®), Version 3.0.* IEEE Computer Society, 2014. Available online at http://www.swebok.org (last access 2018-01-07).
6. R. Chillarege, I. S. Bhandari, J. K. Chaar, M. J. Halliday, D. S. Moebus, B. K. Ray, and M.-Y. Wong. Orthogonal defect classification—a concept for in-process measurements. *IEEE Transactions on Software Engineering,* 18(11), November 1992.
7. T. Gilb. *Software Metrics.* Winthrop Publishers, Inc., 1977.
8. ISACA. *COBIT® 5. A Business Framework for the Governance and Management of Enterprise IT,* 2012.
9. R. S. Kaplan and D. P. Norton. Using the balanced scorecard as a strategic management system. *Harvard Business Review,* pages 75–85, January–February 1996.
10. R. Kneuper. Gokyo Ri: Messung und Bewertung der Qualität von Entwicklungsprozessen am Beispiel des V-Modell XT. In O. Linssen and M. Kuhrmann, editors, *Qualitätsmanagement und Vorgehensmodelle: 19. Workshop der Fachgruppe WI-VM der Gesellschaft für Informatik e.V. (GI),* pages 25–34. Shaker-Verlag, Aachen, 2012.
11. R. Kneuper. Messung der Qualität von ITSM-Prozessen — Eine Fallstudie. *it Service Management,* (33):23–29, 2015.
12. C. Ladas. Scrum-ban. http://leansoftwareengineering.com/ksse/scrum-ban/ (last access 2018-01-02), 2008.
13. R. Schuette and T. Rotthowe. The guidelines of modeling—an approach to enhance the quality in information models. In T.-W. Ling, S. Ram, and M. L. Lee, editors, *Conceptual Modeling—ER '98. 17th International Conference on Conceptual Modeling, Singapore, November '16-19, 1998. Proceedings,* number 1507 in Lecture Notes in Computer Science (LNCS), 1998.
14. G. M. Weinberg. *Quality Software Management. Vol. 2: First-Order Measurement.* Dorset House Publishing, 1993.

Chapter 7
Tool Support for Software Processes

Abstract Since software processes can become very complex, both process engineers and project teams need suitable tool support for developing, managing and enacting these processes. As a result, a large range of tools is available, from process design tools via tools supporting the enactment of entire life cycles, to tools supporting selected process steps, such as test automation or refactoring. Apart from the scope of tasks supported by the various tools, tools differ in how much support they provide for these tasks. For example, a tool to support process modelling might be a simple editor, or it might include various consistency checks, generate different views of the process as needed for different roles, and perhaps even generate some support for enacting the process. This chapter provides an overview of the options to provide process support, distinguishing the two groups of support for process modelling and management, and support for performing and enacting software processes in different stages of the software life cycle.

7.1 Introduction

Since software processes tend to be quite complex, there is an obvious need for tool support for defining, managing and performing these processes. Indeed, some processes are not even feasible in practice without suitable tool support. For example, without tools and an environment that supports frequent testing etc., agile processes are difficult to implement (which is one of the reasons why agile development only started to become wide-spread in the late 1990s). Accordingly, there is a large number of tools available that support these tasks in various forms. The focus in this chapter will be on tools that support a whole sequence of process steps, such as development environments, and not just individual development steps.

We distinguish these tools into different groups, as shown in Fig. 7.1. It is important in this context to note that tool support does not only refer to development processes but may be needed, or at least very helpful, for earlier and in particular

© Springer Nature Switzerland AG 2018
R. Kneuper, *Software Processes and Life Cycle Models*,
https://doi.org/10.1007/978-3-319-98845-0_7

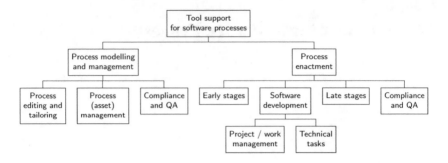

Fig. 7.1 Tool support taxonomy

later software processes as well. Application Life Cycle Management (ALM) tools try to combine such support across the entire life cycle into a single tool.

Tools can support the process to very different degrees, ranging from a simple editor to support the syntactically correct definition of a process, to automated enactment of the process or at least parts of it. As discussed in Chap. 2, tool support will need a certain amount of formality of the process notation, with more support usually requiring more formality. At least those aspects of a process that are to be supported will need to be formalised.

Tool support for process enactment. Regarding tool support for the enactment of processes, two different approaches can be distinguished: on the one hand, support may be under the control of the process performer, e.g. the developer, who decides which tool support to use when. Alternatively, the tool may take more or less control, disallowing certain process steps or even trying to enforce certain steps and their sequence.

As discussed in Sect. 1.3.2, the topic of software processes became quite prominent in the 1980s, which led to a strong interest in different kinds of support environments for software processes at the time, such as *(Process-Centered) Software Engineering Environments* (PCSEE or SEE), *Computer-Aided Software Engineering* (CASE), and *Integrated Project Support Environments* (IPSE). To some extent, there was a trend that such tools should go beyond plain *support* for software development and, to a larger or smaller extent, *enforce* the expected processes. However, this trend was never very successful in practice, and with the growing importance of agile development (which, according to the Agile Manifesto, values "individuals and interactions over processes and tools", see Sect. 3.5.1), it was reversed and most environments nowadays leave control to the development team rather than trying to enforce any particular process.

Nevertheless, a certain amount of enforcement of process steps is not unusual even in agile development, e.g. by disallowing the check-in or commitment of code into the configuration management system if certain required information is not included, such as a reference to the relevant sprint backlog item, or the appropriate unit test results.

Rather than trying to enforce a certain process, it is usually much more effective and efficient to convince the people involved about its advantages. This will be made much easier by providing an easy-to-use, helpful tool-set supporting the enactment of the process. This will increase acceptance of the processes and their deployment, while inadequate tool support will make process deployment difficult to impossible, even if the process is declared mandatory.

7.2 Support for Process Modelling and Process Management

The first group of tools to support software processes helps to support the modelling and management of such processes, starting with editors that help to document a process, based on the various notations as introduced in Chap. 2. Apart from documenting processes, tools can also help to manage them, supporting e.g. versioning and the release process for process assets. The final group of support tools includes various tools for checking compliance and assuring the quality of the process documentation.

In the following, each of these groups of tools will be discussed in more detail.

7.2.1 Process Editors

In order to define processes, some kind of editor is needed, suitable for the process notation to be used. For text-based notations, a standard text editor will usually be sufficient. If the notation used is more complex then the editor should reflect this complexity. Notations built on a complex meta-model such as SPEM or the V-Model XT meta-model (cf. Sect. 2.4) are, in practice, almost impossible to use without a bespoke editor, even though in theory any standard XML editor will do.

The level of support provided by these tools can differ considerably, starting from pure text editing, perhaps supplemented by some suitable text templates. A more advanced type of editor will help to keep the process definition at least syntactically correct, e.g. for an XML-based notation the editor may help to ensure that the process description is valid XML, with balanced start and end tags etc..

Semantic support. An editor providing semantic support, finally, will help to maintain relevant relationships between the different process building blocks, e.g. ensuring that every artefact that is used in any process step has been defined as an initial artefact or as the output of a previous process step, or that any role responsible for any artefact is defined. There are may similar consistency conditions relevant in process definitions, and for a reasonably complex set of process definitions it is rather difficult to satisfy these without adequate tool support. However, while defining a process and its various components it is often quite difficult to keep these conditions satisfied at all intermediate steps, which is the reason why editors including such support will usually allow to switch it off, e.g. requiring consistency only when a process description is to be released, or, alternatively, allow these inconsistencies but provide reports listing them.

Process tailoring support. This kind of editing support refers to the tailoring of existing processes when they are to be used in a certain context, e.g. for a certain project. Otherwise, there is a high risk of destroying the consistency that may have existed in a process description by removing components that "are not needed in this project" but that have other components that that depend on the components removed.

Apart from ensuring the consistency of the tailored processes, a second aspect to consider in tailoring is its compliance to defined tailoring criteria which define what tailoring is allowed, and what would result in a process description that deviates too far from the standard process.

When the process notation used is sufficiently complex to need semantic support for editing processes, it will typically also need similar support for tailoring them, to ensure both consistency and compliance. This is particularly true since tailoring will often be done by people such as project leaders who tend to be less familiar with the intricacies of the process notation used.

Example: EPF composer. To support the definition, adaptation and enactment of software processes based on the SPEM meta-model, the open-source *Eclipse Process Framework (EPF) Composer* was developed by the EPF project within the Eclipse Foundation, based on the commercial tool *Rational Method Composer* provided by Rational Software.

EPF Composer is intended to address two separate but related tasks:

- First, it serves as a content management system, allowing to publish process content as a web site in a consistent format. A number of standard processes, such as OpenUP, are provided together with EPF Composer for immediate use.
- Second, EPF Composer supports process engineers in defining processes, and project managers in tailoring such processes to a specific project.

Example: process editing tools for V-Model XT. The V-Model XT supports editing and tailoring of processes by two dedicated tools, the *V-Model XT Editor* and the *V-Model XT Assistant*. The V-model XT Editor was first of all developed as an internal tool to be used by the V-Model XT development team, but is also available as part of the model infrastructure. It supports direct editing of the XML representation of the model, and could be described as a variant of an XML editor with some specialised functionalities. Since the XML representation of the model is fairly complex, this editor is mainly used by advanced users who want to build an organisational standard process based on the original V-Model XT.

The V-Model XT Assistant, on the other hand, has a more restricted functionality but as a result is far easier to use. Its main purpose is to allow project leaders to tailor the model to their specific needs, based on pre-defined tailoring conditions to include or exclude certain optional parts of the model, and helps to generate a project manual as well as a first draft of a project plan.

7.2.2 Process and Process Asset Management Tools

Process descriptions or models are themselves development artefacts whose configurations need to be managed, including versioning, access control, release process, archiving etc., as was described in Sect. 4.2.3. At a minimum, tools similar to the configuration management and versioning tools used in software development are therefore needed, such as Subversion or Git.

Apart from ensuring that developers work with the currently valid version of the software process, there may be a need that long-running projects are able to continue working with the process version that was current when the project started, perhaps with minor updates. In case of problems with the product developed or the service provided, it may even be necessary to prove later (perhaps even in court) which version of the process was used in the development of the product or the delivery of the service, including the tailoring performed.

Similarly, process improvement ideas and requests are similar to the improvement ideas and requests that arise for software products, and should be collected and managed using similar tools such as ticket systems.

Case Study 7.1. (CS Insurance InfoSys) To support the management of process assets, a tool (first Lotus Notes, later a HTML-based tool) is used. Apart from the current released version of a process description or asset as displayed by default, new draft versions may also be seen by all users, and users can review and comment on them. To comment on the currently released or a new version under development, a "comment" button immediately opens a new mail, with recipients and identification information referencing the current document already filled in, so that it becomes very easy for users to send their comments. This mail is also sent to a ticket system so that the comment can be tracked, and the users can check the current status of their comments at any time.

This kind of tool support helped to increase the motivation of users to not just complain about the process assets but to send their comments to those responsible, but of course this at the same time puts pressure on the process team to actually address these comments since it becomes very visible whether or not this is done.

Wikis for process management. Wikis are also commonly used for these tasks since they contain easy to use version control where users can easily check what has changed in a document, and usually also contain discussion pages that support the discussion of improvement ideas and comments.

Wikis use different philosophies about who is allowed to change a document, and the organisation needs to decide whether it allows *all* users to do so, relying on the logging mechanism to address inadequate changes, or to set up (write) access restrictions to prevent such changes from the start. The decision will typically depend on factors such as the size of the organisation and the criticality of the processes and the products developed. For example, in a regulated environment one will typically be rather restrictive about who is allowed to change the process assets, while an individual project in a non-regulated environment will tend to give everyone write access to the process wiki.

7.2.3 Compliance and Quality Assurance Tools

Instead of editing support as described above, syntactic and semantic correctness as important aspects of the quality of a process or life cycle model can be supported by adequate consistency checking tools used at a later stage, for example just before the release of a model.

As a basis for such consistency checking, relevant *consistency conditions* need to be defined for the notation used, stating for example that any work product used in a process must either be an initial product provided from the outside, or it must be created in a previous process step.

Compliance checking and mapping. Another group of important process management tasks to be supported by tools consists of compliance checking and mapping, aligning the compliance requirements with the relevant process components and helping to track that all compliance requirements are addressed, and to trace which compliance requirements may be affected by process changes. These are tasks that are very similar to requirements management and requirements traceability as needed in the development of software or other products, and therefore similar tool support should be provided.

To a limited extent, this kind of tool support can be seen in the appendices of V-Model XT which contain mappings (including links) from various relevant standards (including CMMI-DEV, ISO 9001 and ISO/IEC/IEEE 15288) to the process component where the individual requirements from these standards are satisfied.

One of the major challenges in this context is to keep such a mapping up-to-date, for example all of these mappings included in V-Model XT are no longer current since both the model itself and the mapped standards have since been updated.

7.3 Tool Support for Process Enactment in the Early Stages of the Software Life Cycle

In the early stages of the software life cycle, the processes essentially consist of the definition of the definition of the process landscape and the IT architecture, and of the collection and management of ideas and their transition to different levels of requirements (stakeholder requirements, product requirements, etc.). The main tools to support these processes can be split into three groups: the first group consists of various modelling tools such as business process modelling tools, UML modelling tools, or user interface modelling/rapid prototyping tools. The second group consists of requirements management and ticketing tools that help to manage these ideas and requirements, tracking their status and tracing the relationships between the ideas and requirements and, later, the various artefacts created to implement them. Related and sometimes overlapping with the second group is the third group of tools to support project management, in particular project planning, defining (and later tracking) the different tasks needed to implement the requirements identified.

All these tools may be used on the level of the individual project or development effort, or on the level of the organisation, defining the organisational process landscape and IT architecture and assigning (high-level) requirements or tasks to the individual project or development effort.

7.4 Tool Support for Process Enactment in Software Development

There is a huge variety of tools that support different aspects of the enactment of software processes. Most of them only address a small number of process steps, and are therefore largely independent of the overall processes enacted and life cycles used. Apart from obvious tools such as UML or program editors and test tools, this also includes collaboration tools which provide functionality such as shared calendars, task lists and discussion forums. In the following, however, only tools that address a major part of the software development process will be considered.

7.4.1 Why Tool Support for the Enactment of Software Development Processes?

There are a number of different reasons for using computer-based tools to support software development. The main ones are for example listed in [2, Sect. D 3.2] as follows:

- increase quality of the software developed
- increase maintainability of the software developed
- increase development efficiency
- improve coordination within the development team
- automate creation of documents
- simplify project management

An important aspect to clarify in any tool support for software processes is the degree of obligation of the definitions of the processes supported. As will be discussed in Sect. 7.6 below, there are three different levels of obligation: *suggested*, *recommended*, *required*, which need to be taken into account when supporting the processes by tools. If the process is required, this may be enforced by the tool set, while in the case of a suggested or recommended process, the tool guides the developer but the developer decides what step to perform when.

7.4.2 Process Visualisation

Tools for visualising processes are usually closely related to tools for editing processes, and for process asset management. The most common representation format today is HTML, because it does not need any specific software for readers, and it allows the use of hyper-links between related parts of the description, such as between a task and the result produced from that task.

An important part of process visualisation in most environments is that the visualisation may be adapted to different roles and context, for example allowing a user to filter out any components not relevant for his role, or to extract and export only those parts of the processes that are relevant for an external partner such as a customer or a supplier. For the latter purpose, one often does not use a hypertext format but a linear format, often PDF.

7.4.3 Process-Aware Tools

To some extent, processes may be supported by process-aware tools.

Definition 7.1 (Process-awareness of tools). *A tool is called process-aware if its behaviour can be adapted to a different process by simply modifying the process model, with little or no need for further adaptation of the tool itself.*

Obviously, process-awareness implies a need for an explicit process meta-model, for example a work-flow description.

According to [5, p. 11], process-awareness allows tools

- "to display on-line process documentation
- to cross-reference artefacts according to the process model
- to enact and enforce the process".

Regarding software processes, process-aware tools are mainly used in the form of various types of ticket system where an important part of the process is described as a work-flow based on a state-machine. This applies for example to many requirements management or bug tracking systems in development, as well as ticket systems for managing incidents and problems in IT service management.

7.4.4 Tool Support for Project Management and Technical Tasks

Tool support for software development can be distinguished into two groups: on the one hand, this involves support for project management tasks, while on the other hand, technical tasks need to be supported. To some extent, this is aligned with the project roles such as project manager and developers, but of course, developers will usually also perform certain management tasks, in particular in a self-organising team in agile development, and a project manager may also perform certain technical tasks.

Tool support for project management. This involves support for obvious project management tasks such as generating a project plan and a project manual, and creating a project-specific process representation, possibly by tailoring a standard organisational process. Tools such as the *V-Model XT Assistant* can help to combine these tasks, automatically deriving a draft of the project plan and the project manual from the tailored standard process (cf. p. 290).

Project management tools that developers commonly will work with are for example ticket systems, requirements management systems and application life cycle management (ALM) systems. These typically embed the process in form of some state machine which defines the possible sequence of states / activities.

Tool support for technical tasks. This second group of support tools includes for example configuration management and versioning tools which may implement a certain sequence of product states and therefore process steps. This may go as far as ensuring such process steps by allowing a commit or check-in only after defined consistency checks have been passed, e.g. code is only allowed to be checked in once the requirement has the correct status. Alternatively, the tools may provide messages or warnings if such a consistency check fails, but still allow the developer to decide whether to perform the step at this stage or not.

7.4.5 Development Environments

Development environments provide an environment integrating the different tools needed by developers and possibly project managers as well. Some environments go one step further by combining the (formalised) description of processes and the support of the enactment of these processes in the same tool.

Integration. The integration may go very deep, with tightly integrated tools based on a common repository, or it may be rather superficial, with bilateral interfaces between tools providing loose coupling and possibly manual migration steps needed. In [1, § 11.4], Brown et al. distinguish three aspects of tool integration:

- *User interface integration* addresses the integration of tools where different tools offer the same "look and feel" in their user interface, and possibly may be used from a common interface such as a *Integrated Development Environment*.

- *Process integration* addresses the integration of tools where different tools need the same functions, and at least implement these in the same way, using the same algorithms, or at a higher level of integration use the same code, for example as a calling interface or as s service that may be used by the different tools. For example, once a tool changes a certain artefact it may call the version management service to handle the relevant versioning activities.
- *Data integration* addresses the integration of tools by sharing the relevant data. This may be done using some form of joint repository or document management system, or using a standard interchange format, such as the *CASE Data Interchange Format (CDIF)*, a standard defined by the *Electronic Industries Association* for the exchange of models between CASE tools. CDIF does not only include the definition of the syntax of the interchange format but also of its semantics to ensure that the different concepts interchanged are interpreted consistently by the tools involved. A similar approach, but restricted to the definition of requirements, is the *Requirements Interchange Format (ReqIF)*..

Types of development environments. Over time, a number of different types of such environments have become available, where the distinction between different types is not always very clear. The most common types of integrated development environments include:

- *Software Engineering Environments* (SEE) were widely discussed in the 1980s and describe an integrated environment consisting of a set of common services and integrating different tools into one common environment [1]. Today, this term has largely been replaced by *Integrated Development Environment* (IDE).
- Integrated Development Environments (IDE) describe a similar concept to SEEs and have become very wide-spread. Most serious software development today is performed using some IDE, with *Eclipse* one of the best-known ones. As described in [5, p. 13], typical tasks supported by an IDE include:
  - code editing, usually with syntax highlighting etc.
  - (graphical) design
  - compiling and debugging
  - source code control and build management.

- Computer-Aided Software Engineering (CASE) tools put more emphasis on explicit support for defined development methods, and therefore tend to be more strongly integrated, typically with less support for the integration of tools from different suppliers. Similar to SEEs, CASE tools were popular in the 1990s but are no longer widely used under that name. Nevertheless, some current IDEs that integrate modelling tools such as UML editors perform very similar tasks.

The Portable Common Tool Environment (PCTE) and related models. With the growing number of different tools to support software development, the need arose in the late 1980s and early 1990s for a common platform that would allow the easy integration of these tools, including the exchange of data between them. A number of different such platform were proposed, and in particular the PCTE model became quite popular. This model, also known as the *toaster model* because its reference structure is said to look somewhat like a toaster (see Fig. 7.2) where different development tools from different suppliers could be "slotted in" like a slice of toast, resulting in an SEE. As this reference structure shows, the core of PCTE consisted of a set of interface specifications for these different development tools as well as a set of standard services.

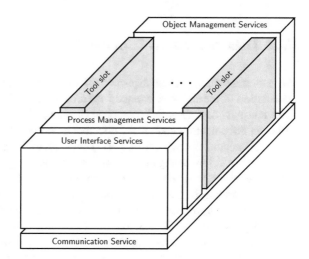

Fig. 7.2 The NIST-ECMA reference model structure (based on [7, Fig. 1])

This platform was later revised by ECMA[1] and this revised version was therefore named the ECMA reference model, which in turn was further revised jointly with the US standardisation organisation NIST and became known as the NIST/ECMA reference model [6]. In 1995, the model was published as ISO/IEC 13719 and revised in 1998.

Closely related to PCTE is *AD/Cycle* which is a set of integration services and support tools by IBM and became quite well-known in the 1990s, using similar concepts to PCTE. In contrast to PCTE, it did not just provide a set of specifications but an actual set of tools.

Nevertheless, neither PCTE nor AD/Cycle in practice was very successful or wide-spread, since both concepts turned out to be very complex and too restrictive on the tool suppliers.

The Open Services for Lifecycle Collaboration (OSLC). OSLC is an open community[2] initiated by IBM that to some extent can be seen as a successor to PCTE and AD/Cycle in that it also defines a set of specifications for integrating different development tools from different suppliers. It leaves more freedom to the individual tools in that they define the format for storing data, not the platform; of course, this

---

[1] ECMA originally stood for the *European Computer Manufacturers Association* but the association was renamed in 1994 to *Ecma International—European association for standardizing information and communication systems*

[2] See `http://open-services.net/` for more information.

has the advantage that there is less integration of the tools, and the exchange of data may become more difficult.

Technically, OSLC is mainly based on web technologies such as W3C linked data, RDF and HTTP. For example, every object such as a requirement or a test case is identified by an URI.

7.4.6 Documentation of Source Code

An important but unpopular aspect of software development is the need for the documentation of the software created.[3] As a result, the technical documentation often does not exist or at least is incomplete or out-of-date. However, spending a lot of effort on documenting code if the documentation will be out-of-date or incomplete when it is needed is obviously a waste of resources. To address this challenge, considerable effort has been put into conventions that help to understand source code without explicit documentation, and into tools for the (semi-)automatic generation of documentation based on such conventions. One of the first such tools was the "WEB" system introduced by Donald E. Knuth for *Literate Programming* [4], based on the TEX system Knuth created around the same time.

Similar ideas were later emphasised in the context of agile development which values "working software over comprehensive documentation" (Agile Manifesto, see Fig. 3.15), in order to concentrate on the technical tasks and reduce the bureaucratic work involved. For example, one of the twelve principles of extreme programming (see Fig. 3.18) requires *coding standards*, first to make the code easier to understand, but also to make tool support possible.

This resulted in tools such as *Doxygen* and *Javadoc* which are quite common today and which generate documentation of software based on the use of coding standards and on structured source code comments. Of course, this still requires some documentation effort, but it is far easier for developers to follow coding standards and to integrate short comments into the code while they are working on it anyway, rather than writing separate documentation afterwards. Since there is no separate documentation of the code, this form of documentation is sometimes called *self-documenting code*.

In addition to helping to generate documentation, the use of coding standards, in particular naming conventions, also enables tool support for certain refactoring tasks, and even for round-trip engineering where different artefacts such as design documentation and source code are synchronised automatically.

---

[3] In this context, we are mainly interested in the technical documentation to be used for later development and maintenance tasks, not in product documentation for the users of the software.

7.5 Tool Support for Process Enactment in the Late Stages of the Software Product Life Cycle

The late stages in the software product life cycle start with the completion of development and the transition into production, also commonly called deployment.

Tool support for deployment, transition and installation. The automation of software deployment using suitable tools has become an important topic over the last few years, mainly in the context of DevOps (cf. Sect. 8.3). Even outside that context, tool support for installation and deployment is important whenever the developed software is to run not only on a single system but on many systems, possibly in different configurations and with different parameters. This may be the case within a single company, where the software needs to run on many different machines (clients or servers), and it is obviously always a relevant topic for COTS software, where typically suitable installation support tools are used.

Tool support for production. Once the software has been deployed and is running, different tools are required for process support. These mainly include ticket systems which help to manage incidents and other types of tickets. Such ticket systems usually include some built-in process or work-flow support in order to deal with the many different kinds of tickets, which may range from simple tasks like explaining to the user how to perform a certain step with the software system, to complex, long-lasting tasks like handling an incident reported by the user which leads to a correction of the software implemented by the development team.

A second type of tool used across many service management processes is the *Configuration Management Database* (CMDB) which helps to manage the information about the configuration of the entire IT infrastructure, including information about which version of which software is running on which machine. This information for example is needed to resolve incidents ("what has been changed about the software that is not working any more?"), as well as manage updates ("which machine still needs the update, and where is the update not allowed to be installed?") and related tasks.

7.6 Compliance and Quality Assurance Tools in Process Enactment

There are different level of expected compliance to defined processes that may be relevant from a quality assurance point of view: if a process definition is *suggested*, quality assurance only has the task to identify whether and how often it is followed, and perhaps in turn recommend a revision of the process if it is not commonly used. In this case, tool support is of little relevance.

A higher degree of obligation is a process definition that is *recommended*. In this case, the task of quality assurance is to ensure that the process definition is followed unless there is adequate reason not to do so. In this case, tools may help to verify that the process definition is followed, for example based on suitable measurements or using process mining as introduced in Sect. 8.1.

Finally, a process definition may be *required*. In this case there are two variants of tool support: adherence to the process definition may either be verified, in the same way as done for a recommended process description. Alternatively, tools may enforce the process so that deviations become difficult or impossible. The latter variant is used only rarely, apart from some individual process steps such as only allowing new code to be checked in if certain conditions are satisfied, such as stating the relevant requirement.

7.7 Privacy (Data Protection)

An issue that is often forgotten when talking about tool support for software processes is the question of ensuring privacy, in the legal context usually called data protection, as explained in Sect. 3.11.

Most process support tools will collect some personal data, for example a history showing what activities or changes were performed when by a certain individual. To satisfy the European GDPR requirements as described in Sect. 3.11.4 (or similar requirements in other countries), one therefore needs to identify in advance to what extent such data are genuinely needed (data minimisation), for which purpose they are needed (purpose limitation), to make this use transparent to users (data subjects), and to limit the use to that defined purpose. Furthermore, to demonstrate compliance with the GDPR, these considerations need to be documented.

In addition to satisfying the GDPR in the use of the tool itself, a tool for software process support should of course also help to ensure and demonstrate compliance in the performance of the processes supported. For example, it will generally be useful if such a process performance support tool also supports the documentation of the personal data stored or processed by the process, and the lawful basis for doing so.

Further Reading

In [1], Brown et al. provide an extensive overview of software engineering environments, in particular ECMA PCTE, with a focus on the concepts behind these environments rather than the details of any particular implementation.

A fairly recent discussion of the concepts used by process support tools can be found in [5].

As discussed before, software processes can be seen as a form of knowledge management. The use of knowledge management concepts and tools to support software processes is discussed in detail in [3].

Exercises

7.1. Which of the tool functions described should be combined into a single tool, and in what cases is it more useful to implement the functions in separate tools?

7.2. It was mentioned before that process support by tools requires formalisation of the process models and meta-models. Using two tool functions as examples, explain why this is the case and which parts of the models exactly need to be formally described.

References

1. A. W. Brown, A. N. Earl, and J. A. McDermid. *Software Engineering Environments. Automated Support for Software Engineering*. McGraw-Hill Book Company, 1992.
2. E. Hering, J. Gutekunst, and U. Dyllong. *Handbuch der praktischen und technischen Informatik*. Springer, 2nd edition, 2000.
3. R. Kneuper. Supporting software processes using knowledge management. In S. Chang, editor, *Handbook of Software Engineering and Knowledge Engineering*, volume 2, pages 579–608. World Scientific Publishing Co., 2002.
4. D. E. Knuth. Literate programming. *The Computer Journal*, 27(2):97–111, 1984. http://www.literateprogramming.com/knuthweb.pdf (last access 2018-07-01).
5. M. Kuhrmann, G. Kalus, and G. Chroust. Tool-support for software development processes. In M. Cruz-Cunha, editor, *Social, Managerial and Organizational Dimensions of Enterprise Information Systems*, Business Science Reference, pages 213–231. IGI Global, 2010.
6. F. Long and E. Morris. An overview of PCTE: A basis for a Portable Common Tool Environment. Technical Report CMU/SEI-93-TR-1, Software Engineering Institute, Carnegie Mellon University, March 1993. https://resources.sei.cmu.edu/library/assetview.cfm?assetid=11821 (last access 2018-02-19).
7. NIST and ECMA. Reference model for frameworks of software engineering environments, 2nd edition. Technical Report ECMA TR/55, NIST National Institute of Standards and Technology, December 1991.

Chapter 8
Selected Current Trends in Software Processes

Abstract Although software processes have been around for decades, software processes still constitute an emerging field in which practice and research are on the quest for new (better) approaches. In this chapter, we collect some trends and emerging approaches and provide an introduction to these topics. We address current research activities as well as initiatives initiated from practice. Topics covered include Process Mining, Statistical Process Control (SPC), and Continuous Delivery and DevOps. Furthermore, we relate the topics presented in this chapter to the foundations set in the previous chapters.

8.1 Process Intelligence and Process Mining

Process mining is a discipline that has recently become quite popular in Business Process Management but is also relevant for software processes. The core of process mining is the evaluation of data from event logs to derive information about the underlying processes and their relationship to process models. It is related to data mining but specifically addresses the mining of process data. This restriction of the kind of data to be analysed allows specific methods and algorithms as well as dealing with specific, process-related questions such as deriving the actually performed process from event logs, comparing it to a defined process, or identifying bottlenecks.

8.1.1 Basic Concepts of Process Mining

Usage types: The three main usage types of process mining, as described e.g. in [25], are

- *discovery*: discover or identify the process as actually performed from the event data available. This is particularly relevant if there is no defined process avail-

© Springer Nature Switzerland AG 2018
R. Kneuper, *Software Processes and Life Cycle Models*,
https://doi.org/10.1007/978-3-319-98845-0_8

able (yet). The main types of information that can be mined from event data are the control flow of the process, and the organisational structure underlying the process.

- *conformance*: compare the process as actually performed against the defined process, as a form of quality assurance. Again, this may refer to the control flow of the process (or, closely related, the life cycle of the work products), or the organisational structure underlying it (e.g. was the work product released by the correct role / person?).
- *enhancement*: use information derived from the event data to improve the process, e.g. to reduce bottlenecks, to identify and analyse the business rules used for decisions taken in the process, to adapt the defined process if there are non-conformances which actually improve the currently defined process.

A discipline very similar to process mining is (business) process intelligence (BPI) which refers to the application of business intelligence techniques to (business) processes. BPI attempts to derive information used for decision making from process data typically contained in a data warehouse (cf. [3]). There is a large overlap between process intelligence and process mining, but process intelligence does not necessarily relate the processes and their analysis to process models. Instead, process intelligence also derives metrics and other information regarding the processes from relevant data.

Process mining tools. In order to handle the large amounts of data relevant in process mining, appropriate tools are needed. The process mining tool best known and most widely used is the open source tool *ProM* [20] for which many plug-ins are available from different research groups so that ProM supports a very large percentage of all process mining techniques and methods. However, as a research tool it is somewhat difficult to use, and there is little documentation on ProM and in particular its plug-ins.

Apart from ProM, there are a number of commercial tools available that provide far less functionality but are easier to use.

Process event logs. The foundation of process mining are event logs that contain information about the individual process steps performed. As described in [25, §4.2], the concept of event logs is based on the following assumptions:

- A process (or its execution) consists of individual cases or instances. For example, a software development process may be looked upon as consisting of different requirements as instances which are dealt with following the same sequence of steps.
- A case consists of different events, where each event belongs to exactly one case. For example, in software development an event may be the completion of the analysis, the implementation or the test of a requirement. An event always happens at a point in time, not during a period of time.
- Events belonging to a case are ordered. This order can then be used to analyse the process control flow.

- Events have further attributes, including at least the process activity performed by the event, plus optional attributes such as the point in time, cost or resources involved.

In order to be usable for process mining, an event log must therefore at least contain the relevant case of each event, the process activity performed and the order of events (as a simple ordering or using time stamps), for more advanced process mining activities also the other attributes mentioned.

In order to generate and handle such event logs with different tools, the standard format *Mining eXtensible Markup Language* (MXML) was defined, later replaced by the *eXtensible Event Stream* (XES) format, see[25, §4.3] and [26]. One of the challenges in applying process mining therefore is to convert event logs from various process support tools into XES, and the tool ProM mentioned above therefore includes a couple of import functions for different event log formats.

8.1.2 Process Mining and Software Processes

Although the first publications on process mining (though not under that name yet) addressed software processes (see [4, 5]), after that process mining was mainly developed for business processes. Transferring the process mining methods and techniques to IT service management processes such as incident or change management is fairly straightforward and has e.g. been the topic of the *International Business Process Intelligence Challenge* in 2013 and 2014 [1, 2]. However, applying process mining methods and techniques to software engineering processes is not as easy since such engineering processes typically are not as structured as business processes.

Nevertheless, some attempts have been made to do so, and different ways of applying process mining in software engineering have been described:

- Applying process mining to the software engineering processes themselves: this is the most obvious and direct usage of process mining in software engineering and will be discussed in more detail in Sect. 8.1.3.
- Using process mining as a tool within the software engineering processes:

  - Using process mining for requirements analysis: mining the relevant business processes can help to support these processes with software systems, as described e.g. in [21, 22]. Similarly, mining the usage of a software system for performing a process can help to improve the system, see e.g. [15]. In iterative development, this mining of the usage of a software system may even be used in the development of new software since a usable version of the system is available at an early stage in development.
  - Mining the execution of software systems: this requires instrumentation of the software to provide event data and investigates the execution of the software, e.g. for performance analysis or to discover control-flow patterns. This ap-

proach, though not under the name process mining, is described for example in [14].

In the current context, we are mainly interested in the first approach, and will discuss that in more detail below.

Closely related but not always referring to processes is the mining of software repositories which is e.g. addressed by the MSR series of working conferences accompanying the ICSE conference series (see `http://msrconf.org`). This field addresses a very wide range of questions referring to developers (e.g. what questions do developers ask in a forum? How well do they cooperate within a project?) as well as products and their quality (e.g. what kinds of bugs, alerts etc. appear repeatedly? What kinds of features are repeatedly moved into and out of the scope of the project?) and processes, the main topic of the work discussed here.

8.1.3 Mining of Software Engineering Processes

As mentioned above, the first publications on process mining were [4] and [5] which actually used these techniques to analyse software engineering processes. These publications described three approaches to process discovery, based on algorithmic grammar inference, Markov models, and neural networks.

While the algorithms and tools used for mining software engineering processes are essentially the same as those for mining general business processes, the main difference lies in the data sources and the necessary pre-processing of the data. Once the data are available in a standard format, the standard toolset can be applied. In software engineering, the relevant data are usually contained in some repository, as part of a configuration management tool such as Git or Subversion, or a requirements management/bug-tracking tool such as BugZilla. Provided that the event logs are not just ordered but include time stamps, one can use this information to analyse the interaction between such different types of tools.

Often also relevant but usually less structured and therefore difficult to mine are mail repositories and discussion forums, as covered by the MSR conferences mentioned above.

The pre-processing of software process event data from repositories was addressed by Poncin as part of his master's thesis [17] and the follow-up publications [18, 19]. As part of this work, he created the framework FRASR which supports the preprocessing of data from common repositories such as Subversion and Git.

After this pre-processing of data, Poncin then investigated the assignment of project roles to individuals based on event log data (e.g. in an open source project where this assignment may not be explicit). As a second question, he analysed the conformance of the actual handling of bugs as shown by an event log to a defined bug life cycle.

A similar approach is described in [8] which uses event data to analyse which process variants are actually used in software development, to analyse conformance to the defined process, and to perform statistical analyses about the stability of the processes used.

There are two main challenges in using process mining on software engineering processes: first, these processes are typically not very well structured compared to business processes, with considerable variation between different instances of the same process. Additionally, the number of repetitions of the same process is typically fairly low. Even in software engineering, there are nevertheless some processes that are repeated quite often, such as the correction of bugs or, in iterative or agile development, the process of handling an individual requirement, user story or similar, with steps such as analysis, test case definition, design, implementation, test performance (possibly on multiple levels) and commit of results. In such cases, process mining can be applied to get feedback on the conformity to the process definitions or on process steps which often take very long and lead to bottlenecks.

Example 8.1. In a group of small development projects, all using the same bug tracking system, process mining was used as an experiment to get a better understanding of the processes used. [13]

The first step to do so was the creation of the event log based on the history table in the ticket system database:

- the *process* under consideration is the handling of tickets in the ticket system
- a *case* is the handling of an individual tickets
- *events* are the individual steps in handling the tickets that are logged in the ticket system.

The main focus was put on the event types that led to a change in the ticket status, while other events such as editing the text, adding a comment or moving responsibility to a different developer were left out of the initial analysis. The process event log in XES format was thus generated from the database underlying the ticket system using a complex SQL statement.

Using this event log for process discovery brought the following result:

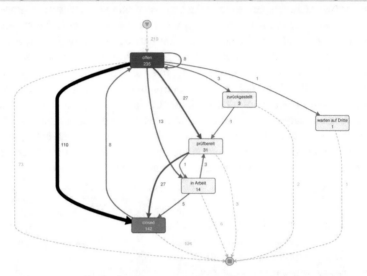

The analysis of this process representation showed that in many cases, tickets were not moved to the status "ready for verification" (prüfbereit), as expected, but moved directly from "open" (offen) to "closed". As a result, the definition of when verification of a ticket and therefore the status "ready for verification" is needed was refined.

Second, the duration of the cases/tickets was analysed, leading to the following result:

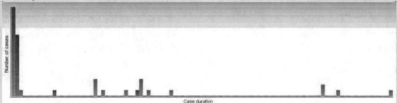

As is immediately visible, case duration varies considerably, with a large proportion of the cases closed very quickly, but some tickets taking a long time. Based on the priorities and the work involved in handling the tickets, this was not surprising. In a next step, the long-running tickets where analysed to see in which status they spend most of the time. Based on the lean principle of keeping work in progress low, it was expected that they may be "open" for a long time, but should not stay long in status "in work" or "ready for verification", which was confirmed by the analysis.

8.2 Statistical Process Control and Six Sigma

Statistical Process Control (SPC) and *Six Sigma* describe two closely related but different sets of techniques for controlling and improving processes that both are based on measurements as introduced in Chap. 6 and have a strong emphasis on statistical methods and techniques. As a result, they are both mainly adequate for processes with large numbers of repetitions, and therefore quite wide-spread in industrial production, but only occasionally used in software processes. In the context of software processes, they are mainly applicable for IT service management, while software development processes are rarely sufficiently standardised to get meaningful statistical data.

8.2.1 Statistical Process Control (SPC)

SPC applies varies statistical methods and tools in order to measure and control processes. One of its core concepts is the regular measurement of important product or process parameters, and the use of different types of quality control charts for monitoring and controlling these parameters. In the context of software processes, relevant process parameters might be the number of phone calls handled by service desk agents per day, or the number of software bugs found in a certain test phase.

(Quality) control chart. In its basic form, a quality control chart, one of the "seven basic tools of quality", includes a central line for the relevant parameter, plus lower and upper control and warning limits, as shown in Fig. 8.1.

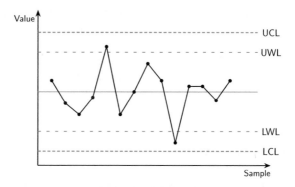

Fig. 8.1 A sample quality control chart

The different types of control charts differ e.g. regarding the rules for calculating the central line and the limits, and the following will descibe a simple form of control chart assuming a normal distribution (bell curve) of the parameter measured, with mean μ and standard deviation σ. In this case, the central line is placed at μ. The warning limits are calculated as $\mu \pm 2\sigma$, and the control limits as $\mu \pm 3\sigma$. This implies that about 5 in 100 measurement samples will deliver values outside the warning levels, and about 3 in 1000 will deliver values outside the control limits.

These warning and control limits now provide heuristics on when to check the process in more or less detail to identify any problems that might occur.

Acceptable values and statistical process capability. In order to judge whether the warning and control limits are adequate for a certain parameter, one needs to identify the acceptable values for this parameter. If the interval from the lower to the upper control limit lies well within the acceptable values, the so-called *tolerance* interval, then the process is considered a *(statistically) capable process*, and there are various definitions used to calculate the statistical process capability, based on the distance from the control limits to the end points of the tolerance interval.

Process improvement based on SPC. There are two parameters that might be addressed by process improvement activities based on SPC:

- the mean of the process might be inadequate, and the goal of process improvement is to move it higher or lower, as required (typically to the middle of the tolerance interval).
- the standard deviation of the process might be too large, implying that there is too much difference between different instances of performing the same process. Statistically speaking, the process capability is too low, perhaps even with the control limits lying outside the tolerance interval.

Both of these parameters may have a stable (but possibly inadequate) value, or they may change over time, describing that the process itself changes. This may be wanted, due to process improvement activities performed, or it may also be a sign that the process is "out of control".

The major goals of process improvement based on SPC are therefore to get processes under control, with stable mean and stable standard deviation, and to ensure they are capable, with suitable mean and low standard deviation.

In SPC one distinguished between common and special causes of variation that need to be addressed by process improvement: common causes apply to all instances of the process and result in higher standard deviation, while special causes change the process in some way, leading to a changing mean and/or standard deviation.

8.2.2 Six Sigma

Six Sigma describes a process improvement approach building on SPC, and its goal therefore typically is one of the goals of process improvement described above. Its focus lies on performing individual improvement projects or activities, rather than an overall improvement programme. The goal is to resolve certain defined problems, with a strong emphasis on using measurement and data. Nevertheless, Six Sigma can also be used as a basis for continuous improvement consisting of a sequence of individual improvement projects.

Overall, Six Sigma can be described as a toolbox of techniques for problem analysis, evaluation of data, with many of them common in quality management and quality assurance. Several of them were already discussed in different contexts in this book, such as SIPOC, Failure Mode and Effects Analysis (FMEA), and of course (quality) control charts. To structure the use of these tools, Six Sigma provides the DMAIC life cycle for improvement activities, or its variant DFSS for design processes:

DMAIC. The DMAIC improvement life cycle consists of the following five phases:

- *Define*: first, the goals and the scope of the improvement project need to be defined, preferably defining quantitative goals.
- *Measure*: next, data that help to understand the underlying problems and their causes need to be identified and collected.
- *Analyse*: once the data are available, they are analysed to identify the problem causes and suitable improvement activities.
- *Improve*: the core of the project is of course to perform suitable improvement activities to resolve the problem.
- *Control*: use data to ensure progress of the improvement project and ensure that the defined problem is genuinely resolved.

This improvement cycle has some similarity to the PDCA cycle, but puts the emphasis on the early phases, identifying suitable improvements, and usually using statistical data to do so.

Design for Six Sigma (DFSS). While Six Sigma and in particular DMAIC focus on improving existing processes, DFSS is a variant that puts the focus on *designing* the processes and products, ideally preventing problems from the start. Like Six Sigma, it puts strong emphasis on using data and statistical methods. There are a number of different project life cycle models for this task, including the Define–Measure–Analyse–Design–Verify approach, where the first three phases are named like those in DMAIC but of course refer to the design task at hand rather than the improvement required.

Qualification levels. Since Six Sigma requires considerable knowledge of statistics and the various improvement tools, as well as experience in their application, different qualification and certification schemes have been created. These usually consist of qualification levels similar to those used in martial arts, including "Yellow Belts", "Green Belts", "Black Belts", sometimes even "Master Black Belts", and "Champions", each with resulting roles and tasks.

8.2.3 SPC and Six Sigma for Software Processes

As mentioned before, SPC and Six Sigma were originally created for industrial manufacturing and therefore are not immediately applicable to software processes. There are two important challenges in applying these concepts to software processes: software processes often vary considerably between different instances, partly for legitimate reasons such as different times of software to be developed, and partly for questionable reasons such as personal preferences of the people involved. At the same time, the number of process instances for software processes is typically rather small, and statistical, data-driven methods are therefore difficult to apply.

As a result, SPC and Six Sigma are therefore mainly adequate for fairly mature, stable processes, as typically found in incident management and similar IT service management processes. Regarding software development processes, such processes can be found in organisations that have achieved a high level of maturity in the sense of the capability maturity models such as CMMI and SPICE.

Example 8.2. The project described in this example was not actually performed as a Six Sigma project, and none of the people involved had any formal Six Sigma qualification. Nevertheless, it used very similar techniques and will therefore be described here as an example of the application of Six Sigma.

An IT service provider was responsible for running the IT infrastructure of its customer, including a large number of PCs. In order to manage this infrastructure, ITIL was used, including routines scanning the network as well as a *Configuration Management Data Base* (CMDB) to document the different components of the infrastructure (configuration items CIs) with their relationships and attributes. However, over time this documentation was no longer up-to-date, due to many changes such as repairs, moving of (components of) PCs and so on. Apart from the fact that this was a problem for managing and resolving incidents, there was a considerable number of PCs provided to the customer that could not be charged because relevant information such as the user, the location or the configuration of the PC was not known. Therefore, a project was set up to address these issues and improve data quality.

- *Define:* the goal of the project was to improve data quality in the CMDB, with particular focus on providing the necessary information such that PCs could be charged to the customer.
  Ideally, one should have defined the number of such PCs but this was impossible: a PC incompletely documented might be a genuine PC to be charged; alternatively, it might for example be a duplicate created by the scan routines after some components of the PC had been exchanged, or it might have been retired some time ago. It was therefore an important task of the *Measure* and *Analyse* phases to clarify these cases.
- *Measure:* relevant data were already available from scanning tools, and no new measurements needed to be set up. Instead, the results from the various scanning tools were collected monthly, and imported into a newly set-up data base, together with the relevant CMDB data.

- *Analyse:* a collection of different SQL reports was drawn from data base, first with a focus on cleaning up address data, and later other inconsistencies. In many cases, the same address had been written in different ways, or the same PC was entered multiple times, leading to duplicate records with different missing attributes. The latter often happened after some component of the PC had been exchanged, and the PC now was recognised as a "new", different PC. Searching for duplicate serial numbers of important components often helped to identify these duplicates.
- *Improve:* reports of inconsistencies identified and missing data were then sent off to the local IT service groups. These were then usually able to correct these inconsistencies, often after inspecting the PC in question.
- *Control:* monthly updates of the scanning data and CMDB data, with updated reports of inconsistencies and missing data, helped to monitor progress of the project and showed that the size of these reports decreased. At the same time, the number of PCs that were charged to the customer increased considerably, and after a short time easily paid for the project.

As happens so often, even though the project clearly was a success, it was eventually stopped before the goals were fully achieved, due to organisational changes.

8.3 DevOps

With the increasing emphasis on time to market and the ability of development teams to deliver (small chunks of) functionality faster by using agile or lean methodologies, the transition of the developed software into production started to become a major bottleneck. At the same time, the different cultures between development and operations in many cases make this very transition rather difficult, typically taking days if not weeks even for small changes. A third challenge was the increase in the number of machines to be operated, moving from a few physical machines to hundreds or even thousands of virtual machines.

Together, these challenges led to the *DevOps* initiative, where DevOps is an artificial word coined from *Dev*elopment and *Op*eration. Although this term is in common use today, it needs to be pointed out that it is not a clearly defined concept, and there are various different interpretations of what "DevOps" means.

8.3.1 From Continuous Integration to Continuous Deployment

An important foundation of DevOps is the automation of the transition from programming to operation, which in the past has been extended in several steps. This path from programming to operation is often called the *deployment pipeline*, or alternatively the *value stream*, see Fig. 8.2. The dashed arrows in the figure denote those parts of the pipeline that are automated in continuous integration / delivery / deployment.

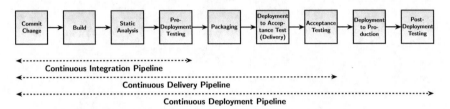

Fig. 8.2 A typical deployment pipeline

- *Continuous integration* has been around since the 1990s, for example as one of the practices used in Extreme Programming. It extends the concept of *nightly builds* by further reducing the size of changes that lead to a new build and test. Rather than performing daily integration, the product is newly integrated and built after each completed small change. One of the best practices of continuous integration is that every developer should check-in his or her changes and integrate them at least once a day.
  Continuous integration thus helps to identify integration problems very quickly. On the other hand, a central requirement for successful continuous integration is that working builds have very high priority in the development team. If any team member creates a change that breaks the build, correcting this break has top priority above everything else, because it prevents the entire team from checking in their changes correctly.
  To implement continuous integration, the integration steps (as shown in Fig. 8.2) need to be automated using suitable tools.
  Continuous integration in a strict sense leads, however, to a conflict with the popular configuration management technique of branching for any larger new functionality and only merging the branch back into the trunk once the functionality is complete. In the context of continuous integration, "feature toggles" are recommended instead so that an incompletely implemented functionality is included in the code but switched off until it is complete and needed. To some extent, this can however lead to additional complexity and resulting problems of its own, and organisations should think about the risks as well as benefits in their context before going for that solution.
- *Continuous delivery* extends continuous integration by also automating packaging of the product and delivery for and performing acceptance testing of the com-

plete package. The challenge here is to automate all these steps so that they can be performed each time a small change to the product has been completed. In particular, this implies that there are no more manual acceptance tests, all acceptance test activities must be automated, including those addressing non-functional requirements.

The result from the continuous delivery pipeline is a releasable and deployable package for each product change, where the customer decides, depending on business needs, whether and when to deploy this package into production.

Again depending on business needs as well as the technical environment, these deployable packages may be cumulative, including all previous changes, or just include an individual change. The latter variant allows more flexibility in deciding which changes to deploy, or possibly to reverse a deployment if wanted, but at the same time leads to a larger number of different possible configurations and therefore a higher risk of quality problems.

- Finally, *continuous deployment* includes that last step of deployment into the production environment, again without any manual intervention. The only exception may be that the customer decides in advance that for business reasons, a certain change or set of changes will only be deployed at a later stage.

  With this exception, every change that the developer deems complete and that passes all automated QA checks and tests will go directly into production, with no manual interference.

  In order to perform continuous deployment, close cooperation between the development team and the operations team is needed, which makes it difficult in an environment where the two teams belong to different companies, for example if development was outsourced to an external supplier, or—making continuous deployment completely impossible—in the development of commercial-off-the-shelf (COTS) software.

  Apart from this organisational challenge, the technical challenge involved in continuous deployment varies from no real challenge at all, if deployment essentially consists of a simple installation on a single server, to extremely difficult if a complex system is to be deployed on a complex mix of (virtual and physical) server, cloud services etc., based on different (versions of) infrastructure software.

Apart from supporting the communication between development and operations, these techniques expand the concepts of agile development and help to reduce some of the risks involved, mainly by getting feedback fast from business as well as about technical (integration) problems. At the same time, however, they introduce new risks, such as insufficiently tested changes that may cause the production environment to fall down—which, when it occurs, tends to be a very expensive problem with high visibility for customers.

In the following, when talking about continuous integration, continuous delivery and continuous deployment, we will summarise them under the name "continuous X".

Continuous X and the development life cycle. While continuous integration today is commonly used in agile and plan-driven development, continuous delivery and continuous deployment work best with development approaches that themselves focus on continuously delivering individual small changes, for example Kanban, rather than methods that deliver a new software version at the end of each release cycle or sprint. Of course, to some extent continuous deployment and continuous deployment can also be used in combination with agile approaches such as Scrum or even some plan-driven approaches, but this is not a natural fit. Nevertheless, it is quite common to combine continuous X with a variant of Scrum which is like standard Scrum except that new increments are not (only) delivered at the end of a sprint but whenever a work item such as a user story has been completed.

8.3.2 The "Three Ways" of DevOps

While the automation of the deployment pipeline is an important component, DevOps goes beyond that. There are various interpretations of what exactly DevOps means, but a common definition is based on the following principles or "three ways" [12]:

- the principles of *flow*, which mainly address the fast delivery of work from development to operation as discussed above.
- the principles of *feedback*, which add feedback of information about problems in operations back to development,
- the principles of *continual learning and experimentation*

As these three ways show, DevOps goes beyond automation of the deployment pipeline and is concerned with ensuring a culture of *cooperation* between the stakeholders involved, mainly development and operations, but in many cases there are other stakeholders that need to be involved as well, such as IT security and quality assurance / quality management.

A different way to view the first way is that DevOps focusses on the interaction between development and operations, aiming to bring newly developed software functionality into productive use more or less immediately. The second and third way try to ensure that this is done without sacrificing the production quality achieved by the lengthy test and roll-out phases once development considers the software "finished", as used in classical development life cycles.

The first way: the principles of flow. The principles of flow essentially consist of continuous delivery or better continuous deployment, and automation of the deployment pipeline as described above. In an ideal DevOps environment, passing through the entire deployment pipeline from committing a change to having it deployed in production will be a matter of minutes, rather than weeks or even months as is common in other contexts. If full automation is not (yet) possible, a first step in that direction is to at least reduce or better eliminate waiting times ("waste") which can sometimes form a large part of the overall time needed for running through the deployment pipeline.

These principles are closely related to lean development, as the following list taken from [12] show:

- *make our work visible*, using techniques such as the Kanban board
- *limit work in process (WIP)* in order to speed up throughput and reduce context changes
- *reduce batch sizes* which helps to reduce WIP
- *reduce the number of hand-offs* since each hand-off involves additional effort, waiting times, and a loss of information
- *continually identify and elevate our constraints* as described in Goldratt's theory of constraints (see Sect. 3.5.6)
- *eliminate hardships and waste in the value stream* which refers to any work that makes life difficult for developers, including for example waiting, correction of defects, or extra processes.

This focus on the flow of changes is particularly suitable for applications with a limited number of dependencies between different work items, such as many large web sites. For example, Amazon was performing 130,000 deployments per day according to [12, p. xxxiv].

While the goal of the first way of DevOps is of course to fully automate the respective parts of the deployment pipeline, just moving towards that goal and reducing waiting times, such as before a manual step of the pipeline, can help to reduce to reduce overall processing time considerably and therefore be extremely helpful.

The second way: the principles of feedback. While the first way refers to the flow of information from development to operations, the second way refers to the flow of information from operations back to development, using the following practices:

- *working safely within complex systems* refers to building up knowledge about how to deal with problems in such complex systems
- *see problems as they occur* emphasises that the system is set up in such a way that problems are identified and addressed quickly
- *swarm and solve problems to build new knowledge*, where swarming refers to bringing in whoever is needed to resolve any problems quickly
- *keep pushing quality closer to the source* emphasises that all QA activities should be by personnel close to the work done, rather than distant (independent) personnel
- *enable optimising for downstream work centres* looks at internal stakeholders further down the value stream, in particular operations, and how the developed products can be designed in a way to ease and support their work, e.g. by designing for performance and configurability.

The third way: the principles of continual learning and experimentation. Even more than the first and second way, the third way is concerned with the culture of the organisation, trying to build up a culture of cooperation, learning and experimentation. According to [12], this is supported by the following practices which are quite similar to what can be found in general process improvement approaches:

- *Enabling organisational learning and a safety culture* puts the emphasis on seeking and sharing information about problems in order to learn from them.
- *Institutionalise the improvement of daily work* ensures a culture of identifying and addressing problems rather than working around them which will lead to the same problems occurring again and again.
- *Transform local discoveries into global improvements* implies that there are mechanisms for collecting and spreading experience collected, ensuring that improvement ideas are incorporated into the processes and process definitions.
- *Inject resilience patterns into our daily work* tries to set processes up in such a way that even if problems occur in the processes, process outputs are not seriously affected.
- *Leaders reinforce a learning culture* requires that leaders set up a culture of learning from experience, without fear if problems occur.

Moving from first to third way. As the description of the three ways shows, they build on each other, and can therefore be seen as three levels of implementing DevOps. Organisations planning to move towards DevOps should first focus on automation of the deployment pipeline, i.e. the first way, and then gradually build on that by implementing the second and finally the third way. Of course, there will always be those who argue that this is too urgent to do so, and implementing the second and third way will anyway help with the implementation of the first way. However, failure because one tries to improve too much in one go is obviously not a better alternative, and there is a good reason why agile methodologies focus on frequent, small steps delivering the basics first. The same concept should be applied in improvement as well, including DevOps-based improvement.

8.3.3 DevOps in Context

Company culture. Implementing the three ways of DevOps requires strong cooperation between the different roles involved, on a day-to-day working level, rather than by repeated escalation of open issues to management for decision. In many organisations, this will lead to a need for change of culture as well as of organisational structure, which of course is a rather difficult undertaking.

Many proponents of DevOps see the "silo organisation" as one of the main obstacles to better cooperation between development and operations, and therefore recommend cross-functional teams as a solution. While a silo mentality of "us against them" certainly is such an obstacle, this should not be confused with an organisation where different tasks (such as development and operations) are assigned to different organisational units. While this may be less relevant for small organisations, large organisations will need some form of internal structure and specialisation, and it seems questionable whether "silos" based on different applications will be any better than "silos" based on development, operations, IT security etc.

Addressing the silo mentality is therefore definitely to be recommended, but one should not expect to resolve the problem just by splitting work into teams in a different way.

Apart from good cooperation between development and operation (including QA and IT security), the success of an organisation also depends on a similarly good cooperation with the business, i.e. the users of the software to be developed and run. This is sometimes addressed under the name of BizDevOps which extends the concepts of DevOps to include the business side. However, so far this is not very wide-spread as an explicit methodology, and will therefore not be discussed any more in this book.

DevOps and system architecture. In order to automate major parts of the deployment pipeline, a suitable systems architecture is needed. On the level of the overall infrastructure, this may be achieved using *infrastructure as code* if the systems in use are mainly based on virtual machines. With infrastructure as code, systems are built and managed as code, e.g. in a cloud environment, without any manual steps.

On a lower level, the applications that run on the infrastructure should be structured into small, largely independent components. Above all, this refers to the deployment units, and only indirectly to development. Of course, if the source code is not well modularised then there is no chance to deploy the object code in small units. However, even well-modularised source code for a large application that is all included in for example the same .exe, .jar or .war file is ill-suited for continuous deployment and therefore for DevOps. This is partly due to the additional effort needed for the deployment itself, but mainly due to the fact that the entire deployment pipeline, including tests etc., in this case needs to be performed for the application as a whole rather than just those parts of it that have changed.

In the context of DevOps, *micro-services* are therefore quite popular, often in combination with *containers*, since they support the physical separation of different functions and thus make fast, automated deployment easier. The platform *Kubernetes* goes one step further and helps to deploy and run containerised services on a large scale, addressing many of the technical challenges mentioned in the description of continuous deployment on p. 315 above.

NoOps or DevOps. Rather than DevOps, the term "NoOps" is occasionally used to describe that no operations (in the classical sense) are used. Nevertheless, this term is not really adequate: operation is still performed, but in a different way, but with an increased degree of automation and possibly sophistication, requiring very different qualifications.

8.3.4 DevOps and CALMS

Another common way to describe DevOps is CALMS, which is an acronym describing five key aspects of DevOps, most of which have already be described above:

- *Culture*: a cooperative, performance-oriented culture is a core part of the DevOps philosophy.
- *Automation* is a basic component of continuous delivery and continuous deployment and therefore also a key component of DevOps.
- *Lean*: the three ways of DevOps, in particular the principle of flow, is directly derived from lean thinking.
- *Measurement*: the principle of feedback includes feedback using metrics, for example providing information about how well an application performs or where the problems in the deployment pipelines occur.
- *Sharing*: closely related to culture, sharing of information between the different people and groups involved is a key aspect of DevOps.

8.3.5 DevOps and ITIL

Although looking at it from different angles, both DevOps and ITIL describe how to transition development results into production and provide quality services based on those results. This leads to the common discussion about their relative merits, and to what extent DevOps and ITIL are in conflict, may be used in combination, or perhaps even support each other [6].

One of the common arguments in this discussion claims that ITIL is an old-fashioned, inflexible approach that should be replaced by a modern approach such as DevOps. On the other hand, ITIL summarises a lot of experience about how to manage large infrastructures successfully, and that experience should certainly be used with modern technology as well as older technology.

A more detailed analysis of the relationship between DevOps and ITIL shows that there is actually no conflict, and both can support each other quite well. In many cases, ITIL defines the tasks that need to be done, and DevOps describes a specific way of how to perform these tasks. Looking at the five phases of the ITIL service life cycle, the following relationships can be identified:

- *Service Strategy* is mainly concerned with clarifying the services to be provided and how to finance them, and therefore has little direct relationship with DevOps.
- *Service Design* has some overlap with DevOps, in particular setting up the environment in which DevOps is to act, such as ensuring the capacity and availability of the infrastructure, and managing information security.
- *Service Transition* is concerned with the transition of services from design / development to operation and therefore has a strong overlap with DevOps. For example, the process "Service validation and testing" is performed to ensure that the services are *fit for purpose (utility)* and *fit for use (warranty)*, i.e. that they are validated and verified. These are important steps within the deployment pipeline as used in DevOps, which aims to fully automate these steps. Put differently, the two approaches emphasise different aspects of this process, but without any conflict but rather supporting each other. The same is true for most other Service Transition processes, such as *Change management* or *Release and deployment*

management. Looking at change management, it is obvious that this is as important a process in a DevOps environment as in an ITIL environment. However, since in DevOps there usually is a large number of small changes, the ITIL processes aligned to small numbers of large conglomerates of changes need to be adapted. E.g. a change advisory board[1] will certainly not want to advise on every minor change but work on the level of types or groups of changes. However, looking closely this is not really much different from advising on large changes that consist of groups of small changes.

A slightly different case is the ITIL process *Service asset and configuration management* which is not addressed explicitly in DevOps, but implicitly is required in order to be able to automate the deployment pipeline, and at the same time the automation (if set up correctly) will help to always have an up-to-date overview of the current (software) configuration items, their version, and their status.

- *Service Operation* includes the most widely used ITIL processes, such as Incident Management, Problem Management and Request Fulfilment. Parts of the DevOps community, however, criticise these processes as too bureaucratic, focussing on e.g. properly documenting incidents in the ticket system rather than resolving them. While this may certainly be true for the way these processes are implemented in some companies, a certain formal overhead is needed to ensure that e.g. all incidents are eventually resolved (or at least rejected explicitly), and to ensure that the knowledge derived from any such incidents is fed back to development. Again, though they look at work from a different angle, the service operation processes or something similar is needed to implement the second and third way of DevOps.

Another important process within Service Operation is *Access Management*. In an ITIL environment, there is a culture of being rather restrictive about access rights, in particular to the production environment, to ensure that changes to this environment are well coordinated and only performed by suitably qualified personnel. This can lead to problems in a DevOps environment if such access rights are granted rather liberally, typically because one wants to have little specialisation within a DevOps team to improve cooperation, with developers also performing operation tasks in the production environment. This involves a high risk that some of these developers have insufficient understanding of the specific needs of a production environment and therefore performs steps that would be OK or even useful in a development environment but lead to problems in a production environment, such as an uncoordinated change of the database structure, or perhaps even side-stepping any documentation steps such that it is no longer traceable which change was performed when. Nevertheless, this is not a fundamental conflict between ITIL and DevOps but a different emphasis where a common solution is certainly possible.

---

[1] According to ITIL 3, the change advisory board is "a group of people that advises the Change Manager in the Assessment, prioritisation and scheduling of Changes. This board is usually made up of representatives from all areas within the IT Service Provider, the Business, and Third Parties such as Suppliers." [16, Glossary]

- *Continual Service Improvement* addresses the same goals as the second and in particular the third way of DevOps, and again, even though DevOps and ITIL emphasise different aspects, they can be setup in such a way to support each other.

Outsourcing. While ITIL is well-suited for an environment where work is outsourced and development and operations are the responsibility of different companies, this certainly is far more difficult with DevOps. In this context, we only look at outsourcing in the sense that a separate company takes full responsibility for operation (or development), not the simplified variant where a separate company provides personnel that works according to the rules and processes set by the other company.

There are essentially two aspects that make outsourcing in combination with DevOps difficult: first and most obviously, close cooperation between development and operations is far more difficult if the two functions are based in different companies, with different goals and processes. In particular operation service providers usually focus on standardising their processes across different customers in order to become more efficient. Once they have to work with different development groups that use different DevOps processes, this efficiency gain will be lost.

Second and usually not quite as serious, good DevOps processes are expected to lead to a competitive advantage, but sharing these processes with a service provider risks that their benefits may also be shared with competitors.

8.3.6 Benefits and Challenges of DevOps

In many ways, the discussion about DevOps resembles the discussion about the use of agile methods in many ways. While there are some that would want to use DevOps for all types of products, applications, and organisations, others see DevOps as the latest fad that may work for small start-ups but not for any "real" work.

There is probably no discussion about the need for good cooperation between development and operations, and the problems of insufficient cooperation seem to be wide-spread. Closely related, speeding up the transition of implemented changes into production is required in many environments, but of course without any loss of quality and reliability. Automation of at least parts of the deployment pipeline therefore is certainly very helpful in most cases.

Testing and analysis. A major challenge is to incorporate sufficient testing and analysis into that automation so that no manual intervention is needed. This requires that the customer (and other stakeholder) requirements are clearly defined in advance so that they can be expressed in the form of test cases. As the agile community rightly argues, in many cases this is not possible, so that in the context of continuous delivery and DevOps close cooperation with the customers (or their representatives such as product management) is needed in order to create and validate those tests in parallel to the development of the software.

Nevertheless, a major part of testing is regression testing, checking that the new change did not break any of the existing functionality. This part of testing of course is fairly easy to integrate into an automated deployment pipeline, and in many cases will lead to a major improvement.

On the other hand, even if it is exactly known what is to be developed, fully automating these tests can become extremely difficult if not impossible in a complex, technical environment such as that described in Example 3.2. In such an environment, there are clear limits to how far DevOps can go.

IT governance. IT governance typically remains an important topic in any organisation even if they start to use DevOps, which leads to the challenge of adapting IT governance to the DevOps environment. One of the main difficulties is to ensure that the various governance and compliance checks and controls that are part of the deployment pipeline do not hold up the work items passing through that pipeline. Put differently, these checks and controls need to be automated as well, or—if that is not possible—they need to be moved such that they can be performed in advance or, based on some sampling strategy, after the work item is in production. For example, certain controls that cannot be automated might be performed as reviews, e.g. on the architecture, before implementation. Where in a more conventional environment, various roles would be responsible for setting up and performing controls as part of the deployment pipeline, these same roles would now be responsible for defining automated controls which are then incorporated into the automated pipeline. Ideally, incorporating these steps in the deployment pipeline will make it easy for DevOps personnel to do the right thing according to IT governance, and make it difficult to do the wrong thing.

Another aspect of IT governance is the need to document what version of a certain application is in production at a certain time, so that this can be traced if any problems occur later. With this task, the automation which is part of the first way of DevOps may actually help since the documentation of all deployment steps can easily be automated as well.

DevOps personnel. Descriptions of DevOps usually mention that this approach needs highly qualified and trained personnel that has a good understanding of development as well as operation. While such personnel certainly exists, it does not exist in large numbers. Initial pilot projects tend to be able to attract such personnel, but obviously, this gets far more difficult once DevOps gets more wide-spread. Training will help, but obviously not every organisation can have large numbers of above-average developers and other personnel.

Suitable organisations, systems and applications. As the discussion so far indicates, DevOps is particularly suitable for development efforts where work can be broken down into small, independent changes, as is mainly true for the continuous revision and extension of an existing application. This is sometimes described as DevOps supporting and requiring more of a product orientation, rather than a project orientation. Therefore, most of the current well-known examples of the application of DevOps concern the on-going maintenance of an existing major website.[2]

A very different development effort that has also become well-known for its successful use of DevOps is the development of the HP LaserJet firmware [10]. Since this referred to the development of an off-the-shelf software package, automation only included the delivery but not the deployment of the software, but apart from that, all three ways of DevOps were implemented and helped to implement new functionality much faster than in the past.

As the discussion about outsourcing above showed, DevOps works best if development and operation belong to the same organisation or company. It is possible to apply DevOps in a context where this is not the case, as for example shown in the HP example, but the implementation of DevOps gets more complex in this case.

Finally, one should note that in some contexts, applying DevOps concepts is only possible to a very limited extent for legal reasons. In certain cases, e.g. large financial institutions, legislation under certain conditions *requires* a strict separation of development and operations in order to ensure a separation of powers and prevent fraud and other illegitimate forms of cooperation, which of course strongly limits the application of DevOps.

Further Reading

Process intelligence and process mining. The main reference on process mining in general is [25]. Regarding process mining of software processes, [17] and [8] provide good introductions to the topic as well as overviews of relevant literature.

Statistical process control. A summary of the use of Six Sigma for software development, specifically in combination with CMMI, can be found in [23] or, more detailed and by almost the same authors, in [24].

DevOps. Very good reading on the ideas of DevOps is [11] which is a novel (!) about DevOps and related concepts. To get a deeper understanding of these concepts, read [12] which is based on [11], with one joint author. Of course, both these books paint a rather positive picture of DevOps. For a more critical discussion see for example [7, 6].

One of the standard references on continuous delivery is [9].

Exercises

8.1. Look at a project that you are involved with. What kind of process data are available within this project that could be used for process mining or similar tasks?

---

[2] For example, Google, Amazon and Netflix are often mentioned in this context.

References

1. BPIC. Third International Business Process Intelligence Challenge (BPIC'13). http://www.win.tue.nl/bpi/2013/challenge (last access 2017-01-09), 2013.
2. BPIC. Third International Business Process Intelligence Challenge (BPIC'14). http://www.win.tue.nl/bpi/2014/challenge (last access 2017-01-09), 2014.
3. M. Castellanos, A. Alves De Medeiros, J. Mendling, B. Weber, and A. Weijters. Business process intelligence. In C. J. and W. M. van der Aalst, editors, *Handbook of research on business process modeling*, Information Science Reference, pages 456–480. Hersey, 2009.
4. J. E. Cook and A. L. Wolf. Automating process discovery through event-data analysis. In *Proc. of the 17th Intern. Conf. on Software Engineering, Seattle, Washington, USA*, pages 73–82, 1995.
5. J. E. Cook and A. L. Wolf. Discovering models of software processes from event-based data. *ACM Transactions on Software Engineering and Methodology*, 7(3):215–249, 1998.
6. R. England. DevOps and ITIL. http://www.itskeptic.org/devops-and-itil (last access 2017-08-25), September 2011. IT Skeptic blog.
7. R. England. DevOps and traditional ITSM—why DevOps won't change the world any time soon. http://www.itskeptic.org/devops-and-traditional-itsm-why-devops-wont-change (last access 2017-08-25), August 2011. IT Skeptic blog.
8. T. Gürgen, A. Tarhan, and N. Karagöz. An integrated infrastructure using process mining techniques for software process verification. In R. Perez-Castillo and M. Piattini, editors, *Uncovering Essential Software Artifacts through Business Process Archeology*, chapter 14, pages 364–382. IGI Global, 2014.
9. J. Humble and D. Farley. *Continuous Delivery: Reliable Software Releases through Build, Test, and Deployment Automation*. Addison-Wesley Professional, 2010.
10. G. Kim. The amazing DevOps transformation of the HP LaserJet firmware team (Gary Gruver). https://itrevolution.com/the-amazing-devops-transformation-of-the-hp-laserjet-firmware-team-gary-gruver/ (last access 2017-09-07), Feb. 2014.
11. G. Kim, K. Behr, and G. Spaffort. *The Phoenix Project: A Novel about IT, DevOps and Helping Your Business Win*. IT Revolution Press, 2013.
12. G. Kim, J. Humble, P. Debois, and J. Willis. *The DevOps Handbook. How to Create World-Class Agility, Reliability, & Security in Technology Organizations*. IT Revolution Press, 2016.
13. R. Kneuper. Process Mining bei Softwareprozessen. In M. Engstler, M. Fazal-Baqaie, E. Hanser, O. Linssen, M. Mikusz, and A. Volland, editors, *Projektmanagement und Vorgehensmodelle 2016. Paderborn, 2016*, number 263 in Lecture Notes in Informatics (LNI) — Proceedings, pages 121–134. Gesellschaft für Informatik e.V. (GI), 2016.
14. D. Lorenzoli, L. Mariani, and M. Pezzè. Automatic generation of software behavioral models. In *Proc. of the 30th International Conference on Software Engineering (ICSE '08)*, pages 501–510. ACM, 2008.
15. L. Maruster, N. Faber, R. J. Jorna, and R. J. F. van Haren. A process mining approach to analyse user behaviour. In *WEBIST 2008, Proceedings of the Fourth International Conference on Web Information Systems and Technologies, Funchal, Madeira, Portugal*, volume 2, pages 208–214. INSTICC Press, 2008.
16. Office of Government Commerce, editor. *ITIL Service Transition*. The Stationary Office (TSO), 2007.
17. W. Poncin. Process mining software repositories. Master's thesis, Eindhoven University of Technology, August 2010. http://www.frasr.org/downloads/2010-08-20_ThesisWouterPoncin.pdf (last access 2017-01-09).
18. W. Poncin, A. Serebrenik, and M. van den Brand. Mining student capstone projects with FRASR and ProM. In *SPLASH 2011 Educators' Symposium, Portland OR, USA*, 2011. http://www.frasr.org/downloads/2011-10_SPLASH-ETS.pdf (last access 2017-01-09).

19. W. Poncin, A. Serebrenik, and M. van den Brand. Process mining software repositories. In *15th European Conference on Software Maintenance and Reengineering, March 1-4, 2011, Oldenburg, Germany*, 2011. http://www.frasr.org/downloads/2011-03_CSMR.pdf (last access 2017-01-09).

20. Process Mining Group, Eindhoven Technical University. ProM tools. http://www.promtools.org/doku.php (last access 2017-01-09).

21. V. A. Rubin, I. A. Lomazova, and W. M. van der Aalst. Agile development with software process mining. In *Proceedings of the 2014 International Conference on Software and System Process (ICSSP 2014)*, pages 70–74. ACM, 2014.

22. V. A. Rubin, A. A. Mitsyuk, I. A. Lomazova, and W. M. P. van der Aalst. Process mining can be applied to software too! In *Proceedings of the 8th ACM/IEEE International Symposium on Empirical Software Engineering and Measurement, ESEM '14*, pages 57:1–57:8. ACM, 2014.

23. J. Siviy, M. L. Penn, and E. Harper. Relationships between cmmi and six sigma. Technical Note CMU/SEI-2005-TN-005, Software Engineering Institute, Carnegie Mellon University, 2005. Available from https://resources.sei.cmu.edu/library/asset-view.cfm?assetid=7389 (last access 2018-01-27.

24. J. Siviy, M. L. Penn, and R. W. Stoddard. *CMMI and Six Sigma: Partners in Process Improvement*. SEI Series in Software Engineering. Addison-Wesley, 2007.

25. W. M. van der Aalst. *Process Mining. Discovery, Conformance and Enhancement of Business Processes*. Springer, 2011.

26. XES Extensible Event Stream. www.xes-standard.org (last access 2017-01-09).

Appendix A
Relevant norms and standards

A.1 A Short Overview of the Most Relevant Process Standards

There is a huge number of different process standards, and Fig. A.1 contains an overview of the most relevant such standards as covered in this book, showing the topics covered. A more extensive list of the relevant standards will be provided in the following section below.

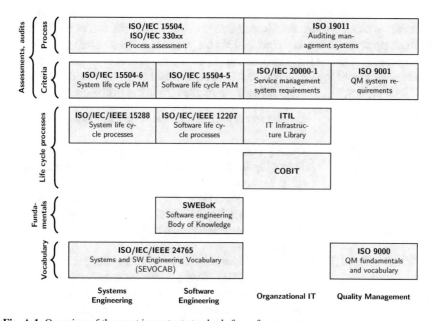

Fig. A.1 Overview of the most important standards for software processes

© Springer Nature Switzerland AG 2018
R. Kneuper, *Software Processes and Life Cycle Models*,
https://doi.org/10.1007/978-3-319-98845-0

A.2 ISO and IEC Standards

The *International Organization for Standardization* (ISO) is the main international standard-setting organisation, working with representatives from many national standard-setting organisations. Standards referring to electrical, electronic and related technologies, including software, are often published jointly with its sister organisation, the *International Electrotechnical Commission* (IEC), but IEC also publishes a number of standards on their own.

Recently, ISO and IEC started to publish relevant standards jointly with the US-American *Institute of Electrical and Electronics Engineers* (IEEE). IEEE also published a number of relevant standards on their own, see Sect. A.3.

The following table lists the main standards that are relevant in the context of software processes. The editions are the latest editions of these standards at the time of writing. The list is ordered by the numbers of the standards, independent of the exact organisation(s) that published it.

Many of the norms and standards in this list were also re-published by other national and international organisations, sometimes after translation into another language. For example, the norm ISO 9001 listed below was also published as a European norm EN ISO 9001, and as a German national norm DIN EN ISO 9001 (and similarly in many other countries as well).

"TR" in the identification of a standard shows that this document is published by ISO as a technical report as opposed to an international standard. Similarly, "TS" identifies a *technical standard* issued by ISO. The year at the end of the ID of any of these standards, after the colon, defines the year when this standard was released.

In general, ISO and IEC standards must be bought and tend to be fairly expensive. However, some of the following standards are available for free download from the ISO web page at [5]. These standards are marked (*) in the list below.

ISO 9000:2015	Quality management systems—Fundamentals and vocabulary
ISO 9001:2015	Quality management systems—Requirements
ISO 9004:2009	Managing for the sustained success of an organization—A quality management approach
ISO/IEC 9126:2001	Software engineering—Product quality—Part 1: Quality model (replaced by ISO/IEC 25010, see below)
ISO/IEC/IEEE 12207:2017	Systems and software engineering—Software life cycle processes
ISO/IEC 13719-1:1998	Information technology—Portable Common Tool Environment (PCTE)—Part 1: Abstract specification
ISO 13849-1:2015	Safety of machinery—Safety-related parts of control systems—Part 1: General principles for design
ISO 13849-2:2012	Safety of machinery—Safety-related parts of control systems—Part 2: Validation
ISO/IEC/IEEE 15288:2015	Systems and software engineering—System life cycle processes

ISO/IEC 15408-1:2009   Information technology—Security techniques—Evaluation criteria for IT security—Part 1: Introduction and general model (*)

ISO/IEC 15408-3:2008   Information technology—Security techniques—Evaluation criteria for IT security—Part 3: Security assurance components (*)

ISO/IEC 15504-1:2011   Information technology—Process assessment—Part 1: Concepts and vocabulary (replaced by ISO/IEC 33001, see below)

ISO/IEC 15504-2:2011   Information technology—Process assessment—Part 2: Performing an assessment (replaced by ISO/IEC 33002, see below)

ISO/IEC 15504-5:2012   Information technology—Process assessment—Part 5: An exemplar software life cycle process assessment model

ISO/IEC 15504-6:2013   Information technology—Process assessment—Part 6: An exemplar system life cycle process assessment model

ISO/IEC TS 15504-8:2012   Information technology—Process assessment—Part 8: An exemplar process assessment model for IT service management

ISO/IEC 15939:2017   Systems and software engineering—Measurement process

ISO/TS 16949:2009   Quality management systems—Particular requirements for the application of ISO 9001:2008 for automotive production and relevant service part organizations. (Withdrawn and replaced by IATF 16949:2016[1])

ISO 19011:2011   Guidelines for auditing management systems

ISO/IEC 19508:2014   Information technology—Object Management Group Meta Object Facility (MOF) Core (*)

ISO/IEC TR 19759:2015   Software Engineering—Guide to the software engineering body of knowledge (SWEBOK®) (*)

ISO/IEC 20000-1:2011   Information technology—Service management—Part 1: Service management system requirements

ISO/IEC 20000-2:2012   Information technology—Service management—Part 2: Guidance on the application of service management systems

ISO/IEC TR 20000-4:2010   Information technology—Service management—Part 4: Process reference model

ISO/IEC TR 20000-10:2015   Information technology—Service management—Part 10: Concepts and terminology (*)

ISO 21505:2017   Project, programme and portfolio management—Guidance on governance

ISO/TS 22163:2017   Railway applications—Quality management systems—Particular requirements for the application of ISO 9001:2015 in the rail sector

---

[1] IATF=International Automotive Task Force is a group of major automotive manufacturers.

ISO/IEC 24744:2014   Software Engineering—Metamodel for Development Methodologies

ISO/IEC TR 24748:2016   Systems and software engineering—Life cycle management—Part 1: Guidelines for life cycle management

ISO/IEC/IEEE 24765:2017   Systems and software engineering—Vocabulary (*)[2]

ISO/IEC TR 24774:2010   Systems and software engineering—Life cycle management—Guidelines for process description (*)

ISO/IEC 25000:2014   Systems and software engineering—Systems and software Quality Requirements and Evaluation (SQuaRE)—Guide to SQuaRE

ISO/IEC 25010:2011   Systems and software engineering—Systems and software Quality Requirements and Evaluation (SQuaRE)—System and software quality models

ISO 26262-6:2011   Road vehicles—Functional safety—Part 6: Product development at the software level

ISO/IEC 27000:2014   Information technology—Security techniques—Information security management systems—Overview and vocabulary (*)

ISO/IEC 27001:2015   Information technology—Security techniques—Information security management systems—Requirements

ISO/IEC 27002:2013   Information technology—Security techniques—Code of practice for information security controls

ISO/IEC 27005:2011   Information technology—Security techniques—Information security risk management

ISO/IEC 29100:2011   Information technology—Security techniques—Privacy framework (*)

ISO/IEC TR 29110-1:2016   Systems and software engineering—Lifecycle profiles for Very Small Entities (VSEs)—Part 1: Overview (*)

ISO/IEC TR 29110-3:2015   Systems and software engineering—Lifecycle profiles for Very Small Entities (VSEs)—Part 3-1: Assessment guide (*)

ISO/IEC/IEEE 29119-1:2013   Software Testing—Concepts & definitions

ISO/IEC/IEEE 29119-2:2013   Software Testing—Test processes

ISO/IEC/IEEE 29119-3:2013   Software Testing—Test documentation

ISO 31000:2009   Risk management—Principles and guidelines

ISO/IEC 33001:2015   Information technology—Process assessment—Concepts and terminology

ISO/IEC 33002:2015   Information technology—Process assessment—Requirements for performing process assessment

ISO/IEC 33003:2015   Information technology—Process assessment—Requirements for process measurement frameworks

---

[2] The definitions from ISO/IEC/IEEE 24765, also known as the Software and Systems Engineering Vocabulary SEVOCAB, are available online at https://pascal.computer.org/sev_display/index.action (last access 2017-12-09) where they are continuously updated.

ISO/IEC 33004:2015	Information technology—Process assessment—Requirements for process reference, process assessment and maturity models
ISO/IEC TR 33014:2013	Information technology—Process assessment—Guide for process improvement
ISO/IEC 33020:2015	Information technology—Process assessment—Process measurement framework for assessment of process capability
ISO/IEC 38500:2015	Information technology—Governance of IT for the organization
IEC 61508-2:2010	Functional safety of electrical/electronic/programmable electronic safety-related systems—Part 2: Requirements for electrical/electronic/programmable electronic safety-related systems
IEC 61508-3:2010	Functional safety of electrical/electronic/programmable electronic safety-related systems—Part 3: Software requirements
IEC 62061:2005	Safety of machinery—Functional safety of safety-related electrical, electronic and programmable electronic control systems
IEC 62304:2006	Medical device software—Software life cycle processes
ISO/IEC 90003:2014	Software engineering—Guidelines for the application of ISO 9001:2008 to computer software

A.3 Other Relevant Standard Documents

- A Guide to the Project Management Body of Knowledge (PMBOK® Guide)—Fifth Edition. Project Management Institute, 2013 [7].
- CMMI® for Development: Guidelines for Process Integration and Product Improvement [2]
- International Requirements Engineering Board (IREB®): A Glossary of Requirements Engineering Terminology, Version 1.6 [3]
- Cobit 5 Framework: [4]
- Software & Systems Process Engineering Metamodel Specification (SPEM) [6]
- DO-178B / ED-12B and DO-178C / ED-12C: Software Considerations in Airborne Systems and Equipment Certification (DO-178B / ED-12B published 1992; DO-178C / ED-12C published 2012)
- IEEE Std 1074-2006 IEEE Standard for Developing a Software Project Life Cycle Process

Further Reading

Appendix B of the SWEBOK® [1] lists the most important standards in the context of software engineering, including a summary of their contents.

Further information on the various ISO standards can be found in the ISO standards catalogue available at `http://www.iso.org/iso/home/store/catalogue_ics.htm`.

References

1. P. Bourque and R. Fairley, editors. *Guide to the Software Engineering Body of Knowledge (SWEBOK®), Version 3.0.* IEEE Computer Society, 2014. Available online at `http://www.swebok.org` (last access 2018-01-07).
2. M. B. Chrissis, M. Konrad, and S. Shrum. *CMMI for Development: Guidelines for Process Integration and Product Improvement.* Addison Wesley, 3rd revised edition, 2011.
3. M. Glinz. *A Glossary of Requirements Engineering Terminology, Version 1.6.* International Requirements Engineering Board (IREB), May 2014. Available online at `https://www.ireb.org/en/cpre/cpre-glossary/` (last access 2018-02-28).
4. ISACA. *COBIT® 5. A Business Framework for the Governance and Management of Enterprise IT*, 2012.
5. ISO. Freely available standards. `http://standards.iso.org/ittf/PubliclyAvailableStandards/index.html` (last access 2018-01-07).
6. Object Management Group (OMG). Software & Systems Process Engineering Meta-Model Specification (SPEM), Version 2.0. Available online at `http://www.omg.org/spec/SPEM/2.0/` (last access 2017-12-20), April 2008.
7. Project Management Institute. *A guide to the project management body of knowledge (PMBOK® guide).* Fifth edition, 2013.

Appendix B
Gokyo Ri Check-lists to Measure Process Quality

This appendix contains some check-lists that help to measure certain characteristics of process quality as defined in the model Gokyo Ri.

Each question should be answered for each process on the scale introduced by SPICE as described in Table 5.4, with values from "fully achieved" to "not achieved".

B.1 Process Quality Characteristic "Process Objectives and Requirements"

Tables B.1 and B.2 provide check items helping to evaluate the two quality sub-characteristics of "Process objectives and requirements", based on [2].

B.2 Process Quality Characteristic "Process Capability"

The quality characteristics in the following Table B.3 are based on a combination of the generic practices of SPICE and CMMI, and the CMMI-based deployment check-list in [1].

References

1. R. Kneuper. *CMMI. Improving Software and Systems Development Processes Using Capability Maturity Model Integration (CMMI-DEV)*. Rocky Nook, 2009.
2. R. Kneuper. Messung und Bewertung des Qualitätsmerkmals "Prozessziele und -anforderungen" von Softwareprozessen. In D. Wuksch, B. Peischl, and C. Kop, editors, *Ausgewählte Beiträge zur Anwenderkonferenz für Softwarequalität Test und Innovation (ASQT 2012)*, volume 295, pages 90–100. Österreichische Computer Gesellschaft, 2013.

© Springer Nature Switzerland AG 2018
R. Kneuper, *Software Processes and Life Cycle Models*,
https://doi.org/10.1007/978-3-319-98845-0

Table B.1 Process quality sub-characteristic: commitments and agreements

	Fully	Largely	Partially	Not
Is the process customer explicitly identified? This applies both to the customer who eventually pays for the process and to the receiver of the process results, if different.				
Have the process results been explicitly agreed with the customer? This may be done as part of a contract, an SLA, a service catalogue, or a process definition document, or at least some informal documentation as an email exchange.				
Have the process stakeholders and their requirements on the process been identified? Including e.g. safety, (IT) security or data privacy officer.				
Have expected process standards, process models etc. been explicitly identified? E.g. ISO 9001. Satisfaction may be expected by management, or because this has been agreed with or promised to customers.				
Have relevant legal and regulatory process requirements been explicitly identified? Depending on the type of process, this may involve a large variety of very different requirements. Examples include tax law, safety regulations etc.				
Have the identified commitments and agreements been addressed in setting up the process? This does not require genuine conformance to these commitments and agreements (this is covered in the process quality characteristic "Conformance"), but at least they were available when defining or performing the process, with the expectation that the process will conform to them.				

Table B.2 Process quality sub-characteristic: support of business goals and defined embedding in the environment

	Fully	Largely	Partially	Not
Is the relationship between the process and the business goals visible? Of course, this this can only be satisfied if the business goals have been defined in the first place.				
Has the business purpose of the process been explicitly defined? Why do we need this process?				
Is the process embedded into a process landscape, architecture or similar? We need to know how the process interacts with other processes, which data are passed etc.				
Have the interfaces between the process and its partner processes been defined and agreed with the partners? This refers to the partner processes as shown by the process landscape and possibly other partner processes.				

Table B.3 Process quality characteristic: process management

	Fully	Largely	Partially	Not
Does the organisation have a documented policy for this process, describing on a top level the goals and general approach of the process? It is not necessary to have separate documents for each process, as long as the process evaluated here is covered by some document. This policy may for example be part of the quality manual, or the introductory part of a process definition document.				
Is the process policy used as the basis for managing the process, including measurement, quality assurance etc.? Many organisations create a nice-sounding policy, e.g. in the quality manual, but without any practical impact. This question therefore investigates whether the policy is not just stated but actually used as a policy.				
Are process performers adequately qualified to perform their work, based on up-to-date process definitions? In many cases, this qualification will consist of two parts: first, a general qualification which may for example be acquired by attending a relevant university course of study or public training courses. Such general training will of course not, apart from a few exceptions, cover the specific processes used in the organisation, which therefore need to be addressed in the second part of the training. This part may also take a variety of shapes, from comprehensive internal training classes to a short email or information at the project meeting in case of minor process changes.				
Is process performance planned and monitored adequately? Depending on the specific process and environment, the planning of the process may be part of project planning or other planning activities. The goal of monitoring is to compare the actual performance of the process against the plan, and to react if there are any relevant discrepancies.				
Are improvement suggestions and data that could help to support improvement of the process collected, analysed, and implemented if adequate? Since the process environment as well as the requirements on the process constantly change, processes need to be adapted and improved continuously.				
Are process results managed adequately? This refers to all work products that are created or modified by the process, as intermediate of final results. Such work products in general need to be versioned, or at least clearly identified; they need to be stored in a way that they are protected against damage and loss, and can be found when needed.				
Are adequate resources available for the process? Resources needed include human resources, which need to be available in the right number and with the right skills and qualifications. Resources needed also include all other resources, such as tool support and raw materials.				

Index

Page references printed in **boldface** refer to the definition or main description of the indexed term.

© Springer Nature Switzerland AG 2018
R. Kneuper, *Software Processes and Life Cycle Models*,
https://doi.org/10.1007/978-3-319-98845-0

Printed in the United States
By Bookmasters